Capitalism in the Ottoman Balkans

The Ottoman Empire and the World, published in collaboration with the British Institute at Ankara

Series editor: Warren Dockter

New and forthcoming titles:

Nationalism and Identity in the Ottoman Balkans: The Impact of Wars and Revolutions from the Sultans to Ataturk, Dimitris Stamatopoulos (ed.)

The Ottomans and Eastern Europe: Borders, and Political Patronage in the Early Modern World, Michał Wasiucionek

As our understanding of Ottoman history continues to evolve, a new generation of scholars are exploring questions of identities, class, society, diplomacy and trade. The British Institute at Ankara (BIAA) is internationally renowned for its support of new independent academic research in the region across various fields, including archaeology, ancient and modern history, heritage management, social sciences and contemporary issues in public policy, and political sciences. I.B. Tauris will now publish work in conjunction with the BIAA a new monograph book series, *The Ottoman Empire and the World*. This collaborative collection of specially commissioned books will focus on the identity, history and society of the Ottoman Empire and the world it inhabited, from the reign of Osman I to the dissolution of the Empire in the early 1920s.

Capitalism in the Ottoman Balkans

Industrialization and Modernity in Macedonia

Costas Lapavitsas and Pinar Cakiroglu

I.B. TAURIS
LONDON · NEW YORK · OXFORD · NEW DELHI · SYDNEY

Published in association with the British Institute of Archaeology at Ankara (BIAA)

I.B. TAURIS
Bloomsbury Publishing Plc
50 Bedford Square, London, WC1B 3DP, UK
1385 Broadway, New York, NY 10018, USA
29 Earlsfort Terrace, Dublin 2, Ireland

BLOOMSBURY, I.B. TAURIS and the I.B. Tauris logo are trademarks of
Bloomsbury Publishing Plc

First published in Great Britain 2019
This paperback edition published in 2021

Copyright © Costas Lapavitsas and Pinar Cakiroglu 2019

Costas Lapavitsas and Pinar Cakiroglu have asserted their right under the Copyright,
Designs and Patents Act, 1988, to be identified as the Authors of this work.

Cover design: Adriana Brioso
Cover image: Trachten-Kabinett von Siebenbürgen – Ein Vornehmer Böyar in der Wallachën.
(© Art Collection 4 / Alamy Stock Photo)

All rights reserved. No part of this publication may be reproduced or
transmitted in any form or by any means, electronic or mechanical,
including photocopying, recording, or any information storage or retrieval
system, without prior permission in writing from the publishers.

Bloomsbury Publishing Plc does not have any control over, or responsibility for, any
third-party websites referred to or in this book. All internet addresses given in this
book were correct at the time of going to press. The author and publisher regret any
inconvenience caused if addresses have changed or sites have ceased to exist, but can
accept no responsibility for any such changes.

A catalogue record for this book is available from the British Library.

A catalog record for this book is available from the Library of Congress.

ISBN: HB: 978-1-7883-1433-6
PB: 978-0-7556-4277-9
ePDF: 978-1-7883-1659-0
eBook: 978-1-7883-1660-6

Typeset by Newgen KnowledgeWorks Pvt. Ltd., Chennai, India

To find out more about our authors and books visit www.bloomsbury.com
and sign up for our newsletters.

Contents

List of Plates	viii
List of Illustrations	ix
List of Abbreviations	xii
Notes on Weights, Measures and Currency	xiii
Notes on Transliteration, Spelling and Pronunciation	xiv
Notes on Archives	xvi
Acknowledgements	xvii

1 The emergence of industrial capitalism in Ottoman Macedonia: A tale to be told — 1
   1.1 Historical development condensed — 1
   1.2 The geographical and historical terrain of Macedonia — 5
       1.2.1 Thessaloniki — 5
       1.2.2 Mount Vermion — 9
           1.2.2.1 The road to Giannitsa and Edhessa — 10
           1.2.2.2 The road to Veroia and Naoussa — 13

2 Analysing Ottoman capitalism: Theoretical and empirical resources — 19
   2.1 Ottoman 'decline' and transformation — 19
   2.2 State, community and religion in the emergence of Ottoman capitalism — 24
   2.3 The broad outlines of textile capitalism in Macedonia — 29
   2.4 Historical literature and original sources — 34
       2.4.1 The yearbooks of the *vilayet* of Thessaloniki (*Selanik Vilayet Salnameleri*) — 37
       2.4.2 Ottoman archives — 40

3 Administrative mechanisms and population changes in the *vilayet* of Thessaloniki — 43
   3.1 Administrative reforms of the Ottoman state in the nineteenth century — 44
   3.2 Administrative structures in the *vilayet* of Thessaloniki during the era of Tanzimat — 49

	3.3 Population trends in Macedonia	51
	3.4 Ethnic and religious composition of the population	58
4	The straightjacket of *çiftlik* agriculture in Macedonia	63
	4.1 Rise and fall of the *tımar* system	63
	4.2 Commercialization of agriculture, spread of tax farming and rise of *çiftlik* estates	66
	4.3 *Ayan* and *kırcalı*	68
	4.4 The disintegration of the *vakıf* of *Gazi* Evrenos *Bey*	71
	4.5 Agricultural output in the *vilayet* of Thessaloniki, 1870–1912	76
	4.6 Agricultural output in Veroia, Edhessa and Naoussa, 1870–1912	81
	4.7 Agrarian relations: The straightjacket of the *çiftlik*	87
	4.8 Muslim and Christian *çiftlik* holding	90
5	The commercial roots of Ottoman textile capitalism	97
	5.1 Merchants and industrial capitalism: Theoretical considerations	97
	5.2 Merchants and capitalism in Ottoman Macedonia	104
	5.3 Thessaloniki trade grows rapidly until the early 1870s	106
	5.4 Fluctuations and growth of trade in Thessaloniki from the 1870s to the 1910s	110
	5.5 Trade in the *kaza* of Veroia and Edhessa	113
	5.6 Who were the Naoussa merchants?	116
6	Private industrial capitalism in Ottoman Macedonia	127
	6.1 Responding to the import wave	127
	6.2 Jewish, Christian and Muslim traders, industrialists and bankers in Thessaloniki	130
	6.3 Emergence of industrial capitalism, 1870–90	138
	6.4 Advance of industrialization, 1890–1902	141
	6.5 Peak of industrial growth, 1902–12	150
	6.5.1 Cotton industrialists expand in Mount Vermion and diversify to Thessaloniki	150
	6.5.2 Expanding into woollens	153
	6.6 The reasons for the ascendancy of the provincial cotton mills	158
	6.7 Explaining the dominance of provincial woollen mills	162
	6.8 Economics of industrial textile capitalism	165
	6.9 A notable and precarious success	172

7	The Ottoman state creates a framework for industrialization	177
	7.1 Rediscovering economic intervention	177
	7.2 A controlling state encourages private industrial investment, 1870–1902	182
	7.3 State and industrialists establish regular relations, 1902–12	191
	7.4 An intrusive, authoritarian, bureaucratic and supportive state	200
8	Ascendant industrialists, emerging working class, turbulent communities	207
	8.1 Social and communal parameters of capitalist transformation	209
	8.2 A nascent capitalist class in Mount Vermion: Controlling the community and dealing with the state	217
	8.3 The emergence of a working class	227
	8.4 The clash of nationalisms	235
9	Precarious capitalism	257

Bibliography	263
Name Index	283
Subject Index	288

Plates

1 European territories of the Ottoman Empire at the end of the nineteenth century
2 The Ottoman *vilayet* of Thessaloniki (*Selanik*) and its provincial urban centres
3 The original plant of Longos–Kyrtsis–Tourpalis in Naoussa, 1870s
4 A drawing of the Bilis–Tsitsis plant in Naoussa in the early twentieth century
5 Commercial publicity of the Goutas–Karatzias plant
6 Commercial publicity of the mill of Longos–Tourpalis in the early 1900s
7 The approved application of Georgios Lapavitsas for a spinning mill in Naoussa
8 The machinery import list for the Kokkinos plant in Edhessa

Illustrations

Figures

1.1 Late Ottoman Thessaloniki viewed from the port	7
1.2 The mosque and the Muslim quarters of Naoussa	16
5.1 Commercial correspondence from Naoussa to Pyrgos in the Peloponnese, 1872	124
6.1 Demetrios Longos, *şayak* trader and industrialist of Naoussa	140
6.2 The plant of Longos–Tourpalis in Naoussa in the early twentieth century	142
6.3 The plant of Bilis–Tsitsis in Naoussa in the early twentieth century	143
6.4 The Tsitsis plant in Edhessa in the early twentieth century	144
6.5 Georgios Kyrtsis, industrialist and merchant of Naoussa and Edhessa	145
6.6 The Kyrtsis clocktower and the *konak* of the mayor of Naoussa	146
6.7 The railway station of Naoussa (*Ağustos*)	148
6.8 The Hadjilazaros–Angelakis (ERIA) plant in Naoussa in the early twentieth century	156
6.9 Locating textile mills next to water for power	168
6.10 The Allatini flour mill in Thessaloniki	169
6.11 The cotton production network in the *vilayet* of Thessaloniki, in the 1890s	170
7.1 Grigorios Longos, industrialist and merchant of Naoussa	189
7.2 Commercial correspondence of Tourpalis company in Thessaloniki	199
8.1 Members of the Longos family, early twentieth century	218
8.2 Bilis–Tsitsis families, early twentieth century	219
8.3 Tsitsis, Kokkinos and Longos families in the 1920s	219
8.4 Young women of Naoussa, early twentieth century	221
8.5 Working conditions in the factories	229
8.6 Child and female labour in the mills	230

8.7 Men working in the mills	230
8.8 a and b Letter by Kiryak Durzhilovich to Georgi Rakovski, 1860	244
8.9 Waiting for Sultan Mehmed Reşad in 1911	255

Tables

3.1 The administrative structure of the *vilayet* of Thessaloniki (*Selanik*)	49
3.2 Population of the *vilayet* of Thessaloniki, 1874	54
3.3 Population of the *vilayet* of Thessaloniki, 1876–1911	55
3.4 Composition of the population of the *vilayet* of Thessaloniki, 1902	59
3.5 Composition of the population of the *kaza* of Thessaloniki, 1902	59
3.6 Composition of the population of the *kaza* of Veroia, 1902	60
3.7 Composition of the population of the *kaza* of Edhessa, 1902	60
3.8 Composition of the population of the *nahiye* of Naoussa, 1902	60
4.1 Selected grains and cash crops in the *vilayet* of Thessaloniki, 1890	79
4.2 Land use in the *vilayet* of Thessaloniki, 1890	80
4.3 Agricultural production in the *kaza* of Veroia, 1886	82
4.4 Agricultural production in the *kaza* of Edhessa, 1886	83
4.5 Agricultural production in the *nahiye* of Naoussa, 1886	84
4.6 Christian *çiftlik* ownership in the area of Naoussa, 1913	93
5.1 Merchant families of Naoussa and the geographical area of their activities, 1911	117
5.2 Prominent merchants in Thessaloniki c. 1902	120
5.3 Prominent banks and bankers in Thessaloniki c. 1902	123
6.1 Jewish, Christian and Muslim traders, industrialists and bankers in Thessaloniki, 1906	134
6.2 Textile mills founded by industrialists from Naoussa, 1874–1912	173
6.3 Equity of Naoussa-owned mills, 1874–1912	174
7.1 Mill applications by Naoussa textile industrialists in provincial Macedonia, 1870–1902	190
7.2 Mill applications by Naoussa textile industrialists in provincial Macedonia, 1902–12	200

Diagrams

3.1 Population trend in the *kaza* of Thessaloniki, 1881–1906   57
3.2 Population trend in the *kaza* of Veroia, 1885–1904   57
3.3 Population trend in the *kaza* of Edhessa, 1885–1906   58

Abbreviations

B.O.A.	*Başbakanlık Osmanlı Arşivleri* (Prime Ministry Ottoman Archives), references followed by the section designation document number, and the *Hicri* date followed by the *Miladi* date in parentheses.
S.V.S.	*Selanik Vilayet Salnameleri* (Provincial Yearbooks of the Province of Salonica)
Ş.D.	*Şura-yı Devlet* (Council of State)
İ.T.N.F.	*İrade Ticaret ve Nafia Nezareti* (The Ministry of Trade and Public Works)
M.V.	*Meclis-i Vükela Mazbataları* (Records of the Council of Ministers)
İ.M.M.S.	*İrade Meclis-i Mahsus* (Decisions of the Special Council)
İ.R.S.M.	*İrade Rüsumat* (Excise Taxes)
B.E.O.	*Bab-ı Ali Evrak Odası* (Document Room of the Sublime Porte)
T.F.R.I.Ş.K.T.	*Rumeli Umum Müfettişliği- Şikayet* (General Inspectorate of *Rumeli*- complaints)
T.F.R.I.S.L.	*Rumeli Umum Müfettişliği- Selanik* (General Inspectorate of *Rumeli*- Salonica)
O.M.Z.M.	*Orman, Maden, Ziraat Mecmuası* (Journal of Forestry, Mining and Agriculture)
C.U.P.	Committee of Union and Progress
E.I.H.N.	Elements of Industrial Heritage in Naoussa

Notes on Weights, Measures and Currency

1 *dirhem* = 3.2 g
1 *kıyye (okka)* = 1.283 kg, taken as 1.3 kg
1 *kile* = 20 *kıyye* = 26 kg
1 *kütle (balya)* = 25–35 kg, taken as 30 kg
1 *zira (arşın)* = 0.757738m, taken as 0.75m
1 *dönüm* = 919.3m^2 also taken as 1600m^2 for some calculations specified in the footnotes
1 Ottoman *Lira* = 100 *kuruş* (or *guruş*) = 4000 *para*
1 British Pound Sterling = 20 shillings
1 British Pound Sterling = roughly 1.1 Ottoman *Lira*

Notes on Transliteration, Spelling and Pronunciation

The geographical area covered in this book is notorious for nationalism that has attached itself vigorously to place names. The choice of name for a town, a city, even a country, is a complex issue with potentially poisonous implications. For consistency and clarity we chose to deploy the contemporary national versions of place names as a matter of course, while occasionally giving original Ottoman names in brackets and typically in italics, all in Latin characters.

For Ottoman place names, but also for other terms and expressions, including words that are Arabic or Persian in origin, or even words that have now entered the English language, we deployed the modern standard Turkish spelling system with very few exceptions. To give an example, *paşa* and *vakıf* were used in preference to pasha and waqf. The vast majority of these words were italicized and, typically, their first mention in the text was accompanied by their common English version or a simple explanation in English in brackets.

For Greek and Slavic place names and other terms and expressions we generally avoided using both the Greek and the Cyrillic alphabet, except on very few occasions. Relevant place names were transliterated using the Latin alphabet in the simplest and clearest phonetic way. In some instances in the text – and when confusion was unlikely – we used place names interchangeably, for instance, Constantinople – *İstanbul*, or Thessaloniki – Salonica – *Selanik*.

Consider, for example, the name of the town at the heart of the book. We used the term Naoussa to render the contemporary Greek Νάουσα, though the variant Naousa can also be frequently found in the English-speaking literature. Moreover, the term *Ağustos* was occasionally used to render the Ottoman Turkish name of the town, آغوستوس. The term *Ağustos* is also the modern Turkish name of Naoussa. Note that an older version of Νάουσα in Greek is Νιάουστα (Niausta), while in Macedonian and Bulgarian the name of the town is Негуш (Negush). It is more than likely that all these terms are etymologically related to each other.

It must be admitted, nonetheless, that in the Balkans very few rules can be rigidly adhered to, especially in matters of language. Some flexibility was inevitably necessary, but care was taken to avoid confusion in all instances. Finally, when referencing Turkish scholars, we used modern Turkish orthography unless the scholars have themselves chosen to use standard English orthography for their names. This was mainly the case for works by Turkish authors that were written or published in English. For Greek or other scholars, we simply transliterated names as simply and clearly as possible in a phonetic way.

Note also that the modern Turkish alphabet contains letters that differ from standard English orthography and pronunciation. The following list should be helpful to the reader:

C, c = 'j' as in 'jet'
Ç, ç = 'ch' as in 'chapter'
Ğ, ğ = soft 'g', lengthens preceding vowel; thus ağa pronounced as a—a
I, ı = undotted i, similar the vowel sound of 'e' in 'open' or the sound of 'io' in 'cushion'
İ, i = 'ee' as in 'see'
Ö, ö = as in German, similar to the vowel sound in 'bird'
Ş, ş = 'sh' as in 'should'
Ü, ü = as in German, or in the French 'tu'

Notes on Archives

Archive references are reported according to the standard methods used for decades by the 'Republic of Turkey Prime Ministerial Ottoman Archives' (*Türkiye Cumhuriyeti Başbakanlık Osmanlı Arşivleri* – BOA). However, the Ottoman Archives have been recently re-organized under the name of 'Republic of Turkey Presidential State Archives' (*Türkiye Cumhuriyeti Cumhurbaşkanlığı Devlet Arşivleri*). It is assumed that the referencing methods of the re-organized Archives will be compatible with the previous long-standing practice.

Acknowledgements

Several people have contributed to putting this book together, knowingly or unknowingly. Special mention should be made of Donald Quataert, who long ago realized the significance of the topic and was quick to offer encouragement. Onur Yildirim, Christos Hadziiossif and Socratis Petmezas read various parts of the text and made important points. Yorgos Dedes solved problems of translating Ottoman Turkish as well as making penetrating comments on the content. Nikos Kokkinos offered constructive comments on the overall argument of the book. The Institute for Mediterranean Studies (IMS-FORTH) was very helpful throughout the lengthy process of research, and a debt of gratitude is owed to Marinos Sariyannis, who kindly made available his extensive expertise of Ottoman archives and texts. Gratitude is also owed to Julia Karadatchka-Simeonova of the Bulgarian National Library for generous help at a critical moment of writing. Finally, Alexandros Oikonomou offered vital insights into the history, the buildings and the sites of factories in the Mount Vermion area, while Takis Baitsis and Lazaros Biliouris were unstinting with photographs and other important local information.

1

The emergence of industrial capitalism in Ottoman Macedonia: A tale to be told

1.1 Historical development condensed

In 1923 the Ottoman Empire came to a formal end after a bitter war that gave birth to the Turkish Republic. Ten years earlier the bulk of the Empire's possessions in Europe – 'Turkey in Europe' – had been lost to the Balkan states, the victors of the First Balkan War. For several decades – even centuries – prior to these cataclysms, the Empire had been perceived in Europe as a decaying society that could barely survive.

The academic perception of the Ottoman Empire has improved considerably in the near century since its death. With the passage of time a fuller picture has emerged of the complex social and political processes that took place as the Empire approached its end, including the sustained reform efforts by the Ottoman state. Historians have conclusively shown that during its final decades the Ottoman Empire made large strides towards modernity. However, age-old prejudices die hard. The Ottomans are not often associated with the dramatic developments that shaped Europe in the nineteenth century – and marked the Romanov and Habsburg empires – including urbanization, growth of wage labour, decline of traditional agriculture and effervescent modernity.

Yet, prejudice aside, the Ottoman Empire exhibited considerable economic dynamism towards its end, much of it due to industrial and commercial capitalism surging from its own domestic wellsprings. The Ottomans began to engage in modernization already in the late eighteenth and early nineteenth centuries. By the time they came to lose their European provinces, the rudiments of an industrial economy were discernible across much of the Empire. Perhaps the clearest evidence of transformation was the emergence of substantial social mobility among the Christian and Jewish communities, which were able to achieve an unprecedented prominence in the Ottoman world.

Macedonia was at the forefront of these economic and social developments. For one thing, the region had great strategic importance for the – rapidly shrinking – late Ottoman Empire, as is apparent from the map in Plate 1. At the end of the nineteenth century, after substantial losses in the preceding decades, Macedonia was the main European territory of the Ottomans, with the exception of Thrace and the imperial capital İstanbul. The port of Thessaloniki (*Selanik*) was the effective capital of Macedonia and a crucial point of contact with the then dominant European economies.

The city of Thessaloniki and its immediate hinterland witnessed profound changes during the second half of the nineteenth century. To be more specific, in 1912, when Ottoman rule in Macedonia came to an end, Thessaloniki possessed several features characteristic of a European city of the turn of the twentieth century including an active industrial and commercial economy functioning along recognizably capitalist lines. It is not surprising that the Macedonian city has long commanded a prominent place in both the historical analysis and the narrative of Ottoman modernity. Precisely because it was a focal point of modernity and lay at some distance from the imperial police machine dominating İstanbul at the beginning of the twentieth century, Thessaloniki provided a natural home for the Young Turks, who brought an end to the absolute power of the Sultan in 1908.

However, Ottoman capitalism in Macedonia had a further notable aspect that has remained practically unknown in the historiography of the Empire. The geographical area with the most dynamic industrial concentration, which stood out in terms of growth and competitive thrust, lay in the Macedonian provinces well to the west of Thessaloniki. The region of Mount Vermion, comprising the three towns of Naoussa (*Ağustos*), Veroia (*Karaferye*) and Edhessa (*Vodina*) – shown in Plate 2 in the next section – registered rapid growth in industrial textiles for four decades prior to 1912, the year when the region was incorporated into the Kingdom of Greece. A subsidiary role was played by the town of Giannitsa (*Yenice-i Vardar*) lying on the plain of Macedonia, roughly halfway between Thessaloniki and the three provincial towns of Mount

Vermion.[1] When Ottoman rule ended in 1912, the region of Mount Vermion had already overtaken Thessaloniki in the core industrial sector of textiles.

This aspect of Ottoman history has barely been noticed in academic and other writing on the economic history of Europe. The lacuna is striking for several reasons, not least because the Ottoman Empire was, even at its end, a significant power in possession of vast territories. Its subsequent demise has left a legacy that continues to shape political events in South-Eastern Europe and the Middle East. The emergence of active industrial capitalism in the Ottoman Macedonian territories would merit thorough historical examination on these grounds alone. After all, both the history and the contemporary reality of the Balkans continue to bear the imprint of emerging industrial and commercial capitalism in what used to be 'Turkey in Europe'.

Beside its importance for European economic history, Ottoman industrialization in provincial Macedonia also repays analysis for reasons directly related to the theory of capitalist development, four of which could be mentioned immediately. First, industrialization occurred spontaneously in the spinning of cotton yarn, led by private capitalists who took advantage of local conditions, global trends and favourable policies by the Ottoman state. Second, industrialization emerged in the upland areas of an essentially agricultural region. While industrialization made great strides, agriculture remained dominated by smallholdings as well as by large estates that relied on sharecropping. There were no significant traces of agrarian capitalism in Ottoman Macedonia. Third, the capitalists that led industrialization were mostly merchants who had accumulated capital by trading in domestically produced woollen cloth. The merchant-capitalists also controlled much of the production of woollen cloth. Fourth, several of the merchants and industrialists acquired substantial landed estates on the Macedonian plain but without transforming them into capitalist farms. Analysis of these

---

[1] Place names – indeed all names – in Macedonia are a fraught issue with a poisonous nationalist pedigree, as was mentioned in the Notes on Transliteration, Spelling and Pronunciation. In this book precedence is given to contemporary national place names (Greek, Turkish, Bulgarian and other) accompanied by their Ottoman variant (Ottoman Turkish in italics and transliterated in the Latin alphabet). However, it is practically impossible to adhere rigidly to this rule, as well as to several others, in Macedonia. Some flexibility has inevitably been necessary in the text. Thus, Naoussa is the transliteration of modern Greek Νάουσα, which can also be rendered as Naousa. Note that the town has also been historically known as Νιάουστα (Niausta) in Greek. Its name in Macedonian and Bulgarian is Херуш (Negush).

aspects of Ottoman Macedonian industrialization can cast an interesting light on the long-standing debates regarding the historical emergence of capitalism.

It is important to note, furthermore, that the merchants and industrialists of Mount Vermion were overwhelmingly Christian Greeks who competed against the Jewish merchants and industrialists dominant in Thessaloniki. Indeed, capitalist development differed considerably between Mount Vermion and Thessaloniki due in part to the dissimilar social origins, internal organization and cultural outlook of the Christian Greek and the Jewish communities. The framework within which industrialization took place in Macedonia reflected the long history of segmentation and discrimination among communities within the Ottoman Empire and provided the seedbed for virulent nationalism at roughly the same time. The ultimate historical demise of the Ottoman Empire is related to these phenomena.

A word of warning is essential at this point. To its very end, the Empire remained a predominantly agrarian society that covered enormous areas of the Balkans, Anatolia and the Middle East. The Ottoman economy was largely dominated by traditional small-scale agriculture, with the cities standing as islands in a sea of peasantry. Provincial Macedonia was a leader in Ottoman industrialization, but compared to the vastness of the Empire, the region amounted to little more than a small pocket of industrial capitalism.

The analysis of textile industrialization in the area of Mount Vermion – and especially in the small town of Naoussa that lay at its heart – constitutes essentially a case study of capitalist transformation under specific conditions. But if there ever was a case study capable of condensing the economic, social, political and historical characteristics of late Ottoman capitalism, this would be it. Analysis of the economic history of Mount Vermion sums up the strengths, weaknesses and inner mechanisms of Ottoman modernization – such as it was – particularly when the integral links between Mount Vermion and Thessaloniki are also considered. Some fresh light can thus be shed on Ottoman economic history as well as adding a piece to the puzzle of European economic development in the nineteenth century. Approached with caution the study even has relevance for the theoretical analysis of the transition to capitalism in general.

1.2 The geographical and historical terrain of Macedonia

A sense of history and a sense of place are vital when it comes to analysing industrial capitalism. The first step, therefore, is briefly to lay out the geographical and historical backdrop of emerging Ottoman industrial capitalism in Macedonia. Plate 2 shows the *vilayet* of Thessaloniki, that is, the Ottoman administrative unit covering the relevant area of Macedonia.[2] In Chapter 3 the administrative and other institutions of the *vilayet* are considered in some detail. Suffice it in this chapter to go over some key aspects of Macedonian geography and history by relying partly on the map in Plate 2.

1.2.1 Thessaloniki

The point of departure is inevitably the city of Thessaloniki. Towards the end of the nineteenth century, Thessaloniki was one of several port cities of the Eastern Mediterranean that embodied Ottoman commercial expansion and modernization. The list also includes İzmir and Beirut, and is obviously headed by İstanbul, the epicentre of Ottoman modernity.[3] However, the capital city has always been a special case in Ottoman history and should be treated accordingly. For our purposes, in the year 1900, Thessaloniki was the largest and most developed city of the European provinces of the Empire after İstanbul.

Thessaloniki is an ancient city established in the late fourth century BC by the Macedonian King Cassander, who gave it the name of his wife, daughter of King Philip and half-sister of King Alexander, the conqueror of Asia. The city was a prominent urban centre of the Roman province of Macedonia and a leading Byzantine metropolis in Europe, for several centuries second only to the capital Constantinople. From 1430 to 1912 Thessaloniki was an Ottoman city, and for most of that time the majority of its population was Jewish.[4]

---

[2] *Vilayet* was the name given to the major provincial units in the late Ottoman Empire in accordance with the Regulation for Provinces (*Teşkil-i Vilayet Nizamnamesi*), discussed further in Chapter 3.

[3] Port-cities of the Eastern Mediterranean (the Levant) have been the subject of several comparative studies; see, for instance, Mansel (2010) and Keyder, Özveren, and Quataert (1994).

[4] The historical literature on Thessaloniki is large and not directly relevant to our purposes. It is worth noting, nonetheless, that Mazower (2004) has written an absorbing overview of the Ottoman history of the city. Also, both the spirit and the social ambience of Ottoman Thessaloniki have been succinctly captured in a few pages by Dumont (2013), who drew on the meticulous work of Anastassiadou (1997).

Those who know and have the choice always approach Thessaloniki from the sea. The boat sails into the Thermaic Gulf from the south, eventually to navigate the narrow mouth of the inner gulf guarded by an Ottoman fort lying on a small promontory to the east. The city appears at the head of the gulf, hemmed in by low hills to the north and bounded by Mount Hortiatis (*Hortaç*) in the east. The great flatlands of Macedonia stretch uninterruptedly to the west all the way to the ring of mountains surrounding the plain. This is a very different land to southern Greece, a place of frequent and low mists, times when sea and sky become one. It can be bitterly cold and rainy in winter, and is hot and bright in summer.

As the boat approaches the docks of the contemporary city the waterfront comes into full view and the Ottoman past of Thessaloniki becomes immediately apparent to the trained eye. The old quay, stretching from east to west, is an Ottoman creation, the outcome of the great symbolic act of demolishing the waterfront section of the ancient Byzantine Wall in the late 1860s and early 1870s. Modernity had arrived in Ottoman Thessaloniki, and that meant forcibly opening the city to the sea, where trade came from. Only a remnant of the old fortifications now stands by the waterfront, the large circular redoubt of the White Tower built by the Ottomans, which the quirks of history have turned into the official landmark of the contemporary Greek city. In other parts of Thessaloniki much of the Wall is still extant, snaking up the low hills to the north towards *Yedikule*, the Ottoman fort at the hilltop. Evidence of the Ottoman past is also apparent to the east of the waterfront in the Victorian hulk of the Allatini flour mill built by the Jewish family of that name, which dominated commerce and industry in Ottoman Thessaloniki. An original picture of the mill is shown in Figure 6.10 of Chapter 6.

To someone approaching by boat in the 1900s the city would have looked vastly different, as is clear from Figure 1.1. For one thing there would have been tens of minarets rising across the urban area but also large expanses of unbuilt space within the Byzantine Wall, especially towards the upper part of the city, near the *Yedikule*, which is clearly visible in the picture. Several bulky western-style buildings would have stood by the quay – a mixture of commercial real estate, hotels and a few private houses. Immediately behind this zone of self-conscious modernity would have spread a warren of narrow alleys, populated mostly by the Jewish poor. Sanitation would

Figure 1.1 Late Ottoman Thessaloniki viewed from the port
Source: A postcard of the city taken from the openarchives.gr.

have been minimal and public services few and modest. In its physical layout, Thessaloniki remained a resolutely Ottoman city until the Great Fire of 1917 that destroyed much of it. Even so, the evidence of capitalist modernity would have never been far away from the visitor. In the middle of the quay – but unfortunately not visible in Figure 1.1 – would have stood the textile mill of Saias Brothers, another prominent Jewish family, its serried roofs and tall chimney reminding the world that this was, after all, a city with industry.

Just before the end of Ottoman rule, in the year 1910 the passenger would have disembarked at the recently built new docks and gone through the Customs House, designed by Eli Modiano, a scion of another of the richest and most powerful Jewish families of Thessaloniki. The Customs House still stands, a broadly neoclassical building, imperial in magnitude, built as the gateway to a large and rapidly modernizing state. Close to it there still remain several late Ottoman commercial buildings that formed the historic heart of commerce in the city. Notable among them is the local branch of the Ottoman Bank, the most powerful financial institution of the late Empire, as well as the offices of the Banque de Salonique, established by the ubiquitous Allatini. Both were built by Vitaliano Poselli, the architect *par excellence* of late Ottoman Thessaloniki, in his distinctive eclectic style. The life of the commercial quarter during Ottoman times would have been dominated by Jewish merchants, industrialists and financiers. The Jewish community of Thessaloniki met an awful end at Auschwitz in the 1940s and very few physical mementoes of its wealth, power and culture remain in the city. There is probably not a single original *mezuzah*, the traditional Jewish providential insertion of the Torah at the entrance of a building, in contemporary Thessaloniki.

Historically the communities of the Ottoman city lived in distinct quarters, but there were no ghettos. The Jews dominated the low, narrow streets near the waterfront, the poorest, least hygienic and most claustrophobic parts of Ottoman Thessaloniki. Things improved after the waterfront section of the Byzantine Wall was knocked down in the early 1870s, allowing the sea breezes to circulate freely. The Greeks lived in the vicinity of their churches found typically in the lower and the eastern part of the city. These were mostly humble affairs built during the centuries of Ottoman rule, since the splendid Byzantine churches of Thessaloniki had all been turned into mosques. The Turks lived in the upper part of the city, where the air was fresher and the views across the gulf expansive. The future founder of the Turkish Republic, Mustafa Kemal Atatürk, grew up in one of the more modest of these neighbourhoods.

By the 1900s life in Ottoman Thessaloniki had changed dramatically as the expansion of commerce and the demolition of the Wall encouraged the wealthy to purchase property close to the waterfront. The area of power and privilege shifted imperceptibly towards the sea and came to be dominated by Jews and Greeks. The traditional Turkish quarters of the upper city took an inexorable turn towards poverty and decline. As industrial capitalism sunk roots and factories emerged, especially among the Jewish community, Thessaloniki acquired the unmistakable aspect of an industrial city in the classic nineteenth century European mould. Mills and other industrial plant emerged in the middle of working class neighbourhoods, the workers walking to work.

Equally notable was the flight of the very rich – Turks, Jews and Greeks – to the eastern part of the waterfront, the 'country' outside the Byzantine Wall. By the early twentieth century an Ottoman suburb had emerged, the *Kelemeriye* (Kalamaria) quarter, an exclusive preserve of the richest bourgeois families dominating real estate, commerce and industry in Macedonia. They have left their mark on the contemporary city with a sprinkling of exuberant Neoromantic, Baroque Revival, Neoclassical and syncretic villas. Their houses certainly stand out among the faceless apartment blocs of the contemporary Greek city but, it must be said, the bourgeois class of Ottoman Thessaloniki would never have won high marks for taste.

1.2.2 Mount Vermion

At the beginning of the twentieth century Thessaloniki dominated Ottoman Macedonia economically, politically and culturally. It was a beacon of capitalist modernity and played a leading part in the Ottoman effort to catch up with 'advanced' Western Europe. Beyond the city, however, the Macedonian plain presented a sharp contrast with the relative sophistication of the port. It was a world dominated by agriculture of poor efficiency, low incomes and generally small urban settlements. Yet, even amidst the general agricultural sluggishness of the plain, industrial capitalism was making rapid advances. By the first decade of the twentieth century the area of Mount Vermion, on the western outskirts of the flatlands, had already surpassed Thessaloniki in core fields of industrial production.

In late Ottoman times the area of Mount Vermion could be reached from Thessaloniki via two roads, both visible on the map in Plate 2. The first crossed the plain in the direction of due west and met the town of Giannitsa (*Yenice-i Vardar*) and then the town of Edhessa (*Vodina*). Beyond Edhessa the road reached Bitola (*Manastır*) deep in the mountainous Macedonian interior, and eventually arrived at the Albanian coast. This was broadly the path of the historic Via Egnatia of the Romans but also of the *Rumeli Sol Kol* of the Ottomans, that is, the trunk road connecting İstanbul to Thessaloniki and then to the Adriatic Sea.[5] It is still one of the main roads linking Thessaloniki to its Macedonian hinterland and beyond.

The second road was smaller, following initially the path of the first but soon branching south-west in the direction of the town of Veroia (*Karaferye*)

---

[5] *Rumeli Sol Kol* means the *Rumeli* Left Arm, that is, the road veering left from İstanbul in the European part of the Empire (*Rumeli*). It was mainly used as a military term.

subsequently to continue towards the southern Macedonian interior. At Veroia, a minor spur of it turned north, arriving at the town of Naoussa (*Ağustos*) and then again at Edhessa. The second road is similarly in existence in contemporary Macedonia but a modern motorway also connecting Thessaloniki to Veroia has been built some way further to the south. After reaching Veroia, the motorway continues west through the Greek mountains and eventually reaches the Ionian Sea, opposite the Italian coast. The same motorway also stretches east from Thessaloniki to reach İstanbul, and on this length it broadly follows the path of the historic Via Egnatia.

Both roads from Thessaloniki to the west still reflect vital social and natural aspects of Ottoman Macedonia that shaped the emergence of industrial capitalism and should be taken in turn.

1.2.2.1 *The road to Giannitsa and Edhessa*

The road from Thessaloniki to Giannitsa and Edhessa crosses endless fields of cotton and corn, and the land is either gently undulating or perfectly flat. In Ottoman times much of the terrain would have been a vast marshland, thick with swaying reeds and a shallow lake in the middle, the Lake of Giannitsa, clearly visible on the map in Plate 2. The rivers coming down from the mountains surrounding the plain created a swampy lake that marked the physiognomy of the land until the 1930s, when it was drained as part of the agrarian policies of the Greek state. The land of the plain has always been fertile, a natural fact that has shaped the history of Macedonia over the centuries, but was also ridden with diseases, especially malaria. Agrarian cultivation often took place close to the marshy lake, and the everyday life of the peasants was moulded by the water's proximity.

Both sides of the road are marked by low earth-mounts, Macedonian tombs from classical, Hellenistic and later times. The principal tombs are near the contemporary village of Pella, site of the last capital of the ancient kingdom of Macedonia and seat of power of Kings Philip and Alexander. A little after Pella, altogether about fifty-five kilometres from Thessaloniki, the road arrives at Giannitsa and the Ottoman past of deep Macedonia is at once evident.

Yenice-i Vardar (Giannitsa) was founded in the 1380s by the Ottoman forces that landed in Europe in the 1350s and took both Thrace and Macedonia within three decades. The town was a Muslim and Turkish urban centre from the very beginning of Ottoman rule, the seat of the most powerful family of the region, the Evrenosoğullari.⁶ The tomb of the founder of the dynasty, *Gazi* Evrenos *Bey*, who apparently died in 1417, still stands in Giannitsa, together with several other Ottoman monuments that include mosques (*camii*) and Turkish baths (*hamam*). The first to establish their historical importance was the Dutch Ottomanist Machiel Kiel.⁷

The descendants of Evrenos dictated the patterns of landownership and shaped political events in Macedonia to the end of Ottoman rule. Their power derived from the religious foundation, the *vakıf* (or waqf in Arabic) founded by *Gazi* Evrenos at Giannitsa and through which they controlled a huge part of the plain. The mode of operation of the *vakıf* and its implications for the development of capitalism in Macedonia will be considered in Chapter 4. The Evrenos family also owned or controlled large tracts of land in Thrace and elsewhere in the Balkans.⁸ Wealth and power allowed the Evrenosoğullari to be governors of Thessaloniki repeatedly during Ottoman rule.⁹ The last scion of the family to play a prominent role in Ottoman affairs was Evrenoszade Rahmi *Bey*, a member of the Ottoman Parliament in the 1870s, one of the first Young Turks, and governor (*vali*) of İzmir during the First World War, after the Evrenos family had departed their ancient seat in Macedonia in 1912.¹⁰

In the eighteenth century the power of the Evrenosoğullari began to decline as the *vakıf* gradually collapsed for reasons that will be discussed subsequently. By the nineteenth century commerce and capitalism had spread across Macedonia and the old Ottoman ways had become increasingly unviable. In the second half of the nineteenth century Giannitsa was a noteworthy commercial centre that also produced domestically manufactured rough cotton cloth. At the turn of the twentieth century it had a sizeable population, a good proportion of which was Christian. So significant had the Christian population become in this most Muslim and Turkish of Macedonian settlements that in the early

---

[6] See Lowry and Erünsal (2010).
[7] See Kiel (1972). Among Greek Ottomanists, the work of Demetriades (1976) has been path-breaking in establishing the history of the surrounding area. The historical importance of Giannitsa is increasingly appreciated by Greek historians, see the excellent account by Androudis (2014).
[8] See Lowry (2008).
[9] See, for instance, Lowry and Erünsal (2010, pp. 58, 68). See also Lowry (2010).
[10] See Mazower (2004, pp. 152–3).

1860s a large church was built in a Christian neighbourhood in the perimeter of the town.

There is, however, a further reason why the Evrenos family were important for our purposes. A grandson of *Gazi* Evrenos by the name of Evrenosoğlu Ahmed *Bey* – a capable bureaucrat and military officer who died around 1500 – established a further, smaller, *vakıf* in Macedonia, as part of the family's estates. The largest settlement on the *vakıf* of Ahmed *Bey* was the town of Ağustos. The founder of Naoussa, the town where Macedonian industrialization emerged in the nineteenth century, was a member of the Evrenos family, and the founding act probably took place sometime in the second half of the fifteenth century.

The new settlement came into existence partly due to Şeyh Abdullah-i İlahi, a celebrated Sufi mystic and spiritual mentor (a *şeyh*), who belonged to the *Nakşibendi* order of Sufism. He had been brought to Giannitsa from Anatolia by Ahmed *Bey*, who was keen to lend to the seat of the Evrenosoğullari some intellectual and religious lustre.[11] To make it easier for the *şeyh* to do his work, Ahmed *Bey* built for him a religious school (*medrese*), a mosque and a Turkish bath in Giannitsa, all of which were integral elements of Islamic cultural life. İlahi spread the *Nakşibendi* beliefs across the southern Balkans until the year of his death in 1491. Sometime before the death of the *şeyh*, Ahmed *Bey* also had a religious retreat built for him, a *tekke*, at a sylvan spot on the foothills of Mount Vermion lying at a considerable distance from Giannitsa, near a small waterfall created by the river Arapitsa. The building of the *tekke* was probably the true symbolic act of the foundation of Naoussa, which soon emerged as a sizeable town of Christians. Centuries later, just below the site of the *tekke*, at a spot called *Tekkealtı* (literally 'below the tekke') there would be built one of the first cotton spinning mills in Macedonia.

After Giannitsa the road continues west, skirting the original site of the drained marshy lake. In Ottoman times this part of the plain would have been sparsely populated, the villages being small hamlets with a few tens of households. Thirty-five kilometres later, the road reaches the hilly area just off the northern spur of Mount Vermion, and there lies Edhessa (*Vodina*). Unlike Giannitsa, Edhessa is an uphill town, built at a significant elevation,

---

[11] See Kiel (1972, pp. 308–10).

and surrounded by dense forests. It is crossed by the river Edhessaios (*Voda*) affording easy access to water. To the north of Edhessa lies the fertile plain of Almopia, an offshoot of the great Macedonian plain. Almopia, known in the Ottoman period – and today – as the *Karacaabad/Karacaova* region, is surrounded by high mountains, the largest being Voras (*Kaymakçalan*).

Edhessa is not an old town and is attested as *Vodina* in the writings of the Byzantine historian Ioannis Skylitzes in the eleventh century. According to Skylitzes, the Emperor Basil II took the stronghold of *Vodina* from Tsar Samuel of the Bulgarians incorporating the town into the Byzantine Empire, probably in the years 1001–2. Skylitzes knew that *Vodina* was built on a precipice and that there were waterfalls in the vicinity.[12] Large waterfalls are the hallmark of Edhessa even today, the name *Vodina* implying the presence of water in Bulgarian and its indigenous Macedonian variant. The abundance of fast-flowing water was the main reason why Edhessa became a leading site of industrialization in the late Ottoman period, with know-how and capital imported from Naoussa. Around 1900 Edhessa was a sizeable town, the population of which was about one third Muslim and two-thirds Christian as is shown in Table 3.7 of Chapter 3.

1.2.2.2 *The road to Veroia and Naoussa*

The main road from Thessaloniki to Veroia and Naoussa today starts as a motorway that heads south through fields of wheat and rice broadly tracing the coastline of the Thermaic Gulf. Soon after it leaves Thessaloniki, the motorway begins to cross the rivers of the plain, visible in Plate 2. The river Axios (*Vardar*) is the largest in Macedonia and after it comes Loudias (*Kara Asmak*) deepened and straightened in the 1930s to provide the main drainage outlet of the plain to the sea. Just before crossing the river Haliacmon (*İnce*

---

[12] See Skylitzes (Basil and Constantine 27) in Thurn (1973, pp, 344–5): 'φρούριον δὲ τὰ Βοδινὰ ἐπὶ πέτρας ἀποτόμου κείμενον, δι' ἧς καταρρεῖ τὸ τῆς λίμνης τοῦ Ὀστροβοῦ ὕδωρ, ὑπὸ γῆς κάτωθεν ῥέον ἀφανῶς κἀκεῖσε πάλιν ἀναδυόμενον. καὶ ἐπεὶ μὴ ἑκουσίως παρεδίδοσαν ἑαυτοὺς οἱ ἔνδον, πολιορκίᾳ τοῦτο κατέσχε. καὶ τούτους ὁμοίως εἰς τὸν Βολερὸν ἀποικίσας, φρουρᾷ δὲ τοῦτο ὀχυρωσάμενος ἀξιολόγῳ, ἐπάνεισιν εἰς Θεσσαλονίκην'. Freely translated it states: 'Vodina is a stronghold lying on a precipitous rock, from which fall the waters of the lake of Ostrovo, flowing unseen under the earth and thither re-emerging. Because those inside did not willingly surrender, he besieged it. And after moving them to Voleron, he strongly garrisoned it and returned to Thessaloniki'. Skylitzes was wrong to think that the waters of Edhessa flow from Lake Ostrovo, which is visible on the map in Plate 2 lying to the west of the town. Rather, the waterfalls drain the surrounding mountains.

Karasu) the motorway branches to the west and begins to skirt the low hills adjacent to the river. Nearby lies Aigai, the first capital of historic Macedonia, with its huge necropolis and the tombs of the ancient Macedonian kings. Dense orchards of fruit trees, mostly peaches, line up both sides of the road, but in Ottoman times almost the whole of the cultivated area would have been given to grains, and much of the land would have looked low, muddy and infested with reeds.

About seventy kilometres from Thessaloniki, the motorway reaches Veroia (*Karaferye*) lying at the foot of Mount Vermion (*Karakamen*) which is also the natural border of the plain to the west. Veroia, built on a low elevation, is a truly ancient town, older than Thessaloniki. It was a thriving centre in Roman times, giving good cause to the Apostle Paul to preach the Gospel there between AD 50 and 60. It was also a noteworthy Byzantine settlement and has a profusion of churches. More relevant for our purposes is that Veroia was the seat of Ottoman administration and the leading town of the region of Mount Vermion.[13] Evidence of the Ottoman past abounds in Veroia, mostly Turkish baths and mosques, none more romantic than the near-ruin of *Orta Camii*, with its evocative and now rare in Greece *alaca* (pied) minaret.

The population of Veroia around 1900 was one-quarter Muslim and three-quarters Christian, as is shown in Table 3.6 of Chapter 3. There was also a sizeable indigenous Jewish contingent that was destroyed in the course of the European disasters of the 1940s but, unlike their coreligionists in Thessaloniki, the Jews were not important to the emergence of industrial capitalism in the local area. The key to the industrial development of Ottoman Veroia was the small river Tripotamos, a tributary of the Haliacmon, passing through the town and providing irrigation and scope for hydropower. The know-how and the motive force of industrialization, similarly to Edhessa, came from Naoussa.

At Veroia the old Ottoman road forms a spur that leaves the motorway and heads north tracing the foothills of Mount Vermion for about twenty kilometres before reaching Naoussa (*Ağustos*). The town is built at a considerable elevation on the mountain and has always been closely associated with it, at times even lending to it its name in Turkish – *Ağustos Dağ*. Naoussa is surrounded by dense forests of beech, oak, hazel trees and black pine, and has a continental

---

[13] See Anastasopoulos (1999, 2002).

microclimate, with harsh and snowy winters. It is crossed by the river Arapitsa, descending from Mount Vermion, a fast stream that creates several small waterfalls, offering potential for hydropower. The Arapitsa proved pivotal to the industrialization of Naoussa in Ottoman times.[14]

At the start of the sixteenth century, Naoussa was a sizeable community of two thousand inhabitants who were overwhelmingly Christian, as will be shown in Chapter 3. During the next two hundred years there was very little to make the town stand out, except perhaps being a major producer of wine and its distillates (*arak*), as was noted in the seventeenth century.[15] Administratively it came under the jurisdiction of the *paşa* (pasha) of Thessaloniki, and according to Evliya Çelebi, the indefatigable Ottoman traveller, in the seventeenth century there was a resident *mütevelli* (trustee) of the *vakıf* of Evrenos as well as a *voyvoda* acting on behalf of the Sultan's mother who had property in the area.[16] Evliya Çelebi also noted the presence of a low-ranking Muslim religious judge, a *naib*, who dealt with criminal and civil cases.[17]

During the decline of central Ottoman power in the late eighteenth and early nineteenth century – the period of the *ayan* (notables) that will be discussed in subsequent chapters – the town had its own Christian armed forces. Inevitably it attracted the tender attentions of the greatest of the *ayan* in the Balkans, Tepedelenli Ali *Paşa* of Ioannina (*Yanya*), who besieged it in 1795, 1798 and 1804, finally bringing it under his control for a decade by treaty. But Naoussa always maintained a measure of self-government, at least according to western travellers.[18] The town also had extensive domestic manufacturing in linen

---

[14] The first reference to the river of Naoussa was perhaps by Aelian in *De Natura Animalium*, who mentioned it as the original site of fly-fishing for trout in the early third century AD; see Hammond (1995). At the time it was called the Astraeus, a name that was maybe also given to some of the surrounding Vermion foothills. Other parts of the foothills near Naoussa were in antiquity associated with the ancient city of Mieza and were called the 'Gardens of Midas', the legendary king of the Frygians with the golden touch. The 'Gardens of Midas' is indeed an appropriate name for a region of exceptional lushness and plentiful water. Şeyh İlahi joined a long tradition when he chose this site for his *tekke*.

[15] See Gara (1998, p. 152).

[16] *Voyvoda* originally designated a commander or a prince in Slavic languages. The term was used to denote rulership in the Christian states of Wallachia and Moldavia, in the northeast of the Balkan peninsula, prior to the Ottoman conquest. During the Ottoman era it was also used to denote the governors of Wallachia and Moldavia appointed by the Porte.

[17] See Demetriades (1973, pp. 30–4, 246, 248).

[18] See Cousinery (1831, p. 73); Pouqueville (1826, vol. III, p. 94).

Figure 1.2 The mosque and the Muslim quarters of Naoussa

Source: Private collection of Takis Baitsis.

towels, wool-fulling, silk, jewellery and weapons.[19] Trade was a significant activity and there were Naoussa merchants in Central Europe.[20]

In 1822, soon after the outbreak of the Greek War of Independence in 1821, Naoussa rebelled against the Sublime Porte. It was immediately besieged by forces from Thessaloniki led by Mehmed Emin Abu Lubut *Paşa*, who sacked it. The town lay in ruins for years and recovery began only in the 1830s, when it was repopulated by returning inhabitants and Christians from surrounding areas. Muslims were also brought in, some from further afield, with the transparent aim of forestalling future disturbances. The Muslims were a poor community of farmers and craftsmen who never played a decisive role in the economic life of the town. Their modest mosque – now long gone – lying close to their humble dwellings is shown in a postcard from 1918 in Figure 1.2.

In the 1830s, however, the Ottoman Empire fully entered the era of its modernization that gradually led to deep transformation of both economy and society. Ottoman reform swept Naoussa in its path. By the end of the nineteenth century this rather insignificant upland Macedonian town had become a focal point of manufacturing and commercial activity, emerging as a centre of Ottoman industrial capitalism. The implications were profound for the entire region of Mount Vermion but also for Thessaloniki and, more broadly, for Ottoman Macedonia. This is the tale to be told.

---

[19] See Cousinery (1831, p. 95); Pouqueville (1826, p. 72); Leake (1835, p. 287).
[20] See Stoianovich (1960).

2

Analysing Ottoman capitalism: Theoretical and empirical resources

2.1 Ottoman 'decline' and transformation

It used to be common in historical studies of the Ottoman Empire to interpret the last three centuries of its existence, from about 1600 to the early 1920s, as a period of relentless 'decline'. The period of 'decline' was presumably preceded by a 'classical age' of robust and aggressive expansion, which lasted roughly from 1300 to 1600.[1] The 'classical age' began with the establishment of the Ottoman state as a sizeable – but still minor – Turkish principality in northwestern Anatolia, and peaked with the emergence of the Empire as perhaps the most powerful state in Europe and the Middle East. The Ottoman Empire at its 'classical' peak – especially during the sixteenth century – was a distinctive social formation, with an autocratic, centralized and efficient government, a regulated agrarian economy and a large and powerful standing army. This formidable polity presumably entered a period of 'decline' after 1600 which lasted until the early 1920s, when the Empire came to an end.

There is little doubt that at the end of the sixteenth century the Ottoman Empire began gradually to face intractable difficulties, including demographic weaknesses, fiscal problems, social unrest and major political upheavals, which led to profound changes in its socio-economic institutions in the ensuing centuries. There is also little doubt that the Empire never again attained the heights of military and political power that it enjoyed circa 1600, and in the nineteenth century it resembled a colony of Western powers. Moreover, from the end of the seventeenth century it began to face successive military defeats,

---

[1] İnalcık and Quataert (1994, p. 1), for instance, propose roughly these two periods in the history of the Ottoman Empire, although they certainly do not subscribe to the view of relentless 'decline'.

which gradually became disastrous. The causes of this grand historical reversal have been much debated, but it is no longer accepted that the Empire was a decrepit social formation during its presumed 'decline' and certainly not during its final decades.

In this connection, considerable analytical attention has been paid to population pressure, or more specifically to the imbalance between population growth and agricultural production (or cultivated land) as the cause of sustained Ottoman weakness.[2] Thus, Akdağ postulated a historic economic weakening of the Empire due to falling crop output, scarcity of precious metals, unfavourable balance of trade and excessive exploitation of the population in the provinces by the Ottoman state and its agents.[3] For İnalcık, on the other hand, the decline in production and the eventual breakdown of social order were due to peasants leaving the land rather than plain economic deterioration or population pressure.[4] Along broadly similar lines, Karpat has more recently claimed that the transformation of the Ottoman Empire was ultimately due to the changing land regime and the ensuing dislocation of the peasantry.[5]

There is no doubt that the Ottoman Empire was a society that remained primarily agrarian to the very end. A vitally important development during the last three centuries of its existence was the relentless decline of the *tımar* system in agriculture. The *tımar* system is discussed in several places in the rest of this book, suffice it here to state that the *tımar* were taxable units of land that belonged to the state and did not afford formal inheritance rights to the holder. The decline of the *tımar* system led to the gradual ascendancy of the *çiftlik* system, *çiftlik* being large agrarian estates with quasi-proprietary features for their holders.[6] The spread of *çiftlik* estates meant that agricultural output began increasingly to find its way towards the market, thus allowing money to penetrate deeply into the agrarian economy. The *çiftlik* system also meant that heavily exploitative relations came to prevail in agriculture altering the terms of attachment of the peasants to the land.

---

[2] An indicative but far from exhaustive list of such writings would include, with variations, Barkan (1970, 1980), Cook (1970), İnalcık (1978) and Erder and Faroqhi (1979).
[3] See Akdağ (1975).
[4] See İnalcık (1980, 1994a).
[5] See Karpat (2002).
[6] See Stoianovich (1953, p. 402); McGowan (1981); İnalcık (1991, pp. 18–26); Veinstein (1991, p. 35).

Equally significant in this respect was the parallel transition to the *iltizam* (farming-out) system of tax collection, whereby the right to collect taxes was allotted to private individuals (*mültezim*) for fixed sums of money typically paid in advance. The transition to the *iltizam* system was driven by the central government's urgent and persistent need for money and was closely related to the emergence of the *çiftlik* system in agriculture. The formal tax-collecting obligations of the *tımar* holder tended to be replaced by the tax-collecting mechanisms of *iltizam*. The *mültezim* bought at public auction the right to collect taxes, a potentially lucrative business which, however, required accumulated capital, access to credit and good connections with market mechanisms. To ensure the return of capital plus profits, the tax farmers exercised enormous pressure on the peasants, who often became heavily indebted. Things became worse in the course of the eighteenth century as the *iltizam* system evolved into life-term tax-farming (*malikane*). The tax farmers were able to pass tax-collecting rights to their descendants, thus acquiring quasi-proprietary and semi-hereditary rights over land and encouraging *çiftlik* formation.[7]

It is also important to note that in the later years of the Empire, especially in the eighteenth and nineteenth centuries, there was a steady weakening and dislocation of the guilds that dominated manufacturing and trade.[8] A crucial development in this connection was the spreading practice of *gedik* certificates. These certificates were introduced at the beginning of the eighteenth century with the aim of affording to craftsmen fuller control over production. The *gedik* formally confirmed the competence of the holder in a certain craft in addition to recording the fixed capital goods required to engage in it. The ostensible purpose was to control the number of workshops and workers in each craft, thus preventing the entry into manufacturing of speculators who held liquid capital and only aimed at profit, such as the *mültezim*. In practice *gedik* certificates strengthened the already existing tendency for a son to inherit his father's craft and capital, regardless of his competence, gradually giving to masters proprietary and hereditary rights over their craft. In later years *gedik* certificates were put up for sale and even turned into equity.[9] The

---

[7] See İnalcık (1980, p. 329).
[8] See Baer (1970a, 1970b); Yi (2004); Faroqhi (2009); Yildirim (2007, 2008).
[9] Yildirim (2000).

urban economy of the Ottoman Empire, particularly in İstanbul and the larger cities, was reshaped by the emergence of independent craft workshops which were, furthermore, able to develop credit relations with merchants and *mültezim*.[10]

Against the background of these transformations, some of the earlier studies of Ottoman development attempted directly to apply Rostow's 'modernization theory' to the Ottoman social formation. For this approach, the Ottoman Empire presumably exemplifies the failure of transition from a 'traditional' to a 'mature' economic structure, because 'take off' from the former to the latter never fully materialized.[11] Yet, Rostow's theory is hardly persuasive in the Ottoman context because, as Akarli has rightly claimed, it amounts to 'a universal model of economic development that is based primarily on the European, and more specifically on the British, experience'.[12] The theory implicitly encourages focusing on real or imaginary divergences of the Ottoman economy from an ideal European model, that is, predominantly from nineteenth-century Britain.[13]

Even without subscribing to Rostow's theory, however, several studies of the economic development of the Ottoman Empire have found it difficult to stay clear of the question: 'What went wrong?'. Needless to say, there are legitimate grounds for posing questions of this type, particularly in relation to the functioning of the Ottoman state, as is shown in later chapters of this book. Yet, if this question was allowed to shape a researcher's approach to Ottoman economic development, there would be a great risk of concluding that the Empire was dysfunctional for roughly three centuries of its 'decline'. Moreover, it would invite comparison with some idealized path to modernity, which would in practice be that of advanced capitalist Western Europe. Inevitably the analytical focus would turn on whether the 'good' institutions and economic practices of the West ever existed in the Ottoman context and, if not, establishing the reasons for their absence.

---

[10] Yildirim (2008, p. 74).
[11] See Rostow (1960). Instances of a Rostowian approach to Ottoman economic history, with variations and speaking broadly, include Hershlag (1964); Issawi (1980); Okyar (1987) and Eldem (1994). Summarizing ruthlessly, these works tend to see the Ottoman past as the antithesis of 'modernity', thus inhibiting a 'take-off' of the Ottoman economy.
[12] See Akarli (2001, p. 6).
[13] See Quataert (1993a, pp. 1–19).

There are merits to historical comparisons, but it is misleading to seek to identify divergences of Ottoman performance from the putative best practice of Western Europe, or elsewhere. The emergence of capitalist modernity exhibits great variety and considerable historical specificity that are integral to it. The real issue is to ascertain the historical peculiarities of Ottoman society which gave a distinctive outlook to Ottoman capitalism in practice. In this light, the analysis in the rest of this book avoids searching for 'Ottoman exceptionalism' and focuses on the social, economic and political processes which accorded to Ottoman capitalism its peculiar and precarious character.

During the last three centuries of the Ottoman Empire, there were periods in which economic activity demonstrated a significant degree of dynamism and growth.[14] The Ottoman state, in particular, made sustained efforts to reform economic practices and instill vitality, especially after the start of the eighteenth century. Spurring the state towards reform was military weakness and successive defeats in war. The pronounced inability of Ottoman arms to stand up to the European powers, especially to Russia, from the eighteenth century onwards forced waves of reforms that at times had remarkable results on economy and society.[15] The most prominent period of such reforms occurred during the second half of the nineteenth century, particularly in the European provinces of the Empire. That was the context in which commercial and industrial capitalism began to emerge, and gradually to transform the outlook of both economy and society.

Steady pressure from Western Europe and Russia had far-reaching implications for the unfolding of Ottoman capitalism. For one thing, it imbued the people and the institutions of the late Empire (both state and community) with a sense of weakness, inferiority and 'backwardness', especially towards Western Europe. Modernity and progress came from Western Europe and were associated with European practices, which set an ideal standard for Ottoman society. This perception had a major impact on the Ottoman state's economic policies, thus shaping the emergence of Ottoman capitalism, as is shown in

---

[14] This point is now well established in Ottoman historiography with respect to different periods, regions and sectors of the Ottoman economy. A research path was beaten by Issawi (1980) and was much developed by Pamuk (1987, 1994) and Palairet (1993). Perhaps the most determined contribution, however, has been made by Quataert (1993a, 1993b, 1994a, 1994b). For a more recent work in similar spirit see Owen (2009).

[15] See Uyar and Erickson (2009).

subsequent chapters. Furthermore, aside from the ideology of 'backwardness', the military, political and economic forces of European imperialism in practice determined the distinctive outlook of Ottoman capitalism. The dominant European countries set the broad parameters of trade, tax and investment policies adopted by the Ottoman state. European influence was at times naked and direct, and at other times indirect. Whatever guise it assumed, the presence of European power was overbearing when the Ottoman state decided its path in economic and social policy. The emergence of Ottoman capitalism is inextricably linked to European imperialism.

In these circumstances, Ottoman capitalism never became a dynamic force that could successfully compete in the world arena. However, the Empire was neither a pawn, nor a mere extra in a play directed by foreigners. In Macedonia, the home of its most vibrant industrial sector of textiles, Ottoman capitalism was aggressive, expansionary and potentially capable of reshaping broader swathes of society, even if in the end it remained precarious. It is shown in the rest of this book that the deeper reasons for the distinctive outlook of Ottoman capitalism were related partly to the Ottoman state and partly to the nature of the religious and ethnic communities that comprised Ottoman society. The region of Mount Vermion offers an excellent terrain over which to examine the interplay of these factors.

2.2 State, community and religion in the emergence of Ottoman capitalism

Max Weber believed that Ottoman 'patrimonialism' – even 'sultanism'– was the opposite of Western European 'rationalism'. The difference apparently lay in the concentration of administrative and military power in the hands of the Sultan who exercised power arbitrarily within a framework of tradition, a practice that was presumably rooted in Islam.[16] This feature of Ottoman polity was thought to inhibit the emergence of socially progressive forces, above all, to prevent the emergence of a bourgeoisie, which in turn accounted for

---

[16] See Weber (1978, pp. 231–2). Also see Weber (1930 [1905]).

the failure of the Ottoman Empire to give rise to advanced capitalism. There are several examples of Weberian analysis of the Ottoman Empire although the influence of Weber's approach has diminished substantially over time.[17] The fundamental reason for the decline in its influence is the realization that the Ottoman state operated far more complexly than Weber imagined. Capitalism did emerge in the Ottoman Empire, even though it was marked by strong peculiarities.[18]

Equally problematic in this respect is the naïve Marxist approach which mechanically postulates a historical succession of modes of production typically from slave-owning to feudal to capitalist. In such a framework the Ottoman Empire would perhaps be an instance of the Asiatic mode of production. This is an ill-thought out concept by Marx and Engels denoting a despotic and unchanging state wedded to a passive and unresisting society.[19] The state's power and control presumably inhibited the emergence of agents of social change, including a bourgeoisie. By implication capitalist transformation could only be initiated from the outside.[20] Such an approach does not do justice to the complexity and inherent dynamism of the Ottoman Empire. As Göçek has remarked: 'Marx's depiction of non-Western social change appears analytically weak when compared to his rigorous analyses of Western European change'.[21] The Asiatic mode of production is far too thin a concept to capture the vast array of societies it purports to cover and provides little analytical help in relation to the Ottoman Empire.

Wallerstein's World-Systems Analysis offers a related but still different approach to Ottoman capitalism focusing on the aggressive expansion of

---

[17] For early examples of the Weberian approach in Ottoman studies, see Mardin (1960); Berkes (1964); Lewis (1979 [1961], 1982) and Ülgener (1981). Typically, these works attributed the economic backwardness of the Empire to a distinctly anti-capitalist or pre-capitalist Ottoman economic mentality that was inherent in its religious culture. More elaborate and refined versions of the Weberian approach based on the concept of patrimonialism include Findley (1980); Barkey (1994) and Göçek (1996). For a general assessment of Weber's analysis of the Ottoman Empire, see İnalcık (1994b). For an example of the analysis that relates Islam and economic underdevelopment in the Middle East, see Kuran (2003).

[18] For critical analysis of Weber's treatment of Islam as an inherently retrograde religion, see Turner (1974); Gellner (1981) and Rodinson (2007).

[19] See Marx and Engels, 1986 [1858], pp. 399–439).

[20] See Turner (1984, pp. 23–51) for a critique of Marxist analyses of the East. Interestingly, there are considerable similarities between Weber's patrimonialism and the naïve Marxist concept of the Asiatic mode of production, as Turner has noted (1978, p. 1).

[21] See Göçek (1996, p. 14).

the European economy on a global scale at the expense of other economies. For Wallerstein, the expansion of Europe was the source of long-term underdevelopment of other areas of the world.[22] The economic evolution of the Ottoman Empire amounted to its incorporation in the expanding capitalist world economy through 'peripheralization'.[23] World-Systems Analysis has gained considerable influence in Ottoman history writing and several studies broadly consistent with it have examined Ottoman 'peripheralization'.[24]

The advantage of Wallerstein's theory is that it stresses the response of the Ottoman Empire to pressures arising from the outside, as it were. There was no inexorable Ottoman 'decline' as the economy adapted to external pressures, and several sectors grew which were capable of fitting into the expanding world economy. This view has considerable strengths, but its weakness is that it turns the Ottoman 'periphery' into a recipient of the pressures of the world economy. The West and Western-dominated global markets were presumably the catalysts of Ottoman capitalist transformation, and the internal dynamics and peculiarities of the Empire played a largely secondary role.[25] This position, however, has very little applicability to Macedonia, as is shown in the rest of this book, thus bringing to the fore a further weakness of Wallerstein's approach. Namely, as soon as one attempts concretely to establish the correspondence between the putative world forces of social change and the specific historical context of capitalist development, the theory becomes nebulous.[26]

It is notable in this connection that several works have appeared during the last three decades that focus on the internal processes of Ottoman society.[27]

---

[22] See Wallerstein (1974, 1980, 1989).
[23] See Wallerstein (1979, pp. 390–1).
[24] The influence of Wallerstein's approach is clear in important works in Ottoman studies. See, for instance, İslamoğlu-İnan (1983, 1987); Quataert (1983); İslamoğlu and Keyder (1987) and Kasaba (1988).
[25] This is not to deny that some works that are broadly within the World-Systems approach also take into account forces internal to the Empire. Thus, Kasaba (1988) shows the involvement of local economic agents, merchants, landlords, bankers, as well as of European capitalists in commercial networks. Keyder and Tabak (1991) consider the transformation of the relations production and property relations in agriculture.
[26] Note though that some authors broadly associated with this current have also provided city-level analyses of the development of the Ottoman Empire; see Keyder et al. (1994).
[27] Thus, Issawi (1980) put together economic data showing that a degree of dynamism existed in several sectors; Pamuk (1987, 1994) established that commercial expansion in the nineteenth century actually had a beneficial impact on the Ottoman economy. Pamuk (1994, 2009) also drew attention to the active role of Ottoman institutions and the state apparatus in inducing the integration of the Empire in the world economy. Quataert (1993a, 1994a, 2014) documented the dynamic adaptation and evolution of several sectors of the economy in the face of fierce European

This literature has attempted to 'normalize' the Ottoman Empire and to avoid the trap of Ottoman exceptionalism. It broadly assumes that, although the Empire did not achieve a successful overall capitalist transformation, Ottoman failure had little to do with a putative cultural, political or social inability to 'modernize'. Even less were Ottoman state and society merely passive participants in capitalist transformation. The trajectory of Ottoman capitalism certainly reflected the pressures of the world market but also derived from the internal development of Ottoman economy and society.

'Normalizing' the Ottoman Empire is a laudable aim, but it is crucial not to neglect the communal and religious dimension of Ottoman capitalism. The communal, religious and ethnic characteristics of Ottoman society and the corresponding features of the Ottoman state were critically important to the nascent capitalism. Ottoman society had a strongly hierarchical nature based on religion. Pronounced social stratification certainly existed within the Muslim, Christian and Jewish communities of the Empire, and a Jewish medical doctor at the Sultan's palace, or a wealthy Christian merchant in the Balkans, were socially superior to a poor Muslim peasant. Nevertheless, it is incontestable that Muslims tended to be at the top of the social and cultural pyramid, enjoying privileged access to state mechanisms for centuries, while adherents to other religions faced discrimination and a raft of restrictions in daily life. It is equally incontestable that spontaneously emerging capitalism in the late Ottoman Empire was led by the subordinate communities. In the case of Macedonia, this meant the Jews of Thessaloniki and the Christian Greeks of Mount Vermion. Their communal characteristics were important in fostering the development of Ottoman capitalism and lent to it a distinctive character that must be taken explicitly into account.

It is important to note in this connection that communities were able to coexist in relative peace within the Empire, as long as the religious hierarchy was broadly respected. Coexistence, however, did not necessarily mean broad and multifaceted interaction. Communities often maintained a relative independence and even indifference towards each other. The internal

competition. In other work, Quataert (1993b) examined the role of traditionally silent sections of the population, including peasants and workers. Akarli (2001), finally, demonstrated that certain sectors of the economy grew while others at the same time contracted, especially in the region of late-nineteenth-century Thessaloniki.

organization and power structures of the subordinate communities acquired considerable weight in social and economic life, especially in view of the limited and variable access these communities had to the Ottoman state. Thus, the internal mechanisms of the Jewish and the Christian Greek communities in Macedonia proved important to the region's capitalist transformation.

The role of the Ottoman state in the process of capitalist transformation should be assessed in this light. Several historians have stressed the differences between the Ottoman state and other European states, and Genç has claimed that the defining principles of Ottoman statecraft were fiscalism, provisionism and traditionalism.[28] Fiscalism has been defined as 'the endeavour to maximize public revenues at all times for other than economic purposes'.[29] According to İnalcık, 'the benefits to the state treasury and the needs of the internal market seem to be the only concern of the Ottoman government'.[30] Provisionism, on the other hand, has been defined as 'the maintenance of a steady supply so that all goods and services in the country were cheap, plentiful and of good quality'.[31] For Genç, the Ottoman state was unique among contemporary states in deploying provisionism to regulate economic relations.[32] McGowan has even maintained that the provisioning of İstanbul was the first policy priority of Ottoman authorities.[33]

In contrast, other historians have tended to treat the Ottoman state as one state among many, even if with its own particularities. Such studies have typically emphasized the flexibility and pragmatism of the politics, social organization and institutions of the Ottoman Empire.[34] Flexibility was considered a rational attitude for a multi-ethnic and multi-religious Empire. Thus, for Pamuk the longevity of the Ottoman Empire, as is demonstrated by its economic institutions and performance, was a consequence of 'the state's pragmatism, flexibility, and willingness to compromise, even before the nineteenth-century Tanzimat reforms'.[35] Far from being ignorant, the Ottoman state was aware of global tendencies and ideological currents and decided to intervene (or not) in

[28] See Genç (1991, 1994, 2000).
[29] See İnalcık and Quataert (1994, p. 44).
[30] See İnalcık (1970, p. 212).
[31] See Genç (1994, p. 60).
[32] See Genç (2000, p. 9).
[33] See McGowan (1981, p. 11).
[34] See, for instance, Barkey (1994, 2008); Pamuk (2004, 2009) and Eldem (2006).
[35] See Pamuk (2004, p. 246).

economy and society according to the balance of internal and external forces. As Eldem has claimed, 'the Ottoman government's attitude stemmed more from the marginality and reduced incidence of Western trade on the economy than from an ignorance of mercantilist and protectionist principles'.[36]

For our purposes, perhaps the most important point in this respect is that the Ottoman state became considerably weaker in the course of the eighteenth century. In contrast to the West, where the rise of absolutism in the seventeenth century prepared the ground for the emergence of capitalism, the Ottoman Sultan faced enormous difficulties in imposing his will across the territories of the Empire for much of the eighteenth and the beginning of the nineteenth centuries, that is, precisely at the time when the forces of capitalist transformation began to take shape. Far from oriental absolutism being the problem, the delay in the emergence of Ottoman capitalism coincided with the lack of a powerful and organized central authority. By the second half of the nineteenth century, the Ottoman state had recovered its ability to dictate policy across the Empire and was able to give a boost to commercial and industrial capitalism. The state, when it commanded sufficient power, proved capable of fostering social conditions that were amenable to the rise of capitalism. It was also capable of applying sophisticated economic policies, as will be shown in the Macedonian context.

2.3 The broad outlines of textile capitalism in Macedonia

In the final decades of the nineteenth century, Ottoman Macedonia presented a complex and varied picture of capitalist transformation. The development of the city of Thessaloniki but also the changes that had taken place in the region of Mount Vermion were a microcosm of the forces that sustained industrial capitalism in the Ottoman context. A series of economic, social and political transformations had taken place in Macedonia, due to factors internal and external to the Empire, which underpinned the rise of capitalism in the area. Several of these transformations naturally had roots in developments that had occurred in earlier centuries. It is important at this point to provide a

---

[36] See Eldem (2006, p. 308).

brief outline of the characteristic features of industrial capitalism in Ottoman Macedonia, pivoting on textiles.

The focal point of industrial development was inevitably the city of Thessaloniki. Historians have examined the trajectory and the characteristic features of Ottoman Thessaloniki using a variety of primary sources, including Turkish and Greek archival material, consular reports, the archives of the Alliance Israélite Universelle, as well as local journals and newspapers.[37] The role of textile manufacturing in the economy of Thessaloniki can be traced to the migration of Sephardic Jews from the Iberian Peninsula in the fifteenth century. The immigration of Jews was facilitated by commercial and manufacturing concessions by the Ottoman state, above all, by the awarding of privileges in trading wool and manufacturing woollen cloth. Macedonia had extensive sheep and goat flocks and thus abundant supplies of raw material for woollen cloth. Even in the early nineteenth century, the Jewish woollen cloth manufacturers of Thessaloniki, who were mostly guild-based, were the main suppliers of the Janissary Corps as well as exporting their goods to Italy and France. The penetration of Western European goods into the Ottoman markets in the first half of the nineteenth century, and the dissolution of the Janissary Corps in 1826, decimated the production of woollen cloth in Thessaloniki.[38]

Despite the collapse of traditional wool manufacturing in Thessaloniki, Macedonia as a whole held the second largest concentration of industrial concerns in the Ottoman Empire towards the end of the nineteenth

---

[37] It took decades after the end of Ottoman rule for academic research to examine this issue, but the literature is now long and varied. An early work that considered the political economy of the region by deploying a Marxist approach was by Svoronos (1956). Turkish historians have placed the development of Thessaloniki in the broader context of the evolution of the Ottoman Empire, including Akarli (2001), Ilicak (2002) and Özdemir (2003). Greek historians tended to have more local concerns, for instance, Gounaris (1993, 1997) and Hekimoglou (1997). However, Anastassiadou (1997) has produced a detailed history of the city during its Ottoman peak of 1830–1912. Furthermore, Quataert (2014), which is in fact a work that was originally published much earlier, made a decisive contribution regarding the role of Thessaloniki in the emergence of late Ottoman capitalism, while Mazower (2004) has written by far the most popular history of the city. Also notable is the analysis of the social role of the Jewish community of Thessaloniki in works by Dumont (1978); Molho (1994); Veinstein (2001) and recently by Naar (2016). Other historians have focused on particular aspects of Thessaloniki society, such as Baer (2010) writing on the Jewish converts to Islam, or placed Thessaloniki within the broader context of political and social Ottoman development as, for instance, Ginio (1998, 2002, 2006).

[38] See Quataert (1994a, p. 98). For an earlier historical analysis of the woollen industry in Thessaloniki, see Braude (1979, 1991). For a general discussion on the woollen industry in the Balkans, see Palairet (1983).

century.[39] Indeed, it is probable that by the early twentieth century the region possessed the largest industrial capacity in the Empire, bigger than İstanbul and its environs, even though the imperial capital had received substantial government investment.[40] The leading manufacturing activity was in textiles, and the industries of Thessaloniki focused mainly on woollen cloth, cotton yarn and cotton cloth. Macedonia represented the densest concentration of cotton-spinning mills in the Empire.[41] The loss of the region in the Balkan wars of 1912–13 was a severe blow to the Ottoman economy.

The most dynamic area of industrial textile capitalism in Macedonia was in the region of Mount Vermion with its three towns of Naoussa, Edhessa and Veroia, which in 1912 could justifiably be described as the Empire's main industrial hub for textiles. Quataert has shown that just before the end of Ottoman rule Macedonia possessed nearly half of the Empire's total cotton-spinning capacity.[42] Furthermore, Palairet's data for machine-based cotton spinning for the whole of Macedonia in 1912 indicates that there were ten spinning mills in Macedonia, with a sum total of 70,000 spindles.[43] As will be shown in detail in subsequent chapters of this book, three of these mills (with a sum total of 22,800 spindles) were in Thessaloniki but the rest (with 47,200 spindles) were located in the area of Naoussa, Edhessa and Veroia.

To be a little more specific, in the 1870s the cotton mills of Thessaloniki represented the pre-eminent indigenous capacity of the Empire, such as it was at the time. By the 1900s they had been overtaken by their competitors in Naoussa, Edhessa and Veroia. The mills of provincial Macedonia initially met local demand, providing yarn to villagers and others for home weaving. In time the provincial mills, but also the mills of Thessaloniki, started to ship yarn to other markets within the Empire but also outside it, for instance, to Albania, Serbia, Bulgaria and Anatolia, and significantly to İstanbul, İzmir, Bursa and Edirne.[44] In the 1890s the provincial mills were competing directly with imported Italian and even English yarn, especially at the lower end of the quality range. As the production of cotton yarn increased, so did the commercial

---

[39] See Ilicak (2002, p. 115).
[40] This claim has been made by Quataert (2014, p. 223) but it is difficult to test it.
[41] See Quataert (1993a, pp. 44–5).
[42] Ibid., pp. 1, 44.
[43] See Palairet (1993, p. 351).
[44] See Quataert (1993a, p. 45).

production of raw cotton in Macedonia, though not in the immediate area of Mount Vermion. The rapid growth of cotton spinning meant that local yarn producers eventually had to obtain raw cotton from other Ottoman markets, mostly İzmir, Adana and Aleppo.

The weight of provincial Macedonia in Ottoman textile capitalism is even clearer when the wool sector is considered. In the late nineteenth century Bulgaria produced most machine-made woollen cloth in the Balkans, but significant mechanization of woollen cloth also took place in Macedonia. Provincial Macedonia had a strong tradition in domestic manufacturing and trading of good quality woollen cloth already in the eighteenth century. A few years after the emergence of mechanized cotton spinning in the 1870s it became possible to extend mechanization to the production of woollen cloth. In the years following the effective independence of Bulgaria in 1878, there emerged four wool-weaving mills in the European part of the Empire situated in Thessaloniki and Naoussa. The most important wool-weaving mill was established in Naoussa in 1908, followed by two further mills in the ensuing three years.[45]

By 1912, when Ottoman rule ended in Macedonia, perhaps 30 per cent of the Empire's domestic cotton-spinning capacity was under the control of capitalists from Naoussa. Moreover, the bulk of the mechanized woollen cloth sector of the European part of the Empire was controlled by Naoussa capitalists. In sum, significant textile industrialization emerged during the last decades of the Ottoman Empire, much of it based in Macedonia and to a large extent driven by the little town of Naoussa.

It hardly needs stressing, however, that the total Ottoman capacity in cotton spinning and wool weaving in 1912 represented a very small part of world capacity. At that time Britain, which was by far the leading power in textiles, possessed 55.3 million spindles, or 39.1 per cent of the world total. Another 43.1 million were located on the European continent, 33.64 million in America and 9.44 million in Asia.[46] The Ottoman total – and the seventy thousand spindles of Macedonia – looked puny in comparison. Nonetheless, a more balanced picture of the industrial transformation of the Empire could be obtained by comparing its total capacity with that of countries that were not

---

[45] See Quataert (1994a, p. 98).
[46] See Farnie (2004, p. 23).

leading textile producers. Thus, in 1907–8, Japan held 1.54 million and Belgium 1.2 million spindles, making Ottoman industrialized textile capacity roughly 10 per cent of that of Japan and 13 per cent of that of Belgium.[47] Ottoman textile capitalism in the 1900s was certainly small but far from negligible. On the other hand, despite the surge of growth, there was still no comparison between textile industrialization in the Ottoman Empire and in the two rival European empires of the time. In 1907–8, Romanov Russia held roughly 7.6 million spindles, while Habsburg Austro-Hungary held 3.6 million spindles.[48]

Notable as the rise of textile industrialization in Ottoman Macedonia was, it remained a speck on the world economy prior to the outbreak of the First World War. Ottoman capitalists would have had to traverse a long path before they could compete even with the smaller powers in the world market. A similar picture emerges when data on Gross Domestic Product (GDP) per capita is considered. According to the estimates by Pamuk, GDP per capita in the Ottoman Empire increased from $680 in 1820 to $880 in 1870 and $1200 in 1913, implying a growth rate of 0.5 per cent for 1820–70 and 0.7 per cent for 1870–1913.[49] Obviously, a certain economic dynamism was present in the Ottoman Empire. However, the annual increase of GDP per capita in Western Europe during the same period was twice as large. Thus, according to Pamuk, the GDP per capita of 'Turkey' was 54.6 per cent of Western Europe in 1820, falling to 42.2 per cent in 1870 and 32.5 per cent in 1913. The weight of the Empire in the world economy generally tended to decline.[50]

The modest presence of the Empire at the global level should not detract from the dynamism and significance of the capitalist transformation that took place in Ottoman Macedonia. By the standards of the Empire an economic revolution occurred in the region of Mount Vermion, much of it originating in the town of Naoussa. Crucial to the success of the town were its economic advantages in producing and trading textiles. Equally crucial was its communal

---

[47] See Saxonhouse and Wright (2004, p. 130).
[48] Ibid.
[49] Pamuk's data refers to 'Turkey' and probably relates to the geographical area of the contemporary Republic of Turkey, although in Western writings of the time 'Turkey' tended to imply a far bigger entity, as in the map in Plate 1. Furthermore, the data for Greece probably refers to the area of the Kingdom of Greece in the nineteenth century rather than modern Greece.
[50] All calculations were made in 1990 Purchasing Power Parity (PPP) in USD based on the GDP per capita series developed by Angus Maddison; see Pamuk (2016).

character – strongly Christian Greek, indeed unusually so among Macedonian towns – and its corresponding relations with the Ottoman state.

It is shown in the remainder of this book that the economic, political and social factors underpinning the industrial transformation of Ottoman Macedonia were products of Ottoman society during the final decades of its existence. Industrial development gave rise to a new social stratification of capitalists, wage workers, landlords and sharecroppers that lent considerable forward thrust but also precariousness to the nascent capitalism. The study of industrial capitalism in provincial Macedonia can thus throw fresh light on Ottoman modernity. It also offers some insight into the persistent difficulty of attaining industrial development when the world market is dominated by powerful and developed capitalist states that determine the tenor of economic policies of others.

Ottoman capitalism never succeeded in fully dominating either the economy or the society of the Empire. To the very end, agrarian and craft activities undertaken on a non-capitalist basis predominated, and Ottoman society retained a pre-capitalist outlook in religion, politics and the law. Even the Ottoman state, which had undertaken successive waves of modernization in the nineteenth century, could not be called properly capitalist in the early 1900s. The emerging capitalist class of the Empire, including the powerful private bankers of İstanbul, did not become a dominant force in the decision-making activities of the Ottoman state. Moreover, the provincial industrialists of Macedonia, and even those of Thessaloniki, played no more than a marginal role in influencing the policies of the Ottoman government.

Still, the Ottoman state strove to facilitate indigenous industrial production, particularly as it had very little practical choice in the matter. Crushing military defeats in the hands of Russia, especially the disaster of 1877–8, but also the financial bankruptcy of 1875, left it with no option but to encourage domestic industry. In that sense, the actions of the state were pivotal to the growth of industrial capitalism in Macedonia.

2.4 Historical literature and original sources

A major difficulty in examining the rise of industrial capitalism in provincial Ottoman Macedonia is that practically no academic literature exists on the subject, and certainly none in English. The magisterial tome edited in 1990 by Halil İnalcık and Donald Quataert, *An Economic and Social History of the Ottoman Empire*, stretching across two volumes and 1010 pages, devoted fewer than ten lines to industrial capitalism in Ottoman Macedonia. Inevitably these were written by Quataert, an inveterately curious student of Ottoman manufacturing, who was aware of developments in the area of Mount Vermion at the end of the nineteenth century but did not examine them in depth.[51] Lest it be thought that the gap in İnalcık and Quataert's volume was an aberration, the equally magisterial and remarkably thorough, *The Balkan Economies*, by Michael Palairet, published in 1993, also paid scant attention to Macedonia and the area of Mount Vermion.

This curious lacuna reflects in part the evolution of historical writing in the successor states of the Ottoman Empire. The main culprits of neglect have been the historians of Turkey and Greece. To a degree this is excusable for Turkish historians, who have directed their attention to Ottoman areas within the boundaries of the contemporary Turkish Republic, that is, effectively to Anatolia. Historians from the other successor states of the Ottoman Empire have more or less shared the same attitude focusing on their 'own' geographical areas. The true mystery, therefore, is the neglect shown by Greek historians, perhaps reflecting the turbulent way in which Macedonia was incorporated in the Greek state in the twentieth century. Whatever the explanation might be, there is little substantive analysis of Ottoman Macedonian capitalism in Greek historiography.

That is not to say that there have been no exceptions, three of which in the post-war years merit immediate mention, namely Vassilis Gounaris, a methodical researcher of the economic history of Macedonia, Evanghelos Hekimoglou, a prolific writer on various aspects of the history of Thessaloniki, and Christos Hadziiossif, the doyen of contemporary Greek economic historians who has advanced some characteristically trenchant insights on Ottoman Macedonian industrialization.[52] The work of all three informs the analysis of this book, though in different ways.

---

[51] See Quataert (1994b, p. 902).
[52] See, for instance, Gounaris (1993); Hekimoglou (1996, 2005) and Hadziiossif (1993).

It would be unfair in this connection, however, to ignore Kostis Moskoff, who was less a historian and more an intellectual in the long-standing tradition of Thessaloniki. Moskoff was keenly aware of the exceptional historical development of the area of Mount Vermion and had publicly recorded his observations and analysis already by the early 1970s.[53] Unfortunately he interpreted the industrial development of both Thessaloniki and Mount Vermion as indicating the 'huckstering' – and by implication deficient and parasitical – nature of Ottoman/Greek capitalism. This was a view that was much in vogue in Greece at the time and is deeply misleading, as will be shown in the rest of this book. There was nothing parasitical about industrial capitalism in late Ottoman Macedonia.

The ground is, thus, by and large virginal, presenting the political economist and the historian with special difficulties and obligations. Not least among these is the relative scarcity of original archival and other sources. This book opens a path by deploying information on the economic development of provincial Macedonia from, first, the Ottoman official yearbooks (*salnameler*) for the *vilayet* of Thessaloniki and, second and more importantly, from the Ottoman Archives of the Office of the Prime Minister (*Başbakanlık Osmanlı Arşivleri* – BOA hereafter).[54] These sources have not been previously researched from the perspective of Macedonian industrialization, and for this reason further discussion of their main features is undertaken below.

Additional information has been derived from Greek sources, particularly from functionaries of the Greek state who moved to Macedonia immediately after its incorporation into modern Greece in 1912–13 and began the demanding process of assimilating the new lands. In general, they were well-trained and capable bureaucrats – even if prone to nationalism – who provided thorough reports and wrote several analytical volumes. Typical among them were Dekazos and Palamiotis, whose work is indispensable to the analysis of Macedonian agriculture. Equally prominent were Kofinas and Tsakalotos, who have left invaluable accounts of the industry of Macedonia immediately after the Balkan wars. It is notable that both were optimistic about the future

---

[53] See Moskoff (1974).
[54] The analysis of the archival and yearbook material draws heavily on the PhD dissertation of Cakiroglu (2015), which has provided much of the empirical backing for this work.

of Macedonian industry, Tsakalotos even hoping to establish a chemical sector in the area. Special mention should also be made of Stougiannakis, who was a schoolmaster in the area of Mount Vermion and an ardent Greek nationalist, but without whose account of local industry and economy it would be impossible to reconstruct the history of the area.[55]

Finally, vital information for this book has been derived from extensive fieldwork. To be able analytically to reconstruct the long-lost world of late Ottoman Thessaloniki and Mount Vermion, it was vital to have command over family histories, local institutions, buildings, physical monuments, natural features and oral traditions. Fortunately, the area of Mount Vermion continues to take great pride in its past thus making the task easier. There is no doubt that such material should always be supplementary to other sources, but when obscurity shrouds historical events, indigenous knowledge can cast a revealing light.

2.4.1 The yearbooks of the *vilayet* of Thessaloniki (*Selanik Vilayet Salnameleri*)

Official yearbooks (*salname*) began to be produced in the Ottoman Empire as the reform efforts intensified in the nineteenth century, indicating a new mindset that gradually emerged among the Ottoman bureaucracy. The first *salname* was prepared in 1847 by the well-known reformist officials Ahmed Vefik Paşa, Ahmet Cevdet Paşa and Mustafa Reşit Paşa.[56] The yearbooks were material evidence of the state becoming 'modern' by providing an annual picture of Ottoman economy and society but also of the state machinery itself.

The yearbooks constitute one of the most important sources for analysis of late-nineteenth- and early-twentieth-centuries Ottoman history and political economy. Indeed, more than one type of yearbook was produced

---

[55] See Dekazos (1913, 1914); Palamiotis (1914); Kofinas (1914); Tsakalotos (1914a, 1914b) and Stougiannakis (1911, 1993 [1924]). The work of these writers and several others in Greek secondary literature has informed the empirical analysis in Lapavitsas (2006), which has been used extensively in this book.

[56] For discussion of the mindset of the reformist officials starting in the early nineteenth century, see Mardin (1960); Ortaylı (1983, 2011) draws a picture of the Tanzimat bureaucrats and society of the time, while Kaplan (2011) describes the Tanzimat intellectuals. For a more recent analysis on the Ottoman intellectuals and the formation of a new economic approach during the Hamidian era, see Kılınçoğlu (2015).

by the Ottoman state. Most prominent were the statistical and descriptive yearbooks, known as *Salname-i Devlet-i Âliyye-i Osmâniye*. The first volume was published in 1847 (1262–63 in *Rumi* and 1263–64 in *Hicri* calendar) and subsequent volumes appeared regularly until 1918 (1334 in *Rumi* and 1336–37 in *Hicri* calendar). During this period there were slight changes in format but in general the yearbooks continued to provide information on the structure of the administration, the practices of government officials and bureaucrats, the size of the population, the construction and maintenance of state buildings and the flows of government revenue and expenditures.[57] Quite naturally these yearbooks were issued in the greatest numbers – sixty-eight volumes in total.

In addition, there were two further types of yearbook, namely provincial yearbooks (*vilayet salnameleri*) and ministry yearbooks (*nezaret salnameleri*). The former provided the main source of information for this book. Provincial yearbooks, as their name indicates, were issued by provincial authorities and offered a detailed picture of administration, education, production, commerce, agriculture, population and geography in their respective area. They have long been a vital source of information for research since they are normally more thorough than central authority yearbooks. Provincial yearbooks have proven indispensable to writing the social and economic history of the Empire.

Provincial yearbooks were first published in 1866, the year when the *salname* for Bosnia appeared (*Bosna Vilayet Salnamesi*). Unfortunately their publication was neither as regular nor as meticulous as that of state yearbooks. For some *vilayet* there might be only a single volume extant, while for others there could be more than twenty. Fortunately, in the *vilayet* of Thessaloniki the publication of yearbooks started relatively early and resulted in several volumes. The first yearbook for the *vilayet* of Thessaloniki was produced in 1870 (1287) and in all twenty volumes have survived, covering the period to 1907 (1325). The quality and quantity of information afforded in each volume improved steadily as the practice of producing yearbooks became better established.

Towards the end of the period the yearbooks began to provide a truly detailed picture of the *vilayet* of Thessaloniki. The improvement is easy to see in the rising number of pages of the yearbooks: the first volume, in 1870, had

---

[57] See McCarthy and Hyde (1979, p. 10).

105 pages but the last volume, in 1907, had 716. By that time the provincial authorities had become incomparably more meticulous, a development that also reflected the transformation of the Ottoman state. Profound changes had taken place in both economy and society that were recorded at increasing length in the yearbooks. During those decades the province of Thessaloniki had acquired a distinctly capitalist sector and the port city had emerged as a model Westernized Ottoman settlement, a hub of economic and commercial activity and one of the most important urban centres and ports of the Empire. Ottoman state bureaucrats were fully aware of these developments and recorded them in the yearbooks.[58]

It is common in the later volumes of the yearbooks to find references to Thessaloniki as the most important economic and commercial centre of *Rumeli* (the European part of the Empire) after İstanbul. Communication and transport facilities had also improved, especially after the construction of the Thessaloniki-Bitola (*Manastır*) railway in the 1890s, making the more remote parts of the *vilayet* easily accessible, and thereby increasing both the flow and the quality of the available information. Furthermore, the growing importance of commercial activities and the increasing integration of the provincial economy in the domestic and the international markets provided more transparent and reliable economic data. While the yearbooks up to the tenth volume, published in 1890, contained no separate sections on the smaller districts and towns of the *vilayet* of Thessaloniki, information on local areas became abundant in the remaining volumes. Evidently things were changing rapidly in the provinces.

The yearbooks make it possible to build a picture of the population and its economic activities in the region of Mount Vermion from 1870 roughly to the end of Ottoman rule in 1912. Yearbook information on commercial activities provides insight into the original sources of capital accumulation in the region. Lists of exports and imports help determine trading strengths as well as the shape of merchant networks. Not least, the changing level of commercial activity reflects the degree of the region's integration in the world economy. In similar spirit, the yearbooks provide data on the number, capacity

---

[58] For the transformation of the Ottoman bureaucracy during the era of rapid reform in the nineteenth century, see Shaw and Shaw (2002); Akyıldız (2004); İnalcık and Seyitdanlıoğlu (2011).

and general economic standing of the region's textile mills. Unfortunately the publication of provincial yearbooks stopped suddenly in 1907, that is, exactly as industrial growth reached its highest point in the region, but the yearbook series still affords a wealth of information on plants, prices and output.

There is no doubt that using the Ottoman yearbooks as a historical source calls for vigilance. It is well known that yearbook information is incomplete and often unreliable. Moreover, it is generally true that the available data on Ottoman history, even at its most reliable, tends to be partial and often weak. However, for the smaller provincial units of the Empire, the yearbooks are often the only available official source of evidence. Sources such as consular reports, official statistics and journals and travellers' accounts are of limited use when it comes to the deep Ottoman provinces. To minimize possible pitfalls in this book, yearbook information on the *vilayet* of Thessaloniki has been cross-checked with other sources as far as possible.

2.4.2 Ottoman archives

A further major source of information was provided by the administrative archives of the Empire. At present there are roughly forty nation states covering the old Ottoman territories, all of which have retained some documentation from Ottoman times. The Archives of the Prime Minister's Office in Turkey (BOA) are by far the most important since they include the bulk of the original documents pertaining to the central Ottoman administration.

The BOA documents relevant to this book were located mainly under the following classifications: *Şura-yı Devlet* (Council of State, ŞD), *İrade Ticaret ve Nafia Nezareti* (Decisions of (the Ministry of) Trade and Public Works, (İ.TNF)), *Meclis-i Vükela Mazbataları* (Records of the Council of Ministers, (MV)), *İrade Meclis-i Mahsus* (Decisions of the Special Council, (İ.MMS)), *İrade Rüsumat* (Excise Taxes, (İ.RSM)), *Bab-ı Ali Evrak Odası* (Document Room of the Sublime Porte, (BEO)), and *Rumeli Umum Müfettişliği* (General Inspectorate of *Rumeli*, (TFR.I.ŞKT and TFR.I.SL)).

These classifications relate to characteristic state institutions of the era of Ottoman reform. Thus, the *Şura-yı Devlet* (Council of State) was founded in

1867 to take administrative decisions and to audit laws and regulations. It was the highest authority for the resolution of conflicts between the state and its subjects. The *Ticaret ve Nafia Nezareti* (Ministry of Trade and Public Works) was responsible for transportation, communications, trade and industry. The *Meclis-i Vükela* (Council of Ministers) was similar to a contemporary Council of Ministers and was often involved in important decisions. The *Meclis-i Mahsus* (Special Council) was a body operating within the Council of State and consisting of senior heads of ministerial departments. The *İrade Rüsumat* (Excise Taxes) issued the imperial orders relating to excise taxes and/or exemptions. Note that the *Rüsumat Emaneti* (Department of Excise Taxes) was founded in 1861 and was subordinate to the *Maliye Nezareti* (the Ministry of Finance). The *Bab-ı Ali Evrak Odası* (Document Room of the Sublime Porte) kept records of all correspondence involving the Grand Vizierate, starting from 1861, the year of its foundation. Finally, the *Rumeli Umum Müfettişliği* (General Inspectorate of *Rumeli*), an administrative unit established in 1902, held all the official correspondence of *vilayet* administration – and of the smaller administrative units within a *vilayet* – in the European part of the Empire.[59]

These archival sources contain petitions, complaints and grievance letters from local people as well as correspondence and reports concerning the administrative, fiscal, economic, political, agricultural and commercial matters of the *vilayet* of Thessaloniki. They also contain documents that reflect the interaction between Macedonian industrialists and the Ottoman state as well as the internal procedures and outlook of the Ottoman administration regarding economic decision making. This historical evidence helps illuminate the rise of industrial capitalism in Ottoman Macedonia by highlighting the role of the state and the importance of community structures. On this basis the political economy of the rise of industrial capitalism in Ottoman Macedonia can be examined with a degree of empirical confidence. A necessary step in this respect is to establish the administrative structures and population features of late Ottoman Macedonia, a task undertaken in the next chapter.

---

[59] For a more detailed account of the changing structure of the Ottoman state and the ruling class during the Tanzimat era, see Shaw and Shaw (2002, especially pp. 71–95).

3

Administrative mechanisms and population changes in the *vilayet* of Thessaloniki

Generally speaking, the rise of industrial capitalism reflects changing social relations, including the emergence of a capitalist class with exclusive property rights over both productive resources and finished output, the systematic growth of wage labour and formation of a working class, the expansion of networks of trade over long distances but also domestically, and the transformation of agriculture as capitalist farming emerges and agrarian labour (free, semi-free or bonded) begins to take the wage form. Moreover, the rise of industrial capitalism also depends on material economic forces, including the availability of an appropriate range of labour skills, suitable technologies of production and communication, access to necessary product inputs and requisite technical facilities of trading.

In the following chapters these social relations and material forces are examined for provincial Ottoman Macedonia to the extent that the available sources allow. In the Ottoman context, furthermore, these fundamental relations and forces operated on a broad canvass determined by the power of the state and the complex interactions between ethnic and religious communities. The commercial and productive practices of the budding capitalists were framed by the policies of the modernizing Ottoman state. The policies of the state were, moreover, filtered by the communal structures of a population that was remarkably mixed as well as strongly marked by religious affiliation that encouraged hierarchical and exclusionary practices.

It is necessary, consequently, to start by sketching a picture of the mechanisms of administration and the composition of the population in the *vilayet* of Thessaloniki towards the end of the nineteenth century. Information is mainly drawn from the provincial yearbooks which allow for a fairly detailed picture to be built of the administrative structures of Macedonia as well as of the population of Mount Vermion and its economic activities from 1870 to the end of Ottoman rule. It is also possible to establish the size and the composition of the population of the towns of Veroia, Naoussa and Edhessa in comparison to Thessaloniki.[1]

3.1 Administrative reforms of the Ottoman state in the nineteenth century

During the first three decades of the nineteenth century, the Ottoman state administration entered a phase of thorough reorganization that gradually had a major impact on the Empire's provinces. A leading role was played by the reformist Sultan Mahmud II reacting against provincial warlords and administrators who had accumulated great power during the preceding period at the expense of the Sublime Porte in İstanbul. The relative weakening of the power of the Porte lasted roughly from the start of the eighteenth century to the start of the nineteenth century and much of this period is known as the age of the *ayan*. The word *ayan* literally means notable and refers to a stratum of landed and urban semi-official state functionaries who also typically had access to military power. The *ayan* were important to the rise of capitalism in Macedonia, and their role will be considered in several places in this work. Suffice it here briefly to indicate their place in the modernization of the Ottoman state.

The political ascendancy of the *ayan* reflected the decline in central Ottoman power and the lack of effectiveness of local administration in the eighteenth century. The growing weakness of the state followed military defeats at the hands of the Habsburgs and other European powers towards the end of the seventeenth century, which were marked by the adverse for the Ottomans treaties of Karlowitz in 1699 and Passarowitz in 1718. The *ayan* rose politically and militarily to fill the gap left by the weakened central state.

---

[1] Empirical analysis draws mainly on Cakiroglu (2015). There are several other works that analyse the population of the *vilayet* of Thessaloniki which will be regularly used for comparison and to strengthen conclusions; see Karpat (1985); Palairet (1993); Eldem (1994); Behar (1996); Anastassiadou (1997) and McCarthy (2000).

Their economic ascendancy owed much to the growing opportunities to trade agricultural output that emerged in the eighteenth century, which they grasped by creating *çiftlik* estates out of publicly-owned land. The *ayan* of Macedonia were instrumental to the proliferation of *çiftlik* estates on the plain, a feature of agrarian development that decisively influenced the path of capitalism in the region.

The *ayan* provided the backbone of a new Ottoman landlordism associated with changes in agrarian labour. The economic and social implications of *çiftlik*-based agriculture will be considered in detail in Chapter 4 but note here that the new landlordism relied on landed estate owners possessing a degree of independent political and military power. In McGowan's pithy terms: 'Official indifference, poor administration, and actual collusion by the courts permitted Ottoman elite figures of all descriptions to alienate estates from the great reservoir of state-owned land (*miri*). Tax-farmers with life-leases and military status were especially well-placed to bring this about. The vast majority of these alienations had been achieved in the course of the eighteenth century'.[2]

The Porte was far from indifferent to the extraordinary power of the *ayan*, and reacted against it already at the end of the eighteenth century. By the first four decades of the nineteenth century the Porte had effectively won the political battle. A landmark in the gradual decline and eventual political neutralization of the *ayan* was the General Consultative Assembly (*Meşveret-i Amme*) convened in İstanbul in 1808 and attended by the leading *ayan* of the Empire. The outcome was the 'Charter of Alliance', or 'Deed of Agreement' (*Sened-i İttifak*), between the central Ottoman state and powerful *ayan*, which aimed to regulate the power of the *ayan* and their relations with the central state. The Deed was not implemented in practice, but signalled the opening of a reform agenda that would in time lead to the restoration of the power of the Porte across the territories of the Empire.[3] Eventually, the *ayan* were either eliminated or integrated into the new mechanisms of Ottoman authority. At the same time the central state made no sustained attempt to change the *çiftlik* system or to constrain the economic power of the landlords. Macedonia, in particular, remained replete with *çiftlik* to the end of Ottoman rule.

---

[2] See McGowan (1994, p. 660).
[3] See Sadat (1969, 1972). A recent analysis stressing the power of the provincial *ayan* and the complex struggle and eventual compromise reached with the Porte can be found in Yaycioglu (2016).

A critical event in the resurgence of central Ottoman power was the disbandment of the Janissary corps in 1826. By that time the Janissaries were far removed from their original military purposes and comprised an insignificant part of the Ottoman army. Moreover, the strict rules of their recruitment and training had long ago decayed. The Janissaries essentially comprised extensive networks of small producers and traders in the capital and other urban centres. They had become 'the most powerful and best-organized advocates of protectionism' since they were directly involved in guild-based production and were both armed and politically minded.[4] The Janissaries proved to be a major obstacle to state-led reform of economy and society.[5] Their elimination and mass slaughter in 1826 had major political, economic and social repercussions since it allowed for the introduction of economic liberalism as well as facilitating political and military reform of the state.

The revival of the power of the Porte was also in response to mounting pressure from European powers after the 1750s. The international weight and the territorial possessions of the Empire had diminished steadily toward the end of the eighteenth century. Russian military aggression had resulted in the treaty of Küçük Kaynarca in 1774 reducing the power of the Porte over its Christian communities. Napoleon's campaign in Egypt in 1798–1801 had ended in failure from the perspective of France, but nonetheless detached Egypt from the Porte which had ruled it since 1517. In the vacuum that ensued arose the greatest of the *ayan*, Kavalalı Mehmed Ali *Paşa*, an ethnic Albanian brought up in Kavala and the island of Thassos (*Taşöz*) in Northern Greece. Mehmed Ali came from a relatively humble background, had experience of tax collecting and had risen through the ranks of the military. He was the exception to the re-establishment of the Porte's authority over the *ayan* in the first decades of the nineteenth century. Mehmed Ali effectively founded the contemporary state of Egypt, adopted policies of modernization and created powerful armed forces manned by native Egyptians. The Ottoman state's weakness against Mehmed Ali resulted in the Anglo-Ottoman Free Trade Convention of 1838, which formally ushered in economic liberalization and forced the opening of

---

[4] See Quataert (1994b, p. 764).
[5] See Uyar and Erickson (2009, pp. 120–8).

domestic markets to foreign trade at the behest of Britain. The Porte had little option but to submit since British gunboats (and Russian land forces) were the only effective means of resisting the encroachments of Mehmed Ali in the Anatolian heartlands of the Empire.

The Ottoman state survived and even managed to revive its fortunes after partly accommodating and partly resisting both the power of the *ayan* and the pressures of the European states.[6] The revival of the Porte was manifest in the era of the Tanzimat, which lasted roughly from 1839 to 1876. This was a period of profound reforms associated with the policies of Sultan Mahmud II and Sultan Abdülmecid I, who were backed by Europe-educated Ottoman administrators. The era of the Tanzimat commenced with the Imperial Edict of *Gülhane* in 1839, promising reform of taxation, creation of a conscript army and individual legal rights of person and property.[7] A further landmark of the Tanzimat was the Imperial Rescript of 1856, which offered assurances of equal treatment to the non-Muslim population in the fields of education, justice, religion and taxation.

The ostensible aim of the Porte during the period of the reforms was to introduce new administrative structures, in part by taking Western Europe as its model, and thus implement economic, educational, institutional and legal changes across Ottoman society. The state machinery that began to take shape around the middle of the nineteenth century had a profoundly different outlook compared to the seventeenth and eighteenth centuries. The state of the Tanzimat aimed at 'modernity' which implied, above all, creating uniform administrative conditions across Ottoman territories. Homogeneity, particularly the elimination of local arbitrary power in economic life, proved vital to the emergence of capitalism in the cities and the provinces.

The first and foremost objective of the Porte in this respect was to set in train the replacement of tax farmers (*mültezim*) by administrators charged with collecting taxes on behalf of the state. Taxation began to be based on income and property, leaving behind the system of imposing taxes on entire

---

[6] See Quataert (1994b, pp. 761–5).
[7] Tanzimat literally means reorganization and the *Tanzimat Fermanı* is the Imperial Edict of Reorganization. This Edict is also known as *Gülhane Hatt-ı Şerif* meaning the Supreme Edict of Gülhane, that is referring to the rose garden next to the Topkapı Palace in İstanbul, where the proclamation was made.

communities considered as single entities, which had greatly favoured the exploitative practices of the tax farmers. Moreover, the system of justice became more 'objective', gradually suppressing some of the ancient forms of confessional and communal discrimination.[8]

To these ends, the reformer Mustafa Reşid Paşa began to reorganize the administrative structures of the provinces as early as 1840.[9] However, the full reorganization of administration took place only after 1864 with the promulgation of 'The *Vilayet* Law of Danube', or '*Tuna Vilayeti Nizamnamesi*', which was initially a pilot scheme initiated by another reformer, Midhat Paşa.[10] The reform was extended to the entire administrative structure of the Empire with the '*Vilayet* Law', or '*Teşkil-i Vilayet Nizamnamesi*', after 1867. Further alterations to the administrative structures of the provinces were made in 1871 by another '*Vilayet* Law', or '*İdare-i Umumiyye-i Vilayet Nizamnamesi*', which shaped the powers of the local state bureaucracy.[11]

The reforms of the 1860s broadcast the spirit of the Tanzimat to the provinces by replacing the traditional Ottoman administrative system of *eyalet* with the new system of *vilayet* taking the French Préfets as a model. Historically the Empire had been divided into *eyalet* (provinces) of which two were by far the most important: *Rumeli* (in Europe) and *Anadolu* (in Asia). Each of these contained several smaller units but without a clear order of administrative hierarchy among them. The reforms replaced the old *eyalet* with several *vilayet* that were approximately equal in size. Each *vilayet* contained several smaller administrative units including, in descending order of importance, *sancak* (perhaps appropriately rendered as district), *kaza* (perhaps best rendered as county), *kasaba* (town), *nahiye* (a small unit perhaps best rendered as village cluster) and *karye/kariye* (village). Thus, a clear administrative structure was established within the new provincial units. *Vilayet* governors possessing substantial power over social, financial, security and political affairs were charged with implementing the relevant laws.[12]

---

[8] The actual success of these reforms was, in most cases, a matter of debate.
[9] See Shaw (1992, p. 33).
[10] The reform excluded places with established *sui generis* administrative structures, such as Serbia, Wallachia, Tunisia, Egypt, Montenegro, Samos and Lebanon; see Shaw (1992).
[11] See Kırmızı (2007, pp. 26–34).
[12] See Shaw (1992, pp. 88–91).

3.2 Administrative structures in the *vilayet* of Thessaloniki during the era of Tanzimat

In the *vilayet* of Thessaloniki, including the region of Mount Vermion, the fundamental administrative reorganization of the Tanzimat period had already taken place by 1867. However, significant changes were further implemented in subsequent years and had an impact on industrialization. Table 3.1 provides an overview of the relevant administrative changes in the final four decades of Ottoman rule.

During the forty-one years that passed from the *Vilayet* Law of 1871 to the end of Ottoman rule in Macedonia in 1912 several administrative reforms

Table 3.1 The administrative structure of the *vilayet* of Thessaloniki (*Selanik*)

Year	Main subdivisions of Thessaloniki *vilayet*	Chain of administrative command for Veroia, Naoussa and Edhessa
1871	4 *sancak*: Thessaloniki, Bitola (*Manastır*), Serres (*Serez*), Drama (*Drama*)	**Veroia** (*kaza*) —> Thessaloniki (*sancak*) —> Thessaloniki (*vilayet*) **Naoussa** (*nahiye*) —> Veroia (*kaza*) —> Thessaloniki (*sancak*) —> Thessaloniki (*vilayet*) **Edhessa** (*kaza*) —> Thessaloniki (*sancak*) —> Thessaloniki (*vilayet*)
1872–6	5 *sancak*: Thessaloniki, Korçë (*Görice*), Bitola, Serres, Drama	**Veroia** (*kaza*) —> Thessaloniki (*sancak*) —> Thessaloniki (*vilayet*) **Naoussa** (*nahiye*) —> Veroia (*kaza*) —> Thessaloniki (*sancak*) —> Thessaloniki (*vilayet*) **Edhessa** (*kaza*) —> Thessaloniki (*sancak*) —> Thessaloniki (*vilayet*)
1876–1905	3 *sancak*: Thessaloniki, Serres, Drama	**Veroia** (*kaza*) —> Thessaloniki (*sancak*) —> Thessaloniki (*vilayet*) **Naoussa** (*nahiye*) —> Veroia (*kaza*) —> Thessaloniki (*sancak*) —> Thessaloniki (*vilayet*) **Edhessa** (*kaza*) —> Thessaloniki (*sancak*) —> Thessaloniki (*vilayet*)
1905–12	4 *sancak*: Thessaloniki, Serres, Drama, Thassos (*Taşöz*)	**Veroia** (*kaza*) —> Thessaloniki (*sancak*) —> Thessaloniki (*vilayet*) **Naoussa** (*nahiye*) —> Veroia (*kaza*) —> Thessaloniki (*sancak*) —> Thessaloniki (*vilayet*) **Edhessa** (*kaza*) —> Thessaloniki (*sancak*) —> Thessaloniki (*vilayet*)

Source: Compiled from SVS I-XX, 1287–1325 [1870–1907].

took place in the *vilayet* of Thessaloniki, but the underlying administrative structure remained essentially the same. The *vilayet* was typically split into three *sancak* (Thessaloniki itself, Serres (*Serez/Siroz*), and Drama (*Drama*)) covering the bulk of the area. In 1871–6 the *vilayet* also included the *sancak* of Bitola (*Manastır*) but Bitola acquired its own *vilayet* in the late 1870s. Note that in the early 1870s Bitola was a significant urban centre in Ottoman Macedonia. For an even shorter period in the 1870s the *vilayet* of Thessaloniki also included the town and immediate region of Korçë (*Görice*) which lies in contemporary south-eastern Albania. During 1905–12, finally, the *vilayet* also came to include a new *sancak*, Thassos (*Taşöz*), a small island of Macedonia which for a short period was elevated into a separate *sancak*.

The three towns of the region of Mount Vermion belonged to the *sancak* of Thessaloniki throughout the period, reflecting their close relations with the main city of Macedonia at the end of the nineteenth century. Of the three, Veroia and Edhessa were the more important places of habitation, each meriting its own *kaza*. Naoussa was never anything more than a *nahiye* and was always administratively attached to Veroia. Interestingly, the same administrative practice has continued to characterize the relationship of Naoussa to Veroia in the successor state of Greece.

The combined effect of the Imperial Rescript of 1856 and the Reform Law of 1867 found a loud echo in the region of Mount Vermion. Under the law of 1867 the *nahiye* of Naoussa acquired the right to appoint a Christian mayor as part of the Ottoman administrative machinery, a step that would have been unthinkable in the urban settlements of Macedonia in the preceding period. Local communal and political conditions had obviously entered a new phase under the Tanzimat. By the late 1860s the Ottoman policy of suppressing particular interests had reached its logical end in provincial Macedonia, making it possible to appoint a Christian mayor as part of the Ottoman administrative structures of a predominantly Christian town.

In sum, the Ottoman state machine of the Tanzimat period treated its non-Muslim subjects in a very different way compared to the historical practices of the Empire. The ascendant power of the Porte successfully ironed out some ancient particularities and discriminatory practices, giving new formal vent to the power of local communities. State power and communal power combined to facilitate the emergence of industrial capitalism in Macedonia within a few years. Industrialization in provincial Macedonia commenced in the lowly *nahiye* of Naoussa and spread first to Edhessa and then to Veroia. In addition to the administrative reform of the area, this development also reflected the characteristics of the population mix and the cultural background of the three towns. It is thus important to examine more closely the population of the region.

3.3 Population trends in Macedonia

A word of warning is necessary at the beginning of this section. Demographic data has always been problematic in Ottoman historiography, in part because population statistics were produced typically to meet the state's fiscal and military purposes. As Quataert states: 'The Ottoman state, before the nineteenth century, counted the wealth of its subjects but not the people themselves. When examining its human resources, it enumerated only those responsible for the payment of taxes (household heads, usually males) or likely to be of military use (young men).'[13] A further difficulty is that population data has been extensively deployed for nationalist purposes, above all, to prove the rights of an ethnic group over a particular geographical area.

In the nineteenth century the Ottoman state began regularly to undertake population censuses, a practice initiated, once again, by Sultan Mahmud II. An early attempt at a census was made in 1826, following the disbandment of the Janissaries, but was not completed due to the Russo-Turkish War of 1828–9. After the war and the wholesale defeat of Ottoman forces, a census was again begun in 1831. This time 'after large-scale preparations, the census was carried out successfully in the various *sancak* and townships of *Rumeli* and Anatolia'.[14]

It is certainly striking that the first census attempt in the Ottoman Empire was made as early as the 1820s, a mere quarter of a century after the introduction of modern census procedures in the United States, Great Britain and France.[15] The Ottoman state evidently found itself under tremendous military and political pressure, and was determined to establish a reliable picture of the available manpower in the hope of building a new army and an operational administrative bureaucracy. Moreover, the state hoped to ascertain

---

[13] See Quataert (2005, p. 112).
[14] See Karal (1943, p. 8).
[15] See Shaw (1978, p. 325).

the precise number of tax payers with the intent of developing a more effective and centralized tax system.[16]

Obtaining a reliable picture of the population was, however, far from easy. Population registers were revised in 1835, 1838, 1844, 1857 and probably in 1864.[17] Official censuses became comprehensive, relatively reliable and consistent only after the enactment of the Regulation of Population Registration (*Sicil-i Nüfus Nizamnamesi*) in 1878. The practice of counting mainly households eligible for taxation as well as young men fit for military service was not completely abandoned until the late 1870s. As Quataert noted, 'Population size for a given area or the Empire as a whole can only be approximated until the 1880s, when the first real censuses appear.'[18]

Thus, while there is no shortage of information on the population of the Ottoman Empire for most of the nineteenth century, it remains difficult accurately to determine its size, trends and ethno-religious mix. Four specific difficulties can be immediately mentioned for the population of the Balkans, including the *vilayet* of Thessaloniki.

First, it is likely that significant errors were made while conducting the official censuses, such as registering areas belatedly, or even ignoring entire areas; in addition, it appears that there were frequent omissions, double counting of data and plain bad arithmetic.[19] Second, since Ottoman authorities were primarily interested in counting households eligible for tax and adult males fit for military service, the official figures have to be translated into estimates of the population as a whole, and this necessarily involves arbitrary assumptions. Third, the available figures on population provided by sources other than the Ottoman state vary greatly in quality and reliability. The estimates provided by Bulgarian, Greek and Serb nationalists, for instance, systematically inflate the numbers of their respective ethnic groups to justify territorial claims. The estimates provided by travellers were typically little more than very rough generalizations from anecdotal evidence collected while journeying through Ottoman lands.[20] The same point applies more or less to estimates by foreign consuls, teachers, business people and others.

---

[16] See Karal (1943); Shaw (1978).
[17] See Palairet (1993, p. 3).
[18] See Quataert (2005, p. 112).
[19] See Palairet (1993, p. 3).
[20] See McCarthy (2000, p. 29).

Nevertheless, some of these estimates remain useful as their compilers usually aimed to provide their respective governments with reliable information for policy purposes. Note that even in such cases it was common for the authors of the estimates to accept that the most trustworthy statistics were those produced by the Ottoman state.[21] Fourth, population figures provided by different official Ottoman sources also vary greatly. Even after 1878, there were various inconsistencies not only between different official sources but also among the figures provided by the same source. This also holds for the provincial yearbooks of Macedonia.

In view of these problems, the official Ottoman statistics are the most reliable source of information on the population. The Ottoman state was the agent with the greatest control and power over the territories of the Empire, despite its manifest deficiencies. It also had the fiscal and military incentives to be as accurate as possible when counting the population. Needless to say, Ottoman population statistics cannot be accepted at face value but must be critically assessed bearing in mind inefficient census methods, administrative changes that affected geographical divisions and boundaries, and migration movements. It is likely that the data systematically underestimated the population, as also tends to happen with contemporary censuses, though errors today are incomparably fewer and less significant.[22]

For our purposes, the guide to the population of the *vilayet* of Thessaloniki are the official Ottoman statistics coupled with some relatively reliable secondary works on the Ottoman population. However, the figures and trends presented below have an indeterminate margin of error, particularly as the original Ottoman figures never provided the actual size of the entire population. Moreover, it is impossible reliably to compare the population figures for Naoussa, Veroia and Edhessa since there is very little accurate information regarding the smaller administrative units of the Empire. With these caveats in mind, the provincial yearbooks provide important insights into the general patterns of demographic change and the ethno-religious composition of the population of both Thessaloniki and Mount Vermion.

---

[21] See Karpat (1985, p. 6).
[22] Ibid., p. 9.

Table 3.2 Population of the *vilayet* of Thessaloniki, 1874

Population (male)	Non-Muslim	Muslim	Total
Thessaloniki (*sancak*)	92,168	65,593	166,741
Thessaloniki (*kaza*)	7,819	12,385	20,204
Veroia (*kaza*)	8,944	1,380	10,324
Edhessa (*kaza*)	1,665	3,331	4,996
Bitola (*sancak*)	113,260	48,842	166,052
Bitola (*kaza*)	39,680	9,494	49,174
Korçë (*sancak*)	48,674	25,403	74,077
Korçë (*kaza*)	10,871	11,953	22,824
Serres (*sancak*)	68,468	43,144	111,612
Drama (*sancak*)	4,303	51,407	55,710
Drama (*kaza*)	1,017	15,010	16,027
TOTAL	326,873	234,389	574,192

Note: It is clearly stated in the yearbooks that until the year 1886 population figures reflected only the male population, thus including only men who were eligible to work, pay taxes and join the army. Other household members – not only women but also children —were omitted from the figures. This explains the huge difference between Table 3.2 and the following tables that refer to the *vilayet* of Thessaloniki. If we consider the average household size to be five, the figures in Table 3.2 are consistent with the corrected estimates of Akarli in Table 3.3. On the other hand, smaller differences, such as those observed in Table 3.3 and other sources, could be explained by population movements and increases due to urbanization and growth, or due simply to measurement errors.

Source: SVS IV, 1291 [1874]. Some obvious inconsistencies of the data, such as the sum of Muslims and non-Muslims not adding up exactly to the supposed total, have been ignored; other minor errors have been corrected.

The first task in this respect is to establish the population of the *vilayet* of Thessaloniki. Based on the administrative structures shown on Table 3.1 and using information from the yearbooks, the male population of the *vilayet* in 1874 was as shown in Table 3.2.[23]

From Table 3.2 it appears that in the early 1870s the bulk of the population of the *vilayet* of Thessaloniki lived in the inland areas rather than on the coast; it is also clear that the non-Muslim element was in the majority. The figures for the *kaza* of Thessaloniki are extraordinarily low, probably due to the problematic ways of counting but perhaps also due to widespread avoidance

---

[23] The figures in the yearbooks refer in practice to one or two years prior to publication since the collection of the data would have taken considerable time under the conditions of the time. The figures for 1874 probably reflect the state of the *vilayet* in 1872–3. Nevertheless, the most sensible thing to do is not to attempt any corrections but use the official dates provided.

Table 3.3 Population of the *vilayet* of Thessaloniki, 1876–1911

1. Population estimates

Year	Official estimates	Corrected estimates
1876	393,000	813,000
1885	990,000	1,069,000
1896	1,010,000	1,091,000
1906	921,000	995,000
1911	1,103,000	1,191,000

Source: Compiled from Akarli (2001: 56).

of census registration by the non-Muslim population. Still, it seems that in terms of population, Thessaloniki, whether as a *kaza* or as a *sancak*, did not dominate Macedonia in the early 1870s: Bitola and Serres were comparable population centres. The figures in Table 3.2 are broadly consistent with the figures by Behar for the *vilayet* of Thessaloniki.[24] They are also consistent with Palairet's estimates for Thessaloniki and other Balkan cities.[25]

However, Thessaloniki was on a different population trajectory from the rest of the urban centres of Macedonia, and soon its population became substantially larger reflecting at least in part the rise of industrial and commercial capitalism. Relevant information for the population of the *vilayet* of Thessaloniki in this respect has been provided by Akarli, shown in Table 3.3 and including corrections for official figures.[26]

According to Akarli, the population of the *vilayet* of Thessaloniki increased dramatically in the 1870s and 1880s but was stagnant and even declined in the 1890s and the first few years of the 1900s. It then grew rapidly again until the end of the Ottoman period in 1912. Akarli attributed these fluctuations to both inward and outward migration.[27] Until the middle of the 1880s inward migration occurred mainly from Bulgaria, Romania and the Caucasus in the aftermath of the Russo-Ottoman war of 1877–8. The stagnation of

---

[24] See Behar (1996), who has compiled population statistics for the Ottoman Empire as part of the 'Historical Statistics Series' of the State Institute of Statistics of Turkey.
[25] See Palairet (1993, pp. 10–13).
[26] See Akarli (2001). Akarli has benefited from the figures provided by Eldem (1994), Palairet (1993) and the yearbook for 1876.
[27] See Akarli (2001, pp. 57–8).

the population in the period 1885–97 was attributed by Akarli to outward migration following the loss of Thessaly by the Empire to Greece in 1881, which presumably encouraged Greek peasants to leave for Thessaly.

Migration pressures were certainly important to the fluctuations in the population of the *vilayet* but the underlying tendency of the population to rise reflected the vigorous economic development of the region. By 1911 the *vilayet* of Thessaloniki was the most urbanized area in the Balkans with strongly expanding economic activities that attracted incomers. It is instructive in this connection to compare population trends in the *kaza* of, respectively, Thessaloniki, Veroia and Edhessa constructed from yearbook data and shown in Diagrams 3.1, 3.2 and 3.3.[28] The estimates commence in 1881 – or the first feasible year after 1881 – because until then the available figures reflect only the male population; minor corrections to the data have been made throughout.

Diagram 3.1 indicates that the population of the city of Thessaloniki rose very rapidly from 1881 to middle of the 1890s and then became stagnant. Veroia presents a similar picture to Thessaloniki in Diagram 3.2; the population of the town even declined in the 1890s. Finally, Diagram 3.3 indicates that Edhessa followed a different trajectory: its population rose rapidly until the middle of the 1890s and then continued to grow. Some of the growth in Veroia and Edhessa could be attributed to inward migration, but the sustained rise of the population of Edhessa was probably also related to rapid industrialization in the town after 1895, partly helped by the construction of the railways. Veroia witnessed much less industrial growth during this period.

Unfortunately it is not possible to construct a figure for the trend of the population of Naoussa. The yearbooks give its population at roughly 5,500 in the 1900s, but this is almost certainly incorrect. Other sources indicate that the population of Naoussa approached 10,000 by the middle, or the end, of the first decade of the 1900s.[29] Rapid growth of population would be consistent with the town becoming the main industrial centre of the region.

---

[28] See Cakiroglu (2015).
[29] See Akarli (2001, p. 61) and Lapavitsas (2006). A significant piece of evidence is that adduced by Biliouris (2014, p. 28) referring to an obscure census of the town in October 1913, perhaps undertaken by school teachers, which recorded 8,580 Greeks and 539 'Ottomans' in Naoussa.

Diagram 3.1 Population trend in the *kaza* of Thessaloniki, 1881–1906

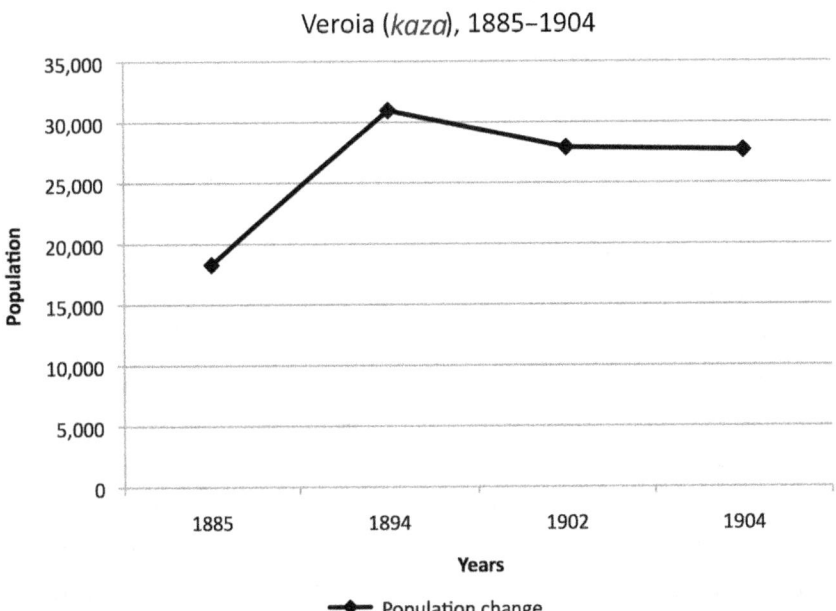

Diagram 3.2 Population trend in the *kaza* of Veroia, 1885–1904

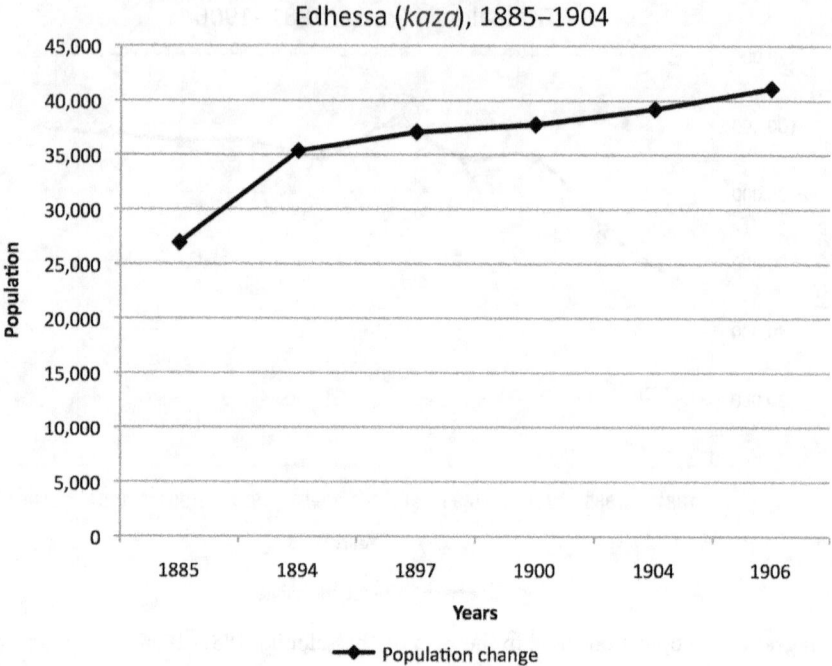

Diagram 3.3 Population trend in the *kaza* of Edhessa, 1885–1906

3.4 Ethnic and religious composition of the population

Establishing the population of Ottoman Macedonia is hard enough but ascertaining its ethnic and religious composition is a veritable minefield in view of the nationalist struggles that have marked the history of the region. The most reliable information can be gleaned from the official Ottoman data despite its multitude of defects. For the *vilayet* of Thessaloniki the provincial yearbooks provided a picture of the composition of the population for the first time in 1890 (in the tenth volume of the yearbooks). Proportions were given for Muslims, Greeks, Bulgarians, Jews and others, and these remained broadly stable throughout the period. Table 3.4 shows the composition of the population of the *vilayet* of Thessaloniki for 1902, according to the yearbooks.

The majority of the population of the *vilayet* of Thessaloniki was Christian. The ethnic distinction between Greeks and Bulgarians, corresponding mostly to their respective religious attachment to the Orthodox Patriarchate and the Bulgarian Exarchate, was also reflected in the statistics. However, the actual

Table 3.4 Composition of the population of the *vilayet* of Thessaloniki, 1902

Thessaloniki (*vilayet*)	Population	Share (%)
Muslim	469,981	44.65
Greek	309,812	29.43
Bulgarian	214,029	20.33
Jewish	47,702	4.53
Total	1,052,493	100.0

Source: SVS XVII, 1320 [1902]. Insignificant proportions of Catholics, Armenians, Protestants, and others have not been included; minor errors have been corrected.

Table 3.5 Composition of the population of the *kaza* of Thessaloniki, 1902

Thessaloniki	Population	Share (%)
Muslim	24,699	30.76
Greek	10,594	13.20
Jewish	44,331	55.22
Total	80,279	100.0

Source: S.V.S, XVII, 1320 [1902]. Insignificant proportions of Bulgarians, Catholics, Armenians and others have not been included; minor errors have been corrected.

kaza of Thessaloniki, which included small villages close to the main urban settlement, presented quite a different picture (Table 3.5).

The population of the *kaza* of Thessaloniki appeared to comprise primarily three ethno-religious groups in 1902: Jews, Muslims and Greeks. It is evident that the character of the city was strongly Jewish, a fact reflected in the personnel and the trajectory of industrialization in Thessaloniki, as is shown in subsequent chapters. The Greek community of Thessaloniki was the weakest of the three main groups.[30]

The population contrast between Thessaloniki and the three provincial towns of Mount Vermion is strikingly apparent in Tables 3.6, 3.7 and 3.8, which were also constructed from the yearbooks.

[30] A broadly similar picture emerges from the work of Anastassiadou (1997). Note that Anastassiadou has relied on two sources: first, detailed municipal population statistics for Thessaloniki in 1890, found in the Historical Archives of Macedonia as a single page document and, second, the provincial yearbook of Thessaloniki for 1321 (1905–6). For some reason we have not been able to identify a yearbook for that date.

Table 3.6 Composition of the population of the *kaza* of Veroia, 1902

Veroia (*kaza*)	Population	Share (%)
Muslim	7,015	25.25
Greek	18,203	65.5
Bulgarian	2,050	7.37
Jewish	485	1.74
Total	27,787	100.0

Source: SVS XVII, 1320 [1902]. Insignificant proportions of Catholics, Armenians and others have not been included; minor errors have been corrected.

Table 3.7 Composition of the population of the *kaza* of Edhessa, 1902

Edhessa (*kaza*)	Population	Share (%)
Muslim	5,263	28.86
Greek	9,820	53.85
Bulgarian	2,424	13.29
Coptic	729	4.0
Total	18,236	100.0

Note: The data shows the population of the *kaza* of Vodina according to the *salname* of 1902. However, Table 3.3 shows a much higher population for the same *kaza*. This is probably a recording error and the sum in Table 3.7 refers to the population of the town – not *kaza* – of Vodina (Edhessa).

Source: SVS XVII, 1320 [1902]. No other ethno-religious groups were recorded for Edhessa.

Table 3.8 Composition of the population of the *nahiye* of Naoussa, 1902

Naoussa (*nahiye*)	Population	Share (%)
Muslim	408	7.76
Greek	4,849	92.24
Total	5,257	100.0

Source: SVS XVII, 1320 [1902]. No other ethno-religious groups were recorded for Naoussa.

In 1902 the population of Veroia and Edhessa appeared to be predominantly Greek Christian, and the population of Naoussa overwhelmingly so.[31] The Jewish community, by far the most dynamic economic force in Thessaloniki,

---

[31] According to Demetriades (1981, p. 50), the Muslims (*Yürük* Turks) who were settled in this region paid certain taxes from which the Christians were exempt. His source is unclear and the reason for such a practice has not been given, but it might help explain the predominance of the Christian population in the region.

was practically absent in the three towns, with the partial (and long standing) exception of Veroia. Both Veroia and Edhessa had substantial Muslim populations, reflecting also the pattern of large landownership on the plain, as is shown in Chapter 4.

The ethno-religious characteristics of the urban centres of the *vilayet* of Thessaloniki were important to industrialization because of differences in internal organization and power among communities. It will be shown in the rest of this book that the dominance of the Jewish community in Thessaloniki and the dominance of the Greek Christian community in Mount Vermion were instrumental to the rise of industrial capitalism in Ottoman Macedonia and accounted for some of its characteristic features. To take the analysis further, however, it is necessary to consider the agrarian economy of the region in some detail.

4

The straightjacket of *çiftlik* agriculture in Macedonia

4.1 Rise and fall of the *tımar* system

The economy of the Ottoman Empire remained overwhelmingly agrarian to the very end, despite the emergence of an industrial sector. Four principal factors historically characterized Ottoman agriculture: abundance of land, scarcity of labour, dominance of smallholdings and prevalence of subsistence production.[1] The first two remained more or less unchanged throughout the Empire's history. However, the dominance of smallholdings and the prevalence of subsistence production began to change dramatically towards the end of the eighteenth century, thus impacting directly on the rise of capitalism.

Studies of the evolution of the Ottoman economy have frequently emphasized the breakdown of the *tımar* system in agriculture as the cause of long-term change, or even 'decline', of the Empire.[2] The *tımar* system was indeed the backbone of both economy and society as the Empire rose to its peak in the fifteenth and sixteenth centuries. The normal practice of Ottoman land tenure at the time was to place most of the available land under state ownership (the term for which was *miri* land), while dividing substantial parts of it into estates, that is, *tımar*. The *tımar* were distributed as temporary prebends to cavalrymen (the *tımarlı sipahi*), who formed the regular cavalry of the Ottoman army at the height of its power.

The *sipahi* cavalryman had the obligation to report for army service upon call with his own retainers, weapons and horses. During the peak of the

---

[1] These features of Ottoman agriculture, particularly during its late period, have been extensively analysed, including by Güran (1998); Keyder and Tabak (1991) and Quataert (1975, 2008).
[2] See, for instance, Barkan (1980); Inalcık (1955, 1991); Cin (1992); McGowan (1981).

Empire, reporting for army service could be an annual event. The peasants of the *tımar* had rights to the usufruct of their smallholdings – which remained the predominant form of cultivation – while the *tımar* holder commanded meadows, vineyards and other fields for the exclusive use of his household. Furthermore, the *tımar* holder had the right to collect certain taxes from the peasants (typically in kind) as personal income. Other taxes belonging to the central state were also collected by the *sipahi* (typically in cash). The obligatory services of the peasants to the *tımar* holders were few and strictly regulated by the central state and its legal representatives at the local level.

The *tımar* system was not an Ottoman invention but rather an adaptation of pre-existing land tenure practices in Anatolia, the Middle East and the Balkans. It resembled the iqta of the Islamic Caliphate and the older Anatolian *Selçuk* Turkish states; it also had similarities with the *pronoia* system of the Byzantine Empire.[3] For one thing, the *tımar* system allowed the Ottoman state to expand the cultivation of available land, expropriating agricultural surplus through taxes and other means. For another, the *sipahi* cavalry together with the standing force of the Janissary infantry corps created an army without equal in the fifteenth and sixteenth centuries, thus enabling the Ottomans to annex enormous expanses of territory in Europe and the Middle East. The *tımar* system could sustain this formidable army without ruining the state budget at a time of limited monetization of the economy. Moreover, the *sipahi* were an effective mechanism for transmitting the commands of central authority to the peasantry as well as ensuring that the peasants remained obedient and at peace. The temporary nature of the *tımar* holding and the formal ownership of the land by the state meant that a genuine feudal class never emerged in the Ottoman Empire.

The *tımar* system began to decline in the seventeenth century for a variety of reasons not least among which was the widespread adoption of individual firearms by the Ottoman army. The *sipahi* cavalry was no longer a match for musket-bearing foot soldiers. The Ottoman state was forced to reorganize and augment the army by expanding the Janissary corps as well as creating large regiments of musketeers recruited from the peasants of Anatolia and elsewhere, who were paid wages.[4] The military contest with rival European powers was

---

[3] See İnalcık (2011, pp. 111–3).
[4] See Uyar and Erickson (2009, ch. 3).

entering a long-term phase which the Empire was bound to lose, in contrast to the fifteenth and sixteenth centuries. Technical progress and military advances had tilted the balance irrevocably in favour of Western Europe as capitalism gradually began to take shape on the Continent.

Even worse for the Ottoman Empire, the transformation of the armed forces required increased monetary expenditures which – together with the steeply rising costs of equipment and other requirements of warfare – placed large fiscal impositions on the state. The fiscal burden kept growing as the *tımar*-holding class became weaker and headed for extinction, thus loosening the control of the state over agriculture and the system of land tenure. The result was gradual loss of central power, especially in the more remote rural areas of the Empire after the seventeenth century. An important manifestation of the decline of state power was the proliferation of *çiftlik* estates as tax collectors began to acquire quasi-proprietary and semi-hereditary rights over land benefiting from the void left by the central state.[5]

The gradual dismantling of the *tımar* system in the seventeenth century placed considerable strain on the Ottoman economic structure that was predominantly based on agriculture. Pamuk has estimated that, in the sixteenth century, perhaps 90 per cent of the population lived in rural areas, while three quarters were actively engaged in agriculture.[6] The economic transformation that ensued upon the decay of the *tımar* system amounted to the proliferation of *çiftlik* estates, that is, large landholdings which effectively had a proprietary character. These estates began to appear in the Balkans already at the end of the sixteenth century.[7] The *çiftlik* estates had a clear commercial orientation since their output was for sale. They came into direct conflict with two crucial features of the *tımar* system, namely state ownership of land and dominance of largely self-sufficient smallholdings in agricultural production.[8]

---

[5] See İnalcık (1980, p. 329).
[6] See Pamuk (2007, p. 40).
[7] See Stoianovich (1953, p. 402); İnalcık (1991, pp. 18–26); Veinstein (1991, p. 35).
[8] There is a well-known debate on the emergence of *çiftlik* estates, focusing particularly on whether the causes were internal or external to the Ottoman economic, political and legal system; see, for instance, İnalcık (1991); Veinstein (1991); McGowan (1981); Keyder and Tabak (1998). In the rest of this chapter the causes of the emergence of *çiftlik* on the Macedonian plain are considered in detail.

4.2 Commercialization of agriculture, spread of tax farming and rise of *çiftlik* estates

Çiftlik estates were already widely spread in the second half of the eighteenth century, and their proliferation continued in the first half of the nineteenth century. The trade of the Empire grew rapidly during this period and there were commercial opportunities for agricultural output which also stimulated petty commodity production in the countryside.[9] There was particularly heavy demand for grain from Western Europe, and rising grain prices made exports more attractive after the 1820s.[10] In addition, market demand for agricultural goods was also increasing within the borders of the Empire. At the end of the nineteenth century the presence of *çiftlik* was pronounced across the European Ottoman provinces.[11]

Note that the export of agricultural goods for much of this period was officially regulated by the Ottoman state due to its strongly 'provisionist' outlook aiming to secure a steady supply of key goods to the domestic economy. Nonetheless, there were no significant obstructions to exporting cash crops from the Balkans in practice. This was probably due to collaboration between the local dignitaries who owned the *çiftlik* – among which the *ayan* stood out – and the merchants who controlled the trading networks.

During the first half of the nineteenth century, in particular, the international terms of trade moved strongly in favour of primary commodity producers in the Empire. Pamuk and Williamson have noted that: 'Over the four decades between 1815–1819 and 1855–1859, the Ottoman terms of trade rose almost 2.6 times, for an annual rate of 2.4 percent.'[12] This spectacular improvement made agricultural commodities very profitable for exporters, thus leading to a boom in agricultural production, especially between 1840 and 1870, during which the volume of world trade increased fivefold. Accordingly, revenues accruing to the Ottoman state from the agricultural tithe quadrupled between 1848 and 1876.[13] In that context, the political turmoil between the *ayan* and the

---

[9] See Teoman and Kaymak (2008, p. 315).
[10] See İnalcık (1991, pp. 24–5); Quataert (1994b, p. 873).
[11] See Güran (1998, p. 123).
[12] See Pamuk and Williamson (2011, p. 175). For an analysis of the terms of trade in peripheral countries during the first wave of globalization, see Williamson (2008).
[13] See Kasaba (1988, pp. 44, 94).

Porte that had marked the preceding century practically disappeared thanks to the liberal reforms of the Ottoman state. Growing revenues and incomes from agriculture ensured the viability of the political and economic compromise between the new (provincial and urban) elites and the state.

The new elites were closely associated with *çiftlik* estates, which induced a pronounced social differentiation in the countryside. Ottoman society had traditionally been divided into two formal social groups, the *reaya* and the *askeri*. The *reaya* were the section of the population that pursued productive activities and were thus liable to paying taxes. Merchants, artisans and peasants, regardless of religious background, belonged to the *reaya*. In contrast, the *askeri* comprised the military and administrative social layers which performed public functions as delegates of the Sultan and were exempt from taxation.[14] The agrarian transformation during the eighteenth and nineteenth centuries led to the emergence of a powerful class of *çiftlik* holders, who were mostly, but not exclusively, Muslim. They owned and controlled much of the land aiming to sell the output in the world market as well as domestically. At the same time merchants who were mostly, but not exclusively, Christian and Jewish, emerged as the winners of the strong commercial expansion. Thus, a new stratification began to appear in Ottoman society comprising powerful landlords and rich merchants.

In addition to commercial opportunities, a catalysing force for the proliferation of *çiftlik* was the deterioration of the fiscal condition of the Ottoman state. The principle of fiscalism that marked the operations of the Ottoman state had a decisive impact on the economy once the monetary needs of the armed forces began to escalate.[15] Fiscalism often amounted to the state collecting revenues as a short-term priority irrespective of other concerns. This encouraged the evolution of tax-farming from the practice of bidding for a tax farm for a limited period of time (*iltizam*) into the practice of bidding for a tax farm for life (*malikane*) when the immediate financial needs of the state became pressing. The new practice reshaped not only the economy but also the balance of power in society, particularly in the eighteenth century. Under the *malikane* system, the collection of public revenues was assigned via auction

---

[14] See İnalcık (1994a, p. 16).
[15] See Genç (1994, pp. 59–60).

to private individuals, mostly from the ranks of the administration and the military (the *askeri*). The contractor paid to the Treasury an initial amount plus a fixed annual sum that was confirmed each year by the state, and in return acquired the right to collect public revenues for life. Merchants, money-lenders and notables who had accumulated capital were also incorporated in the *malikane* system to finance the initial and subsequent payments of money to the state and to collect the taxes with a view to private profit.

Life-term tax farming was put in place at the end of the seventeenth century, and by the eighteenth it had spread to all economic activities that were subject to tax. The main aim of the tax collectors was to augment and commercialize agricultural production hoping to recover their investment and secure a profitable return. The result was enormous pressure on the peasants, even taking violent forms. Local notables who had acquired rights to extract taxes through the *malikane* system created private armies that allowed them to control agricultural land and its peasant communities. The *malikane* system opened the way to the eventual emergence of private property over land in the Ottoman Empire. Fertile plains were under especial danger of falling prey to life-time tax-farming, thus becoming effectively confiscated especially in places where the central power was weakening. Land-grabbing of this type was a driving force behind the proliferation of *çiftlik* on the plain of Macedonia.

4.3 *Ayan* and *kırcalı*

The spread of tax farming and the associated abuses were clear signs of loss of power by the central Ottoman state. By the second half of the eighteenth century the decline in the power of the Porte had reached new levels marked by the ascendancy of powerful *ayan*. The shift in the balance of power in favour of the *ayan* became vividly apparent in the course of the wars against the allied forces of Russia and Austria in 1787–92. The Porte lacked an effective army and was essentially dependent on the forces of the *ayan*, which were not capable of preventing another Ottoman defeat.[16] This was the trigger for military and other reforms that eventually led to the disbandment of the Janissaries in 1826.

---

[16] See Palairet (1993, p. 36).

Thus, at the end of the eighteenth century the Porte ceded military power to the *ayan* as well as losing administrative and fiscal capabilities to tax farmers. However, the central state and the new provincial elites gradually, and through constant struggle, succeeded in establishing a fresh compromise.[17] Slowly, painfully and after a succession of violent events, the Porte consolidated its mechanisms of power, reorganized the mechanisms through which it redistributed economic surpluses, and broadened the space for local elites to pursue their social and economic objectives. During the last decades of the eighteenth and the first decades of the nineteenth century a new form of institutional centralization began to emerge in the Ottoman Empire which eventually gave birth to the modernizing state of the nineteenth century.

From the perspective of the peasants, however, the changing terrain was full of threats and dangers. As the end of the eighteenth century approached the peasants found themselves relentlessly squeezed between the growing revenue demands of the Ottoman state and the ruthless exactions of the tax farmers. The consequence was rising indebtedness of individual peasants to village chieftains as well as to other local notables and tax collectors. For the *ayan*, who had an insatiable appetite for land, these were perfect conditions to expand *çiftlik* estates that effectively became their private property. The peasants became tenants and sharecroppers, or even turned into agricultural labourers.[18] The transformation of agrarian conditions was particularly pronounced in the southern and western Balkans: by the end of the century, *çiftlik* estates and villages had spread throughout Thessaly, Epirus, Macedonia, Thrace, the Marica Valley, Bulgaria, Kosova, the coastal plains of Albania and parts of Bosnia.[19]

Loss of power by the central state and the rise of rapacious and powerful *ayan* contributed to warlordism and widespread banditry in the Balkans at the end of the eighteenth century and the beginning of the nineteenth century.

---

[17] Yaycioglu (2016, ch. 2) draws a detailed picture of the contest between the Porte and the *ayan*, a struggle that varied considerably in the Balkans, Anatolia and the Arab lands further to the south. In the end the Porte prevailed but the Ottoman state that emerged after its victory was in practice quite new. Salzmann (1993, p. 394) notes that: 'The very longevity of the Ottoman state points to a paradox: that long-term institutional decentralization may well be a viable strategy, in fact an integral part, of the socio-organizational evolution of the modern state.'

[18] See Teoman and Kaymak (2008, p. 316); Palairet (1993, p. 38).

[19] See Stoianovich (1953, pp. 402–3).

This period is often referred to as the time of the *kırcalı*, that is, marauding bands of armed men, Muslim and Christian, who paid scant attention to the power of the Porte and often clashed violently with each other. They were particularly active in the region between the Balkan Mountains and the Danube in contemporary northern Bulgaria. The time of the *kırcalı* was a period of continuous political turmoil and nascent rebellion against central Ottoman power.[20] The effect on the peasants was frequently catastrophic since they were forced either to submit to the protection of powerful local landlords, thus becoming dependants of *çiftlik*, or to abandon their holdings and withdraw to safer places, especially upland settlements. The upland settlements were typically not arable and held little interest for the *ayan*. They were also remote and easier to defend, thereby escaping the attentions of the *kırcalı*.[21] The intensity of *ayan* warlordism and the depredations of the *kırcalı* peaked in the early nineteenth century but subsided in the ensuing decades as the Porte reasserted itself.

Macedonian agriculture at the end of the eighteenth century was shaped by these conflicting pressures which lent to it several distinctive features. The advancing commercialization of agriculture, the marketing of agricultural produce in the world market, the persistent inability of the Empire to stand up to pressure from the rising European powers and the power of local elites led to the proliferation of *çiftlik* in Macedonia. By the middle of the nineteenth century the plain of Macedonia, and especially the region of Naoussa, Veroia and Edhessa, were dominated by *çiftlik* estates to a greater extent than most other parts of the Empire. *Çiftlik* provided the agrarian backdrop

---

[20] *Kırcalı* (often transliterated as kirdzhali) means fighter, robber, bandit, rebel in Turkish. These Balkan fighting men have passed into the historical lore of the successor states of the Ottoman Empire. Pushkin's 'Kirdzhali' (Кърджали) is redolent with the romantic glow of the *kırcalı*. It tells the story of Georgii Kirdzhali, a Bulgarian by birth, a robber, who joined the forces of Filike Etairia, led by Alexandros Ypsilantis and Giorgakis Olympios, in their disastrous campaign in Moldavia and Wallachia in 1821, the opening salvo of the Greek Revolution. When the revolt in the Danubian Principalities collapsed, Georgii Kirdzhali took part in the battle of Sculeni with the remnants of the bands of the Etairia that attempted to re-cross the Pruth back onto Russian territory and were cut down by vastly greater numbers of Ottoman cavalry. Kirdzhali escaped the debacle but was eventually handed over by the Russians to the Turks and was put to death. Pushkin, who was struck by the aura of the rebel, used poetic license to make Kirdhzali go free and continue his exploits (Pushkin, 1983, pp. 234–9).

[21] See Sadat (1972, p. 354); Petmezas (1990, pp. 577–80) and Palairet (1993, pp. 34–40). According to Palairet (1993, pp. 38–9), a significant number of the upland settlements in Bulgaria were direct vassals of the Sultan and enjoyed tax and other privileges as 'soldier' or 'pass-defender' villages.

for the emergence of private industrial enterprises in Thessaloniki and the Macedonian provinces.

The main incentive to acquire and establish *çiftlik* in Macedonia – as elsewhere – was 'rising international demand for grain, tobacco and later cotton, which made large-scale farming an attractive proposition'.[22] By drawing on the evidence from the yearbooks and exploring other available sources a picture can be built of the transformation of agriculture in Macedonia, especially in the vicinity of Naoussa, Edhessa and Veroia, during this period. It will then be seen that agrarian relations were a straightjacket on the rise of capitalism in the region.

4.4 The disintegration of the *vakıf* of Gazi Evrenos Bey

Macedonia, and especially the *vilayet* of Thessaloniki, registered an exceptionally high concentration of *çiftlik* compared to the rest of the Empire. A particular reason for intense *çiftlik* emergence on the plain of Macedonia was the disintegration of *the vakıf* of *Gazi* Evrenos *Bey*.

A *vakıf* was a religious foundation allowed to hold land under terms that originated in Islamic law and were incorporated in the Ottoman legal system. Specifically, the *vakıf* land was neither state-owned (*miri* land) as was the case for the vast bulk of Ottoman lands, nor privately owned (*mülk* land) as happened for a small portion of agricultural and other land. Instead it was held in trust under a special dispensation (*vakfiye*) ultimately issued by the Sultan.[23] Crucially, the land of the *vakıf* was inalienable.

The ostensible purpose of a *vakıf*, which could include a mosque, a religious school, a Turkish bath, an inn (*han*), a bazaar and a variety of other establishments, was to provide services to travellers, to the poor and to society in general. Some of these services, including food and medical care, would be provided free of charge and regardless of religious attachment – to Muslims, Christians and Jews. The income from the land but also from the Turkish bath, the inn and the shops as well as from other economic activities

---

[22] See Palairet (1993, p. 36).
[23] See İnalcik (1994a, ch. 4).

that would naturally gravitate to the vicinity of the *vakıf* was free of tax and presumably dedicated to maintaining the *vakıf* services in perpetuity. A trustee superintendent (*mütevelli*) would be appointed to ensure the proper collection of *vakıf* income and its allotment to the declared purposes.

A *vakıf* was an excellent vehicle for the extension and reinforcement of Ottoman rule in conquered lands, delivering a mixture of welfare, charity and commercial services to the population in general. It was an even better vehicle for rich and powerful families or for individuals of the Ottoman upper class, including members of the ruling House of Osman, to hold land and other assets outside the jurisdiction of the official tax mechanisms and to bypass restrictions on hereditary ownership. The *mütevelli* would be a member of the family, or a person of absolute trust, and his position would be inherited, or otherwise managed by the effective holders of the *vakıf*. Some of the income of the *vakıf* would thus find its way into family, or individual, coffers.

Depending on its size, the *vakıf* would ensure the wealth and exceptional social power of its founders, thus defining a social layer within Ottoman society that had privileged access to land and was not subject to the normal constraints of *miri* holdings. Throughout the history of the Empire and particularly during the first centuries of aggressive expansion, *vakıf* were systematically established in the Balkans and elsewhere. The holders of *vakıf* were in a very different social position from the typical *tımar* holders, not least because they had more stable private rights over land and drew agricultural rents that were subject to fewer state exactions. The Porte was typically very circumspect when it came to losing tax revenue – not to mention control – and often tried to reclaim *vakıf* land. This was a marked feature of the reign of the autocratic and powerful Mehmed II, the conqueror of Constantinople, who was the true founder of the Ottoman Empire and champion of centralization.

The *vakıf* of the Evrenos family in Macedonia emerged in the fourteenth century when the Ottomans conquered the area from the Byzantines and the Serbs. Its founder was *Gazi* Evrenos *Bey*, one of the historic leaders of the *akıncı*, irregulars who would raid enemy territory in the name of *gaza*, the war against the unbelievers.[24] The *akıncı* were instrumental to the rapid expansion

---

[24] *Akıncı* literally means raider. The name was typically given to light cavalry units of the Ottoman army based in the border regions and used to attack neighbouring countries.

of Ottoman power in the Balkans in the second half of the fourteenth century. Penetrating deeply into Byzantine, Bulgarian and Serb territory, they caused enormous disruption, while establishing themselves permanently as soon as the opportunity arose. In effect, they prepared the ground for the Ottoman army to arrive and for the state formally to annex entire areas. The *akıncı* were not necessarily of Turkish, or Turcoman origin. Evrenos is not a Turkish name, although the ethnic origin of the founder of the family line, Piranki Isa *Bey*, the father of *Gazi* Evrenos, is entirely unclear.[25] He might even have been a descendant of a mercenary of the notorious Grand Catalan Company that ravaged the Balkans and the coastal areas of Asia Minor in the early fourteenth century.[26]

The *vakıf* of the Evrenos family in Macedonia was enormous, covering a huge part of the plain of Thessaloniki and beyond. In geographical terms – shown on the map of Macedonia in Plate 2 – the seat of the *vakıf*, and capital of the Evrenosoğulları, was the town of Giannitsa (*Yenice-i Vardar*). Its lands stretched from the outskirts of Thessaloniki (*Selanik*) in the East to the outskirts of Veroia (*Karaferye*) in the West; it included parts of Gynaikokastron (*Avrethisar*) in the north-east and reached Edhessa (*Vodina*) in the north-west. To be precise, there were three separate *vakıf* held by the Evrenos family: first, the *vakıf* of *Gazi* Evrenos, the original founder, second, the *vakıf* of Isa *Bey*, the son of *Gazi* Evrenos and, third, the *vakıf* of Ahmed *Bey*, the grandson of Evrenos.[27] The first, and largest, comprised fifty-nine villages, the second nine villages and the third five villages; the last two *vakıf* were added to the original family foundation at some point in the fifteenth century. The number of settlements is evidence of the great size of the *vakıf* of Evrenos, but the true weight of the estate would become clear only after considering its income.

A *tapu tahrir defter* (tax census register) of 1519 provides the earliest available information regarding the economic significance of the *vakıf* of

---

[25] See Lowry (2003, pp. 58–9).
[26] The non-Turkish origins of the Evrenos family was far from unusual during the period of aggressive expansion by the Ottoman state. Four families stood out as leaders of the *akıncı*, the Mihaloğulları, the Evrenosoğulları, the Malkoçoğullari and the Turahanoğullari, and it is certain that the first two did not have Turkish origins. All became established in the Balkans and were the closest thing that the Empire had to a hereditary nobility, providing functionaries to the Ottoman state. For further discussion see Lowry (2003).
[27] See Lowry and Erünsal (2010, pp. 162–4).

the Evrenos family.[28] The *tahrir* were essential instruments of power for the Ottoman state since they recorded with considerable accuracy the tax-paying capacity of given geographical areas for administrative and military purposes.[29] The document recorded an annual income of 460,983, 86,488 and 113,531 *akçe* (aspers, the Ottoman currency of the time) for, respectively, the first, second and third *vakıf* of the Evrenos family; total income rising to 661,002 *akçe*. To appreciate the significance of that sum, note that 1519 was the penultimate year in power of the formidable Sultan Selim I, who had just annexed Syria, Mesopotamia and Egypt. He was followed in 1520 by Sultan Süleyman, probably the most powerful of all Ottoman Sultans, who ruled for nearly five decades. In 1527–8, a few years into Süleyman's rule, the total tax and other public revenues of the Empire came to 537.9 million *akçe*, of which *Rumeli* (essentially the Balkans) provided 198.2 million. Out of the total for *Rumeli* the various *vakıf* and freehold lands provided 10.88 million.[30] At the time *Rumeli* was the most important province of the Empire for tax purposes, ahead of Anatolia, Egypt and Syria. The total population of the Balkans in 1520–35 has been estimated at 195,000 Muslim households and 863,000 Christian households.[31] Thus, the combined income of the *vakıf* of the Evrenos family in the early 1500s appeared to be roughly 6 per cent of the income provided by all the *vakıf* and freeholds in the European part of the Empire. The Evrenosoğulları were very wealthy.

A final point of interest for our purposes is that one of the five villages mentioned in the *tapu-tahrir defter* as belonging to the *vakıf* of Ahmed Bey Evrenosoğlu was *Ağustos*.[32] Indeed, Naoussa was not a village at all but the largest of the seventy-three settlements of all three *vakıf*, recorded as having 372 Christian and 11 Muslim households. Using the standard conversion rate of five persons per household, in 1519, Naoussa was a sizeable Christian town of nearly two thousand people on the western edge of the Macedonian plain. Quite naturally it provided the largest source of income for the *vakıf*, estimated at 69,332 *akçe* annually.

---

[28] Ibid., p. 119.
[29] See İnalcık (1994a, ch. 5).
[30] Ibid., p. 82, using figures by Barkan.
[31] See İnalcık (1993, p. 85) in İnalcık and Kafadar (1993).
[32] See Lowry and Erünsal (2010, p. 164).

The actions of *Gazi* Evrenos *Bey* and his role in the establishment of Ottoman rule in the Balkans are well-known to historians of the early Ottoman era. However, the history and the evolution of the *vakıf* of the Evrenos family have not been studied systematically, and the trajectory of the estate in the sixteenth and seventeenth centuries remains unclear. From the only available study, it appears that at the start of the eighteenth century only 10 per cent of the arable land of the *vakıf* comprised *çiftlik*.[33] During the eighteenth century, however, a large part of the estate was turned into *çiftlik*, and by the end of the nineteenth century at least 60 per cent of the arable and the pasture land of the *vakıf* had become *çiftlik*. Fundamental to this process was the depopulation of the area in the seventeenth century as tax pressures on the peasants increased partly from the tax-farmers working on behalf of the *vakıf* and partly from the central government. Peasants often had to borrow from Muslim moneylenders residing in Thessaloniki, who exercised relentless pressure on borrowers. The peasants were also subjected to the depredations of marauding Turcoman bands in the early eighteenth century.

The two *mütevelli* of the *vakıf* of Evrenos, both of whom were members of the family by tradition, were primarily concerned with ensuring a steady flow of income to the *vakıf* coffers. They had an incentive to turn over both cultivated and abandoned land to whomever would assume the transactions costs of collection while guaranteeing payment of the taxes and rents due. Under the conditions of the eighteenth century, acquisitive Muslim *ayan*, with the power to extract taxes and control agriculture and animal herding on the plain, were good candidates for the task. Entrusting the collection of rents to *ayan* was probably the catalyst for the gradual disintegration of the *vakıf* of Evrenos and its transformation into a remarkable number of *çiftlik* in the *vilayet* of Thessaloniki. The proliferation of *çiftlik* in the area also reversed the depopulation that had occurred in the eighteenth century. The population of the plain rose significantly in the nineteenth century and the majority of the peasants spoke Bulgarian and its local Macedonian variant.[34]

It is important to note that in the nineteenth century non-Muslims were also given the right to hold land securely, particularly after the Imperial

---

[33] See Demetriades (1981, pp. 44–5).
[34] Ibid., pp. 54–5.

Rescript of 1856 and the Land Law of 1858, which granted official sanction to individuals holding private property in land. The Land Law was one of the most important pieces of legislation of the Tanzimat era since it facilitated the transfer of property rights in land as well as strengthening inheritance rights, thus paving the way for a market to emerge in real estate.[35] Indeed, during the preceding decades the system of land tenure had in practice become quite similar to private property. The Law of 1858 could be interpreted as largely a formalization of already existing practices.

The class of *çiftlik* holders in the nineteenth century came to include sizeable numbers of Christians and Jews in addition to Muslims, a development that had significant implications for trade and industry in Macedonia. At the same time there emerged a fragmented class of agricultural producers, ranging from independent smallholders to sharecroppers and agricultural labourers (day and seasonal contracts). Both sharecroppers and agricultural labourers operated under a variety of terms agreed with the *çiftlik* owner, which are briefly discussed below.

In the following sections the evolution of agricultural production and the emerging agrarian relations in Macedonia during the last four decades of Ottoman rule are analysed in detail using material from the yearbooks and other sources. The aim is to establish the role of agriculture in the rise of industrial capitalism in the region. Particularly important were the changing volume and composition of agricultural production, including the relative weight of food and cash crops, and their complex impact of *çiftlik* relations and production networks.

4.5 Agricultural output in the *vilayet* of Thessaloniki, 1870–1912

Agricultural output in Macedonia was dominated by grains. In the early 1860s, 90 per cent of the arable land in the district of Thessaloniki was allotted to wheat, maize, barley, rye and millet. Output comprised grains to the tune of 70 per cent even in the district of Serres, which was the main tobacco and

---

[35] See Aytekin (2009, pp. 939–40). See also Aytekin (2008).

cotton-growing area of the Balkans.[36] Land reserved for the cultivation of cash crops in Macedonia was initially very limited but steadily expanded throughout the nineteenth century.

Until the 1870s, the cultivation of cash crops was almost exclusively aimed at meeting world demand, and hence was subject to severe shocks. Silk was the chief export from Thessaloniki in the 1840s; it was replaced by cotton in the 1860s mostly because the American Civil War had disrupted world supplies. Following the end of the Civil War, demand for cotton dropped precipitously (as did its price), but demand for tobacco and opium rose. Finally, after the 1870s the expanding domestic market began to have an impact on the cultivation of cash crops.

Much of the increase in agricultural output across the Empire in the nineteenth century was simply due to the expansion of cultivated land. There was no significant increase in productivity even in Macedonia which had several natural advantages, such as fertile land, abundant water sources and a favourable climate. Various structural problems hindered the increase of productivity, including weak infrastructure and transport, lack of fertilizers and modern tools, backwardness of technique and absence of agrarian financial institutions. The proliferation of *çiftlik* brought little improvement in these respects, as shall be seen in detail below. Traditional agricultural practices, structural inadequacies and the *çiftlik* mentality placed a ceiling on cultivation, leaving much agricultural potential unexploited.[37]

Nevertheless, between 1820 and 1870 Macedonian agriculture was integrated more firmly into the world economy thanks to intensified trade with Western Europe. Agricultural exports continued to grow and became fundamental to the economy. The beneficiaries were primarily landowners and merchants, even if peasants also began to feel the impact of trade. However, agrarian relations remained hidebound and dominated by the practices of the *çiftlik* estates that were shaped by the social and political power of the landowners. It is notable that there was little capitalist transformation of agriculture in the area. The motive for capital accumulation and the associated relentless push to increase productivity were missing from agriculture to the end of Ottoman rule in Macedonia.

---

[36] See Gounaris (1993, p. 100).
[37] For further discussion, see Gounaris (1993, pp. 15–24).

The first four volumes of the yearbooks, covering 1870–5, simply report the output of agriculture in the *vilayet* of Thessaloniki. Agricultural activity comprised mostly the cultivation of grain as well as a range of other crops; the rearing of silkworms and an annual output of silk cocoons were also mentioned.[38] The yearbooks recorded a sharp overall decline in agricultural output during this period, with very few individual exceptions.[39] The evidence of decline is consistent with the historical literature mentioned in the previous two sections, according to which there was a general fall in agricultural production in the 1870s, especially in the Balkans.

Grain prices were kept high in the following years due to the Russo-Turkish War of 1877–8 and the crop failure of 1879.[40] The worldwide depression in cereal prices began to hit Thessaloniki markets in full earnest in the early 1880s, after which cereal exports never recovered their former pre-eminence. Nonetheless, the export of cash crops remained on an upward trajectory as demand stayed strong. Rising income from exports in turn gave a boost to the domestic markets for food crops.

The tenth volume of the yearbooks, covering 1890, presents a very detailed picture of agriculture in the *vilayet* of Thessaloniki allowing for comparative analysis. It is notable that while food crops were widely cultivated across the *vilayet*, cash crops were confined to specific regions. The most important cash crops were cotton, grapes and tobacco. Table 4.1 provides details of grain and cash crop production.

The combined land share of the major grains – wheat, maize, barley, rye and oats – stood at 65 per cent, much below the 90 per cent for grains in the 1860s mentioned in the previous section of this chapter. It is apparent that a change in the terms of trade against grains had taken place after 1870. The share of cash crops – mostly grapes, cotton and tobacco – began to increase in the 1870s and the 1880s, as peasants moved away from grains. The underlying reasons for this change in land use were fully understood by the compilers of the yearbook for the previous year, 1889, and were duly recorded:[41]

---

[38] Products included wheat, barley, rye, feed, maize, bitter vetch, millet, sesame, cotton, grapes, beans, chickpeas, lentils, rice and tobacco. See SVS I, 1287 [1870]; SVS II, 1288 [1871]; SVS III, 1290 [1873]; SVS IV, 1291 [1874].
[39] See SVS I, 1287 [1870]; SVS II, 1288 [1871]; SVS III, 1290 [1873]; SVS IV, 1291 [1874]. The only considerable increase was in the production of maize.
[40] See Akarli (2001, p. 79).
[41] See SVS X, 1307 [1890]. Translated by the author in Cakiroglu (2015).

Table 4.1 Selected grains and cash crops in the *vilayet* of Thessaloniki, 1890

	Land share (%)
Wheat	14.5
Barley	17.2
Rye	13.3
Oats	5.6
Maize	14.2
Vines	7.6
Tobacco	1.3
Cotton	2.6

Source: S.V.S. X, 1307 [1890]. Land share has been estimated as a percentage of the total land under cultivation.

Since grains were not able to compete with those from Europe and America [in the international markets] and the production of cash crops became more rewarding, cultivators began to cultivate cash crops more, as a result of which production of silk cocoon, opium, cotton, red pepper, etc. developed rapidly.

Even so, grains continued completely to dominate agricultural output in terms of value. Relative shares cannot be calculated because the total value of agricultural production is not known, but if the values of the agricultural products recorded in the yearbook of 1890 were summed up, the share of cash crops would stand at only 13 per cent compared to 87 per cent for grains. It is clear that agriculture in the *vilayet* of Thessaloniki in the 1890s was heavily dependent on food crops, that is, on grains. Food production was by far the most important economic activity in the region of Thessaloniki. The *vilayet* was completely self-sufficient and indeed marketed the surplus of its food crop, which came to about half the total output.

The predominance of food crops even in 1890 – despite the fall in international grain prices – was probably because production aimed at the expanding domestic markets instead of focusing on exports as had typically happened until 1870. At the same time the ratio of cultivated to arable land in the *vilayet* was still quite low, suggesting that agricultural production had hit a ceiling set by domestic demand. Table 4.2 confirms the low utilization of available land and the continuing heavy emphasis on grains despite the rise of cash crops.

Table 4.2 Land use in the *vilayet* of Thessaloniki, 1890

Arable land as % of total acreage	31%
Cultivated land as % of arable land	42%
Grains as % of cultivated land	67%
Cash crops as % of cultivated land	14%
Other uses as % of cultivated land	19%

Source: SVS X, 1307 [1890].

The decline in grain cultivation and the rise of some cash crops were also observed in the 1890s. It is instructive in this connection to consider agricultural data published by the statistical journal of the Ministry of Forestry, Mining and Agriculture (OMZM) for the year 1905.[42] OMZM data indicates that between 1890 and 1905 the cultivation of grains continued to fall in both acreage and volume of production even for the most important grains, that is, for wheat and maize. Interestingly, the cultivation of cash crops also declined, except for tobacco and silk cocoons, both of which rose very strongly in the 1890s and early 1900s.[43] The period from 1890 to 1912 became known as the 'tobacco boom' and handsome profits were made in tobacco cultivation.[44]

Finally, cotton hit a low point in the 1890s but then began to recover 'because the development of a local cotton industry offered growers a secure outlet for their produce'.[45] Neither the volume nor the quality of cotton were adequate for the needs of cotton yarn producers of Macedonia as manufacturing expanded rapidly in the 1900s. In 1905, the share of land reserved for cotton cultivation

---

[42] The Statistical Journal of the OMZM of 1323 (1907), prepared for the European part of the Empire, is an important source of information on agriculture for the last two decades of Ottoman rule in Macedonia.

[43] Annual agricultural production is notoriously difficult to estimate accurately since the official figures are of debatable reliability. The figures provided by Akarli (2001, pp. 52–3) for annual production in 1890 are, for instance, different from those estimated from the yearbooks. Note also that there are problems with converting original Ottoman units of measurement, such as *kıyye* and *kile*, into kilograms. It is likely that the annual production figures reported in the yearbook of 1890 were heavily exaggerated. The data from OMZM [1323] seems more accurate, as was also surmised by Petmezas (2010) following comparison with the agricultural statistics compiled by the Greek Kingdom for the 'new provinces' annexed after 1912. Be that as it may, these problems do not affect our conclusions about the trends in agriculture.

[44] The boom in tobacco cultivation is also reflected in its large share of land reported in 1905, see (OMZM, 1323 [1907]: 86–7). On the fluctuations and the expansion of tobacco cultivation in the nineteenth century, see Hadar (2007) and Nacar (2010).

[45] See Gounaris (1993, p. 105).

among industrial crops in Thessaloniki stood at 19.2 per cent– the highest for the several European *vilayet* of the Ottoman Empire.[46]

Recapping, Ottoman agriculture generally shrank in the 1870s as the world economy entered the 'Great Depression' thus resulting in weaker demand for agricultural goods and lower agricultural prices. The decrease in wheat prices between 1873 and 1894 was 60 per cent in the Ottoman markets compared to a 65 per cent fall in the British markets; moreover, prices never fully recovered in subsequent years.[47] Agricultural contraction became very pronounced in the *vilayet* of Thessaloniki after 1890, resulting in the lowest proportion of land devoted to grain cultivation in the European provinces.[48] Grain output in the *vilayet* of Thessaloniki was primarily channelled to the domestic market and exports were minimal.[49] In contrast, several cash crops began to increase significantly in the 1890s due to rising domestic and foreign demand.

Agriculture in the *vilayet* of Thessaloniki felt the pressures emanating from the world market that had entered a period of stagnation and even decline after the 1870s. Furthermore, there were no systematic productivity increases, and productivity might have even declined for some products. Assessing the significance of these developments for the broader performance of the economy as well as for the emergence of industrial capitalism requires a closer analysis of agriculture in the region of Veroia, Edhessa and Naoussa.

4.6 Agricultural output in Veroia, Edhessa and Naoussa, 1870–1912

Reliable data on agriculture in the smaller administrative units of the *vilayet* of Thessaloniki is hard to obtain. The yearbooks contain some vital information allowing for a first approximation of the agrarian economy of the region. Table 4.3 shows agricultural output in the *kaza* of Veroia based on the yearbook of 1886.

The yearbook estimated the total area of cultivation in the region of Veroia at 90,300 *dönüm*. There is no fixed value for the *dönüm*, which is probably the

---

[46] See OMZM (1323 [1907], pp. 86–7).
[47] See Gounaris (1993, p. 104).
[48] See OMZM (1323 [1907]). This is consistent with the figures of Akarli (2001: 39).
[49] See OMZM (1323 [1907], pp. 28–35).

Table 4.3 Agricultural production in the *kaza* of Veroia, 1886

	% of cultivated land
Wheat	33
Rye	1
Animal feed	2
Barley	16
Maize	35
Bitter Vetch	2
Sesame	5
Vines	6

Source: SVS IX, 1303 [1886].

Turkish equivalent of the Byzantine Greek *stremma*, and presumably measured the land that a team of oxen could plough in a day, or forty by forty standard paces. A *dönüm* in Anatolia was typically considered as slightly more than 900 square metres, but in the Balkans and elsewhere it was frequently bigger.[50] Table 4.3 shows that, in 1886, grains (mostly maize, wheat and barley) comprised the great bulk of agricultural production, close to 90 per cent of the cultivated land in Veroia. In addition, there was wine-making, silk cocoon production and animal husbandry. On the whole the *kaza* of Veroia had a rather sluggish agrarian economy, with few cash crops and even fewer signs of dynamic change.

Agricultural production in the *kaza* of Edhessa in 1886 presented a similar picture. Cultivated land in Edhessa was estimated at 55,900 *dönüm*. Table 4.4 shows that grain (mostly wheat, rye, barley and maize) dominated production, but the share of grains in the cultivated land came to 80 per cent and was significantly smaller than in Veroia. The agrarian economy of Edhessa appeared to be more diversified, with some cash crops, including wine-making and silk cocoon rearing. Perhaps the most significant difference was prominent animal husbandry, which resulted in substantial volumes of wool production, much greater than in Veroia. Even so, it is not really possible to speak of a dynamic agrarian economy in the *kaza* of Edhessa in the 1880s.

---

[50] Lapavitsas (2006), following the early practice of the inspectors of the Greek Kingdom in Macedonia takes the *dönüm* at 1,600 square metres.

Table 4.4 Agricultural production in the *kaza* of Edhessa, 1886

	% of cultivated land
Wheat	14
Rye	10
Animal feed	3
Barley	14
Millet	2
Maize	37
Rice	1
Tobacco	1
Cotton	2
Sesame	2
Vines	14

Source: SVS IX, 1303 [1886].

Finally, and again from the same yearbook, agricultural production in the *nahiye* of Naoussa can be seen in Table 4.5. Cultivated land was estimated at 17,000 *dönüm*, much less than Veroia and Edhessa, but the real difference lay elsewhere. The agrarian economy of Naoussa was far less dependent on grains, which nonetheless covered 59 per cent of cultivated land in the 1880s; the balance was largely taken up by vines and sesame. The most notable agricultural activity in the vicinity of the town was specialized and intensive viticulture. Great quantities of wine were annually exported to Alexandria (Egypt), İstanbul and Thessaloniki; in later yearbooks the list of export destinations came to include Western Europe. Naoussa has long been known for producing high-quality wine, which was traded as far as Germany already in the early nineteenth century and was mentioned by several Western European travellers.[51]

Grapes were a leading cash crop towards the end of the nineteenth century as grape cultivation in the Empire expanded further thanks to the involvement of the Ottoman Public Debt Administration (OPDA). The OPDA was an administrative structure established and run in 1881 by the European creditors to oversee the payments on Ottoman public debt, and which came to control

---

[51] See Pouqueville (1826, p. 95); Cousinery (1831, p. 72); Leake (1835, pp. 284–7).

Table 4.5 Agricultural production in the *nahiye* of Naoussa, 1886

	% of cultivated land
Wheat	12
Rye	9
Feed	8
Barley	15
Maize	15
Sesame	6
Vines	35

Source: SVS IX, 1303 [1886].

a wide range of revenue sources, including tobacco, silk, salt, and so on.[52] The OPDA circumscribed the fiscal powers of the state, transferred accumulated capital abroad, and hindered the ability of the government to implement wider reform programmes and development policies. Nevertheless, this instrument of Western European imperial power played an important role in boosting particular industries, sectors and products with the aim of securing returns to make payments on the debt. Its efforts were noteworthy in tobacco, sericulture and viticulture, contributing to disease control and better technique. It is probable, though not certain, that viticulture in Naoussa benefited from the activities of the OPDA at least indirectly.

Other intensive agricultural activities in Naoussa were sericulture and stockbreeding. Although the annual amount of silkworm seeds in 1886 was not high compared to the rest of the region, the yearbooks explicitly stated that, after combating silkworm disease, the development of sericulture was very substantial in the vicinity of Naoussa and mulberry trees had been extensively planted.[53] Animal husbandry was also part of the local economy, but the output of sheep's wool and goat's hair was perhaps less than what would be expected considering the intensity of woollen textile manufacturing. Naoussa imported wool from outside its immediate region.

In sum, agriculture was more specialized in Naoussa compared to Veroia and Edhessa. Furthermore, the share of cash crops in cultivated land was

---

[52] See Birdal (2010).
[53] See SVS X, 1307 [1890]; SVS IX, 1303 [1886].

far higher, mostly on account of viticulture. Still, it is likely that the ratio of cultivated to arable land was quite low for all three towns. The ratio is impossible to calculate for Naoussa and Edhessa, but in Veroia it stood at slightly less than half of the arable land. About half the available land was left uncultivated following the ancient agricultural practice of protecting the fertility of the soil and pasturing livestock. There was little technological advance in agriculture in the region.

The yearbooks do not contain agricultural information of similar detail for 1907–12. Fortunately, data from OMZM for 1907 casts some additional light on the development of local agriculture, even though it is not really possible to make a reliable comparison with the yearbooks. The OMZM data, moreover, offers no specific information for Naoussa but refers to the *kaza* of Veroia and Edhessa. On this basis it appears that in 1907 in Veroia more than 90 per cent of cultivated land was given to grains, and the remainder to sesame and vines. Roughly the same allocation of cultivated land obtained in Edhessa. In short, the OMZM data gives no reason to think that agriculture in the region had undergone any profound transformation from the 1880s to the 1900s.

Some further insight, finally, can be gained by comparing OMZM data with agricultural statistics prepared by functionaries of the Kingdom of Greece in 1914, following the annexation of the largest part of Ottoman Macedonia.[54] The administrative units were broadly comparable, namely the *kaza* in the Ottoman data corresponded roughly to *eparchia*, or *ypodioikisis* in the Greek statistics.[55] It appears that in Thessaloniki and Edhessa agriculture had contracted in 1907–14, judging by the arable and cultivated land as well as land given to grains. In Veroia, on the other hand, arable and cultivated land had increased, but land sown with grains had actually fallen. Note that Thessaloniki and its region were quite unique in registering a decline in all three types of land use, while every other region of Macedonia registered a rising trend.[56] On this evidence too, agriculture in Thessaloniki but also in the provincial area of Naoussa, Veroia and Edhessa seems to have gone into reverse towards the end of Ottoman rule.

---

[54] See Petmezas (2010).
[55] Respectively, province and sub-governorship.
[56] See the table in Petmezas (2010, pp. 362–3).

The diminishing importance of agriculture and the decline of food crops in the *vilayet* of Thessaloniki contrasted starkly with the overall performance of Ottoman agriculture. The output estimates by Eldem suggest considerable dynamism in Ottoman agriculture, especially during 1889–1907.[57] Estimates for cereal output, for instance, indicate growth of as much as 50 per cent during this period.[58] Agricultural production in the region of Thessaloniki, especially food crops, exhibited the opposite trend. In fact, by the mid-1900s the region had become a regular importer of cereals and flour from the rest of the Empire, imports covering roughly 40 per cent of the total urban wheat consumption circa 1911.[59] This development must have been partly due to the rapid population growth of Thessaloniki.

The stagnation of agriculture in the *vilayet* of Thessaloniki highlights the dominant presence of *çiftlik*, particularly in the region of Edhessa and Veroia. In the *vilayet* of Thessaloniki the number of *çiftlik* estates and villages was the highest in Europe, as is shown in the next section. Moreover, the area close to Veroia had by far the highest percentage of *çiftlik* settlements and households in the *vilayet* of Thessaloniki. It is clear that industrial capitalism in provincial Ottoman Macedonia made its emergence amidst a sea of *çiftlik*.

Intense *çiftlik* formation and advancing commercialization of agriculture gave rise to a variety of production relations that existed side by side. In the *vilayet* of Thessaloniki there were great numbers of market-oriented smallholdings operating alongside a profusion of *çiftlik* estates, which relied on sharecropping but also used wage labour. The ownership of *çiftlik* had also begun to change in the second half of the nineteenth century. Christian and Jewish owners of *çiftlik* emerged who had made their money in commerce or money lending.[60] Remarkably, some of the industrialists of the provincial area also became *çiftlik* holders. It is likely that towards the end of Ottoman rule these changes contributed to a shift in the composition of the agricultural labour force away from sharecroppers and smallholders toward landless wage

---

[57] See Eldem (1994).
[58] Ibid., p. 37.
[59] See Akarli (2001, p. 97).
[60] This trend was noted by Demetriades (1981, p. 57). Especially at the beginning of the twentieth century, rich Jews and some Greeks from Thessaloniki began to acquire *çiftlik* in the Macedonian hinterland, including the area that was formerly part of the *vakıf* of the Evrenos family. Among the Jewish buyers were capitalists from Thessaloniki who began to invest in land after making their fortune in trade and industry.

earners.⁶¹ To take the analysis further, the next section considers property and labour relations in the agricultural sector of Mount Vermion after briefly placing *çiftlik* agrarian relations in theoretical context.

4.7 Agrarian relations: The straightjacket of the *çiftlik*

The role of agriculture in capitalist industrial transformation has been the subject of various studies, often at country level.⁶² Byres's authoritative work tackled the issue of 'what makes accumulation possible, and so enables capitalist transformation'. Byres sought the answer through 'an exploration of the nature, prerequisites and the class agents of that accumulation'.⁶³ He postulated that the form of capitalist industrialization depends on the form taken by the capitalist transformation of agriculture. Specifically, he believed,

> That [*capitalist*] industrialisation depends intimately, and in a variety of ways, upon agriculture. It cannot be understood without reference to agriculture and agrarian change, and to the way in which capitalism penetrates agriculture – whether with the establishment of capitalist relations of production or not.⁶⁴

On this basis Byres considered the agrarian transition to capitalism, and assessed its implications for capitalist industrialization. His specific aim was to establish 'the nature of any individual path of agrarian transition' – and the subsequent transformation of the entire economy – by examining four analytical issues: the emerging class structure, the nature of capital accumulation, the forms taken by the productive forces in the countryside, and the features of capitalist industrialization.⁶⁵

In this approach the capitalist transformation of agriculture and capitalist industrialization can be expected to assume a variety of historically specific

---

[61] See Lampe and Jackson (1982, p. 134).
[62] The literature on agrarian transformation is vast. A prominent place is occupied by Marxist analyses, which are the bedrock for the discussion of agriculture in this section, drawing particularly on Marx (1992); Kautsky (1988); Lenin (1964 [1907]); Dobb (1972 [1946]); Hilton (1985); Brenner (1977) and Byres (1995). The influence of Chayanov (1986) on these debates is also evident.
[63] See Byres (1996, p. 419).
[64] Ibid., p. 423.
[65] Ibid., pp. 420–4.

forms. To establish the characteristic features of each of these forms it would be necessary to deal with several questions, including 'Is the landlord class resident or absentee?', 'How differentiated is the peasant class?', 'How extensive is sharecropping relative to, say, family-operated smallholdings?', and so on. Byres stressed that the state has typically played a crucial role in determining the forms and outcomes of capitalist transformation in agriculture. The tax practices of the state, its personnel, its policies relative to production and trade, its organic links with particular classes and social groups are determining factors in the emergence of both agrarian and industrial capitalism.

Byres's approach offers an appropriate way to consider agrarian relations in Ottoman Macedonia, particularly *çiftlik* estates, always bearing in mind the general paucity of evidence. It should further be mentioned that Byres's work relied on a seminal argument put forth by Lenin in connection with the rise of agrarian capitalism in Russia at the end of the nineteenth century.[66] Focusing on social differentiation among the peasantry, Lenin distinguished between two broad paths of capitalist development. On the one hand, there was capitalism 'from above' (the Prussian path), in which a class of capitalist farmers emerged out of a landlord class. Along this path the landlords acquired a capitalist outlook toward agricultural investment, raising productivity and marketing the output, as the Prussian Junkers had done on their estates. On the other, there was capitalism 'from below' (the American path), in which capitalist farmers emerged out of a broad layer of differentiated peasantry. Along this path the richer peasants moved beyond self-sufficiency, or the simple selling of surplus crop, and focused on managing costs, acquiring land, investing capital, raising productivity and marketing the output. They gradually became capitalist farmers.

Lenin's insight is important to analysing the *çiftlik* of Macedonia at a time when industrial capitalism had begun to emerge in the Ottoman Empire, as it also did in Romanov Russia. The *çiftlik* was neither a feudal estate in the manner of medieval Europe, nor a capitalist farm. To be sure its output was marketed and therefore the holder had a pecuniary motive to acquire the estate. The *çiftlik* generated a monetary return and in this regard its acquisition could be considered a form of investment that was expected to generate a return for the buyer. However, the acquisition of *çiftlik* in the eighteenth and

---

[66] See Lenin (1964 [1907], pp. 238–43).

early nineteenth centuries often involved the use of political power and even outright force. The management of the *çiftlik* and the forms of land tenure on the estate, furthermore, involved non-economic processes. The outlook of the *çiftlik* holder was marked by a ruthless search for monetary returns, but the *çiftlik* did not become a capitalist farm. Similarly, Ottoman *çiftlik* holders never became Prussian Junkers, nor were there signs that they were moving systematically in that direction.

The prevalent form of land tenure in Macedonian *çiftlik* was sharecropping, of which there were two main categories: *ortakçı* and *kesmeci*.[67] The dominant category of sharecroppers was that of the *ortakçı*, who typically provided animals, implements and labour, while the landlord provided land, shelter and seed. The produce was shared equally after deducting the seed and taxes, including the land tithe (*öşür*). Landlords typically allowed the peasant to have a smallholding that could be privately cultivated, perhaps in exchange for services, such as gathering firewood, or transporting the produce of the landlord. The *kesmeci* sharecroppers had quite a similar agreement with the landlord but were obliged to pay a fixed quantity of the product irrespective of the volume of output, and thus had an incentive to increase production. There were also other forms of labour deployed on the *çiftlik*, including farm labourers (*ter oğlanlar*, 'sweat boys'), monthly hired immigrant labourers (*aylıkçılar*) and day labourers (*günlükçüler*) who were typically employed when there was a labour shortage during the ploughing or harvesting season. The sharecroppers and others attached to the processes of agricultural production lived in *çiftlik* villages that often belonged to the *çiftlik* holder, who also had the responsibility for the upkeep of the housing stock.

The *çiftlik* holder in Macedonia certainly sought monetary profit, but non-economic relations were rife in the running of the estate. The *çiftlik* holder would maintain a large residence in the estate, a *konak*, while typically living in a nearby town, or even in a city further afield; in the latter case the owner would be fully an absentee landlord. The eyes, ears – and arms – of the *çiftlik* holder in the estate would be the *kethüda* or *kahya/kehaya*. Power would be frequently displayed, and violence would never be far from the surface, particularly at the time of dividing the crop. The *çiftlik* holder would arrive at the village with his retinue,

---

[67] See Gounaris (1993, p. 18).

an imposing and menacing presence, taking up residence at the *konak*. A formal ritual would follow of measuring and dividing the output at the threshing floor, usually not far away from the *konak*. The manifest power of the landlord would be countered by the native cunning of the peasant – concealing, disguising and excusing output. That would be a key moment for the *kethüda* to earn his keep.

Sharecroppers in Macedonia were partly protected by chronic labour shortage, a notable feature of agriculture in Naoussa, Veroia and Edhessa, where *çiftlik* villages were typically small hamlets. However, the protection afforded to the peasant by the scarcity of labour was undermined by the other regular activity of the *çiftlik* owner: money lending. Even small debts carried compound interest – a practice commonly adopted by the Muslim *çiftlik* owners – thus rapidly leading to a crushing burden on the peasant, which was often carried across the generations. The result was bonded labour, not too dissimilar to slavery. The state of the Macedonian sharecropper and his family was frequently appalling – living in unsanitary and badly kept hovels, facing persistent malnutrition, malaria, scrofula and worms for the children.

In these conditions, and despite the commercial aspect of the *çiftlik*, there was little capitalist agrarian transformation in Macedonia, and certainly no Prussian 'capitalism from above'. Specifically, there was no regular use of wage labour, no integration of dispersed strips of land, no improved crop rotation and use of better seeds as well as insignificant mechanization and use of chemical fertilizers.[68] The typical landlord treated the estate as an investment that had to produce a substantial monetary return through the sale of output, but securing the return relied on exploitative sharecropping arrangements and the use of extra-economic power, rather than systematic investment and deployment of wage labour. There was to be no class of agrarian capitalist landlords in Macedonia to the very end of Ottoman rule.

4.8 Muslim and Christian *çiftlik* holding

Historical evidence indicates that *çiftlik* formation (*çiftlikleşme*) was high in Macedonia, as has already been mentioned in earlier sections of this chapter.

---

[68] See Lapavitsas (2006).

Accurate information regarding the size and the number of çiftlik is lacking but there is no doubt that the *vilayet* of Thessaloniki stood out among the rest of the Empire in this respect. It has been estimated that 42 per cent of all villages around Thessaloniki were attached to big farms.[69] Akarli, who is critical of sweeping generalizations about landholding patterns in Macedonia and rightly insists on the persistence of smallholdings, argues that çiftlik were unusually common in the district of Thessaloniki.[70] According to his estimates, the area of Mount Vermion recorded the strongest presence of çiftlik in the *vilayet* of Thessaloniki: in Veroia 89 per cent of the rural settlements and 52 per cent of the rural population belonged to çiftlik; the equivalent figures for Edhessa were 54 per cent and 25 per cent. Note, finally, that despite the heavy weight of çiftlik in the area of Mount Vermion, smallholding agriculture was still strongly present in the *vilayet* of Thessaloniki: only 33 per cent of the rural population belonged to çiftlik.

The exceptional weight of çiftlik in the *vilayet* of Thessaloniki was due to the disintegration of the enormous *vakıf* of *Gazi* Evrenos *Bey*, discussed in Section 4.4. The *vakıf* had given rise to a multitude of çiftlik, typically held by Muslim *ayan*. The çiftlik estates proliferated further as rising grain prices made exports more attractive in the 1840s and 1850s.[71] A revealing light on agrarian property relations at the end of Ottoman rule can be cast by considering materials produced by the incoming Greek administration in 1913. The evidence refers to the 'police district' of Naoussa, which was a large part of the old *kaza* of Veroia, and thus relates to a substantial segment of the Macedonian plain.[72]

In 1913 agricultural smallholdings were found mostly on the foothills around Naoussa. They were owned by the inhabitants of the town, Christian and Muslim, who either cultivated the land themselves, or rented it out. Hired agricultural labour was rarely used in smallholdings. This sector produced primarily cash crops, including grapes, wine and mulberry leaves for silkworm. In contrast to smallholdings, the çiftlik estates stretched out on the plain beyond the foothills and were owned primarily by Muslim notables who resided in

---

[69] See Quataert (1994b, p. 873); see also Lampe and Jackson (1982, p. 135).
[70] See Akarli (2001, p. 213). Gounaris (1993, pp. 119–20) also observes that large farms dominated the *vilayet* of Thessaloniki, unlike the *vilayet* of Bitola and Kosova; Dekazos (1914, p. 53) makes essentially the same point.
[71] See Palairet (1993, p. 43).
[72] Specifically, Stougiannakis (1911) and Dekazos (1913, 1914).

Veroia and Edhessa. More than 95 per cent of the çiftlik land was given to grains. A significant number of çiftlik was held by Christians, most of whom came from Naoussa. To be precise, 81 per cent of the arable çiftlik land in the 'police district' of Naoussa lay in Muslim hands, while the remaining 19 per cent belonged to Christians.[73] Significant ownership of çiftlik by Christian landlords had probably begun during the Tanzimat era reflecting greater security of property but also the accumulation of wealth through trade and industry.[74]

It is highly instructive to consider more closely the Christian holders of çiftlik. There were 19 çiftlik villages in the 'police district' of Naoussa in 1913, covering the bulk of the arable land of the area, ten of which belonged exclusively to Muslim owners while nine had mixed Muslim–Christian ownership. Without double counting, there were at least forty Muslim and twelve Christian landowners in the area. Most of the Muslims resided in Veroia and Edhessa, while most of the Christians hailed from Naoussa. The Christians held 43 per cent of the arable land in villages that were jointly owned by Muslims and Christians. This breakdown reflects the strong Muslim component of the population of both Veroia and Edhessa that was shown in Chapter 3, but it also reflects the unusual local prominence of Christian Naoussa in çiftlik holding. The çiftlik villages with mixed ownership and their Christian owners are listed in Table 4.6.

The size of a çiftlik given in the table was not an accurate guide to its monetary value since the fertility of the land varied widely. Unfortunately it is impossible to estimate the value of the individual estates given the information available. It is notable, however, that eight out of the twelve Christian landlords came from Naoussa. Several among them were heavily involved in woollen cloth trading and cotton spinning: Pehlivanos, Kokkinos, Platsoukas, Yamalis and Lapavitsas. Their names will come up again and again in subsequent chapters as the forces and relations of industrial capitalism are considered in depth. It

---

[73] See Lapavitsas (2006, p. 690).
[74] Large ownership of çiftlik by Christians probably began with the Imperial Rescript of 1856 and the Land Law of 1858. It appears, however, that some çiftlik ownership was present among local Christians at an even earlier date. Official documents referring to the sack of Naoussa in 1822 record the existence of large scale land ownership by Zafirakis Theodossiou Logothetis; see Lapavitsas (2004) drawing on Vasdravellis (1967). Zafirakis was the leader of the Christian community of Naoussa, in command of sizeable armed forces, probably operating as a Christian *ayan* in the area. The processes through which Christians in Macedonia were able to become çiftlik owners as early as the 1820s are unknown, but they were perhaps related to the gradual disintegration of the *vakıf* of Evrenos.

Table 4.6 Christian *çiftlik* ownership in the area of Naoussa, 1913

Çiftlik village	Christian-owned arable land	Christian owners
Diavornitsa	2,000	Salfatas, Hadjigogos (Veroia)
Kato Kopanos	4,000	Kionses, Petsos (Edhessa)
Ano Kopanos	3,250	Pehlivanos (Naoussa)
Monospita	2,200	Kokkinos, Platsoukas (Naoussa)
Episkopi	1,100	Lapavitsas (Naoussa)
Giannakovo	1,050	Hadjidimitriou (Naoussa)
Tsarmorinovo	1,500	Hadjidimitriou (Naoussa)
Golesiani	1,500	Hadjinotas (Naoussa)
Golo Selo	1,800	Yamalis, Markobitsis (Naoussa)

Source: Lapavitsas (2006). Land measured in 'Turkish' *stremmata* (1,600 square metres).

is clear that the commercial and industrial capitalists of Naoussa invested in *çiftlik* in the second half of the nineteenth century as well as actively trading in land. There were profits to be made, since Macedonian *çiftlik* generated returns of 18–25 per cent on investment in the years around 1900.[75]

The average size of the *çiftlik* estate and the average property held by each landlord in the region were quite large by Ottoman standards. Average available, arable and cultivated land per *çiftlik* owner were, respectively, 3,200 *dönüm*, 1,800 *dönüm* and 1,000 *dönüm* – all of which lay at the higher end of the spectrum for the Balkans.[76] The averages for arable and cultivated land per family living in *çiftlik* estates were also quite high, at 158 and 87 *dönüm*, respectively.[77] If we take İnalcık's figure of 60–80 *dönüm* of fertile arable land per household as the typical benchmark for the Empire, this is a very high average.[78] Given the abundance of land, it is probable that, despite the landlords' exactions, the standard of living of Macedonian sharecroppers was better than the average for the *çiftlik* of the Empire, particularly in view of the generally fertile soil of the area. However, the lack of mechanization and the

---

[75] See Issawi (1980, p. 208).
[76] According to the calculations of Lapavitsas (2006), who takes a *dönüm* at 1,600 square metres, and compared to the calculations of Lampe and Jackson (1982).
[77] See Lapavitsas (2006, p. 687).
[78] See İnalcık (1984, p. 106) who takes the *dönüm* at 920 square metres.

generally mediocre agricultural technique meant that productivity was low, at least compared to the potential of the land.

There were no signs of capitalist transformation of agriculture 'from above' in the region of Naoussa. It made no difference at all in this respect whether the *çiftlik* actually belonged to Christian traders and industrialists. Indeed, it seems that Muslim-owned had higher productivity than Christian-owned *çiftlik*.[79] During the final period of Ottoman rule, especially in the 1900s, there was ceaseless buying and selling of *çiftlik* estates, particularly as the nationalist unrest in Macedonia led frightened Muslim landlords to emigrate to Anatolia, or at least convert their immovable property into cash. In 1912, following the arrival of the Greek army but long before the population exchange of the 1920s, even the Evrenosoğulları left Giannitsa and were resettled in several places in Anatolia and İstanbul.[80] Especially notable was the acquisition of *çiftlik* across Macedonia by Jewish capitalists from Thessaloniki who had emerged out of a thoroughly urban population and had recently begun to acquire *çiftlik* estates.[81] These were speculative purchases aiming at financial profits without transforming agricultural practices.

There is even less evidence of capitalist agrarian transition 'from below' in the region. At times peasants bought *çiftlik* estates collectively and proceeded to re-divide the land. There was monetary wealth among the agricultural population, no doubt boosted by strong emigration to the United States at the end of the nineteenth and the start of the twentieth century. However, there is no evidence of capitalist farming spontaneously emerging among the differentiated layer of peasant smallholders. The changes that were observable in agricultural property relations toward the end of Ottoman rule did not indicate a clear movement in the direction of agrarian capitalism.

In sum, the *çiftlik* economy had a thoroughly restrictive logic that was partly commercial but not capitalist, and was resistant to change. The *çiftlik* estates acted as a straightjacket hindering the emergence of agrarian capitalism, while also presenting an obstacle to the development of industrial capitalism. At the very least *çiftlik* estates did not encourage the integrated production of cotton

---

[79] See Lapavitsas (2006, pp. 689–93).
[80] See Lowry and Erünsal (2010, p. 101).
[81] See Demetriades (1981, p. 57).

and cotton yarn, despite cotton textile industrialists often owning large estates. Moreover, the *çiftlik* economy slowed down the growth of domestic markets in clothing and food both of which could have provided further outlets for capitalist industry. It is conceivable that, if Ottoman rule had continued in Macedonia after 1912, the industrialists and merchants who owned *çiftlik* would have taken steps to introduce capitalist methods of agricultural production, perhaps engaging in some variant of 'capitalism from above'. However, that would have been impossible without major social ructions and must remain in the realm of the 'what if'.

For industrial capitalism to grow vigorously in the Ottoman Empire, the agrarian economy would have had to escape the straightjacket of the *çiftlik*, either from 'above' or from 'below'. It is remarkable, therefore, that by 1912 a sizeable capitalist textile industrial sector had successfully emerged on the uplands of Mount Vermion overlooking the *çiftlik*-dominated plain. Decades of trading in textiles and other commodities were at the root of this phenomenon, which had occurred in spite and not because of developments in agriculture.

5

The commercial roots of Ottoman textile capitalism

5.1 Merchants and industrial capitalism: Theoretical considerations

The role of merchant capitalists in the emergence of industrial capitalism has attracted much scholarly attention in general as well as in relation to the Ottoman Empire.[1] In the Ottoman context the role of merchants is reminiscent of the classic Marxist debate on the transition from feudalism to capitalism which sprang from an aphorism by Marx that two broad historical paths are known in that transition.[2] Along the first, artisan producers began to buy inputs as well as hiring labour and trading the finished output, thus becoming industrial capitalists. This path was supposed to be the truly revolutionary way of establishing industrial capitalism and transforming both economy and society. Along the second, merchants gained direct sway over production dictating terms to producers and hiring labour, thus acquiring the characteristics of industrial capitalists. This was, supposedly, a less dynamic path to industrial capitalism.

Spurred by Marx's observation, Maurice Dobb made a seminal contribution to this topic which elicited a response by Paul Sweezy, thus starting the classic Dobb–Sweezy debate on the transition from feudalism to capitalism.[3] The gist

---

[1] See, for instance, van Zanden (1997) and Mielants (2007) for a general theoretical discussion of merchant capitalism. For Ottoman merchants, see İnalcık (1969), an invaluable source discussing capital formation in the Ottoman Empire; Keyder (1987) tackles the issue of the existence of an Ottoman/Turkish bourgeoisie; while Pamuk (1987) assesses the rise of the Ottoman merchant class during the expansion of European capitalism in the nineteenth century.
[2] See Marx (1993 [1894]), pp. 917–53).
[3] See Dobb (1972 [1946]) and Sweezy (1950). The debate has attracted powerful international contributions, including those by British Marxist historians. For a discussion of the Dobb–Sweezy debate, see Hilton (1985).

of that debate is remarkably apposite to Ottoman Macedonia, since there is no doubt that Macedonian industrial capitalists came largely from the ranks of merchants. Both Dobb and Sweezy were concerned, first, to establish a conceptual definition of capitalism and, second, to identify the prime social force that induced the transition from feudalism to capitalism. Both also accepted that the transition from feudalism to capitalism represented a historic change in the mode of production. However, the similarities in their respective approaches were fewer than the differences.

Dobb, focusing on England, paid close attention to class conflict occurring over feudal production and its associated property relations.[4] The prime cause of the decline of the feudal mode of production was, for Dobb, the clash between the expanding demands of the feudal lords for revenue and the relative inefficiency of feudal production in generating the surpluses that the lords required. The result was class conflict and increasing pressure on workers in the countryside to intensify surplus extraction. Deepening polarization led to the expansion of trade as a fresh source of surplus and encouraged the emergence of capitalist forms of ownership over the means of production.[5]

According to Dobb, the new capitalists were not the great merchants of the international trading companies that characterized late feudalism. The great merchants were organic members of the ruling feudal elite and had benefited from its order: they had no incentive to change it. The new capitalists were, rather, the 'small men' of the rural economy, springing out of the gentry and the yeomen of England, who accumulated capital and land, engaged in trade and gradually became substantial capitalist farmers. Analogously, the small men of the craft economy took advantage of the expansion of trade in the seventeenth century to become part-merchants, thus accumulating capital and gradually dominating production, on the way to becoming industrial capitalists. In brief, the great merchants of feudal society, despite playing an important role in the transition, were not the 'revolutionary' element of change. That honour belonged to small men of production (agricultural and craft) who rose from the ranks to become industrial capitalists. The mirror

---

[4] See Dobb (1972 [1946]).
[5] Ibid., pp. 33–123.

image of their ascendancy was the creation of a class of wage labourers out of the serfs and craftsmen of feudal society.[6]

In response, Sweezy, while also focusing on England and northwestern Europe, turned his attention to the growth of international trade and the emergence of towns as the solvents of capitalism. The catalyst of capitalist transition came from outside the feudal mode of production. Sweezy based his claims on Henri Pirenne's groundbreaking, but non-Marxist, view of the emergence of capitalism in Western Europe, which saw capitalism as the result of the growth of towns and the ascendancy of merchants.[7] For Pirenne, the merchants were imbued with the 'spirit of capitalism', that is, the calculation of costs and risks to provide the basis for the rational pursuit of profit. In Pirenne's approach capitalism could hardly be distinguished from expanded trade. Sweezy, a leading Marxist political economist, never fell into this trap, but under the influence of Pirenne considered feudalism to be a largely static mode of production that needed an external jolt to change. That was provided by long-distance commerce, which tended to boost production with the aim of supplying the objects of trade. The creative force that led to the transition from feudalism (a system of production for use) to capitalism (a system of production for exchange-value) was commerce.[8]

Sweezy's argument that feudalism turned into capitalism due to an external impulse rather than under its own steam appeared to contradict the canon of Marxist historical theory typically based on the endogenous evolution of modes of production, each mode presumably containing the seeds of the next. In contrast, Dobb's view could be considered as far more 'orthodox Marxist'. This point aside, the real interest of the debate lay in the conceptualization of capitalism, in the significance assigned to wage labour as a defining element of the capitalist mode of production, and in the analytical primacy accorded to the sphere of production over the sphere of exchange in characterizing any 'historical' mode of production. In this respect, it is worth remembering that Marx himself had acknowledged the possibility of a merchant-led transition to capitalism, even if that was presumably not the truly revolutionary way.

---

[6] Ibid., pp. 19–65.
[7] See Pirenne (1956).
[8] See Sweezy (1950); Sweezy and Dobb (1950).

The Dobb–Sweezy debate also had far-reaching implications for the analysis of class struggle, which Marxists typically consider the driving force of history. It is immediately apparent that, depending on the approach adopted, there would be a different assessment of the class content of the English Revolution in the seventeenth century, which opened the way for the rapid capitalist transformation of England. The relevant questions are crucial: 'What was the historical role of the English merchant class in the seventeenth century?', 'What were the actions of the great traders of the Chartered Companies of the City, of the colonial traders, but also of the smaller practitioners of commerce domestically and internationally?', 'How did the merchants relate to the feudal aristocracy and the state?'.

Debating the character of the English Revolution (social, political, religious, ideological) was the distinctive contribution of British Marxism to theoretical and historical writing. The most seminal contribution in this regard, however, was made by Robert Brenner, an American.[9] Brenner rejected Sweezy's characterization of capitalism as a system of production for exchange-value as well as Sweezy's emphasis on urban merchant capital as the dynamic force of capitalist transformation. For Brenner, commerce and a 'capitalist mentality' could not lead to capitalism; on the contrary, it was the rise of the capitalist mode of production that explained the ascendancy of both commerce and the spirit of capitalism.

The decisive process for the transition to capitalism, according to Brenner, was class struggle in the English countryside. The feudal class extracted surplus from the peasants primarily through non-economic ways that were juridical, customary and political, ultimately relying on naked force. Peasant resistance caused a crisis which led the feudal class to seek directly to control land to secure a surplus. Land consolidation led to creation of large estates and the landlords entered into contractual agreements with commercial tenants who employed wage labour. Agrarian capitalism thus emerged as a historical outcome of class struggle in the countryside. That struggle destroyed feudal serfdom but also prevented the rise of independent smallholding property in English agriculture.

Thus, for Brenner, Pirenne's thesis and Sweezy's related arguments were misleading. Capitalist agriculture emerged in feudal England from within, as

---

[9] See Brenner (1976, 1977, 1982).

it were. It relied on the marketing of output, the calculation of cost and return and the regular reinvestment of profits by those who run the estates and had left behind the non-economic practices of feudalism.[10] The aristocracy of England had in essence become capitalistic already by the seventeenth century. It is clear that, in this regard, Brenner also departed from Dobb's emphasis on the small man in agriculture who presumably accumulated land and became a capitalist. In Dobb's approach – and in contrast to Brenner – the English aristocracy in the seventeenth century had remained feudal. For Dobb, the English Revolution was bourgeois but not because of the role played directly by the bourgeoisie, either merchant or agrarian. The decisive aspect of the English Revolution was that it broke the feudal fetters over capitalist accumulation, thus leading to the rapid bourgeois transformation of England.

It is important to note in this connection that the most prominent heir of Pirenne in historical writing on the development of capitalism was Fernand Braudel, and his influence has been felt in the Ottoman literature through Wallerstein.[11] For Braudel, capitalism has historically emerged through a complex interaction of politics, culture, religion and social forces, but with commerce playing the leading part. To be more specific, long-distance trade by European merchants in the nascent world market rebounded on European societies primarily through the extraordinary profits made by merchants. In Western Europe, whose feudal society was already fragmenting and in which commerce was already present domestically, the practice of trading in the world market acted as the catalyst of capitalist development. Braudel's captivating but inevitably broad-brush account of the emergence of capitalism was the bedrock of Wallerstein's theory, which stressed the importance of a presumed international division of labour in supplying Europe with sufficient food and fuel to surmount the material crises of European feudalism, thus developing a capitalist World System capable of self-sustained expansion.

Interestingly, Pirenne's thesis has also reappeared in recent years in the guise of mainstream institutional economics and related economic history.

---

[10] See Brenner (1976, 1977, 1982).
[11] See Braudel (1982); see also Wallerstein (1974, 1979, 1980, 1989).

Institutional economics is closely associated with Douglass North and his work on 'transactions costs'.[12] For North and his collaborators, economic development would occur only if there was an efficient economic organization of society, with efficient institutions and clear property rights. The point of efficiency is to encourage private economic initiatives that would generate private returns to match social returns. If a society could institute the right rules of the game, private initiative would do the rest, thus spurring growth and development. By this token, if institutions were inefficient, development would be hampered. The inefficiency of institutions would typically result from inappropriate decisions taken by the rulers of society who might be motivated by personal benefits and costs.

North's inherently ahistorical approach has frequently been deployed in recent literature to account for 'economic growth', that is, for the rise of capitalism, in Western Europe and elsewhere. Perhaps the most influential contribution in economic history along these lines was made by Avner Greif, who in substance reiterated the Pirenne thesis but from a mainstream economics perspective deploying neoclassical institutionalism and game theory.[13] Summarily put, for Greif, the historic rise of the West was due to trade expansion in the late medieval period which created a host of economic opportunities that relied on efficient institutions. Above all, institutions allowed for efficient long-distance trade, including institutions providing security of trading for the merchants.

Specifically, Greif proposed the existence of 'private-order contract enforcement institutions', namely mechanisms devised by the merchants themselves to monitor, sanction and reward agents who engaged in long-distance trade, thus doing away with the need to rely on the state. Evidence for those spontaneously emerging institutions was found by Greif in the medieval practices of Jewish Maghribi traders, who had established communal methods to punish dishonest behaviour, thus facilitating their communal pre-eminence in long-distance trade. For Greif, the cultural beliefs of the traders were perhaps at the root of these institutional practices.

---

[12] See North and Thomas (1973) and North (1994).
[13] See Greif (1993, 2006).

Quite apart from the difficulty of defining 'an institution' in the abstract, and even setting aside the difficulty of fully demonstrating the actual historical significance of any institution in the rise of capitalism in the West, it is hard to see what has been added to the overall thrust of the Pirenne thesis by Greif's reformulation. Transactions costs are a notoriously slippery adjunct to theoretical and historical analysis. They appear to explain much until the historian, or the social theorist, attempts concretely to specify – not to mention measure – the transaction costs of any given activity. At that point transactions costs usually vanish into thin air. Moreover, transactions costs are typically good at explaining things after the event and tend to provide a veneer of scientific credibility to plain truisms.

Transactions costs aside, the inherent ahistoricism of Greif's resurrection of the Pirenne thesis is equally problematic. Presumably, institutions are abstract and general categories that apply across human history with undiminished validity; they play a putative role as mechanisms of self-reinforcing behaviour and are effectively neutral with regard to social stratification. The analysis of particular historical periods and instances thus becomes an exercise in what might be called institutional materialism. Institutions are considered capable of accounting with equal facility for the conduct of a medieval Jewish Maghribi trader and of a hedge fund operator in the City of London. Typically, the class content of institutions is left out of account. By this token, class conflict, social power and the forceful intervention of the state in social affairs tend to be relegated to the margins of an analysis dominated by the functioning and dynamics of institutions. Sweezy would have had no truck with such ideas, even though he also relied on Pirenne.

The point that truly matters for our purposes is that the emergence of capitalism involves the presence of power (and ultimately force) associated with social classes and often exercised by the state. There is no simple instrumental rationality leading to the emergence of capitalist social mechanisms, and certainly no general principle of efficiency in organizing economic life in practice. For capitalism to emerge, power has to be actively deployed, favouring the interests of some social groups, while harming those of others. Efficiency is only what a historian or a social theorist would come to recognize after the event, particularly if the spirit of capitalism has already taken hold of society. That is not to deny the importance of certain institutional practices in given historical and political contexts preceding the emergence of capitalism. But when class, power and the state are analytically downplayed in favour of abstract institutional materialism, the result is typically a collection of generalities that pass as a theory of the emergence of capitalism.

5.2 Merchants and capitalism in Ottoman Macedonia

In light of these debates, it is vital to stress that the emergence of Ottoman industrial capitalism in Macedonia had four prominent historical features. First, merchants undoubtedly led the transition to industrial capitalism. Second, there was no capitalist transformation of agriculture. Third, the character of the state and the type of access that the merchant-capitalists had to its mechanisms actively shaped the trajectory as well as the form and pace of industrialization. Fourth, the practices of the merchants were typically associated with their communities, which were non-Muslim (Jewish and Christian). In sum, Ottoman capitalism, at least in Macedonia, was marked by the modernizing outlook of the state and by the communal structures of the Empire. Perhaps these features also marked Ottoman capitalism in general, making it decidedly weaker than its competitors at the time. There is no doubt, however, that they lent to Macedonian industrial capitalism its unique and precarious nature.

The absence of capitalist transformation in agriculture was of considerable importance for the path of Ottoman capitalism. The remarkable feature of *çiftlik* development in the eighteenth and nineteenth centuries was that it pushed agriculture in the direction of greater commercialization but without creating agrarian capitalism. Agriculture in Macedonia in the 1900s was monetized through *çiftlik* owners selling the output of their estates (mostly grain but also some cash crops) or through smallholders selling their surplus grain output and producing cash crops, but neither 'great' nor 'small' men accumulated land holdings that were managed in the capitalist manner. The capitalists of the region certainly began to acquire land after making commercial and industrial profits, and Christians and Jews started to replace Muslim *çiftlik* owners towards the end of the nineteenth century, as was shown in the previous chapter.¹⁴ However, these 'great' men relied on sharecropping and non-economic methods of surplus extraction. Moreover, the acquisition of agricultural land, including repeated sales and purchases of *çiftlik* estates, frequently aimed at mere speculation rather than developing capitalist agrarian production. Not least, the *çiftlik* holders – Muslims, Christians and Jews – engaged enthusiastically in money lending and usury. There is no way in which they constituted a bourgeois landed class, even if some of them were capitalist merchants and industrialists.

It is true – and is shown in subsequent chapters – that the social stratum of smallholders and other land-based economic agents provided a vital source of demand for industrially produced cotton yarn in Macedonia. In this sense the increasing monetization of Ottoman agriculture was instrumental to the rise of industrial capitalism. But this is no more than a faint echo of the role played by agriculture in the classic debates of capitalist transition that were summed up in the preceding section. It is similarly true – and is also shown in subsequent chapters – that the labour force of the early textile factories in provincial Ottoman Macedonia came from the agricultural areas, typically as young women and children working for short periods of time. However, this development resembles the great flocking of the agrarian population to the urban centres in search of employment in much of the developed world in the twentieth century. There is no evidence that it was caused by ascendant capitalist forces dispossessing the peasantry in the Macedonian countryside while developing technically more advanced, more efficient and profitable large-scale agricultural production.

This does not mean that the agrarian sector was static. The increase in market-oriented production and especially in cash crops, the monetization of the agrarian economy, and the formation of *çiftlik* with their characteristic relations show that Ottoman agriculture was far removed from self-sufficient subsistence farming. Nevertheless, the transformation of the Ottoman agriculture generally lacked a clear capitalist direction since it was not accompanied by technical advances in production and the characteristic relations of capitalist agriculture.

---

¹⁴ See also Demetriades (1981, p. 53).

Industrial capitalism in provincial Ottoman Macedonia emerged in towns that lay in the uplands and did so despite the lack of capitalist transformation in agriculture. There is no direct parallel with Western Europe in this respect, and certainly none with the Dobb-Sweezy debate. Moreover, industrial capitalism emerged through the initiative of merchants who traded in textiles and other commodities. Powerful merchants became capitalists by controlling production and eventually building industrial mills. These merchants either sprang out of the pre-industrial realm of textile production or were closely associated with it.

The trajectory and fluctuations of commerce were instrumental to the emergence of industrial capitalism in Ottoman Macedonia. The merchants of provincial Macedonia traded internationally – mostly in the Balkans and the Middle East – as well as domestically within the Empire. They were heavily involved in the domestic production of woollen cloth, partly because they competed against imports from Western Europe. They had a Christian Greek outlook, which brought them into distinctive relations with the modernizing Ottoman state. Remarkably, they were ready to acquire *çiftlik* estates in the surrounding plain, thus extracting profits by relying on non-capitalist mechanisms. In these respects, Ottoman capitalism in provincial Macedonia has no direct correspondence with the emergence of capitalism in England or in other parts of Western Europe in the preceding centuries.

In sum, there is no general rule for the emergence of industrial capitalism. The debates of historians and political economists do little more than specify crucial factors capable of shaping the historical emergence of capitalism. Historical specificity rules the roost and defines the particular characteristics of each occasion of capitalist transition. This point is further demonstrated in the remaining chapters by considering Ottoman Macedonian industrialization in detail.

5.3 Thessaloniki trade grows rapidly until the early 1870s

In the first half of the nineteenth century free trade policies, promoted by Britain, gradually took hold of Ottoman commerce. A signal event in this process was the Anglo-Ottoman Trade Convention of 1838, also known as the

Treaty of *Balta* Limanı, signed by the Porte essentially under duress at a time of life and death struggle with Kavalalı Mehmed Ali *Paşa*, the ruler of Egypt.

The Convention removed state monopolies, tariffs and other obstacles barring the way of European merchants into the Ottoman markets, including Egypt. Duties on imports and transit goods were fixed at 3 per cent, other internal duties paid by importers at 2 per cent, duties on exports at 12 per cent, and internal customs duties at 8 per cent but only for Ottoman citizens.[15] This was broadly the framework within which the economy of the Empire operated for decades afterwards. There was a revival of protectionism towards the end of 1860s as the Ottoman state's persistent attempt to renegotiate duties and taxes finally bore fruit; import levies rose from 3 to 8 per cent, which did not merely increase state income but also helped stimulate Ottoman manufacturing, as will be shown in Chapters 6 and 7.[16]

The agreement certainly served the interests of Britain by providing new markets for its textiles and other commodities as well as opening up new sources of raw material supply for its industrialists.[17] It also pushed the Ottoman Empire further toward trade liberalism, a path that had already been taken by the time the Convention was signed. The disbandment of the Janissaries in 1826 had ushered in a new period in Ottoman economic life by destroying 'the most powerful and best-organized advocates of protectionism'.[18] The Convention placed its stamp on the new phase in the economic development of the Empire that lasted from the 1820s until the 1870s. In the words of Quataert: 'The Ottoman trade regime became one of the most liberal in the world.'[19]

In the decades that followed the signing of the Convention the Empire's volume of trade increased at an unprecedented rate. Pamuk has shown that in the 1830s the value of Ottoman exports and imports was relatively small and broadly balanced, with a modest overall trade deficit. From the 1830s to the 1870s, the value of exports quadrupled, and then increased again by about 50 per cent to the 1910s. The value of Ottoman imports had, meanwhile, also

---

[15] See Quataert (1994b, p. 826) and Pamuk (2007, p. 206).
[16] See Quataert (1994b, p. 826).
[17] Ibid., p. 764.
[18] Ibid.
[19] Ibid., p. 826.

quadrupled by the 1870s, and then increased again by nearly 100 per cent to the 1910s. By 1913 the Empire had been firmly integrated into the world market and recorded a large trade deficit.[20]

Expanding commercial relations were critical to the industrial transformation that occurred in Macedonia in the nineteenth century. The Ottoman possessions in the Balkan Peninsula had led the integration of the Empire in the world market in the late eighteenth century due to their geographical proximity to Western Europe and their strategic location in international trade routes. Macedonian trade actually declined in the 1840s perhaps due to bad harvests, and also because Greek merchants had departed following the formal establishment of the independent Greek state in 1830.[21] After the 1840s, however, trade in Thessaloniki and its hinterland expanded rapidly in line with the overall increase in Ottoman trade. Consular reports frequently mention the geographical location of Thessaloniki – at the junction of sea and rail routes connecting the Ottoman Empire to Western Europe – as a key reason for its growing trade. A further contributing factor was that the *vilayet* of Thessaloniki possessed powerful productive forces in both agriculture and manufacturing and was home to a well-established merchant class.[22]

The three decades from the early 1840s to the early 1870s were a period of strongly favourable terms of trade for Ottoman agricultural producers and merchants. The leading exports were grains and some cash crops, while import growth was chiefly in textiles, particularly cotton. Thessaloniki became the most significant port of the European provinces after İstanbul, and the main place for trade between the Balkan provinces of the Empire and Western and Central Europe.

The role of regional merchant groups was crucial to this development. The Balkan merchant class of the Ottoman Empire dated back to the fourteenth century, when Ottoman rule in the Balkans commenced. In the seventeenth century, the trade networks of Balkan merchants became well established, stretching from Central Europe to most of the major urban centres of the Empire. Particularly in the eighteenth century there emerged an Ottoman

---

[20] See Pamuk (1987, p. 149).
[21] See Anastassiadou (2001/1997, p. 93), quoting Vakalopoulos (1983).
[22] See Anastassiadou (2001/1997, pp. 95–9).

Greek merchant class that was powerful in both wealth and numbers extending its operations from Europe to the Middle East.[23]

According to Stoianovich, 'the Thessalo-Macedo-Epirote region produced more carters and merchants in the eighteenth century than any other Balkan area of comparable size', and merchants in this zone were primarily Greeks as well as Vlachs, that is, indigenous latinophone inhabitants of the region who frequently adopted Greek culture.[24] Similarly, 'Balkan wool and cotton were exported overland to Austria and Germany almost exclusively by Balkan merchants, mainly Macedo-Thessalian and Epirote Greeks and Vlachs'.[25] It is even likely that in the course of the expansion of trade after the seventeenth century the appellation 'Greek' began to denote a certain type of businessman who traded over long distances, was Christian Orthodox in religion, and spoke Greek in the public domain.[26] The Greek merchant network became exceptionally prominent during the last quarter of the eighteenth century and in the first two decades of the nineteenth century, mostly due to the hugely profitable opportunities created by the Napoleonic Wars and Britain's Continental Blockade.[27]

The merchants of the *vilayet* of Thessaloniki benefited substantially from the commercial expansion lasting from the 1840s to the 1870s.[28] When the trade of the Black Sea region was severely disrupted by the Crimean War in 1853-6, Thessaloniki merchants were able not only to supply wheat to İstanbul, but also to replace Russian merchants as providers of grain to Europe. Similarly, during the next decade, when a cotton bottleneck emerged in Europe as a result of the American Civil War, Thessaloniki merchants began to export cotton from both Thessaloniki and Serres to meet European demand.[29] The commercial development of the city during much of this period was led by

---

[23] See Stoianovich (1960, p. 234). For a more recent work on Ottoman-Greek merchants, see Chatziioannou (2010).
[24] See Stoianovich (1960, p. 279).
[25] Ibid., p. 260.
[26] See Seirinidou (2008, p. 94).
[27] Ibid., p. 90. For a discussion of the networks and relationships within which Greek merchants operated see Chatziioannou (2010).
[28] 'Thessaloniki merchant' is a broad rubric that includes Jewish and Muslim merchants. There is little doubt, however, that Greek merchants were heavily present in the rural hinterland of Thessaloniki. The literature on the trade of Thessaloniki is large, see selectively Svoronos (1956); Stoianovich (1960); Vlami (1997) and Andronikos (2007).
[29] See Anastassiadou (2001/1997, p. 95).

Jewish rather than Greek merchants, as is discussed in this and the following chapter.

The significance of merchants in the economic life of the *vilayet* of Thessaloniki in the nineteenth century is not in doubt. For our purposes, merchants – though not those specializing in grain – were also instrumental in the emergence of industrial capitalism in both Thessaloniki and provincial Macedonia in the 1870s. To establish this point, it is necessary more fully to consider the patterns, the fluctuations and the personnel of commerce in the *vilayet* of Thessaloniki, and more specifically in the *kaza* of Veroia and Edhessa and the *nahiye* of Naoussa.

5.4 Fluctuations and growth of trade in Thessaloniki from the 1870s to the 1910s

The period of rapid expansion of Ottoman foreign trade came to an end in the 1870s as the Great Depression of 1873–96 took hold of the world economy.[30] Ottoman trade continued to grow in the following two decades but at a slower pace.[31] Several factors contributed to the slowdown of trade: a sharp decrease in primary commodity prices which ruined the terms of trade for Ottoman agricultural producers and merchants; the fiscal crisis of the Ottoman state and its bankruptcy in 1875; bad harvests and the disastrous Russo-Turkish War of 1877–8.[32] Furthermore, in the 1860s Ottoman protectionist policies were revived and became further intensified in the 1870s with a view to supporting domestic production and internal trade. Finally, the declining income of primary commodity producers due to falling export revenues curbed imports and directed consumption towards domestic goods.

Primary commodity prices resumed their upward trend only after the 1890s – especially after the end of the Great Depression in 1896 – thus making the terms of trade once again favourable to Ottoman agricultural producers. The restructuring of Ottoman fiscal debt and the formation of the OPDA also

---

[30] For a general analysis of the Ottoman economy during the Great Depression of 1873–96, see Pamuk (1984).
[31] See Pamuk (1987).
[32] See Quataert (1994b, p. 829).

helped readjust the outflows of finance and indirectly facilitated trade. The rate of increase of trade after the 1890s was lower than in the boom years of the 1840s–1870s but the increase after the 1890s occurred against a much bigger base.

The early provincial yearbooks for the *vilayet* of Thessaloniki simply recorded the trading specialities of the region, such as carpets, towels, leather and socks. Grains and certain cash crops, which were among the most prominent goods in terms of export values, went unnoticed. Only in the tenth volume – that for 1890 – was a detailed overview given of the trade of the *vilayet*, making the point that Thessaloniki had benefited from its location, being the largest port of the European provinces after İstanbul.[33]

According to the yearbook for 1890, the main exports from the port of Thessaloniki were grains, tobacco, silk cocoons, opium, cotton, sesame, wine, beeswax and red pepper. It was specifically stated that exports by the manufacturing industry were insignificant.[34] There could be no doubt that Ottoman industrialization was spurred entirely by domestic demand rather than exports. Domestic demand increased significantly in this period thanks to urbanization and the commercialization of agriculture. The main outlets of the new industries were the domestic markets. This was particularly the case for industries specializing in foodstuffs, but it was also true for the early period of the textile industries in the *vilayet* of Thessaloniki, which similarly focused on domestic markets. Rapid growth in the leading towns of the Levant, such as İstanbul and İzmir, and the gradual abolition of internal customs duties after the 1870s gave a boost to domestic demand and created profit-making opportunities for industrialists.[35] In this connection commercial demand by the Ottoman state was particularly significant for the emerging industrialists, as will be shown further in the rest of this book.

The main imports were various types of cotton, woollen and silk textiles, and other goods including sugar, coffee, petroleum, gas, iron, nails, dye, glass and tableware. The total external trade of the *vilayet* was estimated at

---

[33] See SVS X, 1307 [1890]. The city of Thessaloniki was not the only port of the *vilayet*, but carried more than half of the commercial activities of the region, including the commerce of the other two *vilayets* of Macedonia – Kosova and Bitola – and of the *vilayet* of Ioannina (*Yanya*) in Epirus.
[34] See SVS X, 1307 [1890].
[35] See Akarli (2001, pp. 281–6).

roughly 8 million Ottoman *lira*, which comprised 3.5 million in exports and 4.5 million in imports. The biggest trading partner was Britain, followed by France, Austria, Italy, Belgium and Greece, in that order.[36]

Grains were the leading export from Thessaloniki in 1890, a large part of which went to Britain and France. The annual export revenue from grains was roughly 1.5 million Ottoman *lira* and constituted nearly half the total export revenue. It should be stressed that part of the grain revenue accrued to the neighbouring provinces, such as Serres, which exported their output via the port of Thessaloniki. After grains, the main exports were cash crops – tobacco, cotton, silk cocoons, opium and sesame – with a total value of around 1 million Ottoman *lira*.[37] Note that grain exports were barely 10 per cent of the grain output, while cash crop exports were more than 90 per cent of the cash crop output. It is clear that in the *vilayet* of Thessaloniki in 1890, grain was primarily produced for consumption in the domestic market, while cash crops were heavily exported.

The main imports in Thessaloniki in 1890 were cotton textiles, the annual value of which were roughly 1.5 million *lira*, and 60 per cent of the total represented imports from Britain.[38] This figure alone is enough to make starkly clear the nature of the competition faced by the domestic textile manufacturers. Textile imports from France and Italy comprised largely woollen goods and silk, most of which were subsequently transported to the inland *vilayet*, including Kosova and Bitola. There were also substantial imports of coffee and sugar, worth half a million *lira*, of which a considerable amount was again transported inland using the railways.[39] Coffee came from the Arab lands but also from Britain, which controlled the export of Brazilian coffee; sugar was mainly imported from Marseilles and Trieste.[40]

No dramatic changes had taken place in the patterns of the external trade of Thessaloniki by 1907-8, and in its composition and main trading partners it remained broadly the same. The yearbook for 1907 recorded the total volume of external trade at around 8.5 million Ottoman *lira*, 5 million of which were

---

[36] See SVS X, 1307 [1890].
[37] Ibid.
[38] Ibid.
[39] Ibid.
[40] For a detailed analysis of the importance of coffee in domestic and international trade see Faroqhi (1986); specifically on the coffee trade of Thessaloniki, see Ginio (2006).

imports and 3.5 million exports. The fall in the export share of grains had continued and the trade deficit had increased, but neither exports not imports had changed much, if at all, since 1890.[41] Britain was the leading trading partner, followed by France and Germany, which was a recent arrival in the Ottoman markets.

Domestic trade appeared to have grown during this period, not least because the expanding urban population had to be supplied with grain, cash crops and clothes. Already in 1890 annual trade fairs were in decline, replaced by weekly markets in villages and towns.[42] After 1902 the yearbooks began to draw a clear line between domestic and external trade, providing in-depth information about domestic trade and the state of domestic markets.[43] Commercialization had evidently proceeded apace. It is notable that towards the end of Ottoman rule Thessaloniki imported grain from other *vilayet* but also from abroad. By 1911 the annual grain imports of Thessaloniki had reached 47,500 tons.[44] By then the *vilayet* and the city of Thessaloniki possessed a complex economy in which industrial and commercial activities played a leading role.

5.5 Trade in the *kaza* of Veroia and Edhessa

Travellers in Macedonia in the first half of the nineteenth century typically mentioned both Veroia and Naoussa as places of intense commercial activity.[45] The main export of Naoussa was *şayak*, a woollen cloth that subsequently proved instrumental to the town's industrial ascendancy, and, of course, wine. Veroia was mentioned as a centre of domestic textile manufacturing, more specifically hemp and flax shirts as well as *makrama* (a towel used in Turkish baths). Veroia also exported fulled wool for coarse woollen cloth and carpets that were produced either in the surrounding villages or by the Jews of Thessaloniki. It appears that the textiles of Veroia were mostly consumed in the domestic markets.[46]

---

[41] See SVS XX, 1325 [1907].
[42] See SVS X, 1307 [1890].
[43] See SVS XVIII, 1322 [1905]; SVS XIX, 1324 [1906]; SVS XX, 1325 [1907].
[44] See Akarli (2001, p. 93).
[45] See Cousinery (1831, p. 72); Leake (1835, pp. 284–92); Nicolaidy (1859, p. 282).
[46] See Leake (1835, p. 291).

Şayak was a high-quality, felt-like woollen cloth that was widely used in the Balkans and other parts of the Empire to make traditional clothes. A much cheaper traditional textile was *aba*, a coarse woollen cloth used by peasants and others. The production of *şayak* was a complex process that required a steady supply of good quality wool, which had to be scoured, carded, spun, woven, fulled and finished. The fulling process required large volumes of water and a fast-flowing stream to power the wooden contraptions that were typically used to beat the wool. It was difficult to produce finished woollen cloth in places that were distant from fast-flowing water. Naoussa was in a privileged position to produce *şayak* since it had access to good wool from the large sheep and goat flocks kept by Vlach shepherds on Mount Vermion. It also had abundant supplies of fast-flowing water and possessed good traditional skills in operating handlooms. *Şayak* production and trading was the foundation of its eventual industrial predominance.

Several yearbooks for 1870–90 list Veroia and Naoussa as producers of good quality textiles exported to İstanbul and its environs, but also to the Kingdom of Greece.[47] Trading relations between Greece and Naoussa were of decisive importance for industrialization, as will be seen in subsequent chapters. Edhessa also seemed to have an active trade in textiles, mostly exporting output to Bitola, Thessaloniki and its environs. It is clear from the yearbooks that Macedonian textile producers aimed primarily at the domestic market. Competition with imports from Britain and elsewhere had segmented the Ottoman market creating niches for domestic producers, a development that acted as a catalyst for industrialization after 1870.

The yearbook for 1886 gives detailed information regarding the state of trade in the two *kaza*.[48] For Edhessa only wool/fleece and goat's hair are mentioned, and a good part of the output was probably used by *şayak* producers in the *kaza*. The *kaza* of Veroia had a more diverse trading sector. It produced flour sent to other *vilayet*; textiles sold in the markets of İstanbul, Thessaloniki, Bitola and Serres; tobacco and some wine; it also produced sacks made from goat hair that were vital to the grain trade.

---

[47] See SVS III, 1290 [1873]; SVS IV, 1291 [1874]; SVS V, 1292 [1875]; SVS VI, 1293 [1876]; SVS VII, 1294 [1877]; SVS IX, 1303 [1886].
[48] See SVS IX, 1303 [1886].

There is little doubt that Naoussa had the strongest commercial character of the three towns, and its trade was dominated by four commodities. First, there was wine that had been lauded by travellers. Cousinery, for instance, had declared in 1831 that 'the wine of Naoussa in Macedonia is what Burgundy is in France', while in 1859 Nicolaidy had described Naoussa wine to be 'very similar to Bordeaux wines'.[49] All the yearbooks state that the bulk of Naoussa wine was exported to important urban centres of the Empire, including İstanbul and Thessaloniki, but also Alexandria in Egypt.[50] Naoussa wine was also exported abroad, even as far as Germany.[51] Second, there were cocoons and silkworm, both of which were said in the yearbooks to have set 'an example' for the rest of the region. Third, there was *şayak* which was of the highest quality and a core commercial strength of Naoussa. A considerable part of the annual produce was exported to the Kingdom of Greece and the remainder was sold within the *vilayet* of Thessaloniki. Finally, after 1875, the yearbooks state that the town began to trade heavily in cotton yarn, produced by a single mill. This was obviously the Longos-Kyrtsis-Tourpalis plant that played a pioneering role in the industrialization of the area. The yarn was sold to markets in Bitola, Serres and Thessaloniki as well as to other *kaza* in Macedonia.[52]

In the late 1890s there was a notable change in the commercial patterns and flows of trade in both Edhessa and Naoussa that was probably induced by advancing industrialization.[53] The sluggish economy of Edhessa was transformed by the arrival of the railway in the early 1890s, but also after the establishment of the town's first cotton yarn mill in 1895, which traded in domestic markets.[54] That was the Tsitsis mill, which eventually became one of the largest private textile concerns in the Empire. The textile trade in Naoussa also expanded considerably, including cotton yarn and woollen goods,

---

[49] See Cousinery (1831, p. 72) and Nicolaidy (1859, p. 282).
[50] It is interesting to note that the yearbooks consider Alexandria to be formally a part of the Empire, and certainly not *'haric'* or outside the Empire. The phrase usually deployed to denote exports, *'harice nakil edilur'* is not used for Alexandria.
[51] The expression used translates as 'all the way to Germany', which suggests that wine was also traded *en route* to Germany.
[52] See SVS IX, 1303 [1886].
[53] See SVS XV, 1315 [1897].
[54] See SVS XV, 1315 [1897]; SVS XVIII, 1322 [1905]. A comment in the yearbook of 1905 states that: 'With the establishment of railways, the centre of Vodina has been developing and prospering day by day.'

particularly as the town had six textile mills by the 1900s. In Veroia, however, traditional textile manufacturing had regressed. This was a recurrent cause of concern for the compilers of the yearbooks.[55]

5.6 Who were the Naoussa merchants?

Throughout the history of the Ottoman Empire, commerce was a well-known and significant economic activity. In fact, it was one of the founding blocks of the classical or ideal Ottoman system, since merchants acted as the agents of external trade and the mediators between rural and urban economy in domestic trade. The mediating role of merchants was crucial to the 'provisionist' Ottoman state which aimed to secure a regular supply of foodstuffs and other goods to the cities and, above all, to İstanbul. Entire groups of merchants and merchant guilds across the Empire strove to take part in the provisioning of the Ottoman capital.[56] Domestic trade was a vital part of the Ottoman economy.

The merchant networks acquired a different character in the nineteenth century as a result of advancing commercialization and the integration of the Empire in the world economy. The eighteenth century had already marked a turning point in the commercial activities of Thessaloniki, recording an increase in the volume of commercial transactions with Western Europe, but also a profound change in the composition of traded goods and trade partners.[57] Ginio asserts that 'one of the main characteristics of Thessaloniki commerce was its diversity and its reliance on various networks of merchants', who were split along religious lines.[58] The distinction between Greek and Jewish merchants proved important to the eventual rise of industrial capitalism.

In the nineteenth century, a new layer of Greek merchants came to the fore as trade expanded with Western Europe, Egypt and elsewhere. Naoussa

---

[55] See SVS XIII, 1312 [1894]; SVS XIV, 1313 [1895]; SVS XV, 1315 [1897].
[56] There is a large literature on Ottoman merchant guilds and provisioning; see, indicatively Baer (1980) for a broad analysis of guilds in history of the Middle East; Yi (2004) for details on the development of guilds, focusing on İstanbul; Faroqhi (2009) for perhaps the most comprehensive research on Ottoman guilds and Yildirim (2002, 2007, 2008) for analysis of specific institutions and functions of the guilds.
[57] For a detailed analysis of eighteenth-century Thessaloniki trade, see Svoronos (1956).
[58] See Ginio (2006, p. 100).

Table 5.1 Merchant families of Naoussa and the geographical area of their activities, 1911

Area of commercial activity	Families
Ottoman Empire	Kyrtsis, Longos, Tourpalis, Platsoukas, Pehlivanos, Angelakis, Lamnides, Lanaras, Petrides, Tsitsis
Egypt	Goutas, Lappas, Mathaiou, Kokkinos, Pehlivanos
Bosnia	Sefertzis, Gourgouliatos
Greece	Lapavitsas, Longos, Tsitsis

Source: Lapavitsas (2006).

was in a favourable position to take advantage of the new conditions. In the late eighteenth century it had already engaged in strong trading activities undertaken by its native Greek merchant class. In the nineteenth century, the town emerged as a significant domestic trading centre, well connected to prominent export destinations, including Western Europe, Egypt and the Kingdom of Greece. In 1911, near the end of Ottoman rule, this small Macedonian town of fewer than ten thousand people had twelve large and more than twenty smaller trading houses.[59]

Table 5.1 lists merchant families of Naoussa that possessed significant commercial capital, also indicating the main geographical area of their commercial activities. Egypt had a prominent position in the international networks of Naoussa merchants, a feature that was common to other Balkan towns at the time. The transformation wrought to Egypt by Mehmed Ali and the opening of the Egyptian markets after the Anglo-Ottoman Convention of 1838 attracted large numbers of Greek merchants to Egypt, from both the Kingdom of Greece and the lands of the Ottoman Empire. The family businesses of Balkan merchants frequently had one member based in Egypt for commercial purposes, even if the others resided elsewhere.[60] Table 5.1 shows that there were at least five merchant families from Naoussa that were heavily involved in trade with Egypt in 1911. Regular emigration from Naoussa to Egypt took place in the second half of the nineteenth century,

---

[59] See Lapavitsas (2006, p. 678).
[60] See Stoianovich (1960, p. 296).

and traders set up offices in Alexandria and Cairo to deal especially in wine, foodstuffs and *şayak*.⁶¹ Also important to Naoussa was trading with the Kingdom of Greece, which was facilitated by cultural and ethnic affinity and proved vital to industrialization after 1870.

It is instructive to compare the list of prominent Naoussa families in Table 5.1 with Table 5.2 listing prominent Thessaloniki merchants and Table 5.3 listing prominent Thessaloniki bankers circa 1902. Both of these tables were extracted from the Ottoman archives in İstanbul.

The lists in Tables 5.2 and 5.3 register only some of the merchants and bankers of Thessaloniki, and there are glaring omissions, above all, of the Allatini as traders and the Modiano as bankers. A different but related list that casts further light on Thessaloniki merchants, industrialists and bankers appears in Table 6.1 in Chapter 6. Furthermore, the justification for listing in Table 5.3 several wealthy individuals as 'bankers' alongside powerful institutions such as the Ottoman Bank is far from obvious. With these provisos in mind, the tables show clearly the dominant position of Jewish merchants and bankers in Thessaloniki in 1902, followed at some distance by their Turkish counterparts. Greek merchants were perhaps even weaker than their Turkish competitors, although the Greeks had a strong presence in banking.

In view of the relatively weak position of the Greek merchants and bankers of Thessaloniki, the presence among them of merchants and bankers from Mount Vermion is notable. Thus, among the bankers in Table 5.3, *Perikli Hacilazari* (Pericles Hadjilazaros) stands out, a trader whose family had strong interests in manufacturing woollen cloth in Naoussa. Hadjilazaros will appear frequently in the analysis in subsequent chapters. Another banker was *Atnaş Sosidis* (Athanassios Sossidis), a rich merchant and cotton spinner from Veroia, whose exploits will also be considered in subsequent chapters. The list of merchants in Table 5.2 also includes '*Longo, Kirci and Turbali*', evidently Longos, Kyrtsis and Tourpalis who established the first cotton mill in Naoussa in 1874–5. They engaged in purchasing miscellaneous goods in Thessaloniki, that is, they were general importers-exporters. Finally, the list included the company of '*Dimitri Durbali and Sons*' (Dimitrios Tourpalis) which engaged

---

⁶¹ See Lapavitsas (2006, p. 678).

in cereal and cotton trade. The Tourpalis family were among the leading traders and cotton spinners of Naoussa.

The merchants and bankers of Mount Vermion operating in Thessaloniki had integral connections with textile manufacturing and trading. Furthermore, practically all the textile trading families of Naoussa in Table 5.1 were also involved in industrial textile production. At the very least, the merchants owned the watermills that provided the foundation for the textile plants. The Ottoman archives leave no doubt on this score: textile factories were established over already existing watermills that were typically owned by the founders of the industrial enterprises.[62] The watermills were a natural source of power for both *şayak* production and the subsequent spinning of cotton. The *şayak* merchants who led industrialization in Naoussa had close connections with *şayak* manufacturing, perhaps through a putting-out system, or otherwise.

The prominence of *şayak* production in Naoussa was first testified by the traveller Nicolaidy in the 1850s: 'There is here a factory producing thick woollen cloth, quite similar to felt, which is called *saïak*.'[63] The production of *şayak* continued strongly throughout the nineteenth century and was notable even in 1912, in spite of the emergence of extensive industrial cotton spinning and wool weaving.[64] This is a characteristic feature of emerging textile capitalism: it is rare for the rise of mechanized factory production completely to destroy the already existing capacity in textiles. As traditional production declined, some of the cloth producers adapted to the new conditions and found new niches in the emerging markets. The *şayak* makers and traders of Naoussa were the social layer from which industrial capitalism emerged in spinning cotton yarn and weaving woollen cloth. They continued to produce and trade *şayak* for decades afterwards.

In this regard, Naoussa was similar to several places in Bulgaria that had played a decisive role in the development of Ottoman manufacturing in the

---

[62] See, for instance, SVS XII, 1311 [1893]; BOA.İ.MMS.52/2274, 2 Rabiulahir 1292/ 26 Nisan 1291 (08.05.1875); BOA.İ.MMS.117/5004, 28 Rabiulahir 1308 (11.12.1890); BOA.İ.MMS.52/2274. Private ownership of mills in the Ottoman Empire went back as far as the seventeenth century. The Ottoman legal system considered mills as well as vineyards and gardens to be the private property of individuals; see Avcıoğlu (1996, p. 17); İnalcık (1977); Faroqhi (2006, p. 382).
[63] See Nicolaidy (1859, [vol. 2] p. 282).
[64] See Stougiannakis (1911, p. 152).

Table 5.2 Prominent merchants in Thessaloniki c. 1902

Name	Location of the Commercial House	Type of commerce
Emin, Receb, Aziz Efendiler	*Kitabcılar içi* (Inside the bookmakers/booksellers)	Drapery
Fisde Yako Şalom (Sialom)	*Papuşci Hanı civarı* (In the vicinity of the Han of the shoemakers)*	Pharmaceuticals
Kapani Ahmed Efendi (Kapancı)	*Katibler Çarşısı* (Clerks' Market)	Drapery
Hasan Akif Efendi	Purchaser	Tobacco
Hüsnü ve Mustafa Efendi	*Site-i Saul* (Cite Saul)	Drapery
Maryo Fernandes	*Allatini Hanı* (Han of Allatini)	Miscellaneous
Şimo Şimote	*Lombardo Hanı* (Han of Lombardo/Lombardo Passage)	Drapery
İsak Yako Yahil and Co.	*Site-i Saul* (Cite Saul)	Drapery
Hristo Gorgiyadis	*Vardar Kapusu harici* (Outside the Vardar Gate)	Drapery
Tehma Aron Melah (Mallah)	*Sabri Paşa Caddesi* (Sabri Pasha Boulevard)	Drapery
Dilberzade Brothers	*Site-i Saul* (Cite Saul)	Miscellaneous
Mehmed Karakaşzadeler	*Frenk Mahallesi* (Frankish Quarter)	Drapery
Mehmed Balcı Brothers	*Frenk Mahallesi* (Frankish Quarter)	Drapery
Edhem Derviş	*Frenk Mahallesi* (Frankish Quarter)	Drapery
Merkado Haneyşuh	*Site-i Saul* (Cite Saul)	Drapery
Mişon Şalom (Sialom)	*Karılar Pazarı* (Women's Bazaar)	Pharmaceuticals
Vasu Kardeşler	Purchaser	Leather
Fratelli Yuan Şiftolof	*Lombardo Hanı* (Han of Lombardo/Lombardo Passage)	Leather
Telci Mehmed Sami Efendi	*Sabri Paşa Caddesi* (Sabri Pasha Boulevard)	Drapery
Perikli Beşnigidi	Purchaser	Leather
Dimitri Yuanidis	Purchaser	Miscellaneous

Name	Location of the Commercial House	Type of commerce
İpekçi Kardeşler	*Sabri Paşa Caddesi* (Sabri Pasha Boulevard)	Haberdasher
Mustafa Cezar and Sons	*Sabri Paşa Caddesi* (Sabri Pasha Boulevard)	Haberdasher
Longo, Kirci ve Turbali	**Purchaser**	**Miscellaneous**
Sazlu Değirmenci	*Frenk Mahallesi* (Frankish Quarter)	Drapery
Yako Fransez and Son	*Frenk Mahallesi* (Frankish Quarter)	--
Yuşuh İlya Fransez	*Oryantal Hanı* (Oriental Han)	--
Yusuf Alyon (Aellion)	Purchaser	Silk cocoons
Davi Neyfus	Purchaser	Cereals
Yusuf Benrubi (Benroubi)	Purchaser	Leather
Yako Mişon Filorenti and Co. (Florentin)	*İstanbul Çarşısı* (İstanbul Market)	Drapery
Cafer Sadık Efendi	*Hamidiye Mahallesi* (Hamidiye Neighbourhood)	Timber
Evruzdi Bak (?) and Co.	*Sırçeciler* (at glassmakers/sellers)	Miscellaneous
Yusuf Alyon Sons	*Frenk Mahallesi* (Frankish Quarter)	Drapery
Şamlı Mustafa Sons	*Frenk Mahallesi* (Frankish Quarter)	Miscellaneous
Nuri ibn Musa Efendi	*Saulzadeler Hanı* (Han of the Saul family)	--
Dimitri Serafa	Purchaser	Leather
Lyon Karasu	*Yalı Kapısı* (Yalı Gate)	Sugar and coffee
Metalon bin Benisti	*Site-i Saul* (Cite Saul)	Drapery
Yako Fransez	Purchaser	Iron
Hristo Riyago/Rigo Sons	*Rıhtımın ikinci caddesi* (Second street of the Port)	Miscellaneous
Yoda Namyaz	*Saulzadeler Hanı karşısı* (Opposite of the Han of the Saul family)	Miscellaneous
Panayotidi Brothers	*Sabri Paşa Caddesi* (Sabri Pasha Boulevard)	Miscellaneous
Gebaroğlu Brothers and Sons	*Yalı Kapısı* (Yalı Gate)	Mnk dealer
Dimitri Turpali and Sons	***Yalı Kapısı* (Yalı Gate)**	**Cereals and cotton**

Name	Location of the Commercial House	Type of commerce
Menteş Asyu	Yalı Kapısı (Yalı Gate)	Iron
Ebranol Kapanu and Benbenisti	Purchaser	--
Yusuf Serfani	Purchaser	Leather
Fisde Gedalya Evram Erere Co.	Site-i Saul (Cite Saul)	Miscellaneous
Atarfik Co.	Site-i Saul (Cite Saul)	--
Osman Derviş & Hayim Manu	Site-i Saul (Cite Saul)	--
Hristidi Menekşe	İstanbul Çarşısı (İstanbul Market)	--
Manta Şuf/Mantaşof	İstanbul Çarşısı (İstanbul Market)	Gas
Şenger and Co.	Kirci Hanı (Krytsis Han)	Shipping agent
Yako İsak Filorenti (Florentin)	İstanbul Çarşısı (İstanbul Market)	Drapery
Yusuf Filorenti, Sapurta ve Braca	Frenk Mahallesi (Frankish Quarter)	Drapery
Sivrihisaryan Azban Vayan	Frenk Mahallesi (Frankish Quarter)	Drapery
S. Eva/Ava Acemyan	Purchaser	Iron

Source: SVS XVII-XX, 1320–1325 [1902–7]. *Han was a large commercial building.

Balkans. Proto-industrial production of textiles and other commodities had already emerged in various rural settlements in the Balkans in the second half of the eighteenth century as 'part of a major rearrangement of the larger regional equilibrium' although they declined after the end of the Napoleonic wars in the face of Western European competition.[65] There is no hard evidence of proto-industrial activity in Naoussa and its surrounding area, but there is little doubt that wool-working skills and processes were well established already at the beginning of the nineteenth century.[66] They provided the basis for capitalist industrialization, even if cotton spinning constitutes a very different production process from wool weaving.

The Greek merchants that led Ottoman industrialization in provincial Macedonia were inextricably linked to şayak production and trading. The

---

[65] See Petmezas (1990, p. 593).
[66] See Lapavitsas (2006).

Table 5.3 Prominent banks and bankers in Thessaloniki c. 1902

Name	Location
Ottoman Bank	*Frenk Mahallesi* (Frankish Quarter)
Bank of Selanik	*Frenk Mahallesinde Allatini Bazergan Hanı* (Trader Allatini Han in the Frankish Quarter)
Bank of Mytillini	*Frenk Mahallesi* (Frankish Quarter)
Uryan Bank	**Kirçi Hanı (Kyrtsis Han)**
Allatini Bros.	*Frenk Mahallesi* (Frankish Quarter)
Saulzadeler	*Site-i Saul* (Cite Saul)
Kapani Mehmed Efendi (Kapancı)	*İsmail Paşa Hanı* (Ismail Pasha Han)
Hikmet Haşmet Azat Co.	*Site-i Saul* (Cite Saul)
Vidal Fernandez	*Frenk Mahallesi* (Frankish Quarter)
Avram Hayim Amar	*Frenk Mahallesi Teyanu Hanı* (Tiano Han in the Frankish Quarter)
Mişon Teyanu (Tiano)	*Frenk Mahallesi Teyanu Hanı* (Tiano Han in the Frankish Quarter)
Perikli Hacılazari	***Frenk Mahallesi Saias Hanı* (Saias Han in the Frankish Quarter)**
Atnaş Sosidis	***Sosidi Hanı* (Sossidis Han)**
Salomon Hassid	*İstanbul Çarşısı* (İstanbul Market)
Papasoğlu Bros.	*Frenk Mahallesi Rungot Hanı* (Rungot Han in the Frankish Quarter)
Salomon Davi Fransez	*Lombardo Hanı* (Han of Lombardo)
Şinasi Murtaza Vahidzadeler	*İstanbul Çarşısı* (İstanbul Market)
İsak bin Susam ve Mahdumlar	*Frenk Mahallesi Yıldız Hanı* (Yıldız Han in the Frankish Quarter)
Mişon Avram Saltil	*Frenk Mahallesi Allatini Hanı* (Allatini Han in the Frankish Quarter)

Source: SVS XVII-XX, 1320–1325 [1902–7].

historical evidence is not strong enough to establish whether the producers of *şayak* became commercial traders, or the merchants became aware of profitable opportunities and gradually entered *şayak* production. But there is no doubt that powerful Naoussa merchants traded *şayak* and were deeply implicated in its production, not least by owning watermills and controlling land with privileged access to fast-flowing water. It is more than likely that the merchants operated a putting-out system in the production of şayak.

Figure 5.1 shows the rare text of commercial correspondence in the trade of şayak between a seller from Naoussa and a buyer from Pyrgos, a town in the Peloponnese in the Kingdom of Greece.

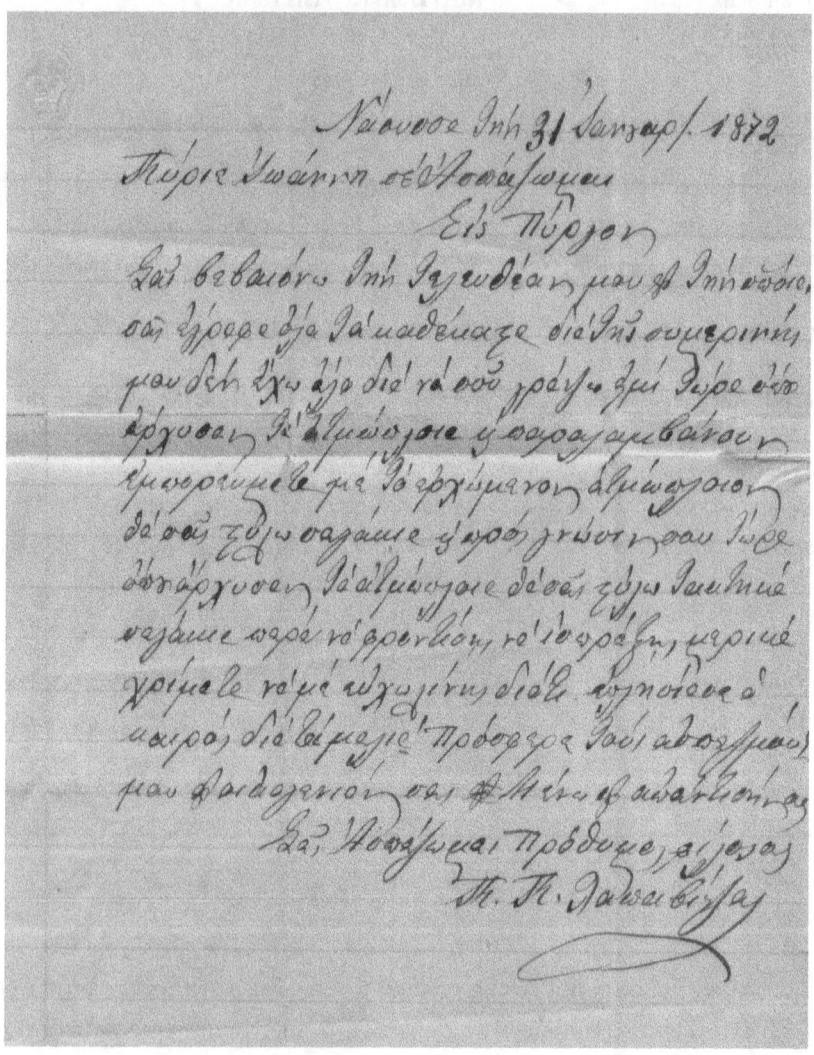

Figure 5.1 Commercial correspondence from Naoussa to Pyrgos in the Peloponnese, 1872

Source: Private collection.

The sender was Constantinos Lapavitsas, a powerful merchant and landowner who controlled much of the trade with the Kingdom of Greece, as was indicated in Table 5.1. The letter was written on 31 January 1872 and had travelled by private means to Thessaloniki. It was then forwarded by an agent to Piraeus by boat – probably entrusted to the captain – arriving on 14 February. It left again on the same day from Athens to Pyrgos using the Greek postal service. Lapavitsas was pleased to inform the recipient that steamboats had just been introduced on the Piraeus route making it possible to send *şayak* 'regularly'. It would, however, be helpful if the purchaser could send some money promptly as the time was fast approaching to pay for raw wool. There was clearly a putting out system in place.

The letter, quite apart from the information it conveys on the mechanisms of long-distance trade and *şayak* production in Naoussa, also casts light on the type of merchant who became a capitalist industrialist in provincial Ottoman Macedonia in the decades after 1870. It was written in fairly formal Greek and, despite several spelling mistakes, there is no doubt that it flowed from the pen of an educated man who conducted his own commercial correspondence. That was probably the characteristic outlook of the leading merchants of Naoussa in the 1870s. Moreover, some among the merchants were not only involved in *şayak* production and trading but also owned huge *çiftlik* on the plain, as did the author of the letter, whose name appears on the list of *çiftlik* owners in Chapter 4. Other merchants possessed sizeable real estate in the town of Naoussa. Merchants, industrialists, landowners and real estate holders formed the local elite, the *çorbacı*, who also run the political and social affairs of the town.

6

Private industrial capitalism in Ottoman Macedonia

6.1 Responding to the import wave

The economic preponderance of the Balkans in the development of commercial and industrial capitalism in the Ottoman Empire is not in doubt. In the second half of the nineteenth century, there was considerable industrial development in the Balkan territories of the Empire, particularly in the regions that in 1878 formed the *de facto* independent state of Bulgaria. The most prominent area of industrial development after Bulgaria was Macedonia. By the 1900s the city of Thessaloniki and the region of Mount Vermion were at the forefront of industrial activity in the Empire.[1] Other regions, such as Western Anatolia, South-Eastern Anatolia and Northern Syria and the Black Sea coast had also moved along the path of industrial capitalism, but Macedonia led the way.

Ottoman industrialization in the Balkans in the late nineteenth century was rooted in developments that had occurred in the second half of the previous century. The political and social turmoil of the late eighteenth century placed peasants under intolerable strain, forcing them either to submit to the protection of powerful landlords, or simply to abandon their holdings and withdraw to safer places, including in upland settlements.[2] The resulting population shifts 'were to become of profound significance in shaping the evolutionary path of the Balkan economy'.[3] Balkan upland settlements were generally unfavourable to agricultural production forcing their populations to resort to a pastoral or semi-pastoral living, directing economic activities

---

[1] See Quataert (1993a, p. 1).
[2] See Sadat (1972, p. 354); Petmezas (1990, pp. 577–80); Palairet (1993, pp. 34–40).
[3] See Palairet (1993, p. 37).

towards animal husbandry, viticulture, commerce and manufacturing. Already in the late eighteenth century the Balkans presented several features of proto-industrial development induced by several sizeable upland communities which placed heavy demographic pressure on an inadequate supply of farmland.[4]

More generally, rural industries and commerce expanded in the second half of the eighteenth century despite the generally restrictive policies of the Ottoman state. According to Genç,[5]

> Rural industry obviously was active before this, but because of the classical Ottoman economic system and the provisionist policy, never had the chance to develop. Factors such as state policies promoting family plots, low labour to land ratios, the nature of agricultural land as state property exempt from confiscation, and state policies restricting the mobility of agricultural workers, all contributed to the underdevelopment of rural industry. Thus, rural industry developed only in mountain villages where agriculture was not possible and animal husbandry dominated, and in some populated areas.

In Macedonia, cotton and woollen domestic manufacturing were prominent already in the eighteenth century. Lowland towns and cities, such as Drama, Veroia and Thessaloniki, were important centres of yarn and cloth production in cotton, wool and silk, with significant export capacity. In the region of Thessaloniki the production of cotton trebled between 1740 and 1790. A significant proportion of raw cotton was exported unprocessed, but roughly a third was spun into yarn; half of the yarn was woven into cloth within the region, and the remainder was exported to Central Europe.[6] There was a remarkable increase in the number of small towns and villages in the region of Thessaloniki that specialized in washing, dyeing and weaving of yarn. It is more than likely that a network of proto-industries, perhaps organized on the basis of a putting-out system led by merchants, underpinned much of this growth.[7]

The conditions of Ottoman manufacturing changed dramatically after the Anglo-Ottoman Convention of 1838, which led to a flood of mostly British

---

[4] Ibid., p. 51; Petmezas (1990, p. 580).
[5] See Genç (1994, p. 64).
[6] Ibid., p. 65.
[7] Cotton cloth production was carried out in similar networks even after the foundation of mechanized industries, as is shown later in this chapter.

textile imports. From the 1840s to the 1860s regular commercial contact with Western Europe became highly detrimental to Ottoman manufacturing, especially to manufactures that were state-operated or based in lowland towns. The influx of cheap manufactured goods from Britain and other countries of Western Europe, and the rising prices of agricultural commodities during this period led to a loss of productive capacity in the Ottoman economy.[8] Some economic historians of the Middle East have claimed that 'de-industrialization' covered the entire nineteenth century as well as the beginning of twentieth century, extending across the Middle East, with a heavily destructive impact.[9]

The actual path of late Ottoman manufacturing was, however, more complex than is sometimes assumed. Sectors that were subjected to European competition generally shrank but some resisted and adapted, especially until the 1850s. Still other sectors flourished in new market niches that appeared particularly after 1870.[10] Ottoman industry displayed a complex development pattern reflecting regional influences and varying according to individual sectors.

In the textile sector British machine-made goods initially squeezed Ottoman producers out of their export destinations and gradually began to dominate the domestic Ottoman markets. The textile manufacturing base of the Empire dwindled after the 1840s and only those producers who found market niches by exploiting natural or other advantages, or producers who were protected by geography, were able to survive. These textile producers were typically located in the upland settlements and provided the substratum out of which industrial textile capitalism eventually emerged in the 1870s. But upland production was far from being the only Ottoman response to the onslaught of imports. In Macedonia, textile capitalism also emerged spontaneously in Thessaloniki, and there was nothing remotely agrarian or geographically isolated about this development. Instead it drew on the resources of the Jewish community, including its long tradition in domestic textile manufacturing.

In the late 1860s the destructive impact of Western manufactured imports and the attendant loss of capacity were ameliorated, in part as the Ottoman state

---

[8] See Pamuk and Williamson (2011).
[9] See Issawi (1980).
[10] See Quataert (1993a, pp. 9–11).

slowly adopted protectionist policies. Its policies were not very comprehensive, as is shown in subsequent chapters, but the immediate and positive response of the domestic economy revealed, first, that there was inherent dynamism to Ottoman production and, second, that even minor protection could have a beneficial effect on domestic industry. The enterprises that sprang during this period competed directly with imported goods and fought for domestic markets.

6.2 Jewish, Christian and Muslim traders, industrialists and bankers in Thessaloniki

In 1912 the *vilayet* of Thessaloniki had a substantial industrial capacity, including both mechanized factories and workshops, thanks to a remarkable boom that began in the late 1870s and continued until the end of the Ottoman period.[11] The city had become one of the most active commercial ports of the Empire, after İstanbul and İzmir and on a par with Beirut. Its natural advantages had been augmented by large-scale infrastructure investments in the second half of the nineteenth century and the start of the twentieth century, including building a railway network, modernizing and enlarging the port, and introducing modern communications, urban transport, and electrification. The construction by the state of a network of *Rumeli* railways was a particularly critical development, since the railways connected the city to both İstanbul and Western Europe.[12] Thessaloniki became a crossroads of transport routes that were vital to international trade. Inevitably, its industrial development was accelerated.

Together with infrastructure improvements and urban expansion went the creation of significant financial capacity. Expanding commercial activities and growing merchant networks had exacerbated the need for financial services. The first modern bank in Thessaloniki, the branch office of the Banque Impériale Ottomane, or the Imperial Ottoman Bank, began operations in 1864. The great bulk of the remaining formal financial institutions were

[11] See Quataert (2014, p. 247).
[12] See Gounaris (1993).

founded after the opening of the Western European rail junction in 1888.[13] The first train to arrive in Thessaloniki from Western Europe carried with it large numbers of prospectors hunting for profit in this 'Eastern Eldorado'.[14] The Banque de Salonique was founded in 1888 as a partnership between the Länderbank of Vienna, the Comptoir d'Escompte of Paris and the Allatini Brothers; it was in practice the bank of the Allatini in the city.[15]

Financial expansion continued apace in the following years. The Agricultural Bank started its operations in 1889 with twenty-two branches across the *vilayet*.[16] In 1895 'the Commercial Club' was formed to fix credit, interest, commission and discount terms for the entire commercial community of Thessaloniki. Two Greek banks followed: the Banque de Mytilene in 1899 and the Bank of Athens in 1905. The Banque d'Orient (Trapeza Anatolis), a joint venture of the National Bank of Greece and the Nationalbank für Deutschland, though the role of the latter was minimal, joined them in Thessaloniki in 1905. The Serb Beogradska Zadruga and the Bulgarian National Bank opened branches in 1908 and 1912, respectively.[17] The city also possessed a substantial number of semi-formal financial mechanisms that were vital to its commercial life already since the middle of the nineteenth century. By 1912 most of these institutions were associated with the Jewish community, and none was more important than the House of Modiano that held the strings of the city's commercial life.[18]

Macedonian industrial capitalism emerged in that context and showed considerable vigour. To establish the mode and the pattern of its development it is necessary briefly to consider the main agents of industrial and commercial capitalism in the region. There is no doubt that the leading capitalists in Macedonia belonged to the Jewish and the Christian communities. There is also no doubt that the largest industrial and commercial concerns were owned by Thessaloniki Jews. The communal aspect of Ottoman capitalism was as

---

[13] See Hekimoglou (1987, p. 58).
[14] See Anastassiadou (2001b, p. 188) for the term 'Eastern Eldorado'. For the opening ceremony of the railway connecting Thessaloniki to Western Europe, see Dimitriadis (2014).
[15] After the 1907 Egyptian crisis, its management passed into the hands of French banks; see Hadziiossif (1993, 173).
[16] See Akarli (2001, p. 152).
[17] See Gounaris (1993, pp. 168–72) and Hekimoglou (1991, pp. 27–8).
[18] See Hekimoglou (1987, p. 38) and Hekimoglou (2012).

integral to its development as were the rise of the upland settlements and the enabling role of the state.

Ladino-speaking Sephardic Jews from the Iberian Peninsula and Italy began to move to Thessaloniki in the sixteenth century as Christian repression in their homelands took a turn for the worse. The Ottoman state gave to the community rights over the manufacture of woollen cloth for the armed forces, thus making it possible for the city to acquire a strong Jewish aspect in the ensuing centuries. The incoming Sephardic Jews rapidly dominated and absorbed the indigenous Romaniot Jews of Thessaloniki, becoming the majority of the city's population until the end of Ottoman rule. However, the most active entrepreneurs among the Jews were fairly recent arrivals. Already in the early eighteenth century Italian Jews from Livorno (Leghorn) had begun to settle in Thessaloniki. In the second half of the nineteenth century, particularly after the incorporation of Livorno in the new Italian nation state and the loss of its free port status in the early 1860s, the trickle became a steady stream.[19] Livornese Jews were the true leaders of commercial and industrial development in Ottoman Thessaloniki.

The Italian arrivals also had distant Iberian roots but spoke Italian at home and were strongly Westernized. For the incumbent Jewish community, they were 'Francos'. Once in Thessaloniki, they learnt inevitably to communicate in Ladino and soon rose to leading positions within the community. The terrain was favourable for the Francos since the Ottoman Jewish community as a whole had declined economically and culturally in the first decades of the nineteenth century, in line with the decline of the power of the Sublime Porte.[20]

Similarly to the local Jews, the Francos relied on family links and communal mechanisms of trust to establish commercial and industrial businesses.[21] However, they had the advantage of extensive international connections, and thus far better information about the practices of rapidly growing industrial capitalism in Western Europe. They also had a further advantage in so far as many had maintained their Italian nationality to benefit from the preferential

---

[19] See Meron (2005).
[20] On the decline of Ottoman Jewry in the early part of the nineteenth century, see Levy (ed.) (1994a, Introduction, Pt. IV, pp. 71–97, written by Levy).
[21] See Meron (2005, pp. 178–81).

treatment afforded to foreigners engaging in trade, a long-standing practice of the Ottoman state, particularly with regard to submitting to the law of the land. Extra-territoriality had long been a coveted privilege in a state that systematically discriminated against non-Muslims. That was the context in which the great Italian Jewish families of Allatini, Modiano, Konfino, Misrachi, Morpurgo and others, together with the older Sephardic families of Almosnino, Aelion and others (some of which might still have older Italian roots) came to dominate the economic life of Thessaloniki in the 1900s.[22]

Table 6.1 offers insight into the relative weight of the three main communities of Thessaloniki in the city's commercial and industrial life in the 1900s.[23] It draws on the records of the Banque d'Orient in 1906 and reflects the bank's assessment of the wealth of its main customers in Thessaloniki and the broader region. As was already mentioned, the Banque d'Orient was established primarily by the National Bank of Greece, the leading commercial Bank of the Kingdom of Greece.[24] Its aim, at least in part, was to compete against the established private banks of Thessaloniki that were dominated by Jewish bankers.

The information casts a revealing light on Ottoman capitalism in the 1900s and helps shape the relevant analytical issues, especially when it is read together with the lists of traders and bankers of Thessaloniki in Chapter 5. The cut-off point of 20,000 Ottoman *lira* has been chosen arbitrarily for ease of presentation and marks a very substantial level of wealth at that time. It could have been lowered to 10,000, thus including many more names without essentially altering the picture. The names in Table 6.1 belonged to some of the richest people in Thessaloniki who sought the services of a powerful bank.

Three features stand out from the table. First, the richest industrialists and traders of Thessaloniki who transacted with the Banque d'Orient in the 1900s were Jews; Christians came second and Muslims a distant third. Within the dominant Jewish group, the Allatini and the Modiano were in a category entirely of their own. These two families were the rulers of Macedonian

---

[22] Ibid., pp. 198–219.
[23] The table is an adaptation of a longer original list by Hekimoglou (1997). The longer list would also have served our purposes, but the shorter one brings out the point more succinctly.
[24] The Banque d'Orient, or Trapeza Anatolis, had offices in Thessaloniki since 1905. The manager of the bank was Cleon Hadjilazaros, son of Pericles Hadjilazaros. Both the bank and Cleon Hadzilazaros played a major role in the economic and political affairs of Thessaloniki even after the end of Ottoman rule; see Hekimoglou (1991, pp. 27–8).

Table 6.1 Jewish, Christian and Muslim traders, industrialists and bankers in Thessaloniki, 1906

Estimated wealth Ottoman *lira*	Jews	Christians	Muslims
300,000 +	Fils Allatini S. Modiano L. Modiano		
80,000	E. Misrachi Fils Konfino	A. Abbott	
60,000	I. Bensussan N. A. Mallah Sides & Cie	C. Kyrtsis & Sons Longos, Kyrtsis & Tourpalis	A. Kapancı M. Kapancı
40,000	J. Benrubi Fils G. Errera	I. Hadjilazaros	
30,000	V. Fernandez Aellion J. & H Sallem J. Florentin & Cie Whital Saltiel & Cie Fils J. Sialom M. I. Sialom G. Almosnino Torres Misrachi & Cie	D. Angelakis Tourpalis Bros	
20,000	A. Amar S. Hassid	A. Sossidis	E.R. Rideb

Source: Adapted from Hekimoglou (1997). Wealth units in nominal Ottoman *lira*.

capitalism, exceptionally wealthy bankers, merchants and industrialists. Their footprint is immediately visible in the infrastructure of the contemporary city, well over a century after the end of Ottoman rule.

The Allatini had developed a dense skein of relations that extended across Western Europe and beyond.[25] In the early twentieth century the family possessed one of the largest fortunes in the Empire. They were related through marriages to the Modiano, the Fernandez, the Misrachi and the Torres, thus having interests in banking, brick manufacturing, tobacco trading, brewing, jute and, above all, in grain trading, flour milling, baking and attendant products. It was not surprising that Sultan Abdülhamid, the last of the Sultans to hold absolute power, who was deposed by the Young Turks and exiled to

---

[25] See Meron (2011, pp. 25–7).

Thessaloniki in 1909, lived out his period of exile in the Villa Allatini, a large mansion in the eastern outskirts of the city close to the massive Allatini plant by the waterfront. The Modiano, on the other hand, who have given their name to a covered market that still plays an important role in the life of Thessaloniki, were dominant in banking and urban real estate as well as being prominent in the buying and selling of *çiftlik* on the Macedonian plain.

The Allatini, the Modiano and the Jewish families that were close to them moved in an social ambience that could be described as *haute bourgeois* by the 1900s. They were strongly intermarrying, conservative in outlook, socializing in exclusive clubs, exceptionally well-connected to the Ottoman state, at home in the markets of Western Europe, familiar with international politics, interested in art and education. They had the accoutrements of an Ottoman bourgeois class, but with all the peculiarities of their religious and ethnic background. They also lived a world away from the great mass of the Jews of Thessaloniki – small shop-owners, workmen, petty hawkers and rough stevedores. The industrial and commercial capitalism that was ruled by the Allatini and the Modiano had sprung out of a community which in the 1830s and 1840s was desperately poor, inward looking and ill-educated. Furthermore, Thessaloniki Jews were determinedly urban, without a trace of agrarian involvement. The wage labour for the activities of the great Jewish capitalists came from the masses of the Jewish urban poor, the urban proletariat of Thessaloniki.

Second, the richest individuals among the Muslims in Table 6.1, the Kapancı, were *dönme*, that is ostensibly Muslim but in practice followers of the seventeenth-century Jewish mystic and self-proclaimed Messiah, Sabbatai Zevi. The *dönme* were viewed with suspicion by other Muslims, but still took the lead in pulling the Muslim community of Thessaloniki into the capitalist world that had begun to emerge in the second half of the nineteenth century.[26] The eclectic villas of the Kapancı family still stand proud amidst the blocks of flats in the eastern part of the contemporary city.

The Muslim upper class of Thessaloniki held a very prominent position in the city. Table 6.1 is misleading in this regard probably because the rich Muslims of Thessaloniki kept their distance from a bank with strong Greek connections. The

---

[26] *Dönme* means convert in general; however, it is typically and specifically used for the followers of Sabbatai Zevi. For a detailed account of the *dönme*, see Baer (2010).

true weight of the Muslim rich is revealed more clearly in the tables in Chapter 5, even if only with respect to traders and bankers. The Muslims derived much of their wealth and power from urban real estate and dominant landownership over the Macedonian plain. The dominance of Muslims in *çiftlik* holding was clearly demonstrated for the region of Mount Vermion in Chapter 4, and was even stronger elsewhere. Muslims were also able to draw wealth by retaining incomparable access to administrative and military positions in the Ottoman state.

Third, and perhaps most striking of all, the Christians in Table 6.1, with a single exception, were related to the area of Mount Vermion. Needless to say, there were also several wealthy Christians in the city, often drawing wealth from urban real estate, who did not appear on the list of the Banque d'Orient. The name on the list that was not associated with Mount Vermion belonged to Alfred Abbott, scion of the Abbott family, and the remnant of a bygone era. The Abbotts were representatives of the Levant Company in the eighteenth century, British nationals who had 'gone native' in Thessaloniki. They had made their money by rearing leeches for the domestic and foreign market, but in truth they were large landowners and moneylenders to the state and others.[27] The time of the Abbotts was well and truly gone by the 1900s as advanced industrial and commercial capitalism had taken root in the city.

The names of the rest of the Christians on the list were all related to emerging industrial and commercial capitalism in provincial Macedonia. They were mostly – but not entirely – provincial entrepreneurs who had cut their teeth in the textile business and had become wealthy and influential enough to operate in Thessaloniki. These capitalists were very different from the *haute bourgeoisie* of the Allatini and the Modiano, with the possible exception of Hadjilazaros and Angelakis who had long moved in the bourgeois circles of Thessaloniki. The provincial entrepreneurs on the list were first- or second-generation capitalists hailing from Christian peasant backgrounds in the area of Mount Vermion, as will be shown subsequently. The same also holds, incidentally, for the origins of Hadjilazaros. These entrepreneurs formed a capitalist layer that had emerged from the very depths of provincial Ottoman society. Moreover, the wage labour that set their enterprises in motion in the

---

[27] For a lively sketch of the Abbotts of Thessaloniki see Mazower (2004, pp. 156–9).

region of Mount Vermion was provided by workers who often still continued their agricultural activities.

It is immediately apparent from Table 6.1 that something extraordinary had happened in provincial Ottoman Macedonia in the second half of the nineteenth century. The agents of provincial capitalism who were active in Thessaloniki had a different social outlook from the Allatini and the Modiano. For one thing, they were typically connected to the domestic production of textiles in the upland areas of Mount Vermion. For another, they possessed far fewer international connections and were much less imbricated into the functioning of the Ottoman state than the Jewish bourgeoisie. Moreover, they had neither the time nor the social space to distance themselves from their humble roots by acquiring the refinements of the *haute bourgeoisie*, such as that was in Thessaloniki at the time. They were certainly bourgeois, but they had also remained provincial people of work, ruthlessly seeking profit, aggressive and ambitious. They were in direct competition with the Jewish capitalists of Thessaloniki, a contest that they were winning by the 1900s.

In light of this discussion, the remainder of this book focuses on the period of 1870–1912, which is essentially the high period of Ottoman industrial capitalism in Macedonia. The period could be usefully split in three allowing for a more structured examination. Specifically:

1. The period of 1870–90, which represented the emergence of industrial capitalism. Private industrial enterprises operating in a recognizably capitalist manner were established in textiles and other fields. Naoussa was the cradle of much of this activity, but Thessaloniki was the indisputable centre during this period.
2. The period of 1890–1902, which showed sustained expansion of capitalist industries in terms of both geographical area and capacity to produce. In provincial Macedonia industrial transformation spread from Naoussa to the surrounding areas.
3. The period of 1902–12, the last decade of Ottoman rule in the Balkans, which represented the peak of industrial growth, especially in the Macedonian provinces. Industrial capacity proliferated and enterprises began to form large concerns able to compete across the Empire.

6.3 Emergence of industrial capitalism, 1870–90

The yearbooks on Macedonia leave no doubt that manufacturing industry was on the ascendant in the *vilayet* of Thessaloniki after 1870. The first volume – for 1870 – devoted a mere two pages to manufacturing, mostly listing a variety of textiles manufactured within the *vilayet*. The *kaza* of Veroia and Edhessa produced linen towels, silk *hammam* sets, *şayak*, various types of socks and leather products; the towels of Veroia were, apparently, of the highest quality.[28] The products were transported to İstanbul and its environs, to Thessaloniki, and significantly, to the Kingdom of Greece. Later volumes indicate that much of the local textile production was based in Naoussa, and that Veroia had gradually lost its pre-eminence. According to the yearbooks, the *nahiye* of Naoussa had commercial relations with the Kingdom of Greece, to which it exported large quantities of *şayak*.

The contrast between the volume for 1870 and that for 1886 is instructive. Manufacturing production had reached a much higher level by 1886, and the compilers of the yearbooks seemed to have grasped the sector's significance. Thus, in 1886, the *kaza* of Veroia had several flour mills, three flour 'factories' and four textile looms, all of which were water-powered.[29] The four textile looms employed sixteen female workers and produced the famed towels of Veroia. The *kaza* of Edhessa had three 'factories' producing flour and soap, and fifty handlooms producing 7,500 metres of *şayak* annually.[30] The town also had several flour mills,[31] several *dink*,[32] and even a water-powered cotton gin.

Manufacturing in Naoussa was reported separately in the yearbook of 1886, which is in itself remarkable for such a small administrative unit as Naoussa.[33] It was noted that the river Arapitsa powered all the mills and 'factories' as it passed

---

[28] See SVS I, 1287 [1870]. In Ottoman terminology product quality came in three categories: *a'la* (highest quality), *evsat* (medium quality), *edna* (lowest quality). In the section on manufacturing the term *a'la* was reserved for the products of Veroia.

[29] See SVS IX, 1303 [1886].

[30] The annual production of *şayak* was around 10,000 *zerağ* (*arşın*), each of which was 0.757738 metres, taken here as 0.75 metre; each *zerağ* (0.75 metre) was sold for 3.5 *guruş*.

[31] Flour mills and flour factories were recorded separately in the archives. The difference probably stemmed from the size and the technology of the flour-making equipment. While flour mills used old technology and were typically modest in size, flour factories were much bigger and usually mechanized.

[32] A *dink* was a contraption for beating wool into felt which could be operated manually or powered by water; see Pakalın (1983, p. 452).

[33] See SVS IX, 1303 [1886]: p. 259.

through the town. Naoussa had a significant number of such establishments, considerably more than Edhessa and somewhat fewer than Veroia. In terms of textiles, the town produced şayak and cotton yarn. The latter was a novel entry in the yearbooks. It was the product of the Longos–Kyrtsis–Tourpalis spinning mill that had actually been established in 1874–5 but was noticed by the yearbook compilers only in 1886. The plant was built on the site of a watermill that had been founded in 1850 and was subsequently incorporated into the cotton mill complex. The establishment of this cotton mill was very much the beginning of textile industrialization in provincial Ottoman Macedonia.

The İstanbul archives contain a remarkable drawing of the original Longos–Kyrtsis–Tourpalis plant as part of an application by its owners, shown in Plate 3. The plant stands proudly in the foreground, a little downhill from the old watermill. The site is at some distance from the town which is faintly drawn on the higher ground, the minaret of its mosque clearly visible. It was a modest three-storey building, with a floor area of only 22.30×11.90 square metres and a height of 7 metres. The basic mode of operation is clear to see: running water was channelled to the watermill from some height using a visible wooden pipe (karouta, in Greek) thus setting the mill's wooden wheel in motion. After moving the wheel, the water flowed downhill and was split into two channels, one going into the cotton mill and the other bypassing it, probably as safety valve. The flow that entered the mill set its own (invisible) wooden turbine in motion. There would have been a complex system of cogs and belts translating the motion of the turbine into that of a central axle running across the mill. All cotton-spinning equipment would have been set in motion by the central axle through other belts. When the water flow came out of the cotton mill, the two channels were again joined up and the water flowed further downhill to be used for agricultural purposes.

The lead applicant for the plant was Demetrios Longos, a powerful and wealthy şayak trader with a dominant position in trading with the Kingdom of Greece. Figure 6.1 shows a photograph of Longos bearing a solemn mien and wearing 'Western' dress.

Modest as the original plant was, it represented a true marvel for its time. The spinning equipment had been bought from a recently failed mill in Pireaus in the Kingdom of Greece, whose owners had originally bought the machinery in Britain. The equipment had been sent by boat to Thessaloniki, and there

Figure 6.1 Demetrios Longos, *şayak* trader and industrialist of Naoussa
Source: Personal collection of Takis Baitsis.

were fifteen hundred spindles altogether.³⁴ It then had to be transported to the site at a time when there was probably not a single mile of hard-surface road in Macedonia. Oxcarts had to negotiate the muddy plain and the uphill tracks to Naoussa.

At the site the spindles were installed by a Greek engineer brought by the owners from Patras, the main city of the Peloponnese, which had witnessed rapid industrial development in the previous decades. The engineer also built the wooden turbine that was made to rotate by the falling water and thus generated the plant's fundamental motion.³⁵ In future years Greek engineers

---

³⁴ See Zografski (1967, p. 482).
³⁵ See Hadziiossif (1993, p. 40).

continued to repair and maintain the machinery and to transfer technical know-how.[36] They also probably provided training for factory workers. In an apposite remark, Stougiannakis called this factory 'an industrial Academy' at which engineers and others were trained.[37] In 1886 the mill's annual cotton yarn output was 65,000–80,000 kg, most of which was consumed in Macedonia.

The Longos–Kyrtsis–Tourpalis cotton mill in Naoussa was the first successful step in industrializing textile production in Macedonia. The pace of further industrialization in 1870–90 was, however, quite slow. A mere two cotton mills were further established during this period, both in Thessaloniki. The first was built in 1879 by the Saias brothers, using a steam engine for the fundamental motion, and employing three hundred workers, all of whom were Jewish. The second was founded in 1884 by Torres and Misrachi, who installed new machinery at the site of an existing plant; the factory was further enlarged in 1886. Female workers, mostly girls, some as young as six years of age, constituted three-quarters of the workforce of all Macedonian spinning mills.[38] Soon the two Thessaloniki mills employed eight hundred workers in total and had a much greater capacity than the modest mill of Longos–Kyrtsis–Tourpalis in Naoussa. Their Jewish founders had brought machinery from Accrington, the heart of spinning and weaving in Lancashire in Britain, and employed competent British managers to run the plants.[39] They were technically more advanced than the provincial mills relying on water power. Things would be very different in the longer term, however, as the provincial mills became more adept in the competitive struggle.

6.4 Advance of industrialization, 1890–1902

Gounaris considers 1888–9 to be the turning point in the industrial development of Macedonia, and 1888–1912 the 'take off' period for industrial production.[40] This is broadly right but it is more informative to split the 'take off' period in two.

[36] See Lapavitsas (2006, p. 677).
[37] See Stougiannakis (1911, p. 149).
[38] See Quataert (1993a, p. 47).
[39] See Gounaris (1993, pp. 135–7); Palairet (1993, p. 350).
[40] See Gounaris (1993, p. 139).

Figure 6.2 The plant of Longos–Tourpalis in Naoussa in the early twentieth century
Source: Private collection of Takis Baitsis.

During 1890–1902 industrialization became increasingly dynamic in Macedonia and especially in its provincial areas, preparing the ground for the rapid growth of the 1900s. For one thing, the three cotton mills that had already been established in Naoussa and Thessaloniki upgraded their capacity extensively during this period. Thus, the Longos–Kyrtsis–Tourpalis mill bore no comparison to the plant of 1874–5. A complex of Victorian buildings had swallowed up the modest original building, as is clear in Figure 6.2. The mill was now a major undertaking that did not only spin yarn but also wove cloth. Furthermore, Kyrtsis was no longer a shareholder.

Moreover, three new cotton mills were founded during this period in the interior of Macedonia: one in Naoussa, one in Edhessa and another one, towards the end of the period, in Veroia. All were effectively spurred by Naoussa industrialists, confirming the leading role of the little town. To be more specific, the yearbook for 1893 tells us that the number of mills in Naoussa had increased to two, and we know from Greek sources that the new mill belonged to Bilis and Tsitsis, established in 1891.[41] This mill was also

---

[41] See Lapavitsas (2006, p. 700) and SVS XII, 1311 [1893].

Figure 6.3 The plant of Bilis–Tsitsis in Naoussa in the early twentieth century
Source: Private collection of Takis Baitsis.

built on the site of a pre-existing watermill, and initially employed a limited complement of workers, similarly to Longos–Kyrtsis–Tourpalis in its early days.[42] By the early 1900s, however, it comprised a sizeable set of Victorian buildings, shown in Figure 6.3. The artificially created water drop, the wooden pipe channeling the water flow to the plant, and the old watermill are clearly visible in the picture. The key features and basic operation of the plant are also accurately depicted in a remarkable old drawing shown in Plate 4.

The true breakthrough in provincial industrialization during this period, however, was the establishment of a cotton mill in Edhessa. The yearbook for 1897 mentions a textile mill in Edhessa without giving further details, although it is clear that it was the Tsitsis mill.[43] The enterprise was established by the Tsitsis family from Naoussa in 1895, using water power, employing five hundred workers and possessing equipment of high quality.[44] It was a large plant with considerable capacity in spinning and weaving and able to withstand comparison with the average spinning plant of Western Europe at the time. Its size is evident in the grainy postcard in Figure 6.4, the only

[42] See SVS XII, 1311 [1893].
[43] See SVS XV, 1315 [1897].
[44] See Lapavitsas (2006, p. 669).

Figure 6.4 The Tsitsis plant in Edhessa in the early twentieth century
Source: Private collection of Takis Baitsis.

evidence that remains of what was probably one of the largest textile plants in the Ottoman Empire.

The real inspiration behind the Edhessa plant appears to have been Georgios Kyrtsis, a restless and entrepreneurial man, with penetrating eyes and a strong chin, shown in bourgeois attire in Figure 6.5. The Kyrtsis family hailed from a small village on Mount Vermion but were established in Naoussa in the early nineteenth century and had some roots in Edhessa. Kyrtsis was familiar with the abundant water supply of Edhessa and understood its potential. He proceeded to acquire suitably located land, which the locals sold to him for a pittance thinking that they were taking advantage of the romantic fool. Apparently, it was commonly said in Edhessa that 'Mad Kyrtsis came and bought all the rocky cliffs'.[45] Little did they know. Kyrtsis became one of the richest people in Macedonia and eventually a paragon of Thessaloniki society, as was shown in Table 6.1.

---

[45] The history of the Kyrtsis family is presumably summed up in a curious publication, part novel, part metaphor, and replete with Christian moralizing, written by Ch. Petridis in 1904 and republished in 1994.

Figure 6.5 Georgios Kyrtsis, industrialist and merchant of Naoussa and Edhessa
Source: Private collection of Takis Baitsis.

In 1895 Kyrtsis had a clocktower built in Naoussa to mark the astonishing transformation that had taken place in recent years. The clock still rings the passage of time today, setting a capitalist order to the life of the town, exactly as he had intended it. Figure 6.6 shows the clocktower, material evidence of Ottoman modernity, next to the *konak* of the mayor, the official site of the Ottoman administration. The *konak* is no longer extant, but the offices of the contemporary Greek local authority are housed in a building on the same site. In the Balkans the geographical sites of political power can be as persistently continuous as those of religion.

It should be noted, nonetheless, that Edhessa was far from an obvious place for industrial capitalism to spread after sinking roots in Naoussa. The

Figure 6.6 The Kyrtsis clocktower and the *konak* of the mayor of Naoussa
Source: Private collection of Takis Baitsis.

yearbooks show that in the 1890s it was the least developed of the three towns of Mount Vermion in terms of commerce, manufacturing and agriculture. However, it had two major advantages in 1895. First, it possessed abundant supplies of fast-flowing water. The know-how of harnessing water power was easily available to Macedonian cotton spinners by the 1890s. Second, it had acquired a reliable means of long-distance transport as the Thessaloniki–Bitola railway line had opened to traffic in 1894.[46]

---

[46] See Gounaris (1993, p. 53).

The building of Ottoman railways was an exercise steeped in foreign political pressure, poor assessment of construction costs and detailed calculation of the political and strategic benefits to the state. Issawi tells us that for every railway line constructed there were several proposals submitted for consideration by the Ottoman state, with widely differing motives for investors, and 'generally, the government seems to have got the worst of the bargain'.[47] It was hardly surprising that the economic benefits of the railway lines, especially in Macedonia, were generally lower than what they might have been. The Thessaloniki-Bitola line was notorious for positioning stations a long way from the major settlements, and thus limiting the usefulness of the railway. This was due to the standard contract between the Ottoman state and the railway builders, which typically charged the state for each kilometre of rail. Quite naturally the state tried to minimize the cost by drawing a route for the railway line that was as direct as possible. Thus, 'Most of the major towns in both central and western Macedonia lay at a considerable distance from the railway line; the stations of Veroia, Naousa, Florina and Giannitsa were reported to be respectively 25 minutes, 2 hours, 1,5 hour and 2,5 hours away from the corresponding towns.'[48]

Fortunately for Edhessa its train station was situated near the centre of the town, thus giving it a considerable cost advantage. The impact on the economic life of the town was felt immediately.[49] The station of Naoussa, on the other hand, was a long way from the town necessitating a long uphill trip in an ox- or horse-drawn cart or coach – an *araba* or a *talika*. Even so, the station – a small building in broadly Central European style – had a major impact on economic activity and was a source of pride, evident in the posture of those standing in its yard in Figure 6.7.

In contrast to Edhessa, the spreading of textile industrialization to Veroia is less easy to ascertain from the extant sources. Gounaris states that the first cotton mill of Veroia was established in 1902 by Sossidis and Faik; it became known as the Vermion mill and employed three hundred workers.[50] However,

---

[47] See Issawi (1980, pp. 194–5).
[48] See Gounaris (1993, p. 53).
[49] The yearbook for 1904 states that 'With the establishment of railways, the centre of Edhessa has been developing and prospering day by day.' (SVS XVIII, 1322 [1904], p. 425)
[50] See Gounaris (1993, p. 140).

Figure 6.7 The railway station of Naoussa (*Ağustos*)
Source: Private collection of Takis Baitsis.

the first relevant reference in the yearbooks was recorded in 1904, at which time, apparently, a factory was under construction in Veroia but had not yet commenced operations.[51] The yearbook for 1906 stated that an establishment, referred to as a spinning mill and situated in the upper part of the town, had actually started to function, while yet another factory was under construction in the lower part of the town.[52] Both plants used fast-flowing water to generate power. It is likely that the former mill was that of Sossidis and Faik, mentioned by Gounaris, while the latter was the mill of Hadjinikolaki Bros. founded in 1907.

According to local oral tradition, the mills of Veroia were established partly due to the intervention of entrepreneurs from Naoussa.[53] The Ottoman archives confirm this oral tradition. An application by Sossidis and Faik was indeed submitted in 1903 with the intention of starting the first cotton mill in Veroia.[54] The plan was to establish the mill on the founders' own property, a certain *Noriçe-i Bala çiftlik* in an area called *Mağaraaltı* (literally, below the

[51] See SVS XVIII, 1322 [1904].
[52] Ibid.
[53] See Lapavitsas (2006, p. 670).
[54] BOA. ŞD.1220/42; BOA. İ.RSM.18/33; BOA. BEO.2219/166390; BOA. ŞD.MLK.74/2; BOA. İ.TNF.21/21; BOA. BEO.3745/280811; BOA. DH.MUİ.92-1/26

cave). The application was approved in the same year and the owners included *Todori Bili* (Theodoros Bilis), who was probably related to the Bilis family of industrialists from Naoussa. In 1910 the enterprise added a further plant to the original mill, and the relevant documents again mentioned Theodoros Bilis.

Athanassios Sossidis belonged to a Vlach family hailing from the mountains to the west of Vermion but living in Veroia. Table 6.1 in this chapter shows that Sossidis was one of the largest merchants of Thessaloniki in the 1900s, as well as one of the bankers in Table 5.3 in Chapter 5. Faik Hoca was a Muslim, and indeed the only Muslim to appear on the list of textile equity holders in provincial Macedonia, and among the few to enter the field of industrialization altogether in Ottoman Macedonia. His participation is a remarkable event, but it is not at all clear why Sossidis went into business with Faik. Maybe Faik was the original owner of the land for the plant, or perhaps was a local notable whose respected name would helpfully expedite the application process.

The Hadjinikolaki mill was significantly smaller than the Sossidis–Faik mill. The Hadjinikolaki were a Veroia family who owned land and also possessed a sizeable water-powered flourmill. They entered industrial textile production in 1907 after being persuaded of the wisdom of the move by the Kyrtsis family.[55] Documents from the archives state that indeed the second textile mill in Veroia was founded by the Hadjinikolaki brothers.[56] On this score too, there is little doubt that the emergence of industrial capitalism in Veroia mills received a boost from Naoussa.

One final point that is worth mentioning is that the historical trajectory of domestic and other manufacturing in Veroia was peculiar, in view especially of the town's pre-eminence in traditionally produced textiles. Once the influx of cheap European textiles had begun in the 1830s, producers in Veroia started buying British yarn to produce the traditional textiles that were 'much esteemed all over Turkey'.[57] Maintaining production by using cheaper imported yarn was a common survival strategy for traditional textile producers across the Empire. Nonetheless, by the end of the nineteenth century traditional Veroia textiles were annihilated in the Ottoman markets, as is clearly stated

---

[55] See Roupa and Hekimoglou (2004, pp. 565–6).
[56] BOA. ŞD.62/50; BOA. TFR.I.MKM.19/1823; BOA. ŞD.2055/12; BOA. İ.RSM.30/50; BOA. BEO.3266/244897; BOA. ŞD.1224/70.
[57] See Quataert (1993a, p. 96).

in the yearbook for 1890 and for several subsequent years.[58] It is remarkable that the traditional producers of Veroia survived the period of fierce foreign competition in the 1840s, 1850s and 1860s, when loss of Ottoman capacity was the order of the day, only to decline rapidly in the 1890s. It raises the question of whether the decline was due to the rise of the domestic textile industries. Unfortunately there is no way of answering it with the available evidence.

6.5 Peak of industrial growth, 1902–12

During the last decade of Ottoman rule in the Balkans industrial capitalism assumed sizeable dimensions in a variety of fields, most prominently in textiles. It is legitimate to consider Macedonia as possessing the beginnings of an industrial economy in 1902–12, even if agriculture remained the dominant economic activity. Naoussa capitalists were at the forefront of industrialization, starting six new textile plants during this decade, three of which were in cotton and the remaining three in wool, a new field of industrial activity. They also successfully transcended the narrow limits of their local region and became active in Thessaloniki, the home ground of Jewish capital. It is notable that no more textile plants were established by Jewish industrialists in Thessaloniki during this period.

Ottoman capitalism seemed to have navigated several difficult straits by 1902–12. A network of banking and financial facilities had been established in Thessaloniki; technical and operational know-how of industrial production had improved; the state's attitude and policies had turned in favour of the industrialists; and there was an overall upswing in economic activity in the *vilayet* of Thessaloniki. That period came to a sudden end when the First Balkan War broke out in 1912.

6.5.1 Cotton industrialists expand in Mount Vermion and diversify to Thessaloniki

A new cotton-spinning mill commenced operations in Naoussa in 1903, the Goutas–Karatzias plant, with substantial capacity.[59] The Goutas family were

---

[58] See SVS X, 1307 [1890].
[59] See Lapavitsas (2006, p. 700).

merchants who had moved to Naoussa from the surrounding hills after the city's sack in 1822. In the second half of the nineteenth century they had made a fortune in Egypt by trading in a variety of commodities, and had considered building a cotton-spinning plant for years before taking the actual step in 1903. Karatzias was an experienced şayak trader related to Goutas by marriage. The international outlook of the owners but also the emerging ambitious perspective of the capitalists of Mount Vermion are apparent in the publicity for the new plant, shown in Plate 5. Hermes, the god protector of commerce, spreads boxes of cotton yarn across the globe, in a poster in several languages printed in Leipzig in Germany.

According to Greek sources, a further cotton mill was also built in Naoussa by the families of Lapavitsas and Kokkinos but did not actually start operations.[60] The Ottoman archives and some communal documents provide further information on this mill, as shall be seen in the next chapter. Sometime after the end of the First World War the Tsitsis family furnished the plant with new machinery and started to operate it under the name of Gr. Tsitsis & Co. It had substantial capacity but cannot be fully included in the industrial base of the Ottoman economy since it started operations only after the First World War.

It is worth noting that, according to the final yearbook – for 1907 – Naoussa capitalists had obtained permission to build a further textile factory in 1906, although its construction had not yet started.[61] The yearbook also indicates that permission for one more plant had been requested and was pending. This information probably relates to woollen mills, as will be shown in both the next section and the following chapter by using Greek sources and the Ottoman archives. Two points, however, are immediately apparent. First, there was a lot more industrial activity in the textile business than is suggested by the number of actually established plants. Second, the role of the state and its relations with the nascent Macedonian industrialists were of critical importance in obtaining permits and developing industrial capacity.

In Edhessa a new cotton mill was also established in 1907 by Lappas and Hadjidimoulas, two industrialists from Naoussa, under the name of Lappas &

---

[60] Ibid., p. 682.
[61] See SVS XX, 1325 [1907].

Co. Similarly to the Tsitsis mill, there is not much information available about the new plant in Edhessa in Ottoman sources. It appears to have been installed as a cotton-spinning and weaving concern and possessed a significant capacity in 1912.[62] Even more more important than the new plant, however, was the capacity upgrade of the existing Tsitsis mill in Edhessa which took place during this period. By 1912 the mill held 16,500 spindles, and also possessed weaving capacity.[63] Finally, a new textile mill was established in Veroia in 1907, the Hadjinikolaki mill, which was already mentioned above.

During this period Jewish industrialists in Thessaloniki seemed to have been constrained by high energy and labour costs. These problems, however, did not prevent Naoussa industrialists from expanding their activities in Thessaloniki. Thus, in 1910 Tourpalis founded a cotton mill in Thessaloniki with significant capacity.[64] Further information on this plant from the Ottoman archives will be given in the following chapters.

The opening of the Tourpalis mill in Thessaloniki was a noteworthy event since it symbolized the confident presence of Naoussa industrialists in the capital of Macedonia. In the 1900s they emerged as a force in Thessaloniki, particularly active in real estate and in retail/wholesale commercial trading. The ever-present Kyrtsis had already moved his activities and residence in Thessaloniki by the end of the 1890s and was actively engaging in new businesses. He came to possess a substantial commercial building, the *Kirci Han*, built partly in the traditional manner of an Ottoman *han* and thus providing sleeping quarters for travellers. In reality it was one of the first modern shopping malls of the Ottoman Empire. It still stands in the historic market area of Thessaloniki, a neoclassical building with ornate metallic gates, in a rather decrepit state despite a half-hearted attempt at restoration. Equally active in commerce and real estate in Thessaloniki were the Tourpalis family who began to acquire substantial property in the city already in the 1880s and built the *Turpali Han*, a major centre at the heart of the commercial area.

Among the more remarkable areas of diversification by Naoussa capitalists in Thessaloniki was commercial ice-making and brewing.[65] The field was

---

[62] See Lapavitsas (2006, p. 669).
[63] Ibid., p. 682.
[64] Ibid., p. 670; Gounaris (1993, p. 141) gives 1909 as the date of establishment.
[65] See Lapavitsas (2006, p. 684).

dominated by the 'Olympos' firm established in 1892 or 1893 by the Jewish families of Misrachi and Fernandez in close collaboration with the Allatini.[66] Longos, Tsitsis and Platsoukas, joined by the inevitable Kyrtsis, branched out and, together with the family of Georgiadis who originated in Anatolia, established a competitor, the Naoussa Brewery.[67] The Brewery also engaged in large-scale commercial production of ice, a vital commodity at a time of non-existent refrigeration.[68] The family of Platsoukas hailed from the hills far west of Naoussa; they were long-standing *şayak* traders, industrialists and sizeable *çiftlik* owners, as was shown in Chapter 4. The concern that was thus established, 'Brasserie Naoussa', competed with 'Olympos' until well after the end of Ottoman rule and the two breweries eventually merged in the 1920s. For several decades the pinnacle of bourgeois dining in Thessaloniki was at 'Olympos-Naoussa', a formal restaurant at the headquarters of the brewery by the seafront.

The arrival of provincial entrepreneurs from Mount Vermion in Thessaloniki was an event for the Greek community, which was numerically small and the weakest of the three main ethnic groups. The industrialists and merchants from the provinces came at a time when economic activity in the city was dominated by Jewish capitalists and helped alter the balance of economic and political power in the city. An echo of that event survived in the popular lore of Thessaloniki for generations after the end of Ottoman rule.

6.5.2 Expanding into woollens

Macedonian industrialization commenced in cotton spinning, but its underpinnings were in domestically produced woollen textiles. Traditional woollen fabrics in the Ottoman context came mostly in two types, *şayak* and *aba*, the former preferred by the better off social layers, and the latter by the poorer strata as well as being in strong demand for army clothes. Until the

---

[66] See Meron (2011, p. 25).
[67] One prominent member of the Georgiadis family, Kostakis Georgiadis, had served in the provincial council of the *vilayet* of Thessaloniki for more than twenty years; see Dimitriadis (2014, p. 67).
[68] See Roupa and Hekimoglou (2004, pp. 118–27). This work relies in good part on reminiscences and oral records by industrial family members and thus suffers from all attendant problems. However, used with care, it can shed much light on obscure aspects of Ottoman industrialization.

end of the nineteenth century Bulgaria produced a large part of the *aba* and somewhat less of the *şayak* consumed in the Empire.

The core strength of textile production in Thessaloniki *vilayet* was also in woollens. The yearbooks stress that *aba* was the most important textile product of the *vilayet*. The *kaza* of Gevgelija (*Gevgeli*) to the north of the city of Thessaloniki acted as the centre of *aba* production primarily for gendarmerie and army clothes.[69] Moreover, throughout the nineteenth century the production of *şayak* in the Balkans showed greater resilience than domestic cotton textiles, not least because it faced far less severe foreign competition. According to Quataert: 'Thanks to this regional speciality, most local producers avoided confrontations in cotton cloth making, the competitive industry par excellence of the age.'[70] Nonetheless, towards the end of the nineteenth century, the early centres of woollen cloth production in Macedonia faced severe decline.

Naoussa was well known for its specialization in *şayak* production, and there is evidence of extensive wool processing in the town already in the 1830s.[71] The yearbooks indicated that Naoussa was the leading producer of the highest quality *şayak* in the *vilayet* of Thessaloniki.[72] Other local producers, such as the Vlachs of Veroia, produced only low-grade *şayak* that was good for their own consumption. The yearbook of 1890 explicitly stated that the leading producers of *aba* and *şayak* were the towns of Gotse Deltsev (*Nevrokob*), Naoussa and Gevgelija.[73] In 1894 the annual *şayak* production in Naoussa was estimated at 150,000 metres, a large part of which was sent to the Kingdom of Greece.[74] The last yearbook – in 1907 – noted that *şayak* from Naoussa was known for its quality and success in various markets.[75] It is clear that traditionally manufactured *şayak* was capable of coexisting with mechanized cotton yarn and cloth for decades.

An attempt to mechanize wool production in Macedonia appears to have been made in 1904, when industrialists from Serres asked permission to

---

[69] See, for instance, SVS X, 1307 [1890], p. 231.
[70] See Quataert (1993a, p. 49).
[71] See Lapavitsas (2006, p. 668).
[72] See SVS IX, 1303 [1886], p. 259; SVS X, 1307 [1890], p. 225.
[73] SVS X, 1307 [1890], p. 227.
[74] SVS XIII, 1312 [1894].
[75] See SVS XX, 1325 [1907].

acquire fulling and carding equipment from an old state factory in Sliven, Bulgaria, with the aim of building a *şayak* factory.⁷⁶ According to Palairet, the first substantial woollen factory was set up in Thessaloniki in 1906 to produce *şayak* for the Ottoman army, while yet another factory was founded in 1911, also in Thessaloniki, to produce army clothes.⁷⁷ However, this information is uncertain, at least according to Quataert and early Greek sources.⁷⁸ Mechanized wool production in Macedonia seems to have commenced in Naoussa in 1907, as is shown below. Indeed, the first attempt to establish a woollen cloth factory was also made in Naoussa as early as the 1870s, though it never came to fruition, as will be shown in subsequent chapters. The first woollen cloth factory in Thessaloniki was actually opened in 1908, using Bielefeld looms and specializing in dyeing and finishing *şayak* for the Ottoman state. Furthermore, a small Thessaloniki mill that was founded in 1911, a joint-stock enterprise financed by Jewish capital, failed almost immediately.

It seems clear that the first mechanized woollen mill in Macedonia was founded by Hadjilazaros and Angelakis in Naoussa in 1907, shown in Figure 6.8. The size of the plant is apparent from the photograph, as is its proximity to the river that had to be crossed by a bridge to reach the plant from the centre of the town. Further details of this important enterprise will be considered in the next chapter, suffice it to note that the concern joined together two already existing manually operated mills and had a large production capacity.⁷⁹ In 1912 the factory produced 100,000 metres of woollen cloth per annum, much of it supplying the Ottoman gendarmerie.⁸⁰ It was probably the largest woollen mill in the Ottoman Empire and technically the most advanced. The mill was converted into a joint-stock company in 1911 and came to be known as ERIA, with an annual production of 200,000 metres of woollen cloth.⁸¹

In 1909, two years after the establishment of the Hadjilazaros–Angelakis mill, a second woollen mill was established in Naoussa. Known as the Pehlivanos–Lanaras mill, it was the town's smallest mechanized factory. This mill produced narrow *şayak* with a width of 0.33 metre, employed

---

⁷⁶ See Palairet (1993, p. 348).
⁷⁷ Ibid.
⁷⁸ See Quataert (1993a, p. 90).
⁷⁹ According to Lapavitsas (2006, p. 700); Quataert's (1993a, p. 90) figures are similar.
⁸⁰ BOA. DH.ID.83-2/7.
⁸¹ See EIHN (1997).

Figure 6.8 The Hadjilazaros–Angelakis (ERIA) plant in Naoussa in the early twentieth century

Source: Private collection of Takis Baitsis.

seventy-five workers and its annual production was 90,000 metres.[82] The Pehlivanos–Lanaras mill provides the strongest evidence in Macedonia to support Dobb's view that industrial capitalism emerges through the 'small' man accumulating capital and controlling production. More information on this mill will be given in the next chapter but it should be noted that the person who stood out among its founders was Christodoulos Lanaras. As his surname immediately suggests in Greek, Lanaras was a carder working for the established *şayak* merchants and industrialists of Naoussa. The diligent carder was able to accumulate capital that was subsequently invested in building the small mechanized establishment of Pehlivanos-Lanaras just before the end of Ottoman rule.

During the 1900s Lanaras was on good terms with the armed bands fighting in the name of Greek irredentism in Macedonia. When the local area was incorporated into the Greek state, the Lanaras family translated their credentials into a fortune. In the interwar years they built a great textile mill

---

[82] See Lapavitsas (2006, p. 700).

in Athens mostly to supply the Greek armed forces, while also maintaining substantial capacity in Naoussa. The family became the industrial patrons of Naoussa and maintained a large textile capacity in the town representing a significant proportion of European output in cotton yarn until the late 1990s, when the Lanaras corporation finally folded.

According to Greek sources, in 1911–12 a further small woollen cloth factory was established in Thessaloniki, the Tourpalis–Kazazis mill. The capacity of this plant was very limited, and it does not substantially alter the picture of woollen production in Macedonia.[83] The bulk of the capital appears to have been provided by a member of the Tourpalis family, but the driving force seems to have been the Kazazis family, hailing from Bitola and active in textiles in Thessaloniki already in the 1900s, especially in the production of *fez*, the characteristic Ottoman headwear of the period. The Kazazis family were also partners of the extremely rich Muslim *dönme* family of the Kapancı – appearing in Table 6.1 – who effectively controlled the production of *fez* (the traditional headdress of men in the late Ottoman period) in Macedonia. Kazazis went into partnership with the Tourpalis family to form the small woollen plant in 1911–12. They remained active in the business world of Thessaloniki for decades.

In sum, at the end of Ottoman rule in 1912 Naoussa capitalists had successfully begun to mechanize woollen cloth production in the European part of the Empire, while the traditional manufacturing of *şayak* continued strongly in the town. They controlled roughly 80 per cent of the horsepower and 90 per cent of the employment in the mechanized woollen cloth sector in the European part of the Empire.[84] The coexistence of mechanized woollen cloth and hand-made *şayak* output was due to the high quality of the latter but also to weak competition from foreign imports. Woollen producers seemed to have secured distinct niches in the Ottoman and wider markets: the Hadjilazaros–Angelakis mill produced cloth for the gendarmerie; the Lanaras–Pehlivanos mill produced narrow *şayak* for a variety of uses; the non-mechanized looms produced *şayak* for traditional clothing.

---

[83] Ibid. See also Roupa and Hekimoglou (2004, pp. 142–51).
[84] See Lapavitsas (2006, pp. 670–1).

6.6 The reasons for the ascendancy of the provincial cotton mills

The cotton mills of Mount Vermion emerged in the early 1870s in conditions that were not exactly propitious to industrial growth: communications, transport, financial services, and even state support for industry left a lot to be desired in the region. Thessaloniki had clear advantages in all these fields, even if industrialized cotton spinning in the city had begun a little later than in Naoussa. Furthermore, the Jewish entrepreneurs were more able to secure tax exemptions and other favourable treatment from the Ottoman state, allowing both the Saias and Torres–Misrachi mills to upgrade their capacity soon after their foundation in the late 1870s and early 1880s.[85]

The provincial mills were initially obliged to concentrate in spinning lower quality thick yarn because such output was less demanding technologically and faced less severe foreign and domestic competition, particularly in the local rural markets. Palairet was right to argue that 'through their advantageous access to cheap raw materials and labour' rural mills could match the growing demand of rural markets and thus 'delivered most of their output to the peasant handlooms'.[86] However, he was less right to state that 'there was little incentive for the spinning mills to integrate into weaving'. By the 1900s the rural mills had moved into weaving and they were winning the competitive struggle with Thessaloniki mills as well as standing up to imports.

During the first two decades of industrialization, the 1870s and 1880s, the provincial industrialists had a rather marginal impact on the operations of Thessaloniki mills. According to the yearbook for 1886 the Longos–Kytrsis–Tourpalis mill had an annual production of roughly 80,000 kilograms; the combined annual production of the two mills in Thessaloniki at that time stood as 450,000 kilograms.[87] This vast difference in output is consistent with the employment figures for the 1870s: eighty for Naoussa versus eight hundred for Thessaloniki. The first mill in Naoussa might have been a remarkable achievement for the little town but it remained decidedly modest for many

---

[85] See Gounaris (1993, pp. 136–9).
[86] See Palairet (1993, p. 350).
[87] Ibid.

years. Even in the 1890s the provincial mills managed to produce only very coarse yarn sold mainly in local markets. The wider markets of Macedonia, but also those of Albania, Bulgaria, Serbia, Anatolia and Greece were the terrain of the mills of Thessaloniki.

This striking disparity was due to continuing favourable conditions for Thessaloniki mills. The city was at the centre of markets, finance and transport in Macedonia, offering major advantages to capitalist investors especially prior to the construction of the railways. The industrialists of Thessaloniki, for instance, were able to meet demand for cotton yarn at Edirne in Thrace, where cloth weaving had remained very active, the cost of their yarn being a third less than that of equivalent English yarn.[88] The predominance of Thessaloniki mills was, however, unlikely to last. The provincial mills had several inherent advantages that would prove telling in the medium term, assuming that their owners had a modicum of capitalist entrepreneurial ability. As it turned out, they had an abundance of it.

The first and crucial advantage of the provincial mills was low cost of labour which will be discussed further in Chapter 8. Suffice it to say that the wages paid in the provinces were around a third of those paid in Thessaloniki.[89] Workers in the rural areas were able to combine industrial with agricultural work, a feature of labour that persisted for decades in the region of Mount Vermion. Moreover, the mills of the interior typically slowed down when the water flow became weaker in the summer, allowing time for agricultural work. The provincial workforce contained a very high proportion of women and children, as was also the case for Thessaloniki mills. The typical provincial Macedonian worker of the early period was a young girl from the surrounding villages working for a short period of time before getting married. The provincial labourers were less dependent on industrial wages than the Jewish workers in Thessaloniki.

Worker organization was also much weaker in the provinces compared to Thessaloniki. The great strikes that took place in Thessaloniki in the 1900s and resulted in substantial wage increases never occurred in the provinces. But there is no doubt that conflict between capital and labour had also emerged in the provinces, leading to remarkable forms of organization and political

---

[88] See Quataert (1993a, p. 97).
[89] Ibid., p. 169.

activity, as will be shown in Chapter 8. Note also that towards the end of the nineteenth century the growth in cash crops began to absorb labour in agricultural work. To attract and keep labour power, mill owners in Naoussa and Edhessa were forced to build workers' housing and to improve working conditions, for instance, by providing meals.[90]

A further cost advantage of the mills of Mount Vermion was relying on water power which, although closely regulated by the state, was practically free. The contrast with Thessaloniki mills that relied on coal to generate steam power was sharp. An added factor was the relative cheapness of land in the provinces, together with the ability of the industrialists to secure access to land that was suitable for using the flow of water. In the summer, when textile operations slowed down, the plants switched to milling flour thus further reducing their average operating costs.[91] Last, but not least, the opening of the Thessaloniki–Bitola railway line in 1894 decisively reduced transport costs for both the inputs and the output of the provincial mills.

In the 1870s and 1880s growing demand from rural areas absorbed the bulk of the provincial output. At the same time segmented demand by low income strata, including in urban areas, took most of the output of Thessaloniki mills. However, things began to change dramatically after 1890 as 'the home market was only lightly protected' and the domestic textile industry came under pressure.[92] Renewed import pressure meant that the cost and other advantages enjoyed by provincial mills proved telling in competition with Thessaloniki mills.

In the 1900s the inland mills emerged victorious. During 1891–1907 annual inland output rose from 800,000 to 2.9 million lbs. (323,000 kilograms to 1,315,000 kilograms), while Thessaloniki output fell from 3 million to 1.5 million lbs. (1,361,000 kg. to 680,000 kg.) of cotton yarn.[93] Thessaloniki mills faced profound difficulties across the full range of their markets, including competition from other Ottoman producers. Thus, when the *Yedikule* mill in İstanbul began to spin coarse yarn, it helped drive Thessaloniki producers out of the Bulgarian market, forcing the Saias mill to suspend operations.[94] In 1901 the Saias mill was actually shut down for several years, re-opening

---

[90] Ibid., p. 48.
[91] Ibid., p. 46.
[92] See Palairet (1993, p. 350).
[93] Ibid. and Gounaris (1993, p. 145).
[94] See Palairet (1993, p. 350).

later in the decade under the name of *Nouvelle Filature de Salonique* with 350 workers.[95] The bankruptcy of the company was made inevitable by the financial difficulties confronting its operations.[96] The output of Thessaloniki mills recovered strongly in 1907–12, but the output of the provincial mills continued to rise powerfully during the same period.

The ascendancy of the provincial mills was apparent in the expansion of their horsepower and employment. The Longos–Kyrtsis–Tourpalis mill had started operations in 1875 with 16 horsepower and 80 workers; in 1912 it had 270 horsepower and 270 workers.[97] By the same date the Bilis–Tsitsis mill had increased its capacity to 148 horsepower and 160 workers. Even the Goutas–Karatzias mill, which had started in 1903 and possessed excess capacity from the beginning – deploying only 200 of its 500 horsepower – had an upgrade in 1906. In 1895 the Tsitsis mill in Edhessa had an initial complement of 500 workers and subsequently upgraded its capacity. The Sossidis and Faik mill in Veroia doubled its capacity between 1903 and 1910, as its owners effectively built another factory within the existing premises.[98]

The provincial mills had also vastly improved the quality of their output by the 1900s. In 1874–5 the Longos–Kyrtsis–Tourpalis plant was capable of producing only the heaviest yarn to use in weaving coarse cotton cloth domestically. At the end of Ottoman rule all the provincial mills produced yarn of considerably higher grade (4–24) and some even produced reasonably high grade (32).[99] Even so, all Macedonian mills operated at the lower end of the market, facing tough competition from imports of British and particularly

---

[95] Gounaris (1993, p. 142).
[96] Akarli (2001, p. 292) describes the bankruptcy as follows: 'In 1896, the Saias family lost 1,000,000 francs upon the collapse of the Karamanos Bank in Marseilles, which administered the financial transactions of the family in Europe. Subsequently, the family started extracting capital from the cotton mill to meet its outstanding financial obligations and deliberately forced the management of the company into growing indebtedness. Under the circumstances, the factory management found it difficult to meet current expenses, about all the cost of the coal and cotton used in the mill. Eventually the firm went bankrupt, and a consortium of Jewish Bankers took the company over and started operations in 1907, under a new joint stock company named *Nouvelle Filature*.'
[97] Capacity and employment estimates have been compiled from Lapavitsas (2006), Gounaris (1993), Quataert (1994a, 1994b, 2014), the Ottoman yearbooks (SVS) and the archives. There are various inconsistencies in the data from the different sources, and thus some informed guesswork has been unavoidable.
[98] BOA. ŞD.MLK.74/2; BOA.İ.TNF.21/21; BOA. BEO.3745/280811; BOA. DH. MUİ. 92-1/26.
[99] See Lapavitsas (2006, p. 682). The lower the classification number of a cotton yarn, the fewer the standard lengths of fibre required to make a pound of weight, and hence the thicker and coarser the yarn. Higher grade yarn would be 40–80.

Italian yarn in the 4–10 range. By the 1900s the provincial mills appeared to have seen off their British competitors, though Italian producers were a different proposition altogether.

The triumph of the mills of the interior in the 1900s is evident in the splendid piece of commercial publicity produced by the Longos–Tourpalis mill (Kyrtsis had left by then) shown in Plate 6. The advertisement was multilingual, as was only appropriate in the Ottoman context (note, however, the absence of English as French was the *lingua franca* of the time). It depicted the expanded plant fairly accurately, while conveying a spirit of industrial solidity and optimism.

Nevertheless, in the 1900s Macedonian cotton mills also faced severe problems of raw cotton supply as the crop often failed, there were frequent global shortages, and local producers switched to more profitable tobacco.[100] The provincial mills developed survival strategies which showed how far they had matured during the preceding four decades. To control cotton supplies, in 1911–12 six of the provincial mills combined in two syndicates, with roughly 41,500 spindles. The cartels aimed to reduce production costs as well as further rationalizing marketing procedures and adopting a division of labour in which each factory would produce only a certain quality of yarn.[101] Specifically, Longos–Tourpalis in Naoussa (by then Kyrtsis had withdrawn) combined with Tsitsis in Edhessa to create the largest cotton-spinning and weaving enterprise of the Empire.[102] Lappas–Hadjidimoulas from Edhessa, Goutas–Karatzias from Naoussa, Billis–Tsitsis from Naoussa and Sossidis–Faik from Veroia combined to form the other cartel. Note that there is no record of these mergers in the archives as they probably were informal arrangements.

6.7 Explaining the dominance of provincial woollen mills

In addition to cotton spinning, the mechanization of wool had made great strides by the 1900s as the Ottoman state had changed its attitude and allowed

---

[100] According to the calculations of Cakiroglu (2015) based on SVS and O.M.Z.M., the land given to tobacco cultivation increased by around 98 per cent between 1890 and 1905 in the *vilayet* of Thessaloniki. The land given to cotton cultivation decreased by around 60% during the same period. See Cakiroglu (2015, p. 73).
[101] See Quataert (1993a, p. 46).
[102] See Hajiiossif quoted in Lapavitsas (2006, p. 683).

provincial manufacturers to move into the field, which they rapidly dominated. The economics of woollen industrialization exhibited considerable similarities with cotton, though the differences were also striking. Competition with European products was not nearly as severe and the production of woollen cloth through domestic methods was able to sustain itself to the very end of Ottoman rule in the Balkans. The survival and even expansion of woollens depended on the flexibility and adaptability of producers, but the key factor was demand for cheap traditional woollen cloth in the Ottoman markets. The Balkans, in particular, continued to wear wool processed in the traditional way until 1912 and beyond.

A major source of demand came from the social layers that had a relatively low income, creating a huge market across the Empire for the woollen output of the *vilayet* of Thessaloniki. The market was price elastic particularly as peasant families were typically able to weave their own clothes. A further source of demand, and much more stable, came from the public sector, since wool was the material for the uniforms of the Ottoman military, gendarmerie and other officials. Demand from the state had always been a determining factor for the size and location of the woollen cloth industry in the Ottoman Empire.

In the nineteenth century Ottoman producers of traditional woollen cloth lost several of their Western European markets, but towards the end of the century they were able to export to countries that were once part of the Empire – Serbia, Bulgaria and Greece. In the domestic market, furthermore, things had changed dramatically. Western European products had no significant advantage over domestic woollen textiles, which remained far more suitable for traditional clothing. Quataert has rightly claimed that 'natural advantages played a larger role in the Ottoman wool cloth industry and survival was somewhat easier'.[103]

To be more specific, two 'natural advantages' were absolutely crucial for the production of woollen cloth: first, abundant and fast-flowing water; second, a plentiful supply of raw wool. Two 'acquired advantages' were also critically important: first, command over the know-how of wool processing, which was far

---

[103] See Quataert (1993a, p. 52).

from universally available, even in the Balkans; second, access to wide merchant networks, both for obtaining the raw wool and for distributing the final output.

At the start of the nineteenth century, the historic domestic manufacture of woollens in Thessaloniki that had been run entirely by the Jewish community was in terminal decline. However, şayak manufacture in the region of Mount Vermion followed a very different trajectory, not least because Naoussa possessed both the requisite 'natural advantages'. First, it had easy access to the abundant and fast-flowing water of Arapitsa; second, it could obtain regular supplies of good quality raw wool from the Vlach shepherds of Mount Vermion. Naoussa and the surrounding region also possessed the necessary 'acquired advantages': first, it had a tradition in domestic spinning and weaving and thus possessed the know-how of textile production; second, the local merchants had a long pedigree of commercial transactions in both foreign and domestic markets.

Domestic production and trade of şayak was the ground upon which cotton industrialization eventually sprang, as was shown in the preceding sections. The industrialization of wool, when it arrived in the 1900s, also took advantage of the accumulated know-how, while exploiting the advantages of the town. The decisive factor, however, was the state's decision to grant a steady market for woollen cloth to the industrialists of Naoussa. The Hadjilazaros–Angelakis mill in 1907 became the main supplier of the regional gendarmerie by tendering the lowest price.[104]

Supplying the Ottoman state was not a very profitable business in the short term, despite providing a regular source of demand for the industrialists. There were two reasons for that. First, suppliers had to squeeze their profit margins very significantly to tender the lowest price. Second, payments by the state were anything but regular, which was hardly surprising given the fiscal difficulties of the period. Thus, in a letter written in 1911, *Atnaş Makri* (Athanassios Makris), the director of Hadjilazaros–Angelakis, which by then had become the Naoussa Textiles Ottoman Inc. Co., addressed the Ministry of Internal Affairs to complain about delayed payments, and raised the spectre of bankruptcy. It appears that the company had made advance cash payments of 4,000 *lira* and delivered miscellaneous goods worth 10,000 *lira* but had not received any money from the state.[105] The problem was hardly confined to the industries of Mount Vermion.

[104] BOA. DH.İD.83-2/7.
[105] Ibid.

Even the Allatini complained bitterly about the impact of delayed payments on the financial health of their enterprise.[106]

State contracts were, nonetheless, highly desirable in the medium to long term. By establishing good relations with the Ottoman state the industrialists could confidently expect steady demand in the future. Moreover, they could look forward to state support in case of financial difficulties. Last but not least, the industrialists could hope to receive concessions or privileges from the state. The masters of this approach were the Allatini of Thessaloniki, who owned the largest flour mill in the Empire, a genuinely sizeable industrial operation. The yearbook of 1890 stated that the labour force of the flour mill was 250 workers.[107] By 1900 capacity had substantially increased but the mill still faced difficulties meeting army demand, particularly as the Russo-Turkish War of 1877 and the Greco-Turkish War of 1897 had turned Thessaloniki into a centre of military operations. The Allatini were responsible for supplying the Ottoman army with a variety of products, including flour, coal and fleece. Their well-established relations with the state allowed them to secure preferential treatment for their enterprises in Thessaloniki.[108] The privileges afforded to the Allatini were explicitly cited in the aforementioned letter by Makris as a reason for similar concessions to be given to the Naoussa Textiles Ottoman Inc. Co.[109] The provincial entrepreneurs had come a long way since the early 1870s and were actively seeking to protect their dominant position.

6.8 Economics of industrial textile capitalism

In light of the preceding analysis, it is possible to sum up the economic forces that catalysed and propelled textile industrialization in Ottoman Macedonia.

---

[106] There is a voluminous correspondence in the archives between the Allatini and the Sublime Porte regarding delays in payments. For some examples, see BEO. 1054/79023; BEO. 1316/98654; BEO. 1334/100022; BEO. 1382.103592; BEO. 1439/107858; BEO. 1709/128109; BEO. 2399/179852; BEO. 2419/181412.

[107] SVS X, 1307 [1890].

[108] The Allatini family was addressed in the archives as '*erzak-ı askeriye müteahhidi*', '*ordu-yu Hümayun müteahhidi*', which means 'contractor/supplier of the Army provisions', or as '*dakik müteahhidi*' meaning 'flour contractor/supplier'; see, respectively, BEO. 1410/105718, BEO. 1505/112865 and BEO. 1728/129531.

[109] BOA. ŞD.1240/35, 19 Şevval 1330 (01.10.1912).

The process began with the opening of the Ottoman markets to British goods, which laid waste to domestic textile manufacturing in 1840–60, although several niche producers continued to exist. These producers served primarily the markets for traditional cloth and clothes, including textiles produced at home by peasants and others. The manufactured textiles were primarily şayak and aba, but there was also substantial domestic production of cloth for own use as well as handloom-produced cloth for commercial purposes in Macedonia and elsewhere.

Mechanization of textiles began in the 1870s with cotton spinning. It aimed at domestic demand, including in rural areas in which domestic woollen production required cotton yarn for better strength and quality. Industrial textile capitalism in Ottoman Macedonia pivoted on selling to low-income strata of the population. It was initiated by merchants who were in command of both trade channels and production processes.[110]

The urban population and the army consumed great quantities of traditional cloth produced by domestic manufacturers, mostly woollen but also cotton. The peasants had limited use for commercial woollen cloth (şayak and aba), since they regularly wove wool for their own clothes. However, both the domestic producers of woollen cloth and the peasants needed strong, coarse cotton yarn to combine with wool to improve the strength of the cloth. Moreover, there were significant numbers of handloom weavers in Macedonia producing coarse cotton fabric for the market, who also needed strong yarn. They provided the sources of demand that made it profitable to mechanize the supply of coarse cotton yarn in the 1870s.

The spur was perhaps given by falling international cotton prices and rising consumption of domestically produced cloth. More specifically, the production of coarse cotton cloth in the Ottoman lands approximately doubled in 1880–1914.[111] It is also likely that the use of cotton yarn for domestic weaving rose as the price of raw cotton fell during the same period. In the words of Palairet: 'The industry developed to supply the hand loom weavers, both subsistence producers and commercial. Demand for cotton yarn was rising,

---

[110] For an analysis of industrialization in cotton textiles in Western Anatolia and its comparison to Egypt, see Panza (2013, 2014).
[111] See Pamuk (1987).

because as its price fell, it displaced woollen and linen warps in domestic mixed cloth weaving.'[112]

Room was thus created for the textile traders and the domestic producers of woollen cloth in Thessaloniki and the region of Mount Vermion to mechanize cotton spinning. The first great leap was made by the şayak traders of Naoussa in 1874–5, but they were immediately overtaken by the Jewish merchants of Thessaloniki in the late 1870s.

The pre-eminence of Jewish textile capitalists did not last long as the competitive advantages of Mount Vermion ensured the return of Greek capitalists in the 1890s, effectively dominating industrialized Ottoman textiles by the 1900s. The cotton spinners of Mount Vermion drew their advantages from much lower labour costs, free energy, low land prices, cheaper water-powered machinery and lower operational costs since they could switch to flour milling in the summer. The typical location of the provincial textile mills, and the advantages offered to Naoussa industrialists by the fast-flowing waters of Arapitsa are apparent in Figure 6.9.

The cotton spinners of Naoussa acted as the catalysts of industrialization in their region. By the 1900s they were beating their Jewish textile competitors and had become well established in the bourgeois circles of Thessaloniki. However, they were still very much in an inferior league compared to the great Jewish capitalists of Thessaloniki, the Allatini and the Modiano. The difference in scale is immediately apparent in Figure 6.10 depicting the central section of the Allatini flour mill in Thessaloniki, which was probably the largest industrial flour plant in the Empire. The Allatini mill was founded in 1854 and relied on 650 steam engines; its capacity had been frequently upgraded, especially when it was rebuilt in 1900 following a destructive fire. The provincials had made great headway in textiles but still had a long way to go before they could measure up to the leading Jewish industrialists.

The cotton spinners of Mount Vermion were also keenly interested in mechanizing woollen cloth already in the 1870s, but the Ottoman state refused to allow it, as is shown in the next chapter. Woollen industrialization emerged only in the 1900s, again in Naoussa, and in connection with supplying the Ottoman security forces. Domestic şayak workshops persisted alongside

---

[112] See Palairet (1993, p. 349).

Figure 6.9 Locating textile mills next to water for power
Source: Private collection of Takis Baitsis.

the woollen industrial complexes until the very end of the Ottoman period. Demand appeared to be strong as the domestic Ottoman economy expanded by further integrating into the world economy, and the high quality of the *şayak* of Naoussa protected its market share. The output of mechanized production met primarily state demand, while that of domestic workshops covered the needs of a broader civilian market.

The establishment of mechanized cotton spinning in Thessaloniki and Mount Vernon created a veritable textile network in Macedonia based on cotton. The

Figure 6.10 The Allatini flour mill in Thessaloniki
Source: Kolonas (2016).

cotton spinners relied primarily on locally produced raw cotton. Thus, in the 1880s and 1890s regional cotton producers turned increasingly towards the domestic market as industrial cotton-spinning grew. Strong cotton demand also encouraged smallholding peasants to switch to cotton, especially food crop producers. The output of raw cotton was supplied to the industrial spinners of Thessaloniki and Mount Vermion, who in turn produced the cotton yarn that sustained several centres of coarse cotton cloth production in Macedonia, as well as the domestic production of woollen cloth by the peasants. A textile network gradually emerged reflecting the capitalist transformation of the Ottoman economy. Even so, in the 1900s Macedonian raw cotton was insufficient for the needs of the spinners, who had to turn to imports from Anatolia and even Aleppo.

Some insight into the textile production network of the *vilayet* of Thessaloniki is offered by Figure 6.11, although it focuses exclusively on cotton. Information for the map was extracted from the yearbooks of the 1890s and therefore it does not reflect the period of greatest industrial expansion in the 1900s. Perhaps by the 1900s the patterns of cotton cultivation and coarse cotton cloth production had become significantly different, particularly as tobacco cultivation grew in importance. Still, the map provides an informative summary of some of the

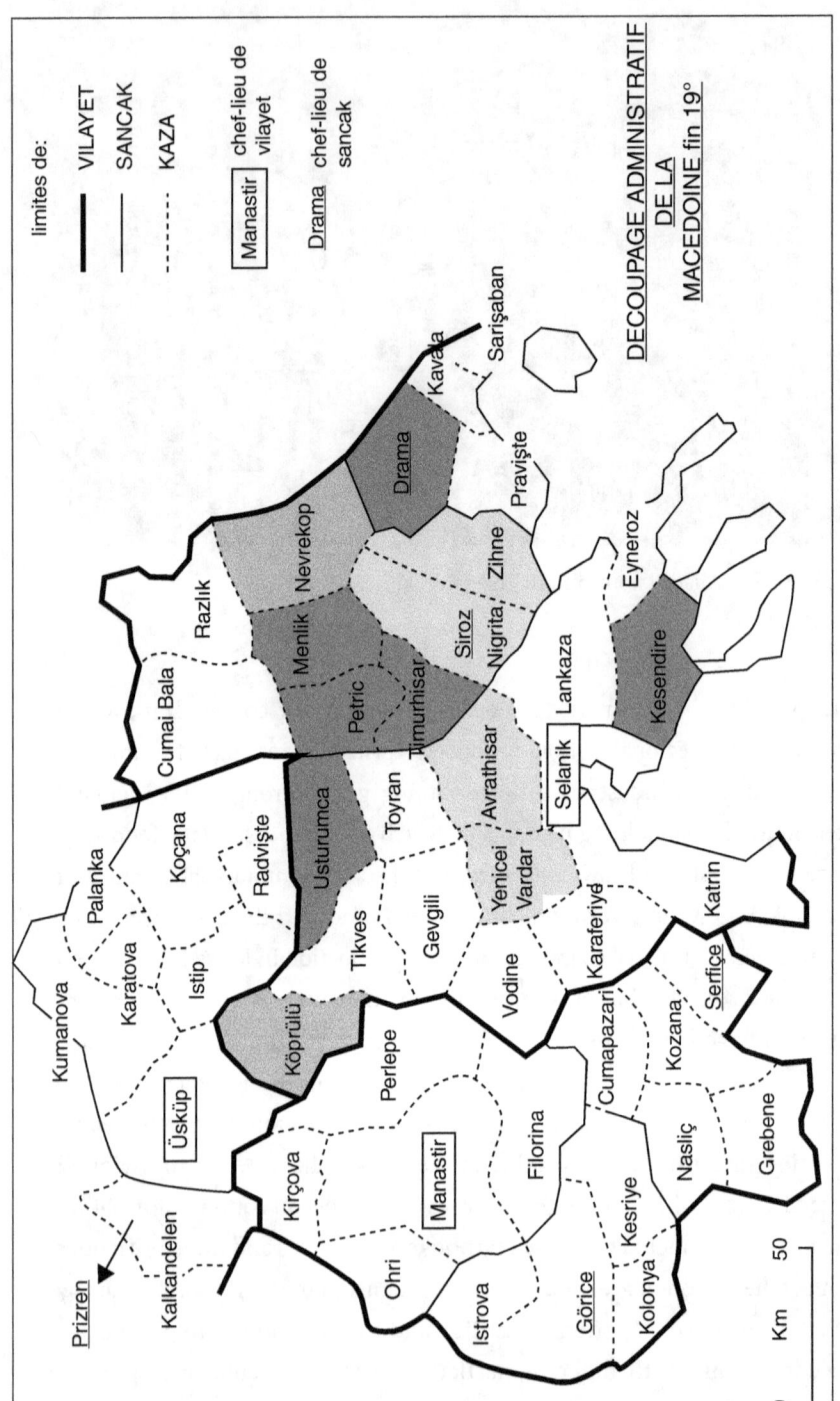

Figure 6.11 The cotton production network in the *vilayet* of Thessaloniki, in the 1890s

Source: Original map taken from D. Panzac, La population de la Macédoine au XIXe siècle (1820–1912), (1992a). Shaded by the authors based on the information from the *salname* in Cakiroglu (2015).

integrated production and trade relations that supported the emergence of Ottoman cotton-spinning capitalism.

The *kaza* shaded with dark gray produced the raw cotton that supplied the cotton-spinning mills of Thessaloniki and Mount Vermion. Cotton gins were probably located in the areas of cotton cultivation. The *kaza* shaded with medium gray produced cotton cloth and thus bought yarn from the cotton-spinning mills. The *kaza* shaded with light gray produced both raw cotton and cotton cloth. The main cotton cloth producing areas were in Eastern and Southern Macedonia, and the main suppliers of raw cotton were found near Serres (*Siroz*) and Zichni (*Zihne*), at least until the early 1900s. Several of the cotton-producing *kaza* also produced cotton cloth. The most prominent urban centres of coarse cotton cloth production were Gotse Deltsev (*Nevrokob*) and Veles (*Köprülü*), which, according to the yearbook for 1897, together held 1,650 textile looms.[113]

It is striking that raw cotton was not produced in the *kaza* of either Karaferye (*Veroia*) or Vodina (*Edhessa*). The lack of locally produced raw cotton might well have been a reason why no new cotton-spinning mills were built in the region of Mount Vermion for more than fifteen years after Longos–Kyrtsis–Tourpalis. Things changed in the 1890s, as the railway made it possible to import raw cotton and export the finished yarn much more cheaply. Even so, the Christian *çiftlik* owners of Mount Vermion, who were also *şayak* traders and cotton spinners, did not integrate their production, and preferred to ship good quality raw cotton from some distance away, particularly as raw cotton production in Macedonia was unable to meet the growing demand.[114] The

---

[113] See SVS XV, 1315 [1897].

[114] Akarli (2001, p. 103) puts the issue in the following terms: 'Regional cotton production turned increasingly towards the domestic markets in the late 1890s and the early 1900s. The establishment of a number of new spinning concerns in Salonica, Ağustos, Vodina and Karaferye increased the demand for cotton, which gave way to a notable increase in cotton prices in Salonica. Moved by the price increase, many farmers, especially the long frustrated cereal producers, switched to cotton production. By 1895 regional cotton production had reached 3,000 tons and probably continued to rise until the early 1900s. However, the degeneration of cottonseeds was now a notorious problem. Local mill owners were seriously considering cotton imports from overseas as the local varieties fell short of meeting the specific technical requirements of the mechanised ring spinners, which were commonly used in local mills. In response, *local authorities, in cooperation with the leading cotton merchants and yarn producers of the region*, imported 40 tons of cotton seed from the United States and İzmir and distributed them to farmers in Siroz and Zihne in 1898. As such, domestic production could be maintained around 3,000 tons throughout the 1890s and the early 1900s. Cotton imports into Salonica remained insignificant during this period.' (Italics added).

traders and spinners of the region also tried to improve the quality of raw cotton by importing better seed varieties from the United States and İzmir, particularly when degeneration of cottonseeds became a major problem in 1895–1900.

6.9 A notable and precarious success

Analysis and evidence in this chapter have shown that in 1912 the economy of Macedonia stood on the cusp of a profound transformation. Agriculture was still predominant, but commercial and, most significantly, industrial capitalism had well and truly taken root. The heart of the capitalist sector in Macedonia was the port city of Thessaloniki, which had boomed in the preceding decades transforming its society and culture. The importance of both the city and the entire region in the Ottoman Empire had grown enormously during the preceding four decades. The economic life of Thessaloniki was dictated by its majority population, the Jewish community.

It was also shown that the most dynamic source of industrial development in Macedonia in the 1900s was in the region of Mount Vermion. With the little town of Naoussa at its core, the region had emerged as the spearhead of textile industrialization in the European provinces of the Empire. Naoussa capitalists had begun to dominate the textile sector, establishing capacity in the other towns of their area, and making a strong mark in Thessaloniki, particularly in commerce, real estate and brewing. The pre-eminence of Naoussa industrialists in the textile sector of Macedonia is depicted in Table 6.2, which sums up the evidence.

In all there were ten active cotton mills in Macedonia in 1912: three in Naoussa (excluding the Lapavitsas–Kokkinos plant since it started operations after the First World War under the name of Tsitsis), two in Edhessa, two in Veroia and three in Thessaloniki. The two Edhessa mills were established with capital and know-how from Naoussa. Of the two Veroia mills at least one had some equity belonging to Naoussa industrialists. Of the three Thessaloniki mills, two belonged to Jewish industrialists and one to a Naoussa industrialist. Thus, Naoussa capitalists controlled at least six of the cotton mills, or approximately 30 per cent of the Empire's total cotton-spinning capacity.[115]

---

[115] See Lapavitsas (2006, p. 670).

Table 6.2 Textile mills founded by industrialists from Naoussa, 1874–1912

	Year	Location	Spindles	Workers
Cotton Spinning				
Longos–Kyrtsis–Tourpalis	1874–5	Naoussa	7,000	270
Bilis–Tsitsis	1891	Naoussa	4,000	160
Tsitsis	1895	Edhessa	16,500	500
Goutas–Karatzias	1903	Naoussa	5,000	160
Lappas–Hadjidimoulas	1907	Edhessa	6,000	–
Tourpalis	1909	Thessaloniki	–	200
Tsitsis (Lapavitsas–Kokkinos)	Operated after the First World War	Naoussa	–	130
Woollen cloth				
Hadjilazaros–Angelakis	1907	Naoussa	1,080	150
Lanaras–Pehlivanos	1909	Naoussa	–	75
Tourpalis–Kazazis	1911–12	Thessaloniki	–	30

Source: Constructed from Lapavitsas (2006) and Gounaris (1993). The figures for the Tsitsis plant in Edhessa refer to 1895 as there is no information about its subsequent upgrades.

Cotton spinning in the late Ottoman Empire was truly the business of Naoussa capitalists. Finally, as far as woollen mills were concerned, the dominance of Naoussa industrialists was absolute, at least in the European part of the Empire.

Equity in the mills was a family affair, some families providing money capital, others land and some both. Different branches of the same family became involved in separate concerns, often reflecting individual decisions by family members. However, the familial bond remained very strong throughout the period. Table 6.3 gives a list of families that held significant equity in the industrial concerns of Ottoman Naoussa.

These families typically belonged to the dominant social group of the town, the Christian çorbacı, which also included landowners and real estate holders. Some of the industrialists were long-established members of the çorbacı, others were recent additions, and still others were reluctant associates, as often happens with self-made men. It is notable that the list of equity-holding families overlaps extensively with the list of families with commercial capital in Chapter 5. There is also a clear overlap with the list of çiftlik owners

Table 6.3 Equity of Naoussa-owned mills, 1874–1912

Mill	Location	Shareholding Naoussa families
Longos–Kyrtsis–Tourpalis	Naoussa	Longos, Kyrtsis, Tourpalis
Bilis–Tsitsis	Naoussa	Bilis, Tsitsis, Kokkinos, Tourpalis, Sefertzis, Tsiomis, Boyatzis
Goutas–Karatzias	Naoussa	Goutas, Karatzias, Tourpalis
Tsitsis (Lapavitsas–Kokkinos)	Naoussa	Kokkinos, Lapavitsas, Bilis, Tsitsis, Sefertzis, Kyrtsis, Longos
Hadjilazaros	Naoussa	Hadjilazaros, Angelakis, Lamnides
Lanaras–Pehlivanos	Naoussa	Lanaras, Pehlivanos, Kyrtsis
Lappas–Hadjidimoulas	Edhessa	Lappas, Hadjidimoulas
Tsitsis	Edhessa	Tsitsis, Kokkinos, Kyrtsis, Sefertzis, Longos, Platsoukas
Tourpalis	Thessaloniki	Tourpalis
Tourpalis–Kazazis	Thessaloniki	Tourpalis

Source: Constructed from Lapavitsas (2006, p. 700).

in Chapter 4. The roots of Ottoman industrial capitalism – certainly in Macedonia – were commercial and mostly to be found in şayak trading, while some among the capitalists also became large landowners. The deeper reasons for these developments will be considered in the following chapter.

To place things in their appropriate order, however, the industrial capacity of Macedonia, important as it was in the Ottoman context, was minute compared to the industrial textile capacity of Western Europe at the outbreak of the First World War. The 70,000 spindles of Thessaloniki and the Macedonian provinces, and even the roughly 150,000 spindles of the whole of the Empire in 1912, were only a small fraction of the capacity of Switzerland, not to mention larger states, such as Austro-Hungary.[116] The industrial transformation of the Ottoman Empire had only just begun, and there were no guarantees that it would be able to unfold successfully in the face of powerful foreign competitors.

Still, the achievement was far from negligible. The average size of the Macedonian mill in 1912, including in Thessaloniki, was roughly seven

---

[116] See Palairet (1993, pp. 351–2) and Landes (1988, p. 215).

thousand spindles. To gauge the importance of that figure, consider that in 1928, at the absolute peak of the global cotton spinning industry, which comprised roughly eight thousand mills across the world, the average size of mill was 22,000 spindles.[117] The Ottoman Macedonian mills, even sixteen years earlier, were not particularly small compared to that average, and actually significantly larger than, say, the Danish mills at the end of the 1920s. But they were midgets compared to the giants of the time, for instance, the Japanese and especially the Russian mills, some of which employed hundreds of thousands of spindles on the eve of the First World War.[118]

Private textile capitalism had made great strides in provincial Ottoman Macedonia, even if its position in the global markets remained precarious. The Ottoman Empire had succeeded in hacking a path towards industrial capitalism, but the distance from the competing empires of the time was still enormous. To establish more fully the causes of this weakness it is important to consider in detail the role of the Ottoman state in the rise of industrial capitalism focusing particularly on its relations with the emerging provincial industrialists.

---

[117] See Farnie and Jeremy (2004, pp. 5–6) in Farnie and Jeremy (2004).
[118] See Thompstone (2004, p. 342), in Farnie and Jeremy (2004).

7

The Ottoman state creates a framework for industrialization

7.1 Rediscovering economic intervention

The economic transformation of the Ottoman Empire after the final decades of the eighteenth century was spurred in part by the growth of international trade and the resultant deep changes in the Empire's social and communal order. Equally important was the decline in the power of the Sublime Porte, followed by its gradual revival, with all the attendant political upheavals. The revived Ottoman state was, however, quite different from its earlier historical forms. By the second half of the nineteenth century the outlook, practices and institutions of Western European states had made deep inroads into the structure and operations of Ottoman state institutions. The modernization of the state prepared the ground for industrial capitalism in material and ideological ways. But the path was far from easy.

The Anglo-Ottoman Convention of 1838 greatly reduced the scope for economic intervention by the Ottoman state, which was forced to surrender its power to influence the volume of trade and to determine the level of import and export taxes.[1] In line with the Convention, taxes on Ottoman exports rose, while import duties became negligible by comparison. To make matters worse, domestic producers had to pay further taxes from which foreign exporters were exempt.[2] Inevitably Ottoman productive units lost competitiveness and manufacturing declined, especially in the urban centres. The manufacturers who were able to survive during this period were either protected by natural advantages, or had special access to market niches, as was shown in Chapter 6.

---

[1] See Pamuk (1987, p. 38).
[2] Ibid., pp. 38–41; Kütükoğlu (1976, p. 22).

It would be wrong to think that the Ottoman state had no understanding of the significance of industry for the economic strength of the Empire. During the first half of the nineteenth century, several industrial enterprises were founded with state support, all in the wider area of İstanbul. The list included a paper and fine felt (*çuka*) factory in Beykoz (founded in 1805), a leather factory (*Beykoz Deri Fabrikası*, founded in 1810), a cotton yarn factory in Eyüp (founded in 1827), an iron factory (*Zeytinburnu Demir Fabrikası*, founded in 1843), a printed cloth factory (*Veliefendi Basma Fabrikası*, founded in the early 1840s), a woollen fine felt factory (*İzmit Çuka Fabrikası*, founded in 1842) and some textile factories (*Feshane* founded in 1835–6 and *Hereke Kumaş Fabrikası*, founded around 1842–4).[3]

The authorities tended to see these plants as the main hope for an Ottoman industrial revolution.[4] The specific motives behind the attempts at state-led industrialization included supplying the needs of the military, reducing imports, constructing a base for the overall industrial development of the Empire, and securing long-term profits from the enterprises.[5] To achieve these ends, several forms of support were given to state-owned enterprises, such as providing technical training and sending personnel to Western Europe as well as conferring various tax exemptions. However, the enterprises proved unable to deliver the expected outcomes: efficiency was low, product quality was poor and profitability remained weak.[6]

The early attempts at industrialization represented the awakening of the Ottoman administration confronted with advancing Western European industrial capitalism. However, they were not part of a wide-ranging and integrated policy, and nor were they accompanied by infrastructure improvements and other supporting measures. The industries faced major problems, including weak supply of capital, lack of skilled workers, irregular provision of good quality raw materials and absence of suitable technology.[7] Without appropriate solutions for these problems, the attempts at state-led industrialization were

---

[3] *Beykoz Deri Fabrikası* (Beykoz leather factory) was originally founded by a private investor, a certain Hamza Bey, but was then bought by Sultan Mahmud II in 1816 to serve the army; see Seyitdanlıoğlu (2009, p. 58).
[4] See Clark (1974, p. 67).
[5] See Güran (1992, pp. 236–8).
[6] See Kala (1993); Güran (1992).
[7] See Güran (1992, p. 235).

destined to fail. Only after the 1860s did industrialization become a deliberate, conscious and – to some extent – general policy of the Ottoman state. By that time there had also emerged several private sector enterprises and individuals with substantial accumulated capital who could tackle some of the problems of industrialization on a private – and communal – basis.[8]

To be more concrete, in the second half of the nineteenth century Ottoman policy towards the economy changed substantially and the state began systematically to support private enterprises after the 1860s. Comprehensive plans were produced for economic reconstruction, and a significant part of the state budget was reserved for the purpose. It has been estimated that perhaps 8.5 per cent of the state budget was allocated specifically to industrial development.[9] Signalling the new attitude was the establishment of the Industrial Reform Commission (*Islah-ı Sanayi Komisyonu*) in 1864 with the aim of protecting and developing manufacturing.[10] The Commission's activities were suspended in 1874, but two years later the Assembly of Commerce and Agriculture (*Ticaret ve Ziraat Meclisi*) assumed the same duties.[11] The efforts of these institutions focused on four main areas relevant to the development of manufacturing: first, managing customs taxes to reverse the destructive impact of the Free Trade Convention on domestic manufacturing; second, launching industrial exhibitions to introduce the technological advances of Western Europe to the Ottoman economy; third, providing technical training to improve the availability of skilled labour; and, fourth, reorganizing the guilds into cooperatives and merchant associations.[12]

Unfortunately for the Ottoman state, modernization during the second half of the nineteenth century proved disastrous for public finances. Creating a sizeable state machine capable of operating in the new conditions, developing a large modern army, and fighting several wars, were tasks that required huge expenditures. However, the tax system remained deeply problematic and failed

---

[8] See Clark (1974); Güran (1992); Seyitdanlıoğlu (2009).
[9] See Güran (1992, pp. 235–6).
[10] The founding date of the Industrial Reform Commission is not certain. It was probably established around 1864–6 but started working effectively after 1868. See Quataert (1994b, pp. 897–8); Ergin (1995 [1927], p. 691); Genç (2000, p. 304).
[11] See Önsoy (1988).
[12] See Yildirim (1998, p. 118) for a discussion on the Industrial Reform Commission; see also Damlıbağ (2012, pp. 203–4) for the role played by the Commission in the industrialization efforts of the Ottoman state.

to raise the required revenues. The Ottoman state began to borrow heavily abroad from the middle of the 1850s, and its external debt gradually became impossible to service, forcing the Empire to declare default in 1875–6.[13] State default meant that it was no longer possible to devote a large part of the budget to financing industrial development. Constrained finances and limited budgets obliged the state to concentrate mostly on vital infrastructural investments. Further to promote industrial development, state policy had to find ways of supporting investment by private entrepreneurs.[14]

During the final decades of the nineteenth century, Ottoman state support for private industries operated on several levels. Enterprises that benefited from a range of state support measures came to be known as 'enterprises with concessions' (*imtiyazlı fabrikalar*).[15] The term is potentially misleading since the range and type of support provided by the state varied among different industries. Not all 'enterprises with concessions' enjoyed the same privileges. There were concessions given to private enterprises founded after 1873 through a law that granted exemption from customs tax on the importation of start-up machinery and factory equipment.[16] This exemption did not extend to all customs taxes but referred specifically to capital goods necessary to establish a plant, aiming to facilitate the inflow of necessary equipment and technology.[17] Provincial Macedonian plants fell clearly within this category.

However, some selected enterprises received far broader concessions granted through informal rather than legal means. We will use the term 'privileged enterprises' to distinguish these from enterprises that simply benefited from legal concessions (*imtiyazlı fabrikalar*). Support for privileged enterprises included broader exemptions from customs taxes and taxes on output sales, exemption from income tax, exclusive rights to obtain certain raw materials, and exclusive rights to produce and trade certain goods.[18] Note that

---

[13] See Birdal (2010) for a comprehensive political and economic account of the Ottoman insolvency and the creation of the OPDA.
[14] See Quataert (1992, pp. 28–31); Kala (1993, pp. 286–301); Martal (1999, pp. 16–33); Seyitdanlıoğlu (2009, p. 65) on the change of state investment policy towards infrastructure as well as on the policy of encouraging private investment.
[15] See Kala (1993, pp. 111–13).
[16] See Quataert (1992, p. 34); Akman (2007, p. 69). The law was initially for a period of fifteen years but was extended continuously until the end of the Empire.
[17] See Damlıbağ (2014, p. 72).
[18] See Kala (1993, pp. 111–13).

customs tax exemptions could be limited or unlimited. Limited customs tax exemptions were valid only within a particular region, and enterprise owners had to pay taxes for goods traded outside it. Unlimited customs tax exemptions allowed producers to sell goods throughout the country free of tax. Privileged enterprises were granted exclusive rights only under exceptional conditions, and presumably remained under close state monitoring to prevent misuse of privileges.

In addition to tax concessions, the infrastructure programmes funded by the financially constrained Ottoman state had a significant impact on the economy of the Empire. In the early 1870s, transport facilities started to improve, and a programme of railway construction was implemented in the Balkans and Anatolia. Transport improvements together with tax and other concessions had a stimulating effect on both commerce and agriculture, partially offsetting the harmful effects of the trade policies of previous decades.[19] The impact was conspicuous in the city of Thessaloniki as the *Rumeli* railways linked it with İstanbul and Western Europe, and the port was substantially enlarged. Substantial inflows of foreign capital were attracted to the city.[20]

The changed outlook and policies of the Ottoman state regarding the economy were vital to the emergence of industrial capitalism in Macedonia in 1870–1912. This is not to suggest that there was an overall development plan for Macedonia or for any other region of the Empire. However, the assumption commonly found in older historical writing that the late Ottoman Empire was run by a decaying state riven with inefficiency and indifferent towards the economy is misleading.

The historical evidence shows that in the decades that followed the default of 1875-6 the Ottoman state kept a very close eye on the economy with a view to promoting industrial and commercial development. The efforts of the autocratic and repressive regime of Sultan Abdülhamid were far from a failure in this respect, especially in Macedonia. In the words of Palairet:[21]

---

[19] See Akarli (1992, p. 450).
[20] See Ilicak (2002, p. 116); Gounaris (1993, p. 157); Tekeli and İlkin (1980, p. 361). See Gounaris (1993), for a comprehensive account of the impact of the railway construction on the region of Thessaloniki.
[21] See Palairet (1993, p. 356).

The post-1878 experience of Ottoman rule in Macedonia and Thrace does not suggest that Ottoman institutions acted as an economically retarding force. The autocracy of Abdülhamid between 1878 and 1908 remained committed to the principles of the Tanzimat, and pushed through large infrastructure programmes... Macedonia was in a prosperous condition on the eve of the overthrow of Turkish rule in 1912.

Indeed, the drive to support industrialization was so deeply rooted that it survived the fall of Abdülhamid, the last of the powerful Sultans. After 1908 the Young Turk regime consciously sought to support industrial capitalism. Immediately after the revolution of 1908, approximately three hundred applications were made to the Ministry of Commerce to establish new industrial plants and other capacity.[22]

Industrialization in Macedonia emerged within the framework created by the Ottoman state in the second half of the nineteenth century. The Jewish merchants and industrialists of Thessaloniki and their Christian Greek competitors in Mount Vermion built a complex array or relations with the local state but also with the centre of power in İstanbul. The private industries of provincial Macedonia did not receive direct state support of the kind available to privileged enterprises, but certainly benefited from tax and other exemptions. The evolving relations of the private capitalist entrepreneurs of Mount Vermion with the transformed Ottoman state helped shape their outlook as a distinct social group and potentially as a separate class. This important point emerges with clarity from the archival material on the provincial mills.

7.2 A controlling state encourages private industrial investment, 1870–1902

When Longos, Kyrtsis and Tourpalis, *şayak* merchants from Naoussa, grasped the opportunity to buy the equipment for the first cotton mill in provincial Macedonia, they could have had no more than a vague idea of what it would take to obtain the requisite permit. The outlook of the Ottoman state had

---

[22] See Ilicak (2002, p. 119).

undergone a sea change in the preceding years as the authorities gradually became aware of the need to support private industry. Even so, the state was ill-prepared to deal with the novel phenomenon of provincial industrial capitalism.

There was no standard and well-established procedure for founding a private mill when the application was submitted to the Provincial Government of Thessaloniki (*Selanik Vilayet Celilesi*) on 15 April 1874. It took more than a year to obtain the final agreement and to receive the permit for the factory on 8 May 1875. A further decision regarding the use of publicly available water by the plant had to await a little longer, until July 1875.[23] This bureaucratic delay was far from an isolated event. Complaints about the long-drawn out and complex nature of applying to start new private enterprises, and particularly about the uncertainties attached, were frequently heard during this period.[24] The Ottoman state was certainly not playing fast and loose with the applications.

There also appeared to be an element of suspicion, or simply lack of familiarity, regarding the provincial entrepreneurs from Macedonia, exacerbating concern about the risks and the social implications of the novel phenomena they represented. In sharp contrast, when two partners, Ahmet Hilmi and Ahmet Bedii, applied in 1880 to establish a textile plant factory in Fenerbahçe in İstanbul, and asked for a list of concessions – including tax exemption for all the machinery and equipment they would import, other materials and goods they would obtain domestically, building the plant and, finally, selling its output – all their requests were approved by the state.[25] Even more striking is that the extensive requests for concessions by the Allatini of Thessaloniki were regularly met with favour, something that could hardly be expected by the provincial Macedonian industrialists.[26] Clearly, not all emerging capitalists were on an equal footing when they approached the central Ottoman state.

---

[23] BOA. ŞD.2006/10, 29 Zilhicce 1291 (06.02.1875).
[24] See, for instance, Balcı and Sırma (2013, p. 31).
[25] See Damlıbağ (2014, p. 72).
[26] Examples abound in the archives; see, for instance, MKT.MHM. 501/20, BEO. 2131/159797, HR.MKT. 152/11 1272, İ.RSM. 11/1, İ.RSM. 2/49, ŞD.2457/37.

It is also important to note that when Longos, Kyrtsis and Tourpalis established their plant, they were not responding directly to investment incentives provided by the state. A law granting concessions to prospective factory founders had indeed been promulgated on 16 September 1873, stating that start-up machinery and factory equipment imported from Europe for the next fifteen years would be exempt from customs tax.[27] This concession was part of the broader scheme of reforms initiated by the Industrial Reform Commission during its rather short lifespan. However, the concession was not the spur for the *şayak* traders from Naoussa to build a cotton mill. The law was never mentioned in correspondence with the authorities, nor were its provisions specifically included in the list of requests made by the applicants to the Ottoman State. Indeed, the law was not even directly applicable to their prospective enterprise. A note in the technical report on the Naoussa application prepared for the Ministry of Public Works (*Nafia Nezareti*) stated that the legislation of 1873 was not intended to cover water-powered factories. Upon the application by Longos, Kyrtsis and Tourpalis, however, the Ministry decided that there would be no harm in extending the scope of the law to include factories using hydraulic energy.[28]

The sequence of notes and correspondence attached to the first application indicates that it traversed a long path from the Provincial Government of Thessaloniki and the Municipality of Veroia (*Karaferye Kaymakamlığı*), to the Ministry of Public Works, the Council of State (*Şura-yı Devlet*), the Special Council (*Meclis-i Mahsus*), the Chief Vizier (*Sadrazam*) until finally reaching the office of the Sultan himself.[29] Equally remarkable were the requests by the authorities for additional documents to be submitted by the applicants. These requests were not to be repeated in any of the subsequent applications to establish industrial enterprises. Thus, the applicants were asked to submit a trust deed, and the local government was asked to supply testimonials about the applicants. A trust deed was indeed signed stating that *Yorgi Kirci* (Georgios Kyrtsis) and *Yani Durbali* (Ioannis Tourpalis) appointed *Dimitri Longo* (Dimitrios Longos) as their representative to construct and operate

---

[27] See Akman (2007, p. 89).
[28] BOA. ŞD.2006/10, 29 Zilhicce 1291 (06.02.1875).
[29] BOA. ŞD.2006/2; BOA. ŞD.2006/10; BOA. İ.MMS.52/2274.

the proposed factory.³⁰ A testimonial was also submitted by several provincial notables stating that they stood witness to the public reputation and the adequacy of the financial resources of the applicants.³¹

It is apparent that the Ottoman state considered the project to be of some gravity due to its social and economic implications. There is also no doubt that the state lacked familiarity with the provincial entrepreneurs and was deeply uncertain about the operation of private enterprises that were beyond its direct control. The distance and lack of trust was also felt on the other side. The British traveller Baker, who visited the first mill soon after its establishment and talked to Longos and Kyrtsis, reported a long litany of complaints by the entrepreneurs: a three month stay in İstanbul to obtain the permit, bribes for officials, and several difficulties with customs authorities in Thessaloniki over the import of machinery.³² The formal and meticulous procedure that is described in the archival documents acquires a rather different perspective when it is seen in this light.

Longos, Kyrtsis and Tourpalis were eventually allowed to establish their pioneering cotton mill on a site that they already owned, and on which there already was a functioning watermill, as was stated in the report by the Municipality of Veroia (*Karaferye Kaymakamlığı*).³³ However, the three traders were not the first to attempt to industrialize textile production in Macedonia. Already in the 1860s powerful Jewish merchants of Thessaloniki, including the Allatini, had given consideration to industrializing textile production. From the archival documents it transpires that similar initiatives had also been undertaken in provincial Macedonia prior to Longos, Kyrtsis and Tourpalis. Thus, an attempt was made by *Yani Hacilazaro* (Ioannis Hadjilazaros) in the early 1870s to mechanize textile manufacturing in Naoussa.³⁴ Ultimately it failed, but the relevant documents and correspondence cast further light on the relationship between Ottoman authorities and prospective private industrialists.

The archives contain a letter signed by *Perikli Hacilazaro* (Pericles Hadjilazaros), the son and İstanbul representative of Ioannis Hadjilazaros,

---

[30] BOA. ŞD.2006/10, 5 Zilkade 1291 (14.12.1874).
[31] BOA. ŞD.2006/10, 2 Zilkade 1291/30 Teşrinisani 1290 (14.12.1874).
[32] See Baker (1877, pp. 408–9).
[33] BOA. İ.MMS.52/2274, 2 Rabiulahir 1292/ 26 Nisan 1291 (08.05.1875).
[34] BOA. ŞD.2402/18, 19 Cemaziyelahir 1290 (14.08.1873).

written on 10 December 1872. The letter had been forwarded to the Ottoman authorities by the Russian ambassador in İstanbul, since Ioannis Hadjilazaros was a Russian citizen as well as a merchant residing in Thessaloniki. In the letter Pericles Hadjilazaros stated that his father intended to build a cotton mill in Naoussa, for which the permission of the Porte was necessary. He stressed that the mill would be the precursor of industrial development in the region, helping to develop industry in the Empire more generally. Special assurances were given that the mill would be under Ottoman jurisdiction.[35] Finally, the letter made the point that, as the project would require a huge sum of capital, the applicant would be grateful to receive substantial tax exemptions.[36] Hadjilazaros was partially successful since permission to build the factory was actually given, but he never received the requested tax exemptions. In fact, he was not even granted the normal tax exemption for imported start-up machinery, which was to be passed as law less than a year later, in September 1873.

The attitude of the Ottoman authorities is revealing because the Hadjilazaros family had already attained a different social standing from Longos, Kyrtsis and Tourpalis. They hailed from the village of Grammatiko on Mount Vermion and thus came from poor mountain peasant stock. By the 1870s they had become large landowners in Eastern Macedonia, wealthy merchants living in Thessaloniki, and traders and financial transactors in İstanbul. They were well connected with the Ottoman state machine, had access to Russian, Austrian and other citizenships, played an important role in Thessaloniki politics, and were in close collaboration with the authorities of the Kingdom of Greece.[37] Pericles Hadjilazaros, who eventually became the US consul in Thessaloniki in the early 1900s, was obviously not in need of local testimonials regarding his 'probity' and 'reputation'. But the Ottoman state refused the tax breaks sought by the applicants, perhaps in part because of their Russian citizenship.

---

[35] By stating that his enterprise would be under Ottoman jurisdiction, Hadjilazaros was probably trying to ameliorate concerns about his Russian citizenship, not to mention the fact that his letter had been handled by the Russian ambassador in İstanbul.

[36] In the letter, Hadjilazaros did not specify the taxes from which he requested exemption. He simply stressed how costly and difficult it would be to establish a plant, and thus asked for substantial tax exemptions in general.

[37] Some insight into the social and political role of the Hadjilazaros family in Eastern Macedonia in the 1890s–1900s can be gleaned from Karavas (2010, pp. 134–43).

The proposed mill was never founded, and the Hadjilazaros family had to wait for another thirty-five years before it could move into industrial textile production.

Following the success of Longos–Kyrtsis–Tourpalis, the archives confirm that the next attempt to establish a factory by Naoussa industrialists occurred in 1890. For fifteen years industrialization in the area of Mount Vermion moved at a snail's pace. In 1890, however, the brothers *Dimitri* and *Diyamandi Bili* (Dimitrios and Diamandis Bilis) submitted an application to build a water-powered cotton mill on the site of an existing watermill in the area of *Tekkealtı* (below the *tekke* of Şeyh İlahi) in Naoussa. The brothers also intended to import the necessary machinery and factory equipment exempt from customs tax.[38] A picture of the plant is shown in Figure 6.3 and a drawing of it in Plate 4 of Chapter 6. The hulk of a more recent plant stands currently on the site as the original Ottoman mill was burned down during the Greek Civil War in the 1940s.

The records for this mill in the BOA are compatible with the information from Greek sources, although there are some discrepancies. One such discrepancy is that the Greek sources give 1891 as the mill's founding date.[39] The archival records indicate that the application was submitted in 1890, and permission was finally obtained in 1892. This implies that the factory might have started its operations before receiving the final permit. A further discrepancy is that the archives mention only the Bilis brothers and contain no reference to the Tsitsis family. That is not necessarily a problem, however, as full lists of shareholders were rarely mentioned in Ottoman documents, which typically recorded only the applicants' names.

The Bilis family came from Naoussa and had apparently lived in the town even before the sack of 1822. By the middle of the nineteenth century they possessed water-powered flour mills and were thus in pivot position to make the move into industrial textiles.[40] The Tsitsis family also hailed from Naoussa and were active in *şayak* trading for decades before applying for permission to build the plant. Grigorios Tsitsis had travelled to Manchester in the 1870s where he had become familiar with industrial textiles.[41] The family became

---

[38] BOA. İ.MMS.117/5004, 28 Rabiulahir 1308 (11.12.1890).
[39] As also do British sources; see Stougiannakis (1911) and PPAP (1890–1, lxxxviii: 231) cited in Gounaris (1993, p. 139).
[40] See Roupa and Hekimoglou (2004, pp. 512–13).
[41] Ibid., p. 293.

actively involved in industrial textile production in Naoussa and Edhessa and were prominent industrialists in Thessaloniki in the 1920s.

An incident that created major difficulties for the Bilis brothers is quite revealing of the manner in which the Ottoman state dealt with prospective industrialists. When they submitted their application, the fifteen-year duration of the tax exemption that was originally announced in 1873 had already lapsed, and the application fell under a new law that had been issued on 4 March 1889 with the aim of continuing to provide tax relief.[42] The permit for the mill was issued quite quickly but securing the tax exemption took more than a year. To obtain the tax exemption the applicants were required to provide a list of the machinery and equipment ordered, which had to be approved by the Ministry of Trade and Public Works (*Ticaret ve Nafia Nezareti*) and the Department of Reforms in the Council of State (*Şura-yı Devlet Tanzimat Dairesi*), and was subsequently forwarded to the Customs Security Department (*Rüsumat Emaneti*). When the machinery and equipment arrived at the port of Thessaloniki, the Customs Office (*Selanik Gümrüğü*) reported that some very minor items did not actually fall within the stipulations of the law, and thus the import of machinery was problematic.[43] To be more precise, the inspectors considered that 'only seven items on the list actually constitute the essentials for founding the factory'.[44] The Customs Office of Thessaloniki further reported that the imported equipment diverged from the submitted list as it included undeclared items – paper, woven fabric, rope and grease.[45] The importation of the equipment, thus, stalled for a while.

Two aspects of this incident are worth noting. First, the Ottoman state appeared to be extremely meticulous and formal in checking applications as well as possessing a complex mechanism to monitor compliance with the law. Second, the state appeared just a little too meticulous and formal to be entirely persuasive. It is not unlikely that, far from being concerned about importing minor items, such as industrial grease, the Customs Officers were seeking their own grease. We shall never know for certain, but there is no doubt that the

---

[42] See Akman (2007, p. 130).
[43] BOA. İ.MMS.117/5004, 18 Rabiulahir 1308/19 Teşrinisani 1306 (01.12.1890); BOA. ŞD.1194/2, 27 Cemaziyelahir 1309/ 16 Kanunusani 1307 (28.01.1892).
[44] BOA. ŞD.1194/2.
[45] See Cakiroglu (2015, p. 186), for the machinery list see BOA. ŞD.1194/2.

Figure 7.1 Grigorios Longos, industrialist and merchant of Naoussa
Source: Private collection of Takis Baitsis.

Bilis brothers had to redraft their list and start the process again. Eventually they succeeded.

The final – third – application by Naoussa industrialists in the archives for the 1890s was for a water-powered textile mill to be built in Edhessa submitted by *Liğor Longo* (Grigorios Longos). From subsequent documents – and from the Greek sources – it is clear that the application referred to the Tsitsis plant in Edhessa. From the Greek sources it appears that other major shareholders included the families of Kokkinos, Sefertzis and Kyrtsis.[46] However, the application was actually submitted in 1896 in the name of Longos, who was one of the shareholders of the new plant, and is shown resplendent in Figure 7.1.[47]

---

[46] See Roupa and Hekimoglou (2004, p. 294).
[47] BOA. TFR.I.ŞKT.15/1465, 10 Temmuz 1319 (23.07.1903). The original phrase is 'tüccar Liğor Longo bazergan' in BOA. ŞD.1207/8, 13 Cemaziyelevvel 1314 (20.09.1896).

Grigorios – 'Galakis' – Longos was the son of Dimitrios Longos, the main applicant for the first mill of the region in 1874–5, whose picture is shown in Figure 6.1 in Chapter 6. As a second-generation industrialist and *çorbacı*, Grigorios Longos probably commanded considerable credibility in the eyes of the Ottoman state in the late 1890s. As was typical of his social class but also due to his personal convictions, Grigorios Longos was closely involved with the affairs of the Church and with the provision of education in the area. In the 1920s, after the end of Ottoman rule, he built a fine primary school in Naoussa, which is still operating. Education was a traditional method for the *çorbacı* to acquire and develop communal power in the Ottoman world.

Summing up, the BOA show that, during the first three decades of relatively slow growth of industry in provincial Macedonia, the applications for textile mills were not very numerous, as is depicted in Table 7.1. Despite the relatively slow rate of industrial advance, by the late 1890s the Ottoman state had become accustomed to the emergence of private industrial enterprises and had developed an appropriate legal framework and associated practices. The procedure of applying had become much less complicated and more uniform. Applicants had to submit a simple request for a permit to establish a mill including a customs-tax exemption for the start-up machinery and equipment to be imported from abroad. A new legal code was issued on 31 July 1896 further regulating the application procedure for the all-important tax exemption for start-up machinery and equipment. The results would soon become apparent.

Table 7.1 Mill applications by Naoussa textile industrialists in provincial Macedonia, 1870–1902

Applicant	Year	Location	Mill	Outcome
1. *Yani Hacilazaro*	1872	Naoussa	Cotton yarn	Did not materialize
2. *Dimitri Longo, Yorgi Kirci* and *Yani Durbali*	1875	Naoussa	Cotton yarn	Longos–Kyrtsis–Tourpalis (1875)
3. *Dimitri* and *Diyamandi Bili*	1892	Naoussa	Cotton yarn	Bilis–Tsitsis (1891)
4. *Liğor Longo*	1896	Edhessa	Textiles	Tsitsis (1895)

Source: BOA, various documents.

7.3 State and industrialists establish regular relations, 1902–12

Following the introduction of the new legal code the administrative procedure for starting an industrial project was finally settled. An application would be initially submitted to the Provincial Government (*vilayet*), which would confirm its *bona fide* nature and forward it, together with the list of machinery and equipment to be imported, to the Ministry of Trade and Public Works (*Ticaret ve Nafia Nezareti*). The Technical Committee of the Ministry (*Heyet-i Fenniye*) would examine the machinery list and, if there were no objections, the application would be passed to, in this order, the Council of State (*Şura-yı Devlet*), the Council of Ministers (*Meclis-i Vükela*), the Chief Vizier and finally even to the office of the Sultan. Once the final approval was given, the Ministry of Trade and Public Works and the Customs Security Department would be notified of necessary actions to be taken. This laborious procedure, at once monitoring, policing and controlling the development of industry, was used for all applications up to 1912, with some minor changes after the 1908 Young Turk Revolution.[48]

The eye of the imperial autocrat in İstanbul was, presumably, the final guarantee of the entire process, but there is little doubt that the efforts of Abdülhamid's police could not prevent bribes and corruption in a bureaucratic procedure of such complexity. Even so, by the late 1890s the Ottoman state had succeeded in developing an institutional framework within which provincial Macedonian entrepreneurs could bring about a more rapid development of industrial capitalism. Aggressive and ambitious merchants-cum-industrialists grasped the economic opportunities and developed closer relations with the state.

During the last decade of Ottoman rule several new textile enterprises were established by provincial industrialists in Macedonia, while several other applications for plants remained inconclusive for a variety of reasons. The capacity of existing mills was also upgraded and diversified beyond cotton spinning. By 1912 Macedonian industrialists had transcended their regional character becoming better connected with the state and beginning to acquire

---

[48] In the documents relevant to Macedonia the procedure first appears in BOA. ŞD.1220/5, 7 Zilkade 1320/ 24 Kanunusani 1318 (05.02.1903).

the outlook of a nascent capitalist class. The archival evidence shows that they had become quite at ease with the mechanisms of the Ottoman state, while retaining important sources of communal power.

At the beginning of the period, in 1902–3, three applications for new plants were submitted by industrialists from Naoussa, all of which followed a revealing path. The first, in 1902, was by *Aristidi Kokino* (Aristidis Kokkinos) who applied for permission to establish a water-powered spinning mill in the area of *Alan* in Edhessa. Kokkinos belonged to a family of rich merchants with extensive operations in Egypt, who had long been implicated in textile manufacturing in Naoussa and were also *çiftlik* owners on the plain. The Kokkinos family were shareholders in most of the major textile undertakings in Naoussa and Edhessa.

Aristidis Kokkinos proposed to establish a new mill in Edhessa but his application faced immediate difficulties. The problem was that Kokkinos intended to build the plant on state land (*arazi-i miriye*) thus requiring the approval of the Ministry of Property Records (*Defter-i Hakani Nezareti*) in addition to that of the other authorities. The land area was eight *dönüm* altogether and its value had been assessed at 50,000 *guruş* by the Municipality of Edhessa. Consequently, the Ministry requested the Municipality to set the appropriate tax for the land, which the Municipality duly calculated as an entirely insignificant sum.[49] It was expected that the procedure would be completed in less than a year.[50] However, the fee for the tax was paid only in 1906, and the official permit was issued subsequently.[51]

A mill in the name of Kokkinos was never built in Edhessa, as is confirmed by the sources considered in Chapter 6. The same sources mention a mill by Lappas–Hadjidimoulas, but no such mill is recorded in the Ottoman archives. The capital for the Lappas–Hadjidimoulas mill would almost certainly have been provided by the Lappas family, wealthy merchants active in Egypt. In the 1920s they built a secondary school in Naoussa, a splendid neoclassical edifice that still dominates the centre of the town. Heracles Hadjidimoulas,

---

[49] The Ministry of Property Records charged 30 para for every 1000 para of the value of the land, which made the tax 37,5 guruş and its fees 10 Ottoman lira. BOA. ŞD.62/37
[50] BOA. ŞD.62/37, 4 Safer 1321/ 19 Nisan 1319 (02.05.1903); BOA. İ.RSM.17/36, 18 Safer 1321/ 3 Mayis 1319 (16.05.1903).
[51] BOA. ŞD.62/37, 2 Rabiulahir 1324/ 13 Mayis 1322 (26.05.1906).

by contrast, was not a wealthy man, but was related to the Longos family on his mother's side and had been trained 'on the job' in the Longos mills. Hadjidimoulas was the driving force not only of the new cotton mill but also of a large jute factory established in Edhessa in 1912, which still stands at the foot of the town's largest waterfall.[52] Perhaps the permit obtained by Kokkinos in 1906 was somehow transferred to Lappas and Hadjidimoulas.

The travails of the Kokkinos application recorded in the archives demonstrate two points. First, command over land was vital to establishing industrial capacity as the plants had to have suitable access to water. This was a major source of social power for the landowning *çorbacı* families in their negotiations with potential merchant-investors. Second, if suitable land happened to belong to the state, the procedure for obtaining the permit could become considerably more complex. By the 1900s, however, the industrialists of the region were perfectly capable of bending the will of the authorities to their interest. Suffice it to note that the tax charged for the Kokkinos land in Edhessa was negligible. There were, however, still more revealing aspects to the Kokkinos application which did not appear in the archive documents and are discussed immediately below. There is little doubt that Kokkinos was a consummate operator whose activities cast light on the social relations and interactions among the *çorbacı*.

A little after Kokkinos, in 1903, *Yorgi Lapaviça* (Georgios Lapavitsas) also submitted an application for a new water-powered cotton mill, but this time in Naoussa.[53] Lapavitsas intended to import the necessary machinery and equipment from Western Europe. The applicant was the son of Constantinos Lapavitsas, the 'Dekapechas' (ten braces tall), *şayak* trader and *çiftlik* holder, whose letter to his trading partner in Pyrgos in the Peloponnese appears in Figure 5.1 in Chapter 5. Constantinos Lapavitsas had probably moved to Naoussa sometime after the sack of 1822, perhaps from the village of Drazilovo on Mount Vermion. This powerful *çorbacı* became the first Christian mayor of Naoussa and played an active part in the fractious political life of the town.[54] The applicant, Georgios, was his second son, who became a leading *şayak* trader, *çiftlik* owner, moneylender and equally powerful *çorbacı* of Naoussa.

---

[52] See Roupa and Hekimoglou (2004, pp. 488–9).
[53] BOA. ŞD.1220/12; BOA. İ.RSM.18/1; BOA. BEO.2109/158126.
[54] The best source on this issue is Goutas (1999, pp. 91–3 and p. 133).

Georgios Lapavitsas planned to build a cotton-spinning mill on land that he already possessed, and the application was approved on 22 June 1903, that is, within six months. The approval form is shown in Plate 7 in all its majestic Ottoman bureaucratic fastidiousness. The document bears dozens of stamps and signatures ascending gradually to the Grand Vizier (*Sadrazam*).

This was hardly the end of the story, however. The imported machinery duly arrived and the plant was built, but failed to operate. The reason was a profound and revealing quarrel with Kokkinos. Historical evidence on the dispute has recently come to light with the publication of the Minutes of the Council of Elders (*Demogerontia*) of Naoussa, whose role and importance in cementing communal power and facilitating the rise of capitalism will be discussed subsequently.[55] The Council also operated as a Church Court and a suit was brought to it on 17 July 1911 by Lapavitsas against Kokkinos.[56]

The plaintiff was actually the father-in-law of the defendant, who stood accused of dishonesty in the matter of the plant of 1903, eight years earlier. According to the depositions, some time before the plant application, Lapavitsas had gone into partnership with A. Sossidis, from Veroia, and D. Bilis, from Naoussa, with a view to constructing a cotton mill. Kokkinos proposed to Lapavitsas to dissolve that partnership and form a new one with himself, a proposal which the plaintiff accepted. The factory permit was obtained, equipment was bought and the plant began to take shape, but Kokkinos showed absolutely no intention of fulfilling his side of the bargain by actively running the business. Repeated entreaties and family councils over several years brought no satisfaction. Eventually the old man realized that Kokkinos was trying to sink the project with a view to protecting his own cotton interests in Edhessa. A new plant in Naoussa would have meant additional competition, which Kokkinos was keen to avoid. Family bonds were important, but profit came first.

---

[55] Publication of the Minutes was the work of E. Valsamides, an indefatigable local researcher in the history of the region of Mount Vermion. The extant Minutes for 1893–1927 have been published fully, and the periods that matter for our purposes are 1893–6 and 1911–15; see Valsamidis and Intzesiloglou (2016). The Lapavitsas–Kokkinos dispute was the most extensive case discussed by the Elders and their decision appears fully in the book, in the original neat Greek handwriting.

[56] See Valsamidis and Intzesiloglou (2016, pp. 190–8, 201–4).

On 24 July 2011 the Church Court decided fully in favour of Lapavitsas. It was, however, far too late for the cotton mill, which was eventually acquired by the Tsitsis family and operated after the First World War, as was noted in Chapter 6. In practical terms, Kokkinos had won. More than the piquant details of the case, however, what is important for our purposes is that such an important dispute was not brought to the Ottoman state courts but was dealt with through the mechanisms of the Christian community. The complex social and political reality of the Ottoman world, which directly impacted on the rise of commercial and industrial capitalism, is immediately evident. The implications will be further discussed in the remainder of this book.

Still in 1903, a further application for a cotton mill was made by *Dimitraki Durbali* (Dimitrios Tourpalis), a scion of Ioannis Tourpalis, one of the founders of the first cotton mill of 1874–5. Dimitrios Tourpalis intended to build a water-powered cotton mill in Naoussa, for which the permit was issued on 2 January 1904.[57] However, a new Tourpalis mill was never founded in Naoussa, even though the machinery was actually imported in 1907, more than four years after the application was submitted.[58] Extant correspondence leaves no doubt that the imported equipment had arrived at the port of Thessaloniki, and even incurred some customs tax due to a mismatch with the submitted lists.[59]

The Tourpalis family were among the oldest *şayak* traders and industrialists of the region, hailing from a village on Mount Vermion and established in Naoussa sometime after the sack of 1822. They held equity in the initial mill of 1874–5 as well as in other local mills, and were among the first of the region's industrialists to make the move to Thessaloniki, as was shown in Chapter 6. Perhaps the equipment that had arrived in 1907 was used for one of the upgrades of the existing Longos–Kyrtsis–Tourpalis plant in Naoussa, or even for the Tourpalis mill that was established in Thessaloniki in 1910.

There is no doubt, however, that a further cotton establishment was founded in Naoussa in 1903, the Goutas–Karatzias mill. Remarkably, there is no relevant application for it in the archives, either for a permit, or for tax exemptions. The

---

[57] BOA. ŞD.1220/47. And also BOA. ŞD.1224/49.
[58] BOA. ŞD.1224/49, 19 Rabiulevvel 1325/ 19 Nisan 1323 (02.05.1907).
[59] BOA. ŞD.1224/49; BOA. MV.117/56; BOA. BEO.3191/239314.

plant was nonetheless mentioned in a document concerning a worker who had been injured in the course of its construction.⁶⁰ The Goutas–Karatzias mill is also probably hinted at in the application by Aristidis Kokkinos in 1902. Kokkinos had requested that the permit he sought should be granted solely by the Provincial Government of Thessaloniki, as had apparently happened for another cotton mill in Naoussa, the application for which had not been forwarded to the Ministry of Trade and Public Works. That was probably the Goutas–Karatzias mill. The request by Kokkinos was rejected on the grounds that his application was for a plant on state land and therefore had to be forwarded to the central government.⁶¹

From that point in time to the end of Ottoman rule in 1912, the archives contain evidence of three new mills that were actually established by provincial Macedonian industrialists. Moreover, there were two further attempts at starting industrial mills that proved ultimately unsuccessful. The key to these developments was the shift in the main field of investment from cotton to wool.⁶² Thus, in 1907, Longos, Kyrtsis and Tourpalis applied to build a woollen mill to produce *şayak* but also *gaytan* (braided woollen cloth) and *kazmir* (cashmere) on their own land. *Gaytan* was widely used in traditional clothing, and its production was instrumental to the growth of industrial capitalism in neighbouring Bulgaria. Moreover, in 1907, the *şayak* trader *Konstantin Lamnidi* (Constantinos Lamnides) applied for a permit to build a textile plant on his own land in the area of *Mandıra* in Naoussa. The two applying parties became involved in a dispute regarding access to the waters of Arapitsa, a perennial point of friction among industrialists but also between industrialists and the town. The dispute is of considerable analytical interest and will be discussed subsequently.⁶³

The 1900s also marked the return of Pericles Hadjilazaros to textile industrialization more than three decades after his first failed attempt in 1872. The archives contain neither a fresh application to build a plant, nor a request to receive tax exemptions by Hadjilazaros. However, they hold an application

---

⁶⁰ BOA. TFR.I.SL.19/1804, 20 Cemaziyelahir 1321/ 30 Ağustos 1319 (13.09.1903).
⁶¹ BOA. ŞD.62/37, 12 Cemaziyelevvel 1320/ 3 Ağustos 1318 (17.08.1902).
⁶² Note that Tsitsis submitted an application in 1904 to establish another mill in the area of *Askala* in Edhessa, and to import the required machinery exempt from tax. It appears that this was no more than an expansion of the original mill of 1895. Presenting a capacity upgrade as a new enterprise was a tactic used by industrialists to benefit from tax exemptions. See BOA. ŞD.2048/34; BOA. İ. RSM.19/40.
⁶³ BOA. TFR.I.SL.161/16085; BOA. ŞD.1225/37.

made in 1911 and seeking to convert an existing unlimited liability enterprise into a joint-stock company, namely the Naoussa Textiles Ottoman Inc. Co., based in Thessaloniki and subject to Ottoman law.[64] This was manifestly the woollen textile plant of Hadjilazaros–Angelakis that was established in 1907, as was shown in Chapter 6. Note that one of the shareholders of the plant was the aforementioned Lamnides. Thus, the permit that had already been obtained by Lamnides in 1907 was actually used for that plant, which was indeed built on Lamnides's land in *Mandıra*.[65] Known eventually as ERIA, the enterprise became a mainstay of woollen production in Northern Greece even after the end of Ottoman rule. It appears that the driving force in the establishment of the enterprise was Athanassios Makris, a textile trader from Thessaloniki who was active in its management and was subsequently prominent in the woollen industry of Thessaloniki.[66]

The information that stands out in the archives about this important plant is that Hadjilazaros succeeded in turning the plant from an unlimited liability company into a joint-stock concern in 1911, which was registered in Thessaloniki as *Ağustos Mensucat Osmanlı Anonim Şirketi* (*Ağustos* Textiles Ottoman Joint-stock Company). ERIA was then added to its official name and it became known as *Ağustos* ERIA.[67] Until then Macedonian mills had typically been family affairs established by sharing out the equity. Towards the end of Ottoman rule, however, industrial capitalism in Macedonia had grown mature enough to support joint-stock enterprises. As will be shown subsequently, mill owners even sought to form oligopolistic concerns to control the domestic market. Ottoman textile capitalism had outgrown its humble organizational beginnings and began to develop along the classic oligopolistic lines of its era.

Furthermore, in 1909 an application for a woollen mill was submitted by *Toşu Pehlivan* (Anastasios Pehlivanos), who requested permission to convert his flour mill in the *Kebir* neighbourhood of Naoussa into a plant to produce *çuka* (a fine felt), *şayak* and *kazmir*. The application was

---

[64] BOA. ŞD(NF.MRF.ML).1234/31, 21 Şaban 1329/ 4 Ağustos 1327 (17.08.1911).
[65] See Roupa and Hekimoglou (2004, p. 440).
[66] Ibid., pp. 203–24.
[67] BOA. ŞD.1234/31; BOA. ŞD.1240/35. There are no records in the archives of other enterprises from Mount Vermion becoming joint-stock companies subject to Ottoman law. However, as is shown in Figure 7.2, the Tourpalis family founded a joint-stock textile company that was based in Thessaloniki.

rapidly approved, as was Pehlivanos's request for customs tax exemption.[68] Pehlivanos was a wealthy *şayak* trader, large *çiftlik* owner and powerful *çorbacı*, whose family remained active in the textile business for decades to come. However, as was noted in Chapter 6, the real force behind this plant was the carder Christodoulos Lanaras and his sons, who manifestly knew the business of wool. This was the smallest among the mills of Naoussa in the Ottoman period, which became the foundation of the massive Lanaras textile enterprises of the next nine decades.

Finally, the BOA show that *Dimitraki Durbali* (Dimitrios Tourpalis) of Naoussa applied for permission to build a cotton mill in the area of *Kelemeriye* (Kalamaria) in Thessaloniki. The application received final approval within three months and the plant, which was a sizeable unit with advanced equipment and operated by gas power, started operations in early 1910, owned by Vasileios Tourpalis.[69] By the early 1900 Naoussa textile capitalists were successful in transferring their activities to Thessaloniki and ready to compete at the core of the Ottoman markets. Figure 7.2 shows a letter by Tourpalis to his bankers (Banque d'Orient, or Trapeza Anatolis) written in French on 23 September 1912. The letterhead reveals that the enterprise had been established in 1910 as a joint-stock company titled '*Société Anonyme Ottomane pour la fabrication de fez & tissus*'. The distance travelled by Naoussa capitalists in the forty years since the commercial correspondence shown in Figure 5.1 was enormous. There is also a certain irony in the fact that the letterhead gives the location as 'Salonique Turquie d'Europe' exactly one month before Thessaloniki became part of the Kingdom of Greece.

Summing up, there is little doubt that 1902–3 was a turning point in the industrialization of Mount Vermion and Thessaloniki. A wave of investment in textiles took place in the following years indicating maturity and breadth of industrial expansion. The attitude of the state had become distinctly favourable towards private capitalists, and the permit and tax exemption procedures functioned smoothly. Table 7.2 summarizes the archival information regarding textile plants that were established or applied for by Naoussa capitalists in 1902–12.

---

[68] BOA. ŞD.1228/10; BOA. BEO.3639/272895.
[69] BOA. ŞD.1229/15.

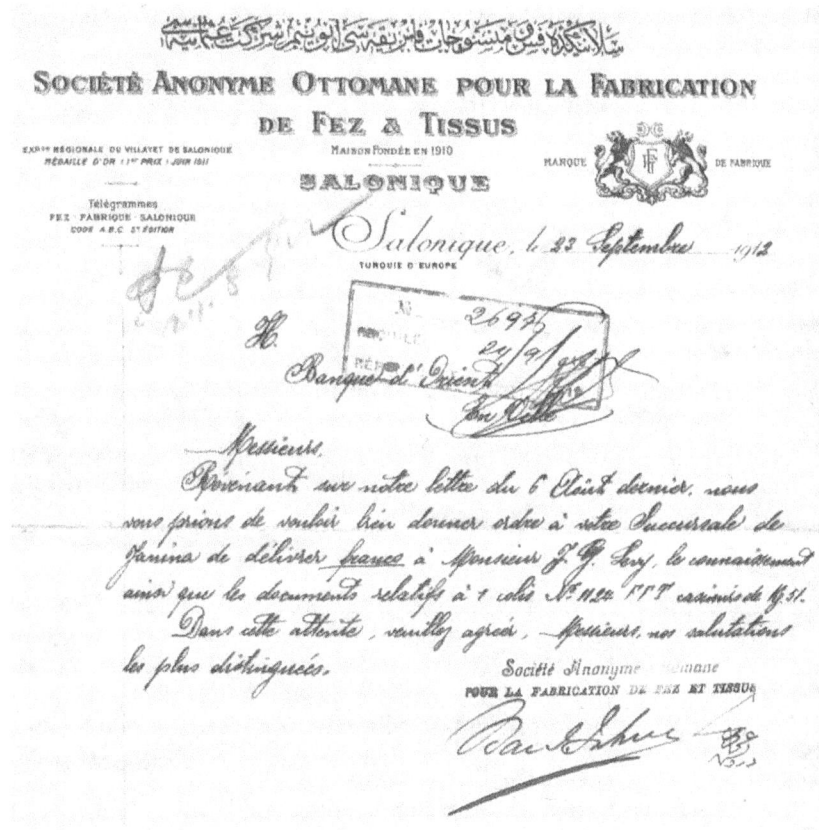

Figure 7.2 Commercial correspondence of Tourpalis company in Thessaloniki
Source: Kolonas (2016).

Relatively minor institutional and administrative improvements continued to be made by the Ottoman state throughout the last couple of decades of its rule in Macedonia as, for instance, with the establishment of the Industrial Administration (*Sanayi İdaresi*), whose presence was first noted in the Kokkinos application of 1902. The relevant procedures for industrial investment did not fundamentally change following the Young Turk revolution in 1908, although the Industrial Administration was replaced by the Directorate of Industry (*Sanayi Müdüriyeti*), which made an appearance in the correspondence of Hadjilazaros in the archives. The Young Turks had a

Table 7.2 Mill applications by Naoussa textile industrialists in provincial Macedonia, 1902–12

Applicant	Year	Location	Mill	Outcome
Aristidi Kokino	1902	Edhessa	Cotton yarn and textiles	Did not materialize
Yorgi Lapaviça	1903	Naoussa	Cotton yarn	Tsitsis after the First World War
Dimitraki Durbali	1903	Naoussa	Cotton yarn	Did not materialize
Longo, Kirci and *Durbali*	1907	Naoussa	Woollen textiles	Did not materialize
Konstantin Lamnidi	1907	Naoussa	Woollen textiles	Hadjilazaros–Angelakis (1907)?
Perikli Hacilazari	1907	Naoussa	Woollen textiles	Hadjilazaros–Angelakis (1907)
Toşu Pehlivan	1909	Naoussa	Woollen textiles	Pehlivanos–Lanaras (1909)
Dimitraki Durbali	1910	Thessaloniki	Cotton yarn	Tourpalis (1910)

Source: BOA, various documents.

deliberate policy of supporting industrialization as is clear from the requests in 1911 by Hadjilazaros to receive favourable treatment for his plant similar to that which had apparently been granted to other applicants. Months before its final demise in Macedonia, the Ottoman state was intent on promoting industrial capitalism in the region. It had no inkling of its impending end.

7.4 An intrusive, authoritarian, bureaucratic and supportive state

The archival evidence shows clearly that the evolving outlook of the Ottoman state after the 1860s had a significant impact on the industrialization of Macedonia. The archives also show that the state had gradually learnt to deal with some of the problems of industrialization as well as relating effectively to the provincial industrialists. It is instructive in this respect to return to the file for the original Longos–Kyrtsis–Tourpalis mill, since it is by far the most important source of information for the state's initial institutional capabilities, its awareness of the communal and social implications of industrial capitalism, and its early relations with a budding industrial class. Even though the original application is not available in the archives, we know its substance, including the specific requests made by the applicants, from the assessment report by *Meclis-i Mahsus* (the Special Council) on 8 May 1875.[70]

The application process in the early 1870s was long and uncertain, and the demand for a trust deed and testimonials was evidence of the suspicion on the part of a state that had hitherto dealt mostly with well-connected industrialists-to-be. Equally important was the bargaining process between two sides groping their way through a novel field. Longos, Kyrtsis and Tourpalis had asked for no less than twenty years of tax exemptions – most probably from all taxes applicable to the project – as well as for seven years of state protection by prohibiting the foundation of similar enterprises in the region. The Ministry of Public Works and the Special Council ignored the request for twenty years of tax exemption and rejected the appeal for protection on the grounds that it would hinder industrialization. The authorities did remark that the requests would be reconsidered if the applicants succeeded in founding the factory. It is impossible to say what that meant in practice.

The state proved quite accommodating when it came to granting exemption from customs taxes on the start-up machinery and equipment, even if the relevant legislation did not technically cover water-powered mills. In effect the authorities did no more than correct their own oversight in drafting the law by extending the concession to the applicants from Naoussa. At the same time the authorities demanded that a record of the imported equipment be submitted to the Provincial Government of Thessaloniki, obviously for purposes of verification. The same requirement was made of all subsequent applicants, and indeed it was included in the relevant tax legislation when that was renewed in 1896.[71]

The requests made by the Naoussa applicants were far from extraordinary or unreasonable in the Ottoman context, falling well within the range of concessions that were typically granted to privileged enterprises. The point is, however, that the privileged enterprises were frequently owned by cadres of the Ottoman bureaucracy. Until nearly the turn of the twentieth century, if

---

[70] BOA. İ.MMS.52/2274.
[71] See Akman (2007), Düstur 20, Safer 1314 (31.07.1896).

applicants were government officials, they were also able to avail themselves of an easier application procedure. Their applications would be forwarded to *Şura-yı Devlet Tanzimat Dairesi* (Department of Reforms in the Council of State) bypassing the *Ticaret ve Nafia Nezareti* (the Ministry of Trade and Public Works).[72] All recipients of such privileges belonged to the administrative bureaucracy. It is not at all surprising, therefore, that the Ottoman state denied the requests made by Longos, Kyrtsis and Tourpalis.

An even more revealing part of the assessment report by the Special Council was that the applicants had actually hoped to manufacture woollen as well as cotton yarn in the 1870s.[73] The response by the Municipality of Veroia was positive on cotton but negative on woollen yarn. Moreover, the Municipality insisted that the new project should not claim more public water than that taken by the flour mill already standing on the site. The Ottoman authorities in Veroia were quite explicitly concerned about the livelihood of the local population in Naoussa, especially women who earned a living by producing woollen yarn and cloth domestically, and wished to protect them. The authorities also intended to regulate the water supply, always a contentious issue in a region with heavy agricultural as well as manufacturing demands on water.

The response of the Municipality of Veroia should properly be seen in light of comments by Stougiannakis, the main Greek source on local industry. Stougiannakis, writing in 1911, lauded the perseverance of Longos, Kyrtsis and Tourpalis, who 'quite naturally' had to fight against 'many difficulties, prejudices and superstitions' and had to overcome 'many obstacles' before they could successfully bring to fruition 'the unprecedented and strange enterprise for those bygone days'.[74] It is apparent that there was disquiet in Naoussa about the project of the *şayak* merchants and parts of the community were opposed to it. The town could probably sense that an economic and social rupture was about to take place that would entail severe dislocation for many of its inhabitants. The Municipality of Veroia acted to prevent social discontent and even unrest.

As the application traversed its path further, the authorities in İstanbul and Thessaloniki concurred with the authorities in Veroia on the issue of wool but found in favour of the applicants on the use of water. The higher echelons

---

[72] See Damlıbağ (2012, p. 207).
[73] BOA. İ.MMS.52/2274.
[74] See Stougiannakis (1911, p. 148).

of the administration decided that, if the water supply to the existing flour mill was not sufficient for the proposed cotton mill, the applicants could lay claim to still more public water as long as they did not cause any harm to local gardens, fields and mills, and if the water was brought to the plant from further upstream.[75] The state did not fully side with the prospective industrialists but sought a compromise to allow the project to proceed, while also affording a degree of protection to the local community. A warning was issued that, if the construction of the factory did not commence within a year, the license would be rescinded.

It is clear that the Ottoman state was loath to relinquish control over economic and social developments that had the potential to disturb existing power structures. It was determined to monitor every stage of the process from the submission of the application to the commencement of operations. To this purpose the central authorities relied heavily on the provincial administrative mechanisms. Consultation and contact between İstanbul, Thessaloniki and Veroia were regular features of all subsequent applications. The final telegram sent by the Council of State to the Provincial Government of Thessaloniki on 2 July 1875, after the permit was granted to Longos–Kyrtsis–Tourpalis, made its attitude perfectly clear: if the new factory proved detrimental to the water supply of the local community and there were any complaints, a report should be immediately filed by the Provincial Government.[76] In the event the applicants brought water from a considerable way upstream through a complex system of channels that is still partially extant, and the provision of the Council of State was never activated.

It is instructive in this respect also to revisit the even earlier application made by Hadjilazaros in 1872, which made a point of stressing that the capital required for his project was huge, thus requesting substantial tax exemptions[77] Lack of capital and the burden of taxation were typical reasons for Ottoman entrepreneurs to ask for state support.[78] The state gave its approval to establishing the plant but granted none of Hadjilazaros's requests for tax relief, even though there had been several precedents of such favours. It is plausible

---

[75] BOA. İ.MMS.52/2274.
[76] BOA. ŞD.2006/10.
[77] BOA. ŞD.2402/18, 19 Cemaziyelahir 1290 (14.08.1873)
[78] See Kala (1993, pp. 109–10).

that the concessions were denied because of the applicants' links to Russia, since Ioannis Hadjilazaros was a Russian citizen. On the other hand, the state did grant concessions to Jewish industrialists and merchants of Thessaloniki who had Italian citizenship, for instance, the Allatini, the Torres, and so on. Perhaps its reaction to Hadjilazaros was due to great tensions in the 1870s as a major Russo-Turkish War was about to erupt in 1877. After all, when the Turco-Italian War of 1911 broke out, the Ottoman state's first reaction was to restrict the activities of its Italian citizens, delivering a lethal blow to the business interests of the Allatini and the Modiano of Thessaloniki.[79]

By the 1890s, however, things had become much smoother and the application of the Tsitsis mill in Edhessa in 1895 was finalized in just three months.[80] Nonetheless, monitoring by the state remained obsessive. The Technical Committee and the Customs Office of Thessaloniki meticulously examined machinery lists included in applications and rarely approved what was originally requested. Their finicky bureaucratic oversight is apparent in Plate 8 showing the machinery list for the proposed Kokkinos plant in Edhessa in 1903. The equipment appeared in both Ottoman Turkish and French, and the diligent pen of the Customs clerk crossed out several items that did not comply with the tax exemption regulations.

Perhaps the most absurd instance of such meddling occurred in connection with the application by Dimitrios Tourpalis in 1903, already mentioned in Section 7.3. When the machinery was actually imported, Tourpalis was forced to pay customs tax as the imports did not match the records. The industrialist subsequently appealed on the grounds of error, and thus the machinery list was dispatched by the Customs Office of Thessaloniki to İstanbul for further consideration. After thorough investigations by the Council of State, the Undersecretary, the Ministry of Commerce and Public Works, the Council of Ministers, the Chief Vizier and even the Sultan himself, it was revealed that Tourpalis had actually imported a *kayış* (machine belt) made of leather which had been erroneously listed as *kamış* (straw).[81] Fortunately for Tourpalis, the correct word appeared on the French version of the list and the issue

---

[79] See Hekimoglou (1991).
[80] BOA. ŞD.1207/8.
[81] BOA. ŞD.1224/49, BOA. BEO.3053/228957, BOA. MV.117/56, BOA. BEO.3191/239314.

was resolved. French had become an official language of the Empire in the nineteenth century and all machinery lists were written in both Ottoman Turkish and French.

Absurdity aside, the monitoring could at times resemble a police investigation. When Aristidis Kokkinos submitted his application in 1902, the Ministry of Property Records was alerted since the land for the plant was publicly owned. A map of the factory had to be produced, the names of the shareholders had to be registered, including their respective shares and title deeds, the appropriateness of the land had to be decided, its value ascertained, the tithe set, and the purposes of land use had to be carefully specified.[82] Similarly, in 1909, when Anastasios Pehlivanos imported tar for the woollen factory that he intended to build in Naoussa, the Customs Office of Thessaloniki objected on the grounds that the imported tar could be used for commercial trading. Pehlivanos appealed against the Customs decision stating that the tar used by commercial decorators, to whom he was accused of selling his imported tar, was of very low quality, unlike the substance that he had purchased.[83] Finally, the upgrade of the Sossidis and Faik plant in Veroia in 1910 required a very special investigation by the authorities. Since the upgrade would take place on state land, it was necessary to determine whether the plot contained any mosques, graveyards or sanctuary ruins.[84]

In sum, by the 1900s provincial industrialists had become adept at navigating the straits of Ottoman bureaucracy, while the state had become much more familiar with private industrial capitalism. The authorities did not object to applications as long as they were not perceived as a threat to the social balance, and no complaints were made by local communities. The Ottoman state had learnt in practice to support private industry and to cooperate with the capitalists, even when they were provincials from non-Muslim communities. A capitalist spirit was discernible in its mode of operation, together with heavy monitoring and control. Society had also profoundly changed as capitalism had taken root.

---

[82] BOA. ŞD.62/37.
[83] BOA. ŞD.1228/10.
[84] BOA. ŞD.MLK.74/2.

8

Ascendant industrialists, emerging working class, turbulent communities

The advance of industrialization brought profound changes to the class structure of Macedonia, most notably in Thessaloniki and the region of Mount Vermion. By the 1900s a class with a distinctly capitalist character had emerged in both places, though its outlook differed between the two, not least due to the cultural and political traditions of their respective communities. Similarly, a working class began to emerge with increasing coherence and ability to project its own views on political and social life. The outlook of the components of the working class also varied according to their respective communities.

Industrial capitalism in Ottoman Macedonia was led by the Jewish community in Thessaloniki and the Christian community in Mount Vermion which also became gradually established in Thessaloniki. Industrialization drew strength from communal practices and institutions, always within the constraints of Ottoman society and under the watchful eye of the Ottoman state. To deal with the problems of emerging capitalism, including class conflict, both communities relied on their own internal mechanisms of power and control that were typically attached to religious structures. They also interacted continually with the Ottoman state and the still dominant mechanisms of the Muslim community.

In Thessaloniki industrialization rested on the bedrock of a thoroughly urban Jewish community led by merchants who had an international outlook and often held foreign citizenship. In Mount Vermion, industrialization was based on a heavily agrarian Christian community and was spearheaded by merchants who had only recently sprung out of the same soil. From the very beginning the Christians tended to compete against Jewish economic power emanating from Thessaloniki and indeed the contest between the two communities went a long way into the historical past.

It was shown in previous chapters that the Jews of Thessaloniki were in a more advantageous position at the initial stages of industrialization due to their favourable relations with the Ottoman state and the superior economic and financial institutions of the port city. The Greek community of Thessaloniki responded partly by mobilizing the support of the Greek Kingdom. The growing power of the Greeks was manifest in the range of financial institutions that appeared at the very end of the nineteenth century, including the Banque de Mytilene, the Bank of Athens and the Banque d'Orient. Furthermore, as Ilicak noted, the Greek 'merchants of the interior' typically sent their sons to Thessaloniki to be installed as commercial agents: 'Greek banks extended credit to these young people and tried to establish contact with Greek clients from their hometown and region.'[1] The rivalry between the two communities intensified after the Young Turk revolution of 1908. There were anti-Jewish campaigns and boycotts by the Greek community, with the Greek press of the city calling on Greek nationals to desist from business transactions with the Jews.

The opposition between the two communities casts light on the social and political development of Ottoman Macedonia as industrial capitalism took root. The dominant form of conflict and struggle during the period of industrialization was between communities and the state as well as among communities. The tensions generated as commercial and industrial capitalism impacted on the social structures of Ottoman Macedonia were a major contributory factor to the nationalist confrontations among Muslims, Jews and Christians. Intense nationalist conflict occurred across Macedonia after 1870, assuming increasingly violent forms towards the end of the nineteenth and the beginning of the twentieth century. The Christian community largely favoured independence from the Empire but was rent asunder by the rivalry between Greek and Bulgarian nationalisms. Thessaloniki and the area of Mount Vermion, but also the area around Giannitsa and the *çiftlik* villages on the plain, witnessed vicious armed struggle in the 1900s, also involving the

---

[1] Ilicak (2002, p. 137). This practice underpinned the expansion of Naoussa capitalists in Thessaloniki in the face of the the city's unfavourable labour and energy costs.

Ottoman state. In contrast, nationalism and secession played a minor role in the life of the Jewish community, which had reached an implicit accommodation with the Ottoman state. Finally, the Muslim community was the last to be drawn to nationalism and tended generally to support the Ottoman Empire and its security forces.

The ethnic tensions in Macedonia and the trajectory of the notorious 'Macedonian Question' – essentially the issue of state control over the European part of the Ottoman Empire – are best considered against the background of rising industrial capitalism in the region. The social transformation wrought by advancing capitalism certainly led to conflict between capital and labour, especially in Thessaloniki, but also fuelled the nationalist struggle in Macedonia.

8.1 Social and communal parameters of capitalist transformation

The clear winners of the profound changes that took place across Ottoman Macedonia during the nineteenth century were the merchants, out of whom emerged the industrialists. It has been estimated that a foreign merchant resident in Thessaloniki could anticipate annual net profits of 200 per cent on investment, while indigenous merchants – provided they were sufficiently cautious – had even greater opportunities for profit making.[2] Jewish merchants became fabulously wealthy and came to control industry in Thessaloniki. Greek merchants from Mount Vermion became very rich, controlled industry in their region and acquired a significant economic presence in Thessaloniki.

Macedonian merchants initiated industrialization in the second half of the nineteenth century in textiles as well as other fields. More broadly, a variety of industrial enterprises emerged across Macedonia: distilleries, brick and tile plants, flour mills, soap factories, in addition to textile mills, and all served domestic markets. At first sight it appears that Sweezy's – and Pirenne's – approach to the emergence of capitalism fits the Ottoman case better than Dobb's, at least in Macedonia, the epicentre of Ottoman industrialization. To an extent this is obviously true, but appearances can be deceptive.

---

[2] See Svoronos (1956, p. 114).

The Jewish merchants of Thessaloniki broadly confirm Sweezy's view since they traded over long-distances and were well-connected internationally as well as being polyglot and often holding foreign passports. To be sure there were substantial numbers of Jewish merchants who did not conform to this type, but the leading ones certainly did. However, the Greek merchants of Mount Vermion were very different from the Jewish merchants of Thessaloniki. They also belonged to a trading tradition with a long international pedigree but were still rooted in the agrarian society of their region. They were from the beginning implicated in the domestic production of woollen cloth, probably reflecting the traditional skills of their birthplaces. These were merchants who had recently sprung out of the ranks of artisanal production and would pose few problems for Dobb's approach.

Furthermore, the wage workers employed by the Jewish merchants – who were often young women – came from the Jewish community and had a thoroughly urban background. In contrast, the wage workers of Mount Vermion – also often young women – came from the surrounding villages and typically worked in the mills for a short period of time. Without question the working class of Ottoman Thessaloniki did not spring out of an agrarian transformation. Equally, there was no wholesale dispossession of the peasantry in the second half of the nineteenth century in provincial Macedonia leading to emergence of wage labour. Capitalist agriculture failed to emerge altogether in Ottoman Macedonia despite industrial capitalism appearing in Thessaloniki and Mount Vermion.

Thus, the classic debates on the transition to capitalism have limited applicability to Ottoman Macedonia. This is further evidence that the specificity and peculiarities of each historical society preclude generalizations regarding the transition to capitalism. Theoretical debates, useful as they are to fix ideas and formulate appropriate questions, offer little more than guideposts to the actual historical emergence of capitalism.

The rise of the merchants and the eventual transformation of some among them into industrial capitalists in provincial Macedonia reflected the upheaval in the social structure of the Ottoman Empire after the second half of the eighteenth century. As *çiftlik* were formed in the agrarian sector, the provincial Muslim elite – the *ayan* – who frequently had military power, accumulated economic and political power in local areas. They obtained tax-farming rights, applied pressure on the peasants directly or through money-lending, and systematically enlarged their land-holdings. The *ayan* acquired vast power over their regions, particularly as central control weakened in the second half of the eighteenth century. That was indeed a time of dispossession of the peasantry in the Balkans, when a hereditary Muslim landlord class began to emerge in the Ottoman Empire.

It is arguable that conditions at the end of the eighteenth or the beginning of the nineteenth century were amenable to the emergence of agrarian capitalism in the Ottoman Empire. Agricultural production increased and became more intensive; control by rich individuals over agriculture (and to an extent over manufacturing) became easier through the *malikane* tax-farming system; layers of the peasantry were dispossessed due to heavy tax exactions and landlord pressure; and trade opportunities kept expanding. And yet, a fully-fledged capitalist transformation of agriculture never occurred in the Ottoman Balkans.

Ottoman agriculture was generally characterized by abundance of land and scarcity of labour. Peasant smallholdings were sizeable and opportunities to sell the crop were readily available. Similarly, the landlords were able to sell the surpluses produced by sharecroppers at a substantial profit. There were few incentives across the sector to transform agriculture on a capitalist basis by unifying strips of land, upgrading agricultural technique, using advanced technology and hiring wage labour. Moreover, the social and political orientation of the Muslim *ayan* was not conducive to agrarian capitalism. Their privileged status was tightly bound with their political position. The *ayan* deployed their wealth with a view to sustaining their political standing and relations, rather than systematically investing profits to raise the productivity of their lands.[3] They sought monetary profit aggressively and engaged in money lending, but their economic activities were heavily conditioned by non-economic power.

Critical to the evolution of the *ayan* was the absence of an ideology that would have allowed them to become a coherent agrarian class. There can be no capitalism without an ideological web uniting the nascent capitalist class around the calculus of monetary gain and loss. As the nineteenth century

---

[3] See Reyhan (2008, p. 138).

progressed, the *ayan* gradually lost social power and were integrated into the bureaucratic structures of the revived central Ottoman state. The landlords remained locally rich and powerful but had missed the historical boat to become capitalist farmers.

The rise of Muslim landlords encouraged further divisions along religious and communal lines in the Balkans. Muslim landlords certainly possessed Christian villages as part of their *çiftlik* and exercised political and social command over the villagers. However, if a non-Muslim *çiftlik* holder attempted to exercise similar command over Muslim peasants, intolerable religious and social tensions would be likely to break out. Furthermore, there is little or no evidence that powerful and prominent Christians – sometimes known as *kocabaşı* in southern Greece – tended systematically to become large landowners similar to the *ayan*. Note that the term *kocabaşı*, and its Macedonian equivalent, *çorbacı*, remained vague, as indeed was the term *ayan*. These were not official Ottoman titles but designations deployed among the communities to denote social standing.

That is not to deny that rich and powerful Christians were able to acquire large estates and became involved in tax farming even in the late eighteenth century in the Balkans and elsewhere.[4] But the power of the Christian notables derived primarily from the web of credit and money lending they were able to weave around the payment of taxes by their community to the state. The system of 'reallocation, or reapportioning' (*tevzi*) of local taxes, which emerged at the end of the eighteenth century as the power of the Porte declined, essentially allowed for local taxes to be paid by the community after deciding the incidence among its members.[5] The *ayan* used their political, military and financial power to mould the *tevzi* system in their own interests. In similar fashion, Christian communal notables had the financial means to provide the liquidity necessary to pay the taxes, subsequently binding the community to their interests through a structure of debts.[6] Their activities were closely related to the Orthodox Church, which had major tax-collecting functions. In this respect the Christian notables were similar to the *ayan*, but

---

[4] See Sadat (1972, p. 350). The case of Zafirakis in Naoussa was also noted in Chapter 4.
[5] See McGowan (1981, p. 159); see also Yaycioglu (2016, pp. 151–6).
[6] This argument has been thoroughly established for southern Greece by Petmezas (2003).

they were not a major landed class and usually possessed estates of smaller size.[7] There was no real comparison with the land-owning outlook of the Muslim *ayan*.

It was shown in Chapter 4 that in the area of Mount Vermion at the end of the nineteenth century there were several large landlords among the Christian notables. Yet, none of them hailed from an established landlord class. They had acquired vast estates in the second half of the century, but via a very different process to the *ayan*. Christian landlords had become wealthy through commerce and industry at a time when the Ottoman state had promulgated legislation that secured private property in land. They were capitalists investing in land, not landlords in the mould of the *ayan*. Remarkably, they did not transform their *çiftlik* into capitalist estates, for the straightjacket of *çiftlik* relations proved too rigid.

The privileged access to land that Muslims enjoyed in the late eighteenth and early nineteenth century pushed sizeable layers of the non-Muslim communities towards artisanal production and in commercial activity. Excluded from the land grab by the *ayan*, the richer and more energetic members of the Christian and Jewish communities 'increasingly entered trade, which reinforced their extraterritorial affiliations'.[8] The Jews had never, in any case, formed a landed community in Macedonia and were mainly manufacturers, traders, small shop-owners, and labourers. Christian peasants, on the other hand, were pushed to the uplands and turned to proto-industrial manufacturing typically organized by Christian merchants, who also engaged in money lending and tax farming. There were even upland Christian settlements that systematically cultivated cash crops under the leadership of communal notables.[9] The provincial Christian elite controlled agricultural production and domestic manufacturing through a complex web of cash advances and money lending that organized the financial affairs of the community. Relations between the Muslim landlord class and the Christian merchant and money-lending class often became cooperative. The *ayan* provided security while the merchants traded agricultural produce from the *çiftlik* of the *ayan*, as well as their own

---

[7] See Petmezas (1990, pp. 583–4).
[8] See Sadat (1972, p. 356).
[9] See Petmezas (1990, p. 584).

manufactured goods. The two groups had a common interest in the expansion of trade.[10]

Under these conditions Jews and Christians in Macedonia engaged in primitive accumulation of capital throughout the first half of the nineteenth century and were in pivot position to make the move to industrial capitalism when the opportunity arose. It is a misconception that indigenous entrepreneurial groups with capital to invest did not exist in the Ottoman Empire. It is a further misconception that the successful capitalists were the beneficiaries of privileged relations with foreign interests in the Empire. The leading Jewish capitalists in Thessaloniki had indeed kept a foot permanently in Western Europe, but the Christian Greek capitalists of Macedonia were not availed of special contacts with Western European interests. Both groups were engaged in a sustained commercial battle against foreign imports. Ottoman capitalists were products of the endogenous development of Ottoman society reflecting its unique historical peculiarities.

The exceptional weight of religious affiliation in determining juridical, political, property and communal rights was a notable feature of Ottoman society. The merchants of the Balkans – Christians, Jews and Muslims – came from communities that were permeated by religious institutions, functioning in a society and a state that had for centuries accorded to Islam a dominant position. Moreover, the core religious structures of the Christian and the Jewish communities were deeply conservative, and indeed functioned as integral parts of the Ottoman state machine.[11] The paradox was that the relatively marginal place of Christianity and Judaism in the Ottoman Empire offered to their respective communities a privileged window to the earth-shattering developments occurring in Western Europe.

Particularly important in this respect was the expansion of communal education which spread literacy but also familiarity with the new ideas that

---

[10] See Sadat (1972, p. 335).
[11] The religious organization of the Jewish community was vastly different to that of Orthodox Christians. Jewish religious institutions were far more horizontal across the community, lacking the hierarchical structure of the Orthodox Church. The Chief Rabbi, or *haham başı*, did not have remotely the same power over the community as the Orthodox Patriarch, and indeed his initial appointment occurred only in 1835 at the express insistence of the Ottoman state which sought a formal head for the Jewish *millet* (see, Levy, 1994b). The Jewish religious structures were generally a conservative force in Ottoman society.

accompanied the growth of capitalism in the West. Thus, barely two decades after the repopulation of the Naoussa in the 1830s, the provision of education preoccupied the leadership of the community and the Church, and a school was built in 1853. The tide truly turned in 1864, with the construction of the 'Naoussa Greek School', whose student numbers increased steadily, reaching almost five hundred in 1896–7.[12] Given that a decade and a half later the population of the town was perhaps ten thousand, the schooling of children had obviously become a widespread and regular practice among the Christians. Industrial capitalism would not be hampered by a lack of literate workers.

This development owed nothing to a presumed inherently 'progressive' character of Christianity or Judaism in contrast to Islam. Indeed there was nothing remotely Weberian to the religious aspect of Ottoman capitalism, whether Jewish or Christian.[13] Rather, the religious dimension was a result of the institutional and cultural evolution of Ottoman society. Dominant Ottoman Islam had an unshakeable belief in its superiority relative to Christianity and Judaism, and paid a bitter price for the conservatism engendered by its ascendancy. The modernizing Ottoman state of the nineteenth century took steps to promote education but ultimately failed to create effective structures across society that could homogenize the cultural outlook of the population. In provincial Macedonia the result was a system of education supported by communal mechanisms which fostered a Christian religious and cultural identity that became synonymous with social progress.

Religion was also important for the stratification of the *reaya*, the main tax paying class in the Ottoman Empire, who were mostly peasants but also artisans and traders. The impositions of the *ayan* and the tax pressures by the state were felt across the body of the *reaya* irrespective of religious affiliation However, in the seventeenth and eighteenth centuries the Muslims were able to escape from taxation in ways that were not available to non-Muslims. They had exclusive access to the Janissary Corps until its disbandment;

---

[12] See Biliouris (2014, p. 14).
[13] In the sense of broadly confirming Weber's substantive approach in his classic work *The Protestant Ethic and the Spirit of Capitalism*.

they enjoyed privileged access to the urban guilds; they were favoured by religious establishments that played a strong economic role, above all, the *vakıf*. In contrast, non-Muslims typically paid additional taxes, including a poll tax, though they were much less likely to be conscripted in the armed forces. Furthermore, as was mentioned earlier, the taxes of Christian peasant communities were determined according to population and were reapportioned internally. Community notables and Church representatives would often collect and pay taxes on behalf of the community, making up shortfalls on behalf of those who could not meet their obligations.[14] The ties of money lending and the obligations of tax paying were inextricably linked, holding Christian communities together, while also creating internal power structures.

As industrial capitalism advanced and the Ottoman state was itself transformed in the second half of the nineteenth century, relations among the communities inevitably changed. Jewish and Christian merchants and industrialists became familiar with the mechanisms and institutions of Ottoman power, as was shown in Chapter 7. However, Muslim merchants and capitalists were also active, at the very least because tax farming and effective money lending had always been a regular practice of Muslim landlords and others. A working class began to emerge, especially in Thessaloniki, that was able to overcome communal barriers, even if it was mostly Jewish and Christian. The capitalist spirit was abroad and the ideological role of religion lost some of its weight. At the same time the rising nationalism of Western and Central Europe entered the Ottoman realm, often through the channels of education, the very conduit of modernity.

The merchants and industrialists of provincial Macedonia gained coherence as a group by being Christian, a cultural identity that also strongly predisposed them to being ethnically Greek. They were certainly not rebels, but they were also not ideal material for an Ottoman capitalist class. The absence of a unifying and homogenizing ideological framework warped the development of capitalism in the Ottoman context.

---

[14] See Petmezas (1990, p. 584).

8.2 A nascent capitalist class in Mount Vermion: Controlling the community and dealing with the state

The Christian Greek upper social layer of Mount Vermion was dominated by landowners, real estate owners, merchants, moneylenders and industrialists, who can be described loosely as the *çorbacı*. The term did not denote an official Ottoman title and nor was it recognized by the state, but it was widely deployed at the time. Gradually it came to acquire negative and even pejorative implications as class, communal and ethnic tensions were exacerbated in the course of capitalist development.

Many of the Naoussa *çorbacı* had moved into the town from the surrounding villages and nearby areas of Mount Vermion when Naoussa was repopulated in the 1830s. Ties among them were cemented through intermarriage, gradually creating a closed and exclusive social layer. It is common for familial links to support the emergence of commercial and industrial capitalism since they provide necessary – and unspoken – mechanisms of trust and monitoring of economic activities. The family and community networks of the *çorbacı*, establishing access and control over capital, land, commercial networks and market information, were vital to the industrial transformation of the area of Mount Vermion. The families of the *çorbacı* were able to secure privileged access to land that was close to fast-flowing water. They were also heavily involved in the management of communal funds as well as being implicated in the collection and payment of local and national taxes.[15]

A flavour of the social outlook of the *çorbacı* of Naoussa can be gained from the photograph of members of the Longos family in Figure 8.1. Surrounded by women of the Longos family, who were relations of the great *çorbacı* 'Galakis' Longos, stands Heracles Hadjidimoulas, erect and confident. The industrialist, who had interests in Edhessa, is formally attired, as is his wife to his left. All the younger women are dressed and coiffed in the 'European' style, as are also the children. The older women, including the mother of Hadjidimoulas and sister of 'Galakis' Longos, are dressed in traditional, if wealthy, Naoussa style.

---

[15] See Lapavitsas (2006, p. 672).

Figure 8.1 Members of the Longos family, early twentieth century
Source: Private collection, made available by Lazaros Biliouris.

The social and cultural leap that had taken place within a single generation is manifest.

A similar image is projected by the Bilis and Tsitsis families, standing to be photographed in the yard of their plant in Figure 8.2. The families, whose members held variable shares of equity, are evidently making a show of their alliance. The men, even the older ones, are dressed in the 'European' style, as are the younger women and the children. One older woman is wearing traditional dress. The scene has a relaxed air, which makes even more apparent the presence of modernity as well as a bourgeois outlook and abundant social power.

However, nothing conveys more clearly the social transformation that had taken place in the preceding decades than the picture in Figure 8.3. The photograph was taken in the yard of the Tsitsis plant in Naoussa, that of the complicated Lapavitsas–Kokkinos provenance. The Victorian design of the plant is clear, but even more vivid is the confident outlook of the Tsitsis, Longos and Kokkinos families posing in their finery, with some of the older women dressed traditionally and at considerable expense. The gathering took

Figure 8.2 Bilis–Tsitsis families, early twentieth century
Source: Private collection of Takis Baitsis.

Figure 8.3 Tsitsis, Kokkinos and Longos families in the 1920s
Source: Private collection of Takis Baitsis.

place under Greek rule well after the end of Ottoman power in Macedonia, but the people in the factory yard had acquired their wealth and high social standing under Ottoman conditions. It is immediately apparent to the trained eye that they were provincials. This is a fleeting – almost ghostly – image of the bourgeoisie that the Ottoman Empire never fully succeeded in forming in provincial Macedonia. At the back and near the middle, surveying all, stands the patriarchal figure of Aristides Kokkinos.

It should further be said that, despite the dramatic social changes wrought by advancing industrial capitalism, the Christian community of Mount Vermion also exhibited great social conservatism. A remarkable picture of a group of young women of Naoussa in the 1920s serves as witness in Figure 8.4. The photograph was taken during Carnival – a major religious and social occasion in the region – and the women posed in what were clearly their best clothes in the traditional style. Modernity had made great strides and was on occasion flaunted in Naoussa, but the traditional background from which the new world had emerged had far from disappeared. Attachment to it was on occasion strongly asserted.

In this rapidly changing world much of the power of the *çorbacı* derived from control over the community, which meant in the first instance control over local administration, the main field of political struggle in Naoussa. The mechanisms of local administration were completely reformed after the Tanzimat as central authority was reasserted. In the 1850s Naoussa had a resident civilian officer, a *müdür*, and a judge, a *kadi*, both of whom were in charge of implementing Tanzimat reforms.[16] The *müdür* guided local administration until the end of Ottoman rule, supported by resident lower-ranking officers for forestry, post and telegraph services, the tobacco monopoly and the police.

The Ottoman administration was further revamped after the *Vilayet* Law (*Teşkil-i Vilayet Nizamnamesi*) of 1867, which allowed Christians to assume official positions in local areas, a natural byproduct of the Rescript of Reform (*Islahat Hatt-ı Hümayunu*) of 1856. The office of mayor was integral to the modernized Ottoman local administration of the Tanzimat since the mayor had formal power over the town's affairs and was entitled to an armed guard.

---

[16] See Nicolaidy (1859, [vol. 2] p. 281).

Figure 8.4 Young women of Naoussa, early twentieth century
Source: Private collection.

But the law was far from easy to implement in view of the age-old traditions of discrimination in the Ottoman Empire and the likely reactions of the Muslim community. Still, the *çorbacı* coveted the post of mayor for the formal role it afforded in the state machine. It thus became an object of political struggle with the workers and the poor of Naoussa.

The reaction of the Muslim community of Naoussa to the administrative reforms was anything but tolerant, even taking violent forms in the 1860s. The first mayor of Naoussa, appointed in 1868, was actually a local Muslim with little social power, a barber. Within a year the *çorbacı* had taken over the position and Constantinos Lapavitsas was appointed as the first Christian mayor of Naoussa, a post he kept for many years. He was followed by Constantinos Antonakis (Perdikaris), another *çorbacı* elected through limited suffrage, and then by *Mici Longo Ağa* (Dimitrios Longos), who was the first mayor to be mentioned in Ottoman documents in 1886.[17] The first mayor to be elected with full male suffrage was Constantinos Hadjimalousis, also a *çorbacı*, whose election in the 1900s signalled the sharpening of social tensions in the area and the growing confidence of workers and the poorer social strata of Naoussa.

While embedding themselves in the local Ottoman structures, the *çorbacı* cultivated the formal communal governance mechanisms fostered by the Tanzimat. The Christian community of Naoussa had a long tradition of self-government, evidence of which is available from travellers for the period before 1822, who also confirmed the existence of Christian armed forces at the disposal of the leader of the community, the *archon*.[18] The revolt of 1822 obviously delivered a body blow to these structures. Yet, by the 1850s the mechanisms of self-government for the Christian community of Naoussa had been re-established, led by ten notables, the Elders (Demogerontes).[19] They operated in conjunction with the mechanisms of the Orthodox Church, the head of which for Naoussa was the Bishop of Veroia.

The structures of self-government in the 1890s and the 1900s, the period of the fastest growth of industrial capitalism, were determined by adult male

---

[17] See SVS IX, 1303 [1886]. For the first mayors see Goutas (1999, p. 133).
[18] See Cousinery (1831, pp. 72–3) and Pouqueville (1826, vol. II, p. 94).
[19] See Nicolaidy (1859, [vol. 2] p. 282).

suffrage in the four main parishes of the town, electing twenty representatives who met with the Bishop of Veroia in the chair. The representatives were in charge of monitoring the economic affairs of a host of committees dealing with town affairs, but mostly religious and education issues.[20] The representatives also elected the Council of Elders (Demogerontia), a formal body that operated as a Court of Law based on the Byzantine and Orthodox legal corpus that was made available by the Patriarchate of Constantinople, in addition to deploying customary law. The suits brought to the Council were typically civil cases referring to marriage, inheritance, communal property, debts and employment contracts, and a host of other minor issues. The Council also dealt with cases relating to the payment of the Church Contribution, a widely disliked imposition on the community.

Much of the power of the *çorbacı* of Naoussa derived from controlling the finances of the parishes, thus availing themselves of access to liquid funds. Power also derived from engaging in the provision of communal education, which relied on the mechanisms of the Church. It was a common practice for powerful and wealthy families to make donations and become involved in the management of the schools and churches that emerged in Naoussa towards the end of Ottoman rule. Control over church and education affairs had profound economic, social, but also ethnic implications. Naturally, it became a hotly contested field between the *çorbacı* and the emerging working class as well as among the rival nationalist movements of the area.

The published Minutes of the Council of Elders for the 1890s and 1900s contain mostly trivial disputes typical of the life of any community. However, they also refer to major cases that involved the *çorbacı* of Naoussa. One of these was the suit brought by Lapavitsas against Kokkinos, discussed in Chapter 7. There were several others that cast an equally revealing light on the life of the community. Thus, in April 1911, the Council heard a case against Dimitrios Tsitsis who had used church funds to acquire property in Thessaloniki, and subsequently refused to return it to the community, or even pay the appropriate rents. In January 1912 another case was brought by several *çorbacı* against Spyridon Lanaras, who was chair of the leading *çorbacı* political society of the town and had kept possession of substantial funds of the society instead of

---

[20] See Valsamidis and Intzesiloglou (2016, pp. 289–96).

making them available to schools. The Council found against the accused in both cases.[21]

Two points from this evidence are important for our purposes. The first is that control over communal mechanisms was of vital importance to the *çorbacı*, and they were keen to acquire it. Their dominant position was continually challenged by communal bodies that had attained considerable independence towards the end of the period. Rising capitalism had led to burgeoning popular discontent that eventually found a political voice. The second is that the *çorbacı* were prepared to seek recourse to the justice mechanisms of the community for significant affairs, while continuing to avail themselves of the judicial procedures of the Ottoman state.

The peculiar duality of Ottoman society is thus made manifest: an authoritarian and prying state coexisted with communal mechanisms that enjoyed remarkable independence and towards which the state often showed little interest. The *çorbacı* negotiated their relations with the Ottoman state in the decades after 1870 and took advantage of its mechanisms, even though these were not entirely free from the prejudices and habits of the past. Furthermore, the *çorbacı* were riven by divisions among themselves arising from the tensions of industrialization and capitalist accumulation. They naturally sought recourse to official justice, and the attitude of the Ottoman state towards their internecine conflicts was indicative of the state's own transformed outlook.

Consider, for instance, the dispute between Longos–Kyrtsis–Tourpalis and Lamnides regarding their respective applications for woollen mills in 1907, already mentioned in Chapter 7. The two sides came into conflict regarding access to the waters of Arapitsa and the issue went well beyond the remit of local administration, the case being eventually taken to the courts. Lamnides succeeded in obtaining permission to build; the application of Longos–Kyrtsis–Tourpalis was rejected on the grounds that the flow of water was insufficient in the summer. The disgruntled applicants sent grievance letters to the Provincial Government of Thessaloniki on 17 July 1907 and to the General Inspectorate of the *Vilayet* of *Rumeli* on 28 July 1907 claiming that the decision was based solely on the misleading testimony of Lamnides.[22] They also filed a case in

---

[21] Ibid., pp. 176–81 and pp. 223–5.
[22] BOA. TFR.I.SL.161/16085.

the Court of the First Instance in Veroia asserting that the use of water by Lamnides would harm those who held land on the opposite bank of the river, such as themselves.

The dispute had actually begun earlier in 1907. Documents indicate that Lamnides had requested an official investigation of a damaged water wheel on suspicion that malefactors were involved. The Municipality of Veroia instructed the builder of the wheel to investigate the incident and he concluded that the causes were natural.[23] The Court of the First Instance, nonetheless, decided that Lamnides should suspend construction of his mill as long as there were complaints about water use. On this basis Longos–Kyrtsis–Tourpalis quickly resubmitted their application, which was however rejected on the grounds that the dispute was still not settled since Lamnides had taken his case to the Court of Appeal.[24] No further evidence is available in the archives but since Lamnides's permit was actually used to build the Hadzilazaros–Angelakis plant, it is probable that Longos–Kyrtsis–Tourpalis let their application lapse. What is important for our purposes is that, much as they tried, none of the warring sides had sufficient strength to swing the authorities in its favour. The Ottoman state acted as an impartial observer and judge, retaining some of the concern for the social implications of the industrial use of water that it had also demonstrated in 1874–5.

The attitude of the state was broadly similar in a further case, namely a complaint by Longos–Kyrtsis–Tourpalis regarding the presumed overvaluation of their industrial operations for tax purposes, submitted to the General Inspectorate of the *Vilayet* of *Rumeli* in 1905.[25] The industrialists argued that valuing the plant and the machinery separately from each other had resulted in overvaluation, and hence their tax obligations had been overestimated. The Ministry of Finance (*Maliye Nezareti*) concurred with the industrialists on the grounds that the relevant laws prohibited the taxation of machinery, even though the Regional Revenue Officer (*Mal Müdürü*) had insisted that the valuation method was appropriate.[26] But there was a caveat: the additional value

---

[23] BOA. TFR.I.SL.140/13923.
[24] BOA. TFR.I.SL.161/16085.
[25] BOA. TFR.I.ŞKT.70/6999.
[26] Specifically, the Public Mandate of *Hazine-i Celile* (Treasury), issued on 17.06.1893, and the *Vergi Emaneti* (Tax Security Department) issued on 20.04.1885.

created by means of the machinery would have to be taken into consideration in ascertaining the amount of tax. This was certainly bad economics, if the point of the tax was to impose a charge on wealth. Yet, once again the state appeared impartial by maintaining a careful distance from the complainants.

For provincial industrialists the task of establishing a close relationship with the state was far from easy. Distance – physical and social – must have been an important factor, and the contrast with the Jewish industrialists was striking. In the voluminous documentation in the archives that refer to the Allatini industrial enterprises there are no demands for testimonials to the family's character or uprightness, despite the fact that they were Italian subjects.[27] The Allatini had at their disposal an entirely different order of contacts and influence in Ottoman society.

Perhaps, however, things had begun to change towards the very end of the period, particularly as some of the provincial industrialists had moved to Thessaloniki and their operations matured, even taking the joint-stock form. This seems to be the evidence from correspondence by Hadjilazaros and Angelakis, who had built the closest relationship with the Ottoman state, mostly by supplying cloth to the gendarmerie. The letter by Athanassios Makris, mentioned in Chapter 6, which had been sent to the Council of State in 1912, stated boldly that the company requested the same favourable treatment given to the Thessaloniki Fez and Textiles Mill Inc. Co., owned by the Allatini. The concessions included a ten-year exemption from property tax, land tax, dividend tax, patent tax and customs tax for all the machinery and raw materials required by the plant. Remarkably, Makris also stated that:[28]

> In fact, the necessity of the requested concessions, in view of competition with foreign products and the resulting economic benefits, has already been acknowledged by the state, which is believed to have included them in the Industrial Encouragement Law (*Teşvik-i Sanayi Kanunu*) that is now being prepared by the Council of Ministers (*Meclis-i Mebusan*).

The letter by Makris was addressed to the government that was formed after the establishment of the Young Turk regime in 1909. Quite apart from its confident tone, it is striking that Makris had already been apprised of

---

[27] And some Austrian, or French; see BOA. MKT.NZD.423/77.
[28] BOA. ŞD.1240/35, 23 Receb 1330/ 25 Haziran 1328 (08.07.1912).

the content of forthcoming legislation. Things had come a long way for the provincials. Nevertheless, when Hadzilazaros applied to build a new road leading to his plant in 1911, the application was initially turned down on the grounds that it would affect public recreation areas. It was eventually approved but on condition that it would neither impinge on the land of other people, nor damage the existing road.[29]

8.3 The emergence of a working class

The counterpart to a rising capitalist class was, of course, an emerging working class. From the 1870s onwards substantial concentrations of industrial workers appeared in the Ottoman Empire, particularly in Macedonia. Information about employment conditions, but also about living and other conditions, is relatively scarce. For Macedonia the most reliable evidence is about Thessaloniki and there is very little on the provincial mills. Information on capital–labour relations in the provinces can only be gleaned from scattered comments as well as from a few references in the archives. The history of the formation of the provincial working class in Macedonia, unlike that of the capitalist layer, is practically impossible to write. It is instructive to remember, furthermore, that Ottoman workers laboured under probably the worst conditions in Europe. There was neither an officially recognized scale of wages nor a single Factory Act issued by the Ottoman state throughout its existence.[30]

The officially recorded number of workers in Thessaloniki varied greatly, but it is certain that a large and active working class was present in the city by the early 1900s.[31] Statistical figures for 1910 together with the estimates by the workers' federations put the number of wage workers in the city, employed in eleven industrial sectors, at around ten thousand; most of the enterprises employed less than ten workers each.[32] The bulk of the labour force comprised Jewish labourers, especially women and children. Ilicak has estimated that, in

---

[29] BOA. ŞD.2075/8; BOA. DH-H.33-1/53.
[30] See Dumont and Haupt (1978, p. 69).
[31] There is a significant literature on the labour movement in Thessaloniki and the Ottoman Empire see Sencer (Baydar) (1969, 1982); Ilicak (2002); Karakışla (1998); Mentzel (1994); Dumont and Haupt (1978); Quataert and Zürcher (1995).
[32] See Ilicak (2002, p. 120).

1893, a total of 640 workers were employed in the cotton mills alone, 480 of whom were women or girls, and all of whom were Jews.[33]

The cotton mills of Thessaloniki operated from sunrise to sunset, and workers only had a thirty-five-minute break for lunch. Wages were low. Hekimoglou considered the annual earnings of a skilled worker in Thessaloniki to be at most 50 Ottoman *lira*, while a skilled accountant would make 150, a high bank executive 200, and a bank manager 300–1,000 Ottoman *lira*, depending on the bank.[34] More reliable seems to be Quataert's estimate of around 5–8 *guruş* daily for unskilled men and 3–8 *guruş* for women and children, which amounted to roughly 20 Ottoman *lira* per annum for men and perhaps 10–15 for women.[35] Men were paid two to three times more than boys and starting wages for girls were 50 per cent lower than for boys.[36] Poverty was the hallmark of workers and the lower social strata in Thessaloniki, and poverty marked the bulk of the Jewish community.

The workers federations in Thessaloniki repeatedly stated that the Ottoman labourers worked under the worst conditions in Europe.[37] Remarkably, employment conditions in the provincial mills were much worse than in Thessaloniki. A large proportion of workers in the Naoussa mills came from the surrounding villages, as was also probably the case in Veroia and Edhessa.[38] There is little doubt that the majority of the workers were young women and girls.[39] Their wages were substantially lower than in Thessaloniki, perhaps only a third, as was already mentioned in Chapter 6. After all, towards the end of 1912 the daily wage for women and children in Thessaloniki had reached 7 *guruş*. Provincial workers were plainly paid a pittance.

Working hours in the provincial mills, as in Thessaloniki, were very long: from 'sunrise to sunset' or 'dawn to dusk'.[40] This meant a fifteen-hour day in summer and a ten-hour day in winter. Things could get much

---

[33] Ibid., pp. 121–2.
[34] See Hekimoglou (1997, p. 177). The estimate by Hekimoglou was taken from Kofinas (1914) and should be treated with the utmost caution. Presumably Kofinas meant indigenous skilled labour, not workers invited from abroad, who typically earned a lot more.
[35] See Quataert (2014).
[36] See Quataert (1993a, p. 47).
[37] See Ilicak (2002, p. 121).
[38] See Lapavitsas (2006, p. 679).
[39] See, for instance, Upward (1908, p. 188) and Quataert (1993a, p. 47).
[40] A point that is generally agreed; see Lapavitsas (2006, pp. 679–80); Quataert (1993a, p. 47); Upward (1908, p. 188).

Figure 8.5 Working conditions in the factories
Source: Private collection of Takis Baitsis.

harder, however, when the pressure of market demand was great. Thus, in correspondence with the Ottoman authorities in 1903, *Liğor Çiçi* (Grigorios Tsitsis) of Edhessa stated that, although his mill usually operated from sunrise to sunset, there were times in winter when it had to continue until midnight.[41] This made the working day seventeen- or eighteen-hours long, and it most probably was a single shift.

The harsh conditions that workers faced during these shifts can be glimpsed from photographs that date from the period after the end of Ottoman rule but still give a taste of the interior of the textile plants during the Ottoman period. Thus, Figure 8.5 shows that textile capitalism in Naoussa, as elsewhere in the world, relied on the nimble fingers of young girls and children. They worked in a gloomy and bare environment that became harsh in winter. The prevalence of child and female labour is even more apparent in the striking image of Figure 8.6. It is probable that a gender-based division of labour existed in the plants, perhaps reflected in the male presence in Figure 8.7. Note that the photograph also shows the central axle providing the fundamental motion of the machinery.

In the same note, Tsitsis requested permission to electrify his plant. The introduction of the note summed up the 'mission statement' of his company as follows:[42]

> Our company, founded seven years ago and comprising solely of Ottoman subjects, has succeeded in establishing a sizeable water-powered yarn and

[41] BOA. TFR.I. ŞKT.15/1465.
[42] BOA. TFR.I.ŞKT.15/1465.

Figure 8.6 Child and female labour in the mills
Source: Private collection of Takis Baitsis.

Figure 8.7 Men working in the mills
Source: Private collection of Takis Baitsis.

fabric factory in Edhessa, thanks to His Majesty's permission. Since then it has spared no sacrifice to compete with European products.

With this lofty ambition Tsitsis kept the plant going until late at night in winter. The problem was that it was impossible to use gas lamps to provide light since there was a great danger of setting the cotton dust on fire. Candles were used, which unfortunately did not illuminate the workplace sufficiently to ensure its efficient operation. Tsitsis must have been aware of the gains made by the Allatini flour mill in Thessaloniki, which was electrified and able to work during the night from as early as 1890.[43] He appeared much less interested in the welfare of his workers – scutching, carding, drawing and spinning cotton for interminable hours, by candlelight and without heating in the freezing winter nights of Edhessa. Dark, satanic mills, indeed.

The response of the authorities to Tsitsis is not known, but there is a further letter in the archives dating from 1907, which again requested permission to electrify the mill. The request was supported by a letter from the Austrian Embassy to the Grand Vizier (*Sadrazam*) which also asked for customs clearance for the electrical equipment. The supplier was the huge concern of Ganz and Co. in Budapest.[44] Efficiency would be served at last.

Workplace accidents that resulted in major injuries attracted the interest of the Municipal authorities and even of the General Inspectorate of *Rumeli*. The Inspectorate was founded towards the end of 1902, mainly to deal with unrest in Macedonia and *Rumeli*, and operated until the Young Turk Revolution in 1908 under the Inspector Hüseyin Hilmi *Paşa* who was responsible for the reorganization of the disturbed provinces.[45] There are at least three files in the archives on factories in Naoussa, Edhessa and Veroia in 1903–4 relating to serious injuries incurred either in the construction or in the operation of the factories.[46] The Ottoman state could be very meticulous on some of these occasions. Thus, the Local Administration of Naoussa was ordered to investigate an incident in which the worker *Marika*, daughter of *Dimitri*, was seriously injured in the Longos–Kyrtsis–Tourpalis plant in

---

[43] SVS X, 1307 [1890].
[44] BOA. BEO.3021/226569; BOA. İ.RSM.28/21; BOA. BEO.3084/231233.
[45] See Adanır (1996).
[46] BOA. TFR.I.SL.19/1804; BOA. TFR.I.SL.22/2133; BOA. TFR.I.SL.44/4382

1904 because her hair was caught in the straps of a machine.[47] It is hardly credible that over four decades there were a mere three accidents, however, especially in view of the harsh labour conditions. It is more likely that the state intervened only when accidents were too serious to be handled tacitly at the plant.

One reason for worse wages and conditions in the provincial mills was the relative abundance of labour power in the provinces. Quataert asserts that:[48]

> Generally, however, there were few other wage-earning jobs near the mills of interior Macedonia and so the operators could rely on cultivators who were available seasonally. During the summer harvest, the number of workers did fall sharply. But, since they had few other opportunities to earn cash wages, their labour remained cheap and available for the yarn factories of the Macedonian interior.

Labour supply became more problematic in the 1900s as migration to the United States of America and elsewhere assumed significant dimensions in rural Macedonia.[49] There were also employment opportunities in agriculture, especially in the booming tobacco industry. Provincial employers were obliged to improve conditions somewhat, but the gap with Thessaloniki remained.[50]

A further reason for better conditions in Thessaloniki was that its workers constituted the most conscious and best organized section of the working class in the Empire.[51] The labour movement of Thessaloniki proved capable of putting upward pressure on wages, especially in the 1900s. Tobacco and textile workers had begun to engage in strike action already in the early 1900s, but the decisive moment came in 1908 immediately after the Young Turk Revolution, when a great strike wave engulfed the city and the Empire. On one count there were 60 strikes in the three months immediately after the Revolution, in which more than 100,000 workers took part;[52] according to Güzel, there were altogether 111 strikes in 1908.[53] The frustrations of the emerging working class

---

[47] BOA. TFR.I.SL.44/4382.
[48] See Quataert (1993a, p. 46).
[49] See Quataert (2014, p. 245).
[50] See Quataert (1993a, p. 48).
[51] See Quataert (2014, p. 245).
[52] See Sencer (Baydar) (1982).
[53] See Güzel (1996, pp. 35–47).

that had accumulated over many years, exploded after the rise of the Young Turks.[54]

A direct result of the strikes in Thessaloniki was the emergence in 1909 of the Socialist Workers' Federation, led by Avraam Benaroya, a Bulgarian Jew. The Federation, as its name signified, hoped for a common front and joint organization of all workers in Thessaloniki and indeed across the Empire. It was broadly supportive of the Empire as a state entity but naturally not as a social or political formation. Among its founding members were Bulgarian socialists and even the socially radical elements among Bulgarian nationalists. The bulk of Federation support came from Jewish and Bulgarian workers, while Greek workers generally kept their distance. In one of those curious twists of history, however, the Federation was instrumental to the eventual creation of the Greek Communist Party in the 1920s, and had an input in the making of the Turkish Communist Party.

The Ottoman state showed no interest in improving employment conditions, despite strict control over the establishment and operation of the factories. The state would become involved only when there was a major incident, such as a dispute over pay. It certainly disapproved of labour movements and attempted to avoid capital–labour confrontations, especially when the state itself was the employer. When the Police Department was established in 1845, several punitive measures were legally promulgated to support its actions in dealing with employee mobilizations.[55] After the 1890s the state became increasingly uneasy about proletarianization in the cities and elsewhere, and was so concerned about new forms of labour organization that it intervened to restrict them.[56]

Equally revealing was the response of the Young Turks to the strike wave of 1908. The government passed the Provisional Strike Law (*Tatil-i Eşgal Cemiyetleri Hakkında Kanun-ı Muvakkat*) in 1909, marking a deliberate change of attitude by the state towards workers.[57] The various prohibitions imposed during the previous era indicated that the Ottoman state understood

---

[54] See Özok-Gündoğan (2012, p. 183).
[55] See Sencer (Baydar) (1969, pp. 97–8).
[56] See Quataert (1993b).
[57] See Ökçün (1982).

little of the generic opposition between capital and labour, and dealt with such conflicts as a matter of public order. In contrast, the new Law was fully aware of the nature of social conflict and attempted to resolve it, but in favour of capital.[58] There would be no social revolution delivered by the Young Turks, certainly none that they had intended.

The organization of labour in the interior of Macedonia was much inferior to Thessaloniki. Important in this regard was that wage labourers in the provinces were often engaged in cultivating their own smallholdings.[59] There is also little doubt that employer pressure on workers was of a different order of magnitude compared to Thessaloniki. Measures were systematically taken to assert employer power, and even 'armed goons were employed by mill-owners to police clocking-in times and intimidate workers'.[60] The fact that the factories of the interior Macedonia had armed guards is also confirmed by the Ottoman archives. In one well-documented case the Tsitsis brothers requested permission to hire four or five armed guards in their factory in Naoussa to protect it from possible Bulgarian attacks, and their application was approved by the authorities.[61].

There were no worker strikes recorded in Naoussa, or elsewhere in the provincial mills, during the Ottoman period. Even so, in Naoussa a grassroots movement emerged in the 1890s, the *Poupoulo*, which had populist and socialist sympathies, as well as a constitution that demanded better conditions for workers.[62] The inevitable conflict between the *Poupoulo* and the *çorbacı* of Naoussa took directly political rather than industrial forms. There was intense rivalry, particularly over controlling the administrative structures of the town, above all the office of the mayor. After protracted political struggles in the 1900s, the *Poupoulo* prevailed and its leader, Constantinos Hadjimalousis, was the first mayor of Naoussa elected with full male suffrage. Unfortunately, there is no information about these events in the archives, which is not surprising as they were generally settled within the Christian community. The absence of involvement by the Ottoman state is itself indicative of the direction of development of Ottoman capitalism.

---

[58] See Boratav (2007, pp. 19–39). For the national(ist) economy policy of the Young Turks, see Toprak (2012).
[59] See Lapavitsas (2006, p. 678).
[60] Ibid., p. 680.
[61] BOA. TFR.I.SL. 154/15376; BOA. TFR.I.SL. 155/15450; BOA. TFR.I.SL. 155/15459.
[62] See Lapavitsas (2006, p. 680).

The Ottoman state, ever vigilant and controlling, kept itself rather aloof from the internal political life of the Christian community, also reflecting its distance from the *çorbacı*. The struggle between the *çorbacı* and the *Poupoulo* in Naoussa was largely handled by the Christian community relying on its own resources, but also by turning to the Kingdom of Greece, including the Athens newspapers and the Greek consul in Thessaloniki. Similarly, the community mobilized the mechanisms of the Church rather than the Ottoman state to tackle sharp disputes about education and schools.[63] The Ottoman state never possessed the ideological means that were necessary fully to integrate the Christian community. The Christians belonged to Ottoman society, but they were still an 'other'. These were the grounds on which nationalism took root in the community.

To sum up, the conditions of the emerging working class in provincial Macedonia were extremely poor. The British traveller Upward was dismayed by the social and working conditions that he saw in Naoussa in 1907–8 and commented in a memorable turn of phrase: 'It is progress, it is civilisation, but even when the Turk has gone there will still be something left for the Labour Party to do in Niausta.'[64] He was certainly right, although there would be no Labour Party in Macedonia after the arrival of the Greek army in 1912. Social, political and economic conditions changed substantially under Greek rule, but industrial and social tensions continued to pile up. When the Democratic Army of Greece, the Communist insurgent army of the Greek Civil War, occupied Naoussa in January 1949, some of the heaviest fighting took place in the fortified mills. Decades of class tension peaked violently when the rebels burnt the factories and mansions of the elite of Naoussa.

8.4 The clash of nationalisms

Nationalism in the Balkans was imported from Western Europe towards the end of the eighteenth century, as the ideas of the Enlightenment and the

---

[63] Ibid.
[64] See Upward (1908, p. 188). Upward was also amazed to discover that 'English football' was keenly practiced in the little Macedonian town. This unmistakable sign of the working class was probably the gift of English engineers brought in to operate the machinery of the factories.

French Revolution began to spread. It was initially most prominent among the Greeks, whose revolt in 1821 had much of the character of a people's rising. Among the Slavic peoples of the peninsula it arrived later, by which time it had acquired a strongly romantic admixture. To be sure the Serbs had revolted against Ottoman power already in 1804 but, unlike the Greeks, their revolt was not initially characterized by a coherent nationalist ideology.

Balkan nationalism developed along two main cultural axes both of which reflected the medieval history of the area, namely religion and language. Of the two, religion proved the main instrument of national differentiation in the Ottoman Empire, though it did not make for a prevalent national outlook among Ottoman Jews.

Religion was the dominant ideology of Ottoman society from the beginning, providing the ethical principle of state organization and the moral means of integrating the many components of the Empire's population. The Ottoman Empire was fundamentally a Turco-Islamic state that never entirely abandoned the ideology of *gaza*, that is, punitive campaigns to spread Islam among the non-believers.[65] It tolerated communities of Christians and Jews within its borders since they were 'the people of the book/scripture', even after the Ottomans had formed a heavily centralized imperial state in the sixteenth century with an increasingly conservative Sunni outlook. However, the other believers had an inherently inferior position marked by a legion of rules and other forms of discrimination.[66]

The Balkans had remained mostly Christian following the Ottoman conquest in the fourteenth and fifteenth centuries, in sharp contrast to Anatolia. Moreover, the Balkan Christians were frequently armed and had for centuries supplied units to the Ottoman security forces.[67] Christianity

---

[65] See İnalcık (1973) for an authoritative exposition. Wittek's (1938) '*gaza* thesis' postulated that the establishment of the Ottoman state was the result of a committed religious struggle against the 'infidels'. This thesis has been challenged by historians and the on-going debate is not directly relevant to our purposes. However, even if it were accepted that the rise of the Ottomans was mostly a sustained campaign of plunder and enslavement, and while acknowledging that Christian warlords went into partnership with Muslim raiders at the time of the initial Ottoman expansion, it would still seem likely that the *gaza* played a crucial ideological role in the fluid frontier zone of Northeastern Anatolia, where the Ottoman statelet emerged at the end of the thirteenth century; see Kafadar (1995).

[66] See Lewis (1984).

[67] The Islamization and Turkification of Anatolia after the Battle of Manzikert in 1071 is a process that is still shrouded in darkness due in part to the scarcity of original sources. Vryonis (1971) has

sustained the separate character of its adherents as well as providing a degree of cultural affinity with Western Europe, notwithstanding the vicious conflicts and the frequently undisguised hatred between Orthodox and Catholic Christians. Substantial numbers of Balkan people, mostly of Slavic ethnic origin, lived in the northern and western parts of the Balkan Peninsula under the jurisdiction of the Austro-Hungarian Empire. The political role of Christianity in the Balkans crucially affected political, social and economic developments in the nineteenth century. Persistent antagonisms between the Ottoman, the Habsburg and the Romanov Empires in the eighteenth and nineteenth centuries, together with the equally persistent meddling of Britain and France in Ottoman affairs, placed their stamp on Balkan nationalisms. National divisions were sharply exacerbated by Great Power politics, especially as the small Balkan states that emerged in the nineteenth century operated under the tutelage of the Great Powers.[68]

The Greek Christian, or rather, the 'Rum', part of the Ottoman population had developed its own aristocracy already by the end of the seventeenth century. Pivotal to it was the Patriarchate of Constantinople, an ancient institution with a complex administrative and economic structure. In the eighteenth century the Great Church could justifiably be called an integral part of the Ottoman state machine. Recent historical research has shown that it was effectively a tax collector, and the position of the Patriarch was in practice an Ottoman state post.[69] Closely connected to the Church was the secular aristocracy of the Phanariot Greeks of İstanbul. They supplied professional services to the ruling Muslim stratum of the Empire ranging from functioning as the Dragomans of the Porte and the Fleet – in practice officers for foreign affairs – to providing advanced medical expertise. In the eighteenth century the Phanariots reached the pinnacle of their power, above all, by securing monopoly control over the rulership of the Danubian principalities of Wallachia and Moldavia, under the suzerainty of the Sultan.

---

produced a classic piece of scholarship stressing the violent and destructive nature of the Turkic invasions. However, the process appears to have been more complex, variable and negotiated, with a common cultural and religious substratum emerging between Christianity and Islam; see Hasluck (1929) and Peacock, De Nicola and Yıldız (eds) (2015).
[68] See Jelavich (1983, ch. 5).
[69] See Papademetriou (2015, chs. 3 and 4).

Western ideas flowed into this realm, even as a trickle, particularly as the Phanariot aristocracy regularly sent its offspring to study in the West. Such was the background of the so-called 'Modern Greek Enlightenment', an explosion of intellectual activity that followed Western European trends in the second half of the eighteenth century.[70] The 'Enlightenment' provided the intellectual backing for the rise of nationalism among the Orthodox Christians of the Empire. Moreover, the Christians had never entirely forgotten their medieval past, whether that was the Byzantine Empire or the independent kingdoms of the Serbs, Bulgarians, and others. They had retained a memory of it in folk songs and customs as well as through Church mechanisms and rituals.[71]

By the late eighteenth century broad layers of Orthodox Christians increasingly perceived themselves as the nation of Greeks, a development fully facilitated by their pre-eminence in trade. The implications were profound, since nationalism relates first and foremost to identity and community, even if these are largely fictitious.[72] The appearance of national identities in the Balkans occurred at a time when the central state was weak, there was widespread landlordism by the *ayan*, and the *kırcalı* roamed the lowlands. Meanwhile, trade, including with Western Europe, was expanding.

Lest it be misunderstood, it was far from inevitable that the constructed national identities of the Balkans would tend to acquire a sharp religious outlook.[73] There is a common cultural bedrock and an affinity of aspirations among the Balkan and the Anatolian peoples, which have been a constant refrain in the history of the area since the tales of *Şeyh* Bedreddin in the fourteenth century. However, Ottoman society was based on undisputed Muslim ascendancy that was institutionally buttressed by a conservative Sunni state. Muslims had a deeply rooted conviction in their own superiority toward Ottoman Christians, who were tolerated as long as they kept their place. Christians reciprocated with disdain mixed with fear. Wealth acquired by Christians would naturally alter the perceptions of relative superiority, but

---

[70] The term 'Modern Greek Enlightenment' was coined by Dimaras (1977). For in depth discussions of its emergence see Kitromilides (1996) and Kondylis (1988).
[71] See Jelavich (1983, pp. 171–8).
[72] Anderson's (1983) analysis of 'imagined communities' certainly fits the extraordinary emphasis on a mythical historical past that is characteristic of Balkan nationalisms.
[73] Todorova (2009, p. 165) has stressed the organic, unifying tradition of popular culture among Christians and Muslims in the region.

divisions still run very deep.⁷⁴ Religious divisions were also prominent among the Balkan Christians, particularly between Orthodox and Catholic.

Language was a secondary principle of national differentiation in the Balkans, constantly leading to fissures in Christian nationalism in the nineteenth century. The Orthodox Church, unlike the Catholic, had allowed mass to be preached in languages other than Greek since the deepest Middle Ages. For the Slavic peoples of the Balkans and Eastern Europe, Orthodox Christianity was the means of acquiring written command over their own languages.⁷⁵ However, the Patriarchate of Constantinople spoke, wrote and delivered the liturgy in Greek, the holy language of the East. Its administrative structures were culturally Greek, regardless of the ethnic origin of those who filled the posts.

The Ottoman state took systematic advantage of the administrative and ideological mechanisms of the Christians in the Balkans to cement its rule. Mehmed II, the first truly powerful Ottoman Sultan, officially reconstituted the Patriarchate of Constantinople in 1454 by personally appointing as Patriarch the monk Gennadios, a sworn enemy of Orthodox union with the Catholic Church.⁷⁶ It is worth stressing that the leading position of the Patriarchate of Constantinople in the late Ottoman Empire was very much a product of Ottoman rule. A decisive step in its ascendancy occurred in 1766-7, when the Ottoman authorities allowed the Patriarchate to absorb the autonomous Slavic churches of Peć and Ohrid in the Balkans. With its influence enhanced and as the authority of the Porte declined amidst the administrative chaos of the eighteenth century, the Church emerged as a reliable tax-collecting mechanism that operated in part by auctioning powerful positions within its institutional structures.

---

[74] Krstić (2011) has carefully traced the sharp religious borders between Ottoman Christians and Muslims despite their coexistence and cultural syncretism. The army of Christian 'neomartyrs' during the Ottoman period has, for instance, served to mark Christian oppression and the unbridgeable gap with Muslims.
[75] A point that was elegantly demonstrated by Obolensky (1982). The first Glagolitic alphabet of the Slavs, devised in the ninth century by Cyril and propagated with the help of his brother Methodius from Thessaloniki, was probably based on the Slavic dialects of Macedonia, the lineal descendants of which can still be heard in Northern Greece.
[76] This is an event shrouded in myth and symbolism reflecting perceptions of 'Turkish tyranny', which has been used to legitimize the ascendancy of the Church among the Orthodox Christians at the expense of the secular Byzantine aristocracy; see Papademetriou (2015, pp. 21–41).

Vital to the rising nationalisms in the Ottoman Balkans was also the concept of the *millet*, which has deep Islamic roots that predate the Ottoman Empire and indicates a religious community.[77] The meaning of the *millet*, despite its undeniable religious associations, has varied over the centuries of Ottoman rule and it would be deeply misleading to confuse it with the modern nation. For our purposes, toward the end of the eighteenth century the *millet* began increasingly to signify a religious group integral to the Empire and possessing its own internal structure, including mechanisms of taxation, as well as having its own leader. The Patriarch of Constantinople became the formal head of the *Millet-i Rum*, which came to include practically all the Orthodox Christians of the Empire – Greeks, Bulgarians, Serbs, Vlachs, Moldavians, Arabs and others – thus enormously augmenting the Patriarch's secular power.

After the Tanzimat the Ottoman state used the *millet* system as a means of confronting the age-old practices of Muslim ascendancy. Seeking modernity was far from the exclusive concern of the Christians. The Muslim community keenly absorbed the ideas of Western Europe already from the eighteenth century. However, among the Muslims the drive toward modernity took peculiarly official forms driven by the desperate need of the state to confront Western military superiority. While the educational mechanisms of the Orthodox Christians were shaped by the Church, the first high educational institutions of the Muslims were military schools established by the reforming sultans. As the Porte reasserted its power in the nineteenth century, the ideology of 'Ottomanism' was promulgated, amounting largely to equality among the *millet*, coupled with individual equality in juridical and electoral rights. Secularism was supposed to replace the religious basis of the *millet* system, and the person of the Sultan was expected to act as the focal point of 'Ottomanism'.

In practice the Ottoman state failed to secure equitable participation of the various millet in the 'reformed' structures of the army, the administration, and education.[78] It is important to note that the Orthodox Church was ambivalent about the Tanzimat reforms since they potentially threatened its traditional

---

[77] The debate on the meaning and the role of the *millet* is extensive and not directly relevant to our purposes. Braude (1982) has argued that the term *millet* became widely used only in the late Ottoman period, particularly the term *Millet-i Rum* to denote the Greek Orthodox. Konortas (1999) has further argued that the Patriarch assumed the role of 'leader' of the Christians only after the decline of power of the Porte in the eighteenth century.

[78] See Findley (1982).

hold over the secular affairs of Orthodox Christians. Individual rights for Christians that were presumably ensured through secular Ottoman courts were not easily compatible with traditional group rights defended in ecclesiastical courts.[79] Partly through its own failings and partly through the resistance of the established mechanisms of the *millet*, the Ottoman state proved incapable of sustaining a new homogenizing national identity similar to those of Western Europe, or even to those of the Balkan states of Greece and Serbia. The half-baked concoction of 'Ottomanism' had no chance against the rising nationalisms of the ethnic and religious groups of the Empire in the Balkans.[80] 'Ottomanism' was briefly revived by the Young Turks after 1909 in an attempt to create an 'Ottoman nation', minus the pivotal role of the Sultan. The Balkan Wars of 1912–13 put a decisive end to that notion. As 'Ottomanism' failed, the Young Turks became open and ardent Turkish nationalists.

Nationalism was imported from Western Europe but the ideological vehicles for it were created by the internal practices of the Ottoman Empire. The conceptual apparatus of the *millet* – inherently based on discrimination – was incapable of dealing with the ideas of equality and liberty emanating from Western Europe, irrespective of the wishes of the Ottoman ruling elite.[81] The ideal notion of the nation triumphed over the religious identity of the *millet*. Armed clashes and the shedding of blood in the nineteenth century firmly fixed divisions between Christians and Muslims but also among Christians. Not least in importance was the role of the small states of Greece, Serbia and Bulgaria acting as powerful poles of irredentist, state-backed nationalism, each with its own historical-religious myth, throughout most of the nineteenth century.

It is important to note in this connection that the Jews of Thessaloniki did not seek to differentiate themselves nationally from the Ottoman Empire, even though their most powerful families carried Italian and French passports. The competing nationalisms of the Balkans offered no advantages to Jews compared to the reforming Ottoman Empire, indeed they represented a palpable threat from undercurrents of intolerant Christianity. Moreover, Zionism was an ideology developed by Ashkenazy Western European Jews

---

[79] See Stamatopoulos (2018). For an older discussion of the impact of the Tanzimat on the Patriarchate of Constantinople, see Augustinos (1992).
[80] See Lewis (1979 [1961], chs. 6, 7).
[81] See Karpat (1982).

that was largely brought over to indigenous Sephardic Ottoman Jews as part of a far broader wave of cultural modernization of Ottoman Jewry in the second half of the nineteenth century. Modernization was led by Western European Jews keen to help their brethren in the Ottoman Empire. Its main domestic agents in İstanbul, Thessaloniki and elsewhere were the powerful Francos of the Ottoman Jewry.[82] The modernizers tended to be assimilationists and keen to promote the learning of Turkish by Jews.

The Zionists assumed a rejectionist outlook toward the modernizing upper layers of the Jewish community, thus promoting the learning of Hebrew and appealing to the youth and the poor.[83] But they made limited headway in a community that had rarely felt threatened where it lived and for which 'the return to Zion' typically meant going to the Holy Land to die, not least as Zion was part of the Empire. In Thessaloniki, in particular, the Zionist message had very little appeal for a majority community that dominated the city's economic and social life. Furthermore, the Jewish youth and poor of Thessaloniki were strongly attracted to the ideas of the Socialist Workers' Federation of Avraam Benaroya. The ground was barren for the Zionists even in the political turmoil that followed the Young Turk revolt.[84]

The Jews of the Empire were the only religious community to embrace the ideology of 'Ottomanism' with any vigour.[85] Education played an important role in this respect since among the Jews it generally lacked the sectarian character that it had for Christians. The main lever for the educational advancement of Ottoman Jews was the Alliance Israélite Universelle, an international educational association established as part of the modernizing efforts of Western European Jews and embraced by the Francos. The Alliance had an assimilationist outlook and generally supported the efforts of the Tanzimat. In Thessaloniki the educational lead of the Alliance was buttressed by the Allatini, thus fostering an educational boom during the final decades of Ottoman rule. In a short period of time and exactly as industrial capitalism

---

[82] See Rodrigue (1994).
[83] See Benbassa (1994).
[84] See Mazower (2004, pp. 405–6) for an account of two separate visits by Vladimir Jabotinsky, the apostle of Zionism, to Thessaloniki. In 1908 Jabotinsky's efforts to instill Jewish nationalism left the community largely indifferent. In 1926 he had more success, but by then Thessaloniki was part of the Greek nation state and conditions were quite different for the Jewish community.
[85] See Cohen (2014).

emerged, the Jewry of Thessaloniki was transformed from a community of low literacy and poor intellectual accomplishment into a paragon of intellectual progress.[86]

Macedonia was also relatively remote from the main centres of Greek nationalism in the south as well as from the centres of the Modern Greek Enlightenment in İstanbul, Bucharest, Trieste and elsewhere. The oldest form of national identity in Macedonia was nonetheless Greek, reflecting the dominance of Greek public culture among the Christians. Independence for Greece in the 1830s lent extra kudos to Greek nationalism. Its most powerful rival was Bulgarian nationalism which arose later but was visibly present by the 1850s.[87] Bulgarian nationalism was a relative latecomer to the Balkans, partly because of the proximity of Bulgarian lands to İstanbul, and partly because of the domination exercised by Greeks over Bulgarian intellectual and religious life. Consequently, two interrelated issues provided the organizing focus of Bulgarian nationalism in addition to confronting the Ottoman state: first, independence from the Greek-dominated structures of the Church and, second, command over education, which meant using the Bulgarian language and altering school curricula accordingly. Greek and Bulgarian nationalisms clashed primarily over these two issues in Macedonia in the second half of the nineteenth century.

Few texts sum up the early outlook of Bulgarian nationalism in Macedonia more succinctly than a letter by Kiryak Durzhilovich to Georgi Rakovski, sent on 25 October 1860, and shown in Figures 8.8a and b. Durzhilovich was born in 1817 in the village of Drazilovo or Derzilovo (in Bulgarian, Държилово – Durzhilovo) on Mount Vermion, the broader area from which several of the çorbacı of Naoussa originated.[88] His family name was Dinka or Dinkov (in Greek, Dingas) but he typically signed his name in Greek as Kiriakos Darzilovitis (or Derzilovitz). Kiryak Durzhilovich and his younger brother, Konstantin (Constantinos), were significant figures in the history of Bulgarian nationalism in Macedonia. Their father was a merchant who moved the family to nearby Edhessa (*Vodina*) sometime in the 1820s. In the 1840s Kiryak entered

---

[86] See Hekimoglou (2012).
[87] The bibliography on this issue is enormous. For a useful summary see Gounaris and Mihailidis (2000).
[88] The village of Metamorfosi on Mount Vermion currently stands on the site of Drazilovo. The contemporary village is a little hamlet, but the original name is still widely used in the area.

Писма до Г. С. Раковски 1860 г.   621

305

От Киряк Държилович[1] — Солун

25 октомври 1860 г.

Отговаря на писмо от Раковски относно получаването на „Дунавски лебед" в Солун. Дава сведения за себе си. Настанен в Солун отдавна като гръцки печатар и книжар. По интриги на гръцки шовинисти и владици печатницата му закрита. Пристигането от Москва на племеника му Георги Динков. Безпомощното положение на християните от Южна Македония

Θεσσαλονίκῃ. 25 'Οκτωβρίου 1860.

'Αξιότιμε κύριε,

Πρό τινων ἑβδομάδων ἔλαβον δύο φύλλα τῆς ὑμετ[έρας] ἐφημερίδος τοῦ πρώτου αὐτῆς ἀρ[ι]θμ[οῦ], πρὸ πέντε δὲ ἡμερῶν ἕτερα μέχρι τοῦ ἀρ[ι]θμ[οῦ] 5. Ἕνεκα ἀπασχολήσεως δὲν Σᾶς ἔγραψα ἐγκαίρως. Ἤδη εὐχαρίστως ἀπατῶ.

Λυπoῦμαι οὐκ ὀλίγον μὴ δυνάμενος νὰ εὐχαριστήσω ὑμᾶς δι'ἐγγραφῆς συνδρομητῶν, ἐλπίζω ὅμως τὸν ἅγιον Πολυανῆς νὰ ἐγγράψω συνδρομητήν. Σήμερον πέμπω εἰς Κουκούσιον τὰ φύλλα, ἴσως ἀκολούθως ἐγγράψω καὶ ἄλλον τινά.

Μεγαλυτέραν λύπην αἰσθάνομαι μὴ γνωρίζων τὴν βουλγαρικὴν γλῶσσαν, καίτοι Βούλγαρος. Πρὸ δέκα περίπου ἐτῶν εἶμαι ἀποκαταστημένος ἐν τῇ πόλει ταύτῃ, ἔχων τυπογραφεῖον, εἰς ὃ τυπώνω ὅλα τὰ ἐν χρήσει τοῖς σχολείοις ἑλλ[ηνικά] βιβλία. Ἐπειδὴ ὅμως, ὡς ἦτο δίκαιον, συνήργησα εἰς τὸ νὰ ζητήσουν οἱ Βούλγαροι Κουκυοσίου ἐπίσκοπον Βούλγαρον τὸν Παρθένιον, οἱ Γραικοί, μάλιστα οἱ ἐν τοῖς πράγμασιν, σὺν τῷ μητροπολίτῃ Θεσσαλονίκης καὶ τῷ μητροπολίτῃ Βοδενῶν, συνήργησαν διὰ τοῦ πασᾶ καὶ πρὸ ἓξ μηνῶν μοῦ ἔκλεισαν τὸ τυπογραφεῖον μου. Ἤδη δὲ μένω μὲ μόνον τὸ βιβλιοπωλεῖον μου. Ἡ ὑπόθεσις μετέβη εἰς Κωνσταντινούπολιν εἰς τὸ ὑπουργεῖον. Ἐκεῖ ἔχω φίλους, πλὴν ἔχω καὶ τοὺς ἀντενεργοῦντας. Τὸ ἀποτέλεσμα μοὶ εἶναι ἄδηλον. Οἱ Γραικοί, βεβαίως βοηθούμενοι ὑπὸ τοῦ κλήρου καὶ τῆς ἐξουσίας, σφοδρῶς καταφέρονται κατὰ τῶν Βουλγάρων, ἐνῷ οὗτοι πράττουν ἐντὸς τῶν δικαιωμάτων των, ζητοῦντες ἀνάπτυξιν καὶ πρόοδον τῆς μητρικῆς των γλώσσης. Ἐγὼ καίτοι ἀγνοῶν τὴν γλῶσσαν ταύτην, ἀνέκαθεν ὡμίλησα ὑπὲρ τῆς διαδόσεως αὐτῆς μεταξὺ τῶν Βουλγάρων. Ἡ σπουδὴ αὐτῆς διευκολύνει κατὰ μέγα μέρος καὶ τὴν σπουδὴν τῆς ἑλληνικῆς. Καὶ γνήσιος Γραικὸς ἂν ἤμην, τὸ αὐτὸ ἤθελον ὁμιλήσῃ. Φαίνεται ὅμως, ὅτι οἱ ἀπαθῶς κρίνοντες εἰσὶν ὀλίγοι, ἑπομένως θεωροῦνται καὶ πταῖσται.

Ὁ Γεώργιος Δίγκωφ κατὰ μῆνα Αὔγουστον ἐρχόμενος ἐκ Μόσχας ἐπέρασεν ἀπὸ τὴν πόλιν σας. Ἴσως ἐγένετο πρὸς ὑμᾶς γνωστός. Οὗτος εἶναι ἀνεψιός μου, δηλ. υἱὸς τοῦ ἀδελφοῦ μου Κ[ωνσταντίνου] Δίγκα. Διὰ συνεργείας μου πρὸ δύο ἐτῶν ἐστάλη εἰς τὴν Ῥωσσίαν. Κατετάχθη μαθητὴς εἰς τὸ σχολεῖον τῆς Σμολένσκης, ὅπου σπουδάζει δι' ἐξόδων τῆς κυβερνήσεως ὡς ὑπότροφος.

Ἐντεῦθεν οὐδὲν νεώτερον δύναμαι νὰ σᾶς μεταδώσω, ἐκτὸς τῆς καταπιέσεως καὶ ταλαιπωρίας τῶν χριστιανῶν. Πολιτικοὶ καὶ ἐκκλησιαστικοὶ ἄρχοντες,

Figure 8.8a Letter by Kiryak Durzhilovich to Georgi Rakovski, 1860

Source: Traikov (1957).

622 Писма до Г. С. Раковски 1860 г.

ἐξαιρέσει ὀλίγων, πάντες εἰς οὐδὲν ἕτερον καταγίνονται, εἰμὴ εἰς ἁρπάξαι καὶ
ξεσχίσαι. Οὐδεμίαν πρόνοιαν περὶ τῆς βελτιώσεως τῶν χριστιανῶν. Μάτην φωνάζουν
οἱ εὐρωπαῖοι, μάτην γράφουν οἱ ἐπουργοί, μάτην δημοσιεύουν κλοπὰς καὶ
σφαγὰς οἱ δημοσιογράφοι, — οἱ Τοῦρκοι μένουν ἀνάληπτοι. Καιρὸν δὲν ἔχω
νὰ γράψω ὑμῖν καθέκαστα.
                    Ἐν τούτοις μένω
                            ὁ ὑμέτερος
                              Κ[υριάκος] Δερζήλοβιτζ.

ДБВК, Ф. Раковски, 1Б 1166/52
(стар инв. № 8184)

Превод

                                      Солун, 25 октомври 1860 г.
    Почитаеми господине!
    Преди няколко седмици получих два екземпляра от първия
брой на вашия вестник, а преди пет дена получих други екземпляри
до брой пети.
    Поради заетост не ви писах навреме. Сега с удоволствие ви
отговарям.[2]
    Съжалявам немалко, задето не мога да ви зарадвам със за-
писване на абонати, но се надявам да запиша св. поленинския
[епископ] като абонат. Днес изпращам броевете в Кукуш. Може би
по-нататък да запиша и някой друг.
    Много голяма скръб изпитвам, че макар и да съм българин,
не знам [да пиша на] български език. От около десет години аз
съм настанен в този град [Солун] и имам печатница, в която печатам
всички въведени в училищата гръцки книги[3], но понеже, както и
беше право, съдействувах на кукушките българи да искат епископ
българин — Партений, гърците, особено първенците, заедно със
солунския и воденския митрополит, направиха постъпки пред па-
шата (окръжния управител) и преди шест месеца ми закриха печатницата. Сега оставам само с книжарницата си. Въпросът бе отнесен
в министерството в Цариград. Там имам приятели[4], но има и такива,
които действуват против мене. Резултатът не ми е известен. Гърците,
разбира се, подпомогнати от духовенството и властите, силно се
нахвърлят срещу българите, макар последните да действуват в
рамките на своите права, като искат да се развиват и напредват
на майчиния си език. Ако и да не владея [писмено] този език, аз
винаги съм говорил в полза на неговото разпространение между българите. Преподаването му улеснява до голяма степен и изучаването
на гръцкия език. И истински грък да бях, пак същото щях да
поддържам. Изглежда обаче малцина са тия, които преценяват без-
страстно и поради това се смята, че сме виновни ние.
    Георги Динков, връщайки се през месец август от Москва,
мина през вашия град. Може би се е запознал с вас. Той е мой
племеник, сиреч син на моя брат К[онстантин] Динката. С мое
съдействие преди две години той беше изпратен в Русия. Постъпи
ученик в училището [семинарията] в Смоленск, където следва на
държавни разноски като стипендиант.[5]

Figure 8.8b Letter by Kiryak Durzhilovich to Georgi Rakovski, 1860

the University of Athens and lived in the Kingdom of Greece probably until 1850. In the 1850s and 1860s Kiriakos Darzilovitis, supported by his brother Constantinos, acted as publisher and bookseller in Thessaloniki promoting the literary use of Bulgarian and the cause of Bulgarian nationalism.

The letter by Durzhilovich was sent to Rakovski, a prominent intellectual and activist in the Bulgarian Renaissance and one of the historic fathers of Bulgarian nationalism. At the time Rakovski lived in exile in Belgrade, hounded by the security forces of the Ottoman state. During 1860–1 he published the newspaper Dunavski Lebed (The Danube Swan), an outlet for rebellious Bulgarian nationalism. Durzhilovich kept a correspondence with Rakovski.[89] The letter in Figures 8.8a and b was edited by Rakovski and published in his newspaper with the evident aim of bolstering Bulgarian nationalism in Macedonia. It is instructive to translate it in full (with contemporary place names in brackets):[90]

> Dear Sir,
>
> A few weeks ago, I received two copies of the first issue of your newspaper, and five days ago several more up to issue number 5.
>
> Due to various obligations I did not write to you promptly. I am now responding with pleasure.
>
> I feel not a little sorrow that I am unable to please you by registering subscribers, but I hope to obtain the subscription of the Bishop of Polyani.[91] Today I will send the copies to Koukoush (Kilkis), and perhaps I might be able to find another subscriber soon.
>
> I feel even greater sorrow that, although I am a Bulgarian, I do not know the Bulgarian language. I have been living in this city (Thessaloniki) for ten years now, and I have a print shop where I publish all the Greek books that are used in schools. However, because I helped, as was only proper, the Bulgarians of Koukoush to request a Bulgarian bishop – Parthenios – the Greeks,[92] especially the notables, together with the

---

[89] There are altogether eight letters by Durzhilovich to Rakovski in the Bulgarian historical archive at the National Library of Bulgaria in Sofia.

[90] See Traikov (1957 [vol. 2], pp. 621–5), which also includes facsimiles of the handwritten letter by Durzhilovich. A partial translation of the letter in English is available at http://www.promacedonia.org/en/vt/index.htm (accessed 31 January 2018). The translation has been completed and slightly amended in the text below.

[91] The Bishopric of Polyani is a historic seat in central Macedonia that includes the town of Kilkis (in Bulgarian, Koukoush), that is, the settlement of *Avrethisar* in the *vakıf* of *Gazi* Evrenos *Bey*.

[92] In the text, Γραικοί, that is, specifically Greek-speaking Ottoman Orthodox Christians.

Bishop of Thessaloniki and the Bishop of Vodina, made representations to the *paşa* and six months ago closed down my printshop. And now I have only my bookshop. The issue was passed on to Constantinople, to the Ministry. I have friends there, but there are also people who are against me. The result is not yet known to me. The Greeks, naturally backed by the clergy and the authorities, are strongly attacking the Bulgarians, though the latter are acting within their rights, demanding development and progress of their mother tongue. For my part, though I am ignorant of this language, I have always spoken in favour of its dissemination among the Bulgarians. The study of this language greatly helps the study of Greek. Even if I were a pure Greek, I would have maintained the same. But it appears that those who form opinions without bias are few, and that is why they are considered at fault.

In the month of August, Georgios Dinkov passed from your city (Belgrade) on his way from Moscow. Perhaps he was introduced to you. He is my nephew, that is, the son of my brother Constantinos Dingas. Partly due to my efforts he was sent to Russia two years ago. He entered school at Smolensk, where he is studying with a government scholarship.

There is no further news to report to you from here, other than the oppression and troubles of the Christians. Political and Church leaders, with few exceptions, are only concerned with one thing, how to grab and tear things apart. No thought is given to improving the condition of the Christians. The Europeans complain in vain, the Ministers write in vain, the journalists report thefts and massacres in vain. The Turks are callous. I have no time to relate to you these events.

I remain

Yours

K. Derzilovitz

This is a remarkable letter, written in natural Greek by a man who had clearly had university training, an extremely rare event at the time. Durzhilovich not only hailed from the same area as several of the merchants and industrialists of Naoussa but also belonged to the same agrarian and trading social layer. Even though he had lived and studied in Athens, he was an ardent Bulgarian patriot in conflict with the Ottoman authorities as well as the Greek notables and clergy. Indeed the problems he confronted in 1860 were not new. In 1851 he had faced charges in the Ottoman courts of Thessaloniki for publishing 'seditious' books.[93] As a Bulgarian nationalist he was concerned to promote education in Bulgarian and independence from the structures of the Patriarchate of Constantinople. He was equally concerned to confront the poor social conditions of the Christians. His nationalism was marked by social radicalism similar to that of Rakovski.

The most striking aspect of the letter, however, is that Durzhilovich openly admitted to having no knowledge of Bulgarian in the course of communicating with one of the fathers of Bulgarian nationalism.[94] He sought to spread the message of Rakovski's nationalist newspaper in Macedonia, even securing a subscription by the new Bulgarian bishop of Kilkis and considered himself a Bulgarian patriot, but could only communicate in Greek. He was also a highly educated man, who run a vital publishing house in Thessaloniki that produced textbooks for Greek schools and could have presumably easily learnt to write in Bulgarian, but apparently failed to do so. From the standpoint of his Greek opponents in Thessaloniki, Kiriakos Darzilovitis would appear to be a Greek (Γραικός) who had become very confused and dangerous.

The ethnic outlook of Durzhilovich was characteristic of the early period of conflict in Macedonia, a time of fluid identities and comparative innocence. The fluidity between Greek and Bulgarian national identities persevered throughout the decades that followed, and further striking confirmation of it is afforded by Durzhilovich's own family. Take, for instance, Kiryak's nephew, Georgi (Georgios) Dinkov, the son of Konstantin Durzhilovich, who is mentioned in the text of the letter. Georgi, also known by the surname Dinkata, was a well-known advocate of Bulgarian education and nationalism, who recorded the folk traditions and geography of Macedonia and was attracted

---

[93] See Vakali (2015), who discusses the trial of 1851 and gives further information on Durzhilovich/Darzilovitis.

[94] The edited Bulgarian text by Rakovski makes two crucial interpolations, namely [ДА ПНША НА] and [ПНСМЕНО], suggesting that Durzhilovich merely lacked command of written Bulgarian, and this was presumably the reason why he wrote in Greek. However, in the letter Durzhilovich stated twice and clearly that he was 'ignorant' of Bulgarian altogether ('μη γνωρίζων την βουλγαρικήν γλῶσσαν' and 'ἀγνοῶν την γλῶσσαν ταύτην'). It is indeed hard to believe that someone like Durzhilovich had no knowledge of Bulgarian, and it would seem plausible that he simply did not know how to write in it. Yet, how plausible could it be that such a committed nationalist, with exceptional academic abilities and keen to promote the use of Bulgarian, failed to acquire written command of the language, if indeed Bulgarian was his mother tongue?

to socialism.[95] Moreover, his sister, Slavka Dinkova, was prominent in the promotion of Bulgarian education, especially for women, in Thessaloniki. The activities of both Georgi and Slavka were of a piece with those of their father Konstantin and uncle Kiryak both of whom had become leading figures in the sizeable Bulgarian community of Thessaloniki in the late 1860s.

However, in the 1870s, following the end of his Bulgarian nationalist exploits in Macedonia, Georgi Dinkov went to live in Athens, where he earned a living as a pettifogger, and in 1876, shortly before his death, had a son. Dimitrios Dingas, son of Georgi Dinkov, grandson of Konstantin Durzhilovich, and nephew of Slavka Dinkova, became a devoted Greek patriot and paragon of the Greek community of Macedonia. He was a Member of the Ottoman Parliament after the Young Turk Revolution, a Member of the Greek Parliament after the incorporation of a large part of Macedonia in the Kingdom of Greece, and a high-ranking Minister in several Greek governments for decades. The great-nephew of Kiryak Durzhilovich, inveterate promoter of Bulgarian education in Macedonia, even served as Greek Minister of Education in the 1920s. Such astonishing fluidity of names and roles was a characteristic feature of national identity in Macedonia.

Fluidity aside, the spirit of comparative innocence marking Durzhilovich's letter would soon come to an end. The conflict between the two nationalisms became venomous once the Ottoman state had acknowledged a separate Bulgarian Church in 1870 (Bulgarian Exarchate). In practice, if not formally, the Porte had recognized the existence of a separate Bulgarian *millet*. Bulgarian nationalism gained further momentum after the Congress of Berlin in 1878 which, at the instigation of Russia, accorded to Bulgaria effective independence and even assigned to it greatly expanded borders that included Macedonia. The Russian plan never came to fruition mostly due to German intervention, but it was clear that Bulgaria was on the ascendant in the Balkans. The struggle between Bulgarian nationalism and the Ottoman state as well as between Bulgarian and Greek nationalisms in Macedonia became armed and murderous in the 1890s and 1900s.

Nationalism in Macedonia certainly had a religious and linguistic pedigree but it would be hopelessly one-sided to analyse it at the level of ideology alone.

---

[95] See Traikov (1957 [vol. 2], p. 626).

As Gounaris has claimed, the adoption of nationalism, the rediscovery by Christian communities of the deep historical past and its re-description in national terms, 'were mostly determined by cleavages which reflected real and vital interests, basically the allocation of material resources'.[96] These cleavages resulted in good part from the socio-economic transformation of Macedonia since the late eighteenth century leading to the emergence of commercial and industrial capitalism. The analysis of the transformation of the region of Mount Vermion in the preceding chapters of this book can cast a fresh light on the social and economic forces engaged in the nationalist struggle.

The frictions attendant to the rise of capitalism inevitably generated class antagonisms. Among the Christians class antagonisms became intertwined with communal conflicts which were marked by nationalist ideologies. Even the Greek Consul General in Thessaloniki was fully aware of this aspect of the nationalist struggle in Macedonia, and explicitly stated that: '... in the villages of Macedonia antagonism of interests takes precedence but later on it is necessarily transformed into a national confrontation'.[97] The social tensions created by commercial and industrial capitalism in Mount Vermion made the region a flashpoint between Greek, Bulgarian, and – much less – Romanian nationalism. Turkish nationalism, which emerged later among the Muslims, was bound up with controlling the Ottoman state and defending the Empire.

The leading bearers of Hellenism in the area of Mount Vermion were by and large the *çorbacı*, irrespective of their ethnic background. Adopting the Greek identity with its close attachment to the Patriarchate of Constantinople was a natural option for the wealthy merchants, landowners and manufacturers of the region already from the early decades of the nineteenth century and long before Bulgarian nationalism had raised its head. This phenomenon was common in the southern Balkans as the Greek identity – mostly in language and education – was adopted by the urban elite, even when its mother tongue was Bulgarian, Vlach, or other. In Plovdiv – Philippoupolis for the Greeks, or *Filibe* for the Turks – an important city in modern day Bulgaria, for instance,

---

[96] See Gounaris (1995, p. 415). Gounaris (2010) has also written a comprehensive bibliographical account of the enormous literature on the 'Macedonian Question'.
[97] See Gounaris (1995, p. 417).

the established section of the merchant elite was strongly Greek, but was challenged by a zealous Bulgarian faction, leading to one of the earliest clashes among the two nationalisms in the 1850s.[98] Similarly, much of the elite of Bitola (*Manastır*) in Macedonia had a prominent Greek character, even though its mother tongue was often Vlach.[99]

Adoption of the Greek identity by the *çorbacı* in the region of Mount Vermion lent to Greek nationalism a whiff of privilege. Bulgarian nationalism appealed to small shopkeepers, petty traders, artisans and other middling layers striving for social ascendancy in a rapidly changing world, and finding themselves under pressure from large merchants and industrialists. They had a visceral dislike of the *çorbacı*, who repaid them with social contempt. It was not surprising, therefore, that some sections of Bulgarian nationalism continually interacted with socialist currents of thought. Greek nationalism was very different in this regard, trapped in a rigid narrative of the glories of ancient Greece and deeply suspicious of socialist ideas.

Amidst the sea of the peasantry that was heavily Slavophone things were less clear. The peasants were naturally opposed to landlords, who were mostly Muslim but could also be Christian, which typically meant Greek. They were sympathetic to agrarian reform and shared the hostility of Bulgarian nationalists towards the *çorbacı*. The peasants were also deeply suspicious of the Greek clergy and infuriated by the exactions and corruption of the Church. Any preference for Bulgarian nationalism was, however, tempered by natural peasant conservatism on matters of religion. The *çiftlik* villages in the region of Mount Vermion were torn between Patriarchism and Exarchism during the last quarter of the nineteenth century. At the end of the Ottoman period, however, Exarchism had gained the upper hand. The Vlachs of the uplands of Mount Vermion and to some extent in Veroia showed some sympathy towards Romanian nationalism.

The nationalist struggle in Macedonia reached its peak in the 1900s, the time of the fastest development of industrial capitalism in the region. The leading role was played by Bulgarian nationalism under the Internal Macedonian Revolutionary Organization (IMRO) which was established in

---

[98] Described in full by Lyberatos (2009; see also Lyberatos (2010).
[99] Discussed by Gounaris (2000).

1893 in Thessaloniki. The IMRO was an organization led by schoolteachers and officers of the Bulgarian army that attracted wide support among the urban layers but also the peasants of Macedonia. Its ideological and organizational development followed a violent and tortuous path, and it contained currents that sought independence for Macedonia, with a strong admixture of socialism.[100] In the late 1890s the IMRO began to prepare for armed revolt against the Ottoman state, especially after the Greek army had been thoroughly beaten by the Ottomans in 1897.

In April 1903 there was a campaign of bombing in Thessaloniki undertaken by anarchist Bulgarian students associated with IMRO. The bombing was followed by a generalized peasant uprising among the Christians of Macedonia, which broke out on 20 July 1903, *Ilinden*, and was at its most intense in the *vilayet* of Bitola (*Manastır*). The revolt failed as the Ottoman state, supported by the Muslim community, suppressed it ruthlessly. Despite its failure, the initiative of IMRO spurred Greek nationalists to intervene more actively in Macedonia. Bands of armed irredentist Greeks, led by Greek army personnel, began to appear in the Macedonian countryside after 1904, engaging in clashes with IMRO bands. The marshy plain of Mount Vermion was a leading area of conflict, one of the most forceful agents of which was Constantinos Mazarakis-Ainian, an officer of the Greek army who led a Greek band and left a book recounting his experiences.[101] For our purposes, the following two points stand out in the officer's memoirs.

First, Mazarakis had little comprehension of the economic and social upheaval occurring in the area. He appeared perfectly content with the stereotypes of his time concerning national character, blending a strong dose of arrogance towards the local people with a virulent anti-Bulgarianism. Second, Mazarakis was dismissive of the *çorbacı* of Naoussa, from whom he had expected much more than he had received. Thus, in May 1905 he met

---

[100] The literature on IMRO is quite extensive and not directly relevant to our purposes. A detailed (if poorly translated) account of its evolution based on Western European sources can be found in Lange-Akhund (1998). Perhaps the most succinct summary of its ideological trajectory in the twentieth century, and still useful, was given by Barker (1950).

[101] See Mazarakis (1963). The memoirs of Mazarakis first appeared in the 1930s and were subsequently subjected to heavy doctoring by the institutions of the Greek state to make them more compatible with the – ever-changing – official view of Macedonia and the national character of its people; see Karavas (1999). They still remain an invaluable testimony to the reality of the struggle for Macedonia in the 1900s.

Longos and Tourpalis, who apparently promised a lot but delivered very little.[102] Indeed, Mazarakis seemed altogether disappointed with the people of Naoussa because they had failed to provide reliable recruits and were more interested in the good life than in the nationalist struggle. Local attitudes to the Macedonian Question did not match the high standards of a low-ranking officer of the Greek army.

The outlook of Mazarakis was perhaps typical of nationalists from the Kingdom of Greece at the time.[103] In contrast, the *çorbacı* of Naoussa were far more aware of the realities of Mount Vermion and Macedonia, which tempered their nationalism. They certainly understood the social and political dangers posed by Bulgarian nationalists in the 1900s and were keen to confront them. To this purpose they requested express permission from the Ottoman state to hire armed guards. In 1907 both Longos–Kyrtsis–Tourpalis in Naoussa and Tsitsis in Edhessa submitted petitions to the local administration and to the General Inspectorate of the *Vilayet* of *Rumeli* asking for permission to deploy armed guards on the grounds that their mills, depots and commercial activities were under threat from Bulgarian irredentists. Longos–Kyrtsis–Tourpalis wanted to hire twelve armed men but the Inspectorate allowed only four and demanded that their names be registered.[104]

The threat was real. In 1907 there was an assault by a Bulgarian band on the Tsitsis mill in Edhessa as a result of which the plant was placed under permanent military protection by the state, and eventually some of its workers were given arms. In spite of rising nationalism, there were no walls separating the industrialists from the Ottoman state. The guards requested by the industrialists soon found further uses in an environment riven by class and national conflicts. In a letter by the Municipality of Karaferye to the General Inspectorate of Thessaloniki it was noted that the armed guards of

---

[102] See Mazarakis (1963, pp. 61–2).
[103] At least Mazarakis had experienced the realities of Ottoman Macedonia at first hand. This is much more than could be said for Penelope Delta, a nationalist from the upper circles of Athenian society who wrote *In the Secrets of the Marsh*, a historical novel about the Greek nationalist effort in Macedonia in the 1900s that has had a tremendous ideological impact in Greece over the decades. The 'Marsh' was, of course, the marshy lake of Giannitsa surrounded by *çiftlik* villages. Written in 1937, the novel was little more than a noxious anti-Bulgarian tale utterly ignorant of the economic and social realities of the area; see Karavas (2014).
[104] BOA. TFR.I.ŞKT.125/12436; BOA. TFR.I.SL.154/15376; BOA. TFR.I.SL.155/15450; BOA. TFR.I.SL.155/15459.

the Longos–Kyrtsis–Tourpalis plant had been used to protect a priest from Naoussa and his entourage during a trip undertaken to the north of Macedonia. The Municipality of Karaferye duly ordered an investigation.[105]

The armed nationalist struggle in the region of Mount Vermion remained in full swing until 1908, when the Young Turk revolt took place. Greek nationalists, including the powerful business community of Thessaloniki, initially assumed an ambivalent stance towards the Young Turks, partly at the instigation of the Greek Kingdom.[106] Both the Greek state and the leaders of the Greek community in Thessaloniki perceived Bulgarian nationalism as their main enemy and were generally accommodating towards the Ottoman state. The Greek industrialists and bankers of Thessaloniki were not prepared to risk upsetting the Sultan's government in İstanbul for the sake of what appeared to be a movement led by mere mid-ranking Ottoman officers and bureaucrats. In contrast to the Greeks, the Jewish community played a significant role in the Young Turk movement.

To general surprise the Young Turks were enormously successful and received support from the Socialist Workers' Federation and the socialist wing of IMRO in Thessaloniki. But the expectation of democratic gains and rapid improvement in communal relations following the overthrow of Abdülhamid proved largely unfounded. It gradually became clear that the Young Turks would in practice give to the Empire a stronger Turkish outlook. Still, the change of regime kept a lid on Christian nationalist unrest in Macedonia for a period as the Bulgarian bands went quiet and the Greek bands largely withdrew. A tense normality returned to the countryside while the Young Turks made sustained efforts to boost 'Ottomanism'.

Thus, in 1911 Sultan Mehmed Reşad, a weak and ceremonial figure who had succeeded Abdülhamid and was entirely beholden to the Young Turk administration, went on an official trip in the Balkans. The aim obviously was to boost the legitimacy of Ottoman rule as the clouds were gathering beyond the imperial borders. Figure 8.9 shows the welcoming of the Sultan at the train station in Naoussa. The town had clearly put on its best clothes for the occasion and there was a palpably festive air.

---

[105] BOA. TFR.I.SL.144/14397.
[106] See Hekimoglou (2015).

Figure 8.9 Waiting for Sultan Mehmed Reşad in 1911
Source: Megas (2011).

The tensions created by industrial capitalism and nationalism were certainly enormous, but the end of the Ottoman Empire in Europe would not come from a nationalist revolt. The lethal blow would fall from the outside. Against all expectations the small Christian states of Bulgaria, Serbia, Greece and Montenegro succeeded in forming an anti-Ottoman alliance in 1912. The First Balkan War broke out in October of the same year. The Ottoman army was rapidly and decisively defeated, and the armies of Greece, Serbia, and Bulgaria took over Macedonia, while the Bulgarians even threatened to take İstanbul. The Ottoman era came to a sudden end in the Balkans and the Macedonian Question was settled through the barrel of a gun, as is the historical norm. In the following decades, the economic and social development of the region of Mount Vermion and the whole of Macedonia would be determined by entirely different factors. It is beyond doubt, however, that the roots of industrial capitalism and modernity in Macedonia are to be found in the late Ottoman period.

9

Precarious capitalism

Ottoman industrial capitalism in Macedonia – the main site of industrialization in the Empire – originated in major political, economic and social upheavals that took place from the late eighteenth to the middle of the nineteenth century. During the first part of that period, the Sublime Porte endeavoured to strengthen its authority against provincial warlords and others. It also sought to restore its fiscal accounts by adopting an outlook in which 'restrictive economic policies dominated, emphasizing monopolies and the retention of raw materials for domestic use'.[1]

Once the nineteenth century was properly in its stride, the Ottoman Empire adopted free-trade liberalism. The turn towards liberalism was signalled in 1826 by the massacre of the Janissaries. During the first decades of the nineteenth century, the Porte reasserted its authority over the provinces and engaged in political reform that led to the Tanzimat proclamation in 1839. It had already signed a Free Trade Treaty with Britain in 1838, which opened the floodgates to Western European industrial goods, above all, British cotton textiles. Domestic manufacturing contracted, especially in the urban centres, an economic reversal that lasted until the 1860s. In several upland areas, however, domestic manufacturing survived and even prospered as producers secured niches for themselves in the new conditions. Notable among these niches was the production of *şayak* and *aba*, types of woollen cloth that covered the traditional needs of the population. At the same time the export of agricultural products expanded thanks to favourable terms of trade for the Empire.

---

[1] See Quataert (1994b, pp. 762–3).

In the 1860s the Ottoman state took steps to reverse the deleterious impact of free trade policies. There was no comprehensive development plan, but the state did seek to protect and strengthen the domestic economy by raising import levies and lowering export taxes, while internal duties on overland commerce were abolished in 1874. A controlling attitude towards trade had already begun to rise across much of Europe at the time. The finances of the state, meanwhile, went from bad to worse, mostly due to the effort to strengthen the armed forces and finance the modern bureaucratic reforms. State insolvency occurred in 1875-6, leading to the formation of the OPDA under foreign management. During the global Great Depression of 1873-96, moreover, both world demand for primary goods and the terms of trade in agriculture became unfavourable to the Ottomans. Agricultural prices recovered in the 1890s but never again became as favourable as in 1820-70.

The cumulative effect of these tendencies and events was a burst of rapid economic development in 1870-1912. Private industrial capitalism emerged, mostly in textiles but also in food production and other sectors. Macedonia, particularly the *vilayet* of Thessaloniki, was the main geographical area of industrial activity in the Empire. The port city of Thessaloniki took the lead, and its Jewish community provided most of the entrepreneurs and the bulk of wage labour.

Fundamental to the rise of industrial capitalism in Ottoman Macedonia was the enormous expansion of trade across the *vilayet* of Thessaloniki after the 1830s. The city became one of the most important ports of the Empire, second only to İstanbul in the European provinces. The main imports were manufactured goods, mostly textiles from Britain, and the bulk of exports were agricultural goods. The period of strongest commercial expansion was 1830-70, laying the foundations for private industrial capitalism in the ensuing decades. Commerce was marshalled by the merchant families of Thessaloniki, typically Jewish but also Muslim and Christian, with extensive networks in both domestic and international markets. The Jewish merchants were well connected internationally and had opportunities to accumulate capital.

Among the Jewish merchants the Allatini, the capitalist kingpins of Macedonia, were able to introduce industrial flour milling already by the mid-1850s. They dominated the grain trade by taking advantage of the steady demand for grain products in both the city and the region as well as by drawing on the pool of wage labour in the Jewish community. The Allatini eventually controlled a broad array of industrial, commercial and banking activities, including brickworks, silk plants and so on. Other Jewish families developed textile industrialization, which became established in the Thessaloniki in the late 1870s. They exploited the plentiful Jewish labour force and sold the output to the domestic markets of the Empire and the neighbouring countries. By the 1900s Thessaloniki had a fairly developed and complex capitalist economy.

The most dynamic area of Macedonian industrialization, however, was in the region of Mount Vermion, a largely agricultural district at some distance to the west of Thessaloniki. Industrial capitalism in provincial Macedonia was led by the local Christian community aiming primarily at the domestic market. Its focus was in industrial textiles – cotton spinning and wool weaving – which took root in the early 1870s mostly in the small upland town of Naoussa. The economic, social, communal and cultural characteristics of capitalism in Mount Vermion were thus quite different from those of Thessaloniki.

Domestic production of textiles in the region of Naoussa was already marked in the 1820s and 1830s. There is no evidence that it declined in the nineteenth century, except perhaps for a brief period after 1822, when the town rebelled and was sacked by Ottoman state forces. By the 1850s that catastrophic event had become a memory, and the town was well known for its domestic production and the export of *şayak*. Its manufacturers were able to market their textiles in domestic and foreign markets, particularly the Kingdom of Greece. That was the basis on which industrial capitalism in cotton spinning emerged in the 1870s and then spread across the region.

In the ensuing four decades the capitalists of Mount Vermion took advantage of very low wages and cheap hydraulic energy as well as the expansion of transport facilities due to the arrival of the railway in the 1890s. They relied on support from the Ottoman state, with which they gradually developed regular relations. By the 1900s they had created a sizeable industrial base in Mount Vermion and diversified their operations in Thessaloniki. Naoussa capitalists controlled a large part of the Empire's capacity in industrial textiles and seemed ready for further expansion.

Despite the emergence of industrial capitalism, however, the Macedonian economy remained heavily agrarian to the end of Ottoman rule in 1912. Agricultural production across the plain of Macedonia, from Thessaloniki to

Mount Vermion, was dominated by smallholdings and, even more significantly, by *çiftlik* estates. The estates were characterized by sharecropping, little use of wage labour, lack of sustained productivity growth, very low land utilization, poor technology and weak agricultural technique. The spread of *çiftlik* estates on the plains of Macedonia generated the agricultural surpluses required to meet the needs of the upland areas, where specialization in manufacturing went hand in hand with food deficiency.[2] Sharecroppers provided the hard work of cultivation, and migrant labourers supplied the harvesting mechanism.[3] The *çiftlik* estates proved resistant to capitalist transformation even when their owners where merchants and industrialists from nearby towns. The agrarian sector of Macedonia produced for the market and even exported a large part of its output, but never became properly capitalist.

In early 1912 Ottoman Macedonia found itself in a contradictory position. Industrial capitalism had emerged with considerable vigour and an energetic and aggressive class of merchants and industrialists set the tone of economic life in the city of Thessaloniki and in Mount Vermion. The *vilayet* of Thessaloniki seemed poised for a true developmental 'take off'. And yet the precariousness of the industrial development of the region was also evident. After more than forty years of industrial development there was practically no vertical integration in textiles; machinery and technology came entirely from abroad and was typically second-hand; the countryside was dominated by *çiftlik* estates and showed no real signs of capitalist transformation; society, moreover, was riven with national and religious divisions, while political conflict had taken murderous forms. It would have taken a huge effort for Ottoman society to make another great leap forward in the direction of capitalist development.

The peculiar historical burden of the Ottoman state is clear in this light, since the state was the only agent that could have forced society to make such a leap. The development of industry had long been the aim of the Ottoman administration, even if its efforts to create state-owned mills had failed. After the 1860s the state had used its limited budget to support infrastructural investment, while also supporting private entrepreneurs through various concessions, mostly tax relief. There is no denying that by the 1890s it had

---

[2] See Palairet (1993, p. 50); Petmezas (1990, p. 586).
[3] See Palairet (1993, p. 50).

succeeded in creating conditions favouring the growth of private industry in the *vilayet* of Thessaloniki. However, forming an integrated bourgeoisie and a homogeneous working class capable of overcoming the manifold divisions of Ottoman society were tasks of an altogether different magnitude.

From the distance of more than a century it is not implausible to argue that the raw materials for such a transformation were available. There was no reason in principle why the ethno-religious divisions among Ottoman capitalists could not be overcome as commercial and industrial capitalism gathered pace in the nineteenth century. After all, great strides had been made among workers in Thessaloniki to transcend nationalist divisions. A shared class character had started to become visible in the labour movement and in the life of wage labourers in the city. As the working class became more prominent in Thessaloniki, the religious and ethnic divisions that had historically marked Ottoman cities began to subside.

However, the Ottoman state was incapable of compelling society to move in the required direction. Despite all the talk of equality in the face of the law, the practices of the Ottoman state remained biased. For one thing, privileged enterprises, often associated with high-standing bureaucrats, were treated more favourably than enterprises created spontaneously, especially those that were far from the centres of power. For another, and far more significant, the ancient autocratic political barriers and the cultural discrimination that traditionally favoured the Muslim community were far from overcome. The task was rendered practically impossible by the poisonous historical legacy of the Empire.

In Ottoman Macedonia the main agents of industrial and commercial advance were Jewish and Greek capitalists embedded in their respective communities. Both had only recently begun to acquire firm political and social rights. As the start of the twentieth century approached, the Ottoman state learnt to relate to merchants and industrialists in supportive ways, and the merchants and industrialists began to acquire the habits of people with easy access to the state. Yet, at least for the Greeks of provincial Macedonia, much of this transformation had come far too late. The ideology of nationalism had already become entrenched by the late nineteenth century, even if not all merchants and industrialists shared equally in it.

'Ottomanism' made some headway during the last four decades of Ottoman rule and had an impact on the Young Turks. In the abstract it seemed to offer the rudiments of a homogenizing ideological force that could support the development of industrial capitalism. In practice it failed to create the required ideological framework as non-Muslim communities reacted with suspicion to the inevitable disruption of their traditional practices and internal mechanisms. The Muslim community was even more apprehensive and hostile to what it perceived as Christian social and economic ascendancy. 'Ottomanism' proved no match for Balkan nationalism.

The Ottoman Empire was caught in a historical bind inherited from its own past. The state's policies of supporting commerce and industry were reasonably effective, and the industrialists of provincial Macedonia soon learnt to swim with the tide. But Ottoman society lacked the wherewithal that could have allowed the creation of an integral capitalist class capable of fully transforming the social order. To be sure the state supported industrial and commercial capitalism and gradually learnt to deal more comfortably with non-Muslims, a process that was important in provincial Macedonia. But the more that the Ottoman state pursued the path of modernity, the stronger became the forces of nationalism. This conundrum was violently resolved from the outside as the Balkan wars of 1912–13 brought an end to more than five centuries of Ottoman rule in Macedonia. There would never be a developed Ottoman capitalism in Europe.

Bibliography

Adanır, F., 1996. *Makedonya Sorunu, Oluşumu ve 1908'e Kadar Gelişimi*. İstanbul: Tarih Vakfı Yurt Yayınları.

Akarli, A. O., 2001. *Growth and Retardation in the Ottoman Economy, the Case of Ottoman Selanik, 1876-1912*. Unpublished PhD Dissertation. London School of Economics and Political Science.

Akarli, E. D., 1992. Economic Policy and Budgets in Ottoman Turkey, 1876-1909. *Middle Eastern Studies* 28: 443-76.

Akdağ, M., 1975. *Celali İsyanları: Türk Halkının Dirlik ve Düzenlik Kavgası*. İstanbul: Bilgi Yayınevi.

Akman, M., 2007. Tanzimat'tan Cumhuriyet'e Osmanlı Hukuk Mevzuatı-I. Tertip Düstur'un Tarihi Fihrist ve Dizini. *Türk Hukuk Tarihi Araştırmaları* 3: 67-224.

Akyıldız, A., 2004. *Osmanlı Bürokrasisi ve Modernleşme*. İstanbul: İletişim Yayınları.

Anastasopoulos, A., 1999. *Imperial Institutions and Local Communities: Ottoman Karaferye 1758-1774*. Unpublished PhD Dissertation. University of Cambridge.

Anastasopoulos, A., 2002. Lighting the Flame of Disorder: Ayan Infighting and State Intervention in Ottoman Karaferye, 1758-59. *International Journal of Turkish Studies* 8: 73-88.

Anastassiadou, M., 2001/1997. *Salonique 1830-1912 [Turkish Version] une ville Ottomane a l'age des Reformes*. Leiden: Brill. 2001. *Tanzimat Çağında bir Osmanlı Şehri Selanik*. İstanbul: Tarih Vakfı Yurt Yayınları.

Anastassiadou, M., 2001b. Yörenin Batılıları, in Veinstein, G. (ed.), *Selânik 1850-1918: 'Yahudilerin kenti' ve Balkanlar'ın Uyanışı*, 183-96. İstanbul: İletişim Yayınları.

Anderson, B., 1983. *Imagined Communities: Reflections on the Origins and Spread of Nationalism*. London; New York: Verso.

Andronikos, F., 2007. Post-Byzantine Greek Merchants of the Fifteenth-Seventeenth Centuries. *Journal of the Hellenic Diaspora* 33: 7-22.

Androudis, P., 2014. The Ottoman town Yenice-i Vardar (Giannitsa) in Macedonia: Historical Trajectory and Monuments (in Greek), in Drakoulis, D. and Tsotsos, G. (eds), *The Analysis of Space from a Historical, Social and Urban Planning Perspective*, 243-68. Thessaloniki: Stamoulis.

Augustinos, G., 1992. *The Greeks of Asia Minor: Confession, Community, and Ethnicity in the Nineteenth Century*. Kent, OH; and London, England: Kent State University Press.

Avcıoğlu, D., 1996. *Türkiye'nin Düzeni*. İstanbul: Tekin Yayınevi.

Aytekin, A. E., 2008. Cultivators, Creditors and the State: Rural Indebtedness in the Nineteenth Century Ottoman Empire. *Journal of Peasant Studies* 35: 292–313.

Aytekin, A. E., 2009. Agrarian Relations, Property and Law: An Analysis of the Land Code of 1858 in the Ottoman Empire. *Middle Eastern Studies* 45 (6): 935–51.

Baer, G., 1970a. Guilds in the Middle Eastern History, in Cook, M. A. (ed.), *Studies in the Economic History of the Middle East: From the Rise of Islam to the Present Day*, 11–30. London: Oxford University Press.

Baer, G., 1970b. The Administrative Economic and Social Functions of Turkish Guilds. *International Journal of Middle East Studies* 1: 28–50.

Baer, G., 1980. Ottoman Guilds: A Reassessment, in Okyar, O. and İnalcık, H. (eds), *Türkiye'nin Sosyal Ve Ekonomik Tarihi (1071–1920): Birinci Uluslararası Türkiye'nin Sosyal Ve Ekonomik Tarihi Kongresi Tebliğleri*, 95–102. Ankara: Meteksan.

Baer, M., 2010. *The Dönme: Jewish Converts, Muslim Revolutionaries, and Secular Turks*. Stanford, CA: Stanford University Press.

Baker, J., 1877. *Turkey in Europe*. London: Cassell Petter & Galpin.

Balcı, R. and Sırma, İ., 2013. *Ticaret ve Ziraat Nezareti Memalik-i Osmaniye'de Osmanlı Anonim Şirketleri*. İstanbul: İstanbul Ticaret Odası Yayınları.

Barkan, Ö. L., 1970. XVI. Asrın ikinci yarısında Türkiye'de fiyat hareketleri. *Belleten* 34(136): 557–607.

Barkan, Ö. L., 1980. *Türkiye'de Toprak Meselesi, Toplu Eserleri*. İstanbul: Gözlem Yayınları.

Barker, E., 1950. *Macedonia*. Connecticut: Greenwood Press.

Barkey, K., 1994. *Bandits and Bureaucrats: The Ottoman Route to State Centralization*. Ithaca, NY: Cornell University Press.

Barkey, K., 2008. *Empire of Difference: The Ottomans in Comparative Perspective*. Cambridge: Cambridge University Press.

Bartholomew, J. G., 1912. *Literary and Historical Atlas of Europe*. London: J. M. Dent.

Behar, C., 1996. *Osmanlı İmparatorluğu'nun ve Türkiye'nin nüfusu, 1500–1927: The Population of the Ottoman Empire and Turkey, 1500–1927*. Ankara: T.C. Başbakanlık Devlet İstatistik Enstitüsü.

Benbassa, E., 1994. Associational Strategies in Ottoman Jewish Society in the Nineteenth and Twentieth Centuries, in Levy, A. (ed.), *The Jews of the Ottoman Empire*, 457–84. Princeton, NJ: The Darwin Press, in collaboration with the Institute of Turkish Studies, Washington, DC.

Berkes, N., 1964. *The Development of Secularism in Turkey*. Montreal: McGill University Press.

Biliouris, L., 2014. *3rd Primary School of Naoussa: Galakeia*. Naoussa: Society of Parents and Guardians.

Birdal, M., 2010. *The Political Economy of Ottoman Public Debt: Insolvency and European Financial Control in the Late Nineteenth Century*. London; New York: Tauris Academic Studies.

Boratav, K., 2007. *Türkiye İktisat Tarihi, 1908–2005*. Ankara: İmge Kitabevi Yayınları.

Braude, B., 1979. International Competition and Domestic Cloth in the Ottoman Empire, 1500–1650: A Study in Underdevelopment. *Review* (Fernand Braudel Center) 2(3): 437–51.

Braude, B., 1982. Foundation Myths of the Millet System, in Braude, B. and Lewis, B. (eds), *Christians and Jews in the Ottoman Empire: The Functioning of a Plural Society*, 69–88. New York: Holms & Meier.

Braude, B., 1991. The Rise and Fall of Salonica Woollens, 1500–1650: Technology Transfer and Western Competition. *Mediterranean Historical Review* 6: 216–36.

Braudel, F., 1982. *The Wheels of Commerce*. Berkeley: University of California Press.

Brenner, R., 1976. Agrarian Class Structure and Economic Development in Pre-Industrial Europe. *Past and Present* 70 (Feb. 1976): 30–75.

Brenner, R., 1977. The Origins of Capitalist Development: A Critique of Neo-Smithian Marxism. *New Left Review* 104: 25–92.

Brenner, R., 1982. Agrarian Class Structure and Economic Development in Pre-Industrial Europe: Agrarian Roots of European Capitalism. *Past and Present* 97 (1): 16–113.

Byres, T. J., 1995. Political Economy, the Agrarian Question and the Comparative Method. *Journal of Peasant Studies* 22: 561–80.

Byres, T. J., 1996. *Capitalism from Above and Capitalism from Below: An Essay in Comparative Political Economy*. London: MacMillan Press.

Cakiroglu, P., 2015. *Industrialisation in Provincial Macedonia in the late Ottoman Era: Economic, Social and Communal Factors*. Unpublished PhD Dissertation. Department of Economics, SOAS, University of London.

Chatziioannou, M. C., 2010. Creating the Pre-Industrial Ottoman-Greek Merchant: Sources, Methods and Interpretations, in Baruh-Tanatar, L., Kechriotis, V. (eds), *Economy and Society on Both Shores of the Aegean*, 311–35. Athens: Alpha Bank Historical Archives.

Chayanov, A. V., 1986. *The Theory of Peasant Economy*. Madison: University of Wisconsin Press.

Cin, H., 1992. *Osmanlı toprak düzeni ve bu düzenin bozulması*. Konya: Selçuk Üniversitesi Hukuk Fakültesi.

Clark, E., 1974. The Ottoman Industrial Revolution. *International Journal of Middle East Studies* 5, 65–76.

Cohen, J. P., 2014. *Becoming Ottomans*. Oxford: Oxford University Press.

Cook, M. A., 1970. *Studies in the Economic History of the Middle East: From the Rise of Islam to the Present Day*. London: Oxford University Press.

Cousinery, E. M., 1831. *Voyage dans la Macedoine*. Paris: Imprimerie Royale.

Damlıbağ, F., 2012. Osmanlı Devleti'nde Sanayi Finansman Metodu Olarak Fabrika İmtiyaz Sistemi. *İstanbul Üniversitesi İktisat Fakültesi Mecmuası* 62(2): 197–222.

Damlıbağ, F., 2014. Osmanlı Sanayisindeki Vergi Muafiyetleri (Ottoman Indusal Tax Exemptions). *OTAM 35/Bahar*, 65–88.

Dekazos, P., 1913. *Naoussa in Macedonia (in Greek)*. Athens: Mantzevelakis.

Dekazos, P., 1914. *Agrarian Relations in Macedonia (in Greek)*. Athens: Leonis.

Demetriades, V., 1973. *Central and Western Macedonia according to Evliya Çelebi (in Greek)*. Thessaloniki: Society of Macedonian Studies.

Demetriades, V., 1976. The Tomb of Ghazi Evrenos Bey at Yenitsa and Its Inscription. *Bulletin of the School of Oriental and African Studies* 39: 328–32.

Demetriades, V., 1981. Problems of Land-owning and Population in the Area of Gazi Evrenos Bey's Wakf. *Balkan Studies* 22(1): 34–57.

Dimaras, K. T., 1977. *The Modern Greek Enlightenment* (in Greek), Modern Greek Studies 2, Athens: Hermes.

Dimitriadis, S., 2014. *The Making of an Ottoman Port-city: The State, Local Elites and Urban Space in Salonika, 1870–1912*. Unpublished PhD Dissertation. Department of History, SOAS, University of London.

Dobb, M., 1972 [1946]. *Studies in the Development of Capitalism*. London: Routledge & Kegan Paul.

Dumont, P., 1978. The Social Structure of the Jewish Community of Salonica at the End of the Nineteenth Century. *Southeastern Europe* 5: 33–72.

Dumont, P., 2013, Salonica and Beirut: The Reshaping of Two Ottoman Cities of the Eastern Mediterranean, in Ginio, E. and Kaser, K. (eds), *Ottoman Legacies in the Contemporary Mediterranean: The Balkans and the Middle East Compared*, 189–208. Jerusalem: The European Forum at the Hebrew University.

Dumont, P. and Haupt, G., 1978. *Osmanlı İmparatorluğunda Sosyalist Hareketler*. İstanbul: Gözlem.

Eldem, E., 2006. Capitulations and Western Trade, in Faroqhi, S. (ed.), *The Cambridge History of Turkey, Vol. 3, The Later Ottoman Empire, 1603–1839*, 283–335. New York: Cambridge University Press.

Eldem, V., 1994. *Osmanlı İmparatorluğu'nun iktisadi şartları hakkında bir tetkik*. Ankara: Türk Tarih Kurumu Basımevi.

Erder, L. and Faroqhi, S., 1979. Population Rise and Fall in Anatolia, 1550–1620. *MES* XV, 322–45.

Ergin, O. N., 1995 [1927]. *Mecelle-i Umûr-ı Belediyye*. İstanbul: İstanbul Büyükşehir Belediyesi Yayınları.

Farnie, D. A., 2004. The Role of Merchants as Prime Movers in the Expansion of the Cotton Industry, 1760–1990, in Farnie, D. A. and Jeremy, D. J. (eds), *The Fibre That Changed the World, The Cotton Industry in International Perspective, 1600–1990s*, 15–56. Oxford: Oxford University Press.

Farnie, D. A. and Jeremy, D. J. (eds), 2004. *The Fibre That Changed the World, the Cotton Industry in International Perspective, 1600–1990s*. Oxford: Oxford University Press.

Faroqhi, S., 1986. Coffee and Spices: Official Ottoman Reactions to Egyptian Trade in the Later Sixteenth Century. *WZKM* 76: 87–93.

Faroqhi, S. (ed.), 2006. The Cambridge History of Turkey, Vol. 3, The later Ottoman Empire, 1603–1839. New York: Cambridge University Press.

Faroqhi, S., 2009. *Artisans of Empire: Crafts and Craftspeople under the Ottomans*. London: I.B. Tauris.

Faroqhi, S. and Veinstein, G. (eds), 2008. *Merchants in the Ottoman Empire*. Leuven: Peeters Publishers.

Findley, C. V., 1980. *Bureaucratic Reform in the Ottoman Empire the Sublime Porte, 1789–1922*. Princeton, NJ: Princeton University Press.

Findley, C. V., 1982. The Acid Test of Ottomanism: The Acceptance of Non-Muslims in the Late Ottoman Bureaucracy, in Braude, B. and Lewis, B. (eds), *Christians and Jews in the Ottoman Empire: The Functioning of a Plural Society*, 339–68. New York: Holms & Meier.

Gara, E., 1998. In Search of Communities in Seventeenth Century Ottoman Sources: The Case of the Karaferye District. *Turcica* 30: 135–62.

Gellner, E., 1981. *Muslim Society*. Cambridge: Cambridge University Press.

Genç, M., 1991. 19. Yüzyılda Osmanlı İktisadi Dünya Görüşünün Klasik Prensiplerindeki Değişimler. *Divan* 1: 1–8.

Genç, M., 1994. Ottoman Industry in the Eighteenth Century: General Framework, Characteristics, and Main Trends, in Quataert, D. (ed.), *Manufacturing in the Ottoman Empire and Turkey, 1500–1950*, 59–86. Albany: State University of New York Press.

Genç, M., 2000. *Osmanlı İmparatorluğu'nda Devlet ve Ekonomi*. İstanbul: Ötüken.

Ginio, E., 1998. The Administration of Criminal Justice in Ottoman Selanik (Salonica) during the Eighteenth Century. *Turcica* 30: 185–209.

Ginio, E., 2002. Migrants and Workers in an Ottoman Port: Ottoman Salonica in the Eighteenth Century, in Rogan, E. (ed.), *Outside In: On the Margins of the Modern Middle East*, 126–48. London: I.B. Tauris.

Ginio, E., 2006. When Coffee Brought About Wealth and Prestige: The Impact of Egyptian Trade on Salonica. *Oriente Moderno,* Nuova serie 25(86): 93–107.

Göçek, F. M., 1996. *Rise of the Bourgeoisie, Demise of Empire: Ottoman Westernization and Social Change.* New York; Oxford: Oxford University Press.

Gounaris, B. C., 1993. *Steam over Macedonia, 1870–1912: Socio-Economic Change and the Railway Factor.* Boulder, CO: East European Monographs.

Gounaris, B. C., 1995. Social Cleavages and National 'Awakening' in Ottoman Macedonia. *East European Quarterly* 29: 409–426.

Gounaris, B. C., 1997. *Thessaloniki 1830–1912: History, Economy and Society, Vol.1 of Thessaloniki, History and Culture* (in Greek). Salonica: Paratiritis.

Gounaris, B. C., 2000. *On the Banks of the Hydragoras* (in Greek). Athens: Stachy.

Gounaris, B. C., 2010. *The Macedonian Question from the 19th to the 21st Century.* Athens: Alexandria Press.

Gounaris, B.C. and Mihailidis, I., 2000. The Pen and the Sword: Reviewing the Historiography of the Macedonian Question, in Roudometof, V. (ed.), *The Macedonian Question: Culture, Historiography, Politics,* 99–141. Boulder, CO: East European Monographs.

Goutas, A., 1999, *Naoussa in the 19th Century,* in Greek. Thessaloniki: Loxias.

Greif, A., 1993. Contract Enforceability and Economic Institutions in Early Trade: The Maghribi Traders' Coalition. *American Economic Review,* 83(3): 525–48.

Greif, A., 2006. *Institutions and the Path to the Modern Economy: Lessons from Medieval Trade.* Cambridge: Cambridge University Press.

Güran, T., 1992. Tanzimat Döneminde Devlet Fabrikaları, in Yıldız, H. D. (ed.), 150. *Yılında Tanzimat,* 235–57. Ankara: Türk Tarih Kurumu Yayınları.

Güran, T., 1998. *19. Yüzyıl Osmanlı Tarımı Üzerine Araştırmalar.* İstanbul: Eren.

Güzel, Ş., 1996. *Türkiye'de İşçi Hareketi, 1908–1984.* İstanbul: Kaynak Yayınları.

Hadar, G., 2007. Jewish Tobacco Workers in Salonika: Gender and Family in the Context of Social and Ethnic Strife, in Buturovic, A. and Schick, I. C. (eds), *Women in the Ottoman Balkans: Gender, Culture and History,* 127–52. New York: I.B. Tauris.

Hadziiossif, C., 1993. *Waning Crescent. Industry in the Greek Economy, 1830–1940* (in Greek). Athens: Themelio Publishers.

Hammond, N. G. L., 1995. The Location of the Trout-River Astraeus. *Greek, Roman and Byzantine Studies* 36(2): 173–6.

Hasluck, F., 1929. *Christianity and Islam under the Sultans,* ed. M. Hasluck, 2 vols. Oxford: Oxford University Press.

Hekimoglou, E., 1987. *Banks and Thessaloniki, 1900-1936* (in Greek). Thessaloniki: Private Publication.

Hekimoglou, E., 1991. *The Modiano Affair, A Banking Crash in Thessaloniki in 1911* (in Greek). Thessaloniki: Th. Altinji.

Hekimoglou, E., 1996. Θεσσαλονίκη, Τουρκοκρατία και Μεσοπόλεμος. Thessaloniki: Έκφραση.

Hekimoglou, E., 1997. The Jewish Bourgeoisie in Thessaloniki, 1906-1911: Assets and Bankruptcies, in Hassiotis, I. K. (ed.), *The Jewish Communities of Southeastern Europe (from the 15th Century to the End of World War II)*, 175-83. Thessaloniki: Institute for Balkan Studies.

Hekimoglou, E. (ed.), 2005. *The History of Entrepreneurship in Thessaloniki, the Ottoman Period*. Thessaloniki: N.G.E.C.S. Publications.

Hekimoglou, E., 2012. *The 'Immortal' Allatini, Ancestors and Relatives of Noemie Allatini-Bloch (1860-1928)*. Thessaloniki: Jewish Museum of Thessaloniki.

Hekimoglou, E., 2015. The Greek Community of Thessaloniki and the Challenge of the Young Turks, 1908-1912, in Stamatopoulos, D. (ed.), *Balkan Nationalism(s) and the Ottoman Empire, Vol. III, 7-32*. İstanbul: ISIS Press.

Hershlag, Z. Y., 1964. *Introduction to the Modern Economic History of the Middle East*. Netherlands: Brill Archive.

Hilton, R. (ed.), 1985. *The Transition from Feudalism to Capitalism*. London: Verso.

Ilicak, H. Ş., 2002. Jewish Socialism in Ottoman Salonica. *Southeast European and Black Sea Studies* 2(3): 115-46.

İnalcık, H., 1954. Ottoman Methods of Conquest. *Studia Islamica* II, 104-29.

İnalcık, H., 1955. Land Problems in Turkish History. *The Muslim World* 45, 221-8.

İnalcık, H., 1969. Capital Formation in the Ottoman Empire. *Journal of Economic History* 29: 97-140.

İnalcık, H., 1970. The Ottoman Economic Mind and Aspects of the Ottoman Economy, in İnalcık, H. (1978), *The Ottoman Empire: Conquest, Organisation and Economy*, 207-18. London: Variorum Collected Studies Series.

İnalcık, H., 1973. *The Ottoman Empire*. London: Weidenfield and Nicholson.

İnalcık, H., 1977. *Adaletnameler*. Ankara: Türk Tarih Kurumu Basımevi.

İnalcık, H., 1978. The Impact of the Annales School on Ottoman Studies and New Findings. *Review, Fernand Braudel Centre* 1(3/4): 69-96.

İnalcık, H., 1980. Military and Fiscal Transformation in the Ottoman Empire, 1600-1700. *Archivum Ottomanicum* VI, 283-337.

İnalcık, H., 1984. *The Emergence of Big Farms, Çiftliks: State, Landlords, and Tenants*, Reprinted in: *Studies in Ottoman Social and Economic History*, 1985. London: Variorum Reprints.

İnalcık, H., 1991. The Emergence of Big Farms, Çiftliks: State, Landlords, and Tenants, in Keyder, Ç. and Tabak, F. (eds), *Landholding and Commercial Agriculture in the Middle East: Globalization, Revolution, and Popular Culture*, 17–34. Albany, NY: SUNY Press.

İnalcık, H., 1993. State, Sovereignty and Law during the Reign of Süleyman, in İnalcık. H. and Kafadar, C. (eds), *Süleyman the Second and His Time*, 59–92. İstanbul: ISIS Press.

İnalcık, H., 1994a. The Ottoman State: Economy and Society, 1300–1600, in İnalcık, H. and Quataert, D. (eds), *An Economic and Social History of the Ottoman Empire, 1300–1914*, 9–410. Cambridge; New York: Cambridge University Press.

İnalcık, H., 1994b. Sultanizm Üzerine Yorumlar: Max Weber'in Osmanlı Siyasal Sistemi Tiplemesi. *Toplum ve Ekonomi* 7: 5–27.

İnalcık, H., 2011. *Osmanlı İmparatorluğu: Klasik Çağ 1300–1600*. İstanbul: Yapı Kredi Yayınları.

İnalcık, H. and Kafadar, C. (eds), 1993. *Süleyman the Second and His Time*. İstanbul: ISIS Press.

İnalcık, H. and Quataert, D. (eds), 1994. *An Economic and Social History of the Ottoman Empire, 1300–1914*. Cambridge; New York: Cambridge University Press.

İnalcık, H. and Seyitdanlıoğlu, M. (eds), 2011. *Tanzimat: Değişim Sürecinde Osmanlı İmparatorluğu*. İstanbul: İş Bankası Kültür Yayınları.

İslamoğlu-İnan, H., 1983. Osmanlı Tarihi ve Dünya Sistemi: Bir Değerlendirme (Ottoman History and the World System: An Assessment). *Toplum ve Bilim* 23: 9–39.

İslamoğlu-İnan, H. (ed.), 1987. *The Ottoman Empire and the World Economy*. Cambridge: Cambridge University Press.

İslamoğlu-İnan, H. and Keyder, Ç., 1987. Agenda for Ottoman History, in İslamoğlu-İnan, H. (ed.), *The Ottoman Empire and the World Economy*, 42–62. Cambridge: Cambridge University Press.

Issawi, C. P., 1980. *The Economic History of Turkey, 1800–1914*. Chicago, IL; London: University of Chicago Press.

Jelavich, B., 1983. *History of the Balkans*, vol. I. Cambridge, UK: Cambridge University Press.

Kafadar, C., 1995. *Between Two Worlds*. Berkeley: University of California Press.

Kala, A., 1993. Osmanlı Devletinde Sanayileşmenin İlk Yıllarında Özel Fabrikalar. *Türk Dünyası Araştırmaları* 83: 107–32.

Kaplan, M., 2011. Mustafa Reşid Paşa ve Yeni Aydın Tipi, in İnalcık, H. and Seyitdanlıoğlu, M. (eds), *Tanzimat, Değişim Sürecinde Osmanlı İmparatorluğu*, 465–75. İstanbul: Türkiye İş Bankası Kültür Yayınları.

Karakışla, Y. S., 1998. Osmanlı İmparatorluğu'nda 1908 Grevleri. *Toplum ve Bilim* 78, 187–208.

Karal, E. Z., 1943. *Osmanlı İmparatorluğunda ilk nüfus sayımı 1831*. Ankara: T.C. Başvekâlet İstatistik Umum Müdürlüğü.

Karavas, S., 1999. The Palimpsest of the Memoirs of Kapetan-Akritas (in Greek). *Historica* 16(31): 291–330.

Karavas, S., 2010. *Blessed Are Those Who Own the Land* (in Greek). Athens: Vivliorama.

Karavas, S., 2014. The Fairytale of Penelope Delta and the Secrets of the Macedonian Struggle (in Greek), in Karavas, S. (ed.), *Secrets and Fairytales from the History of Macedonia*. Athens: Vivliorama.

Karpat, K., 1982. Millets and Nationality: The Roots of the Incongruity of Nation and State in the Post-Ottoman Era, in Braude, B. and Lewis, B. (eds), *Christians and Jews in the Ottoman Empire: The Functioning of a Plural Society*, 141–70. New York: Holms & Meier.

Karpat, K., 1985. *Ottoman Population, 1830–1914: Demographic and Social Characteristics*. Madison: University of Wisconsin Press Madison.

Karpat, K. H., 2002. *Studies on Ottoman Social and Political History: Selected Articles and Essays*. Leiden: Brill.

Kasaba, R., 1988. *The Ottoman Empire and the World Economy: The Nineteenth Century*. Albany, NY: SUNY Press.

Kautsky, K., 1988. *The Agrarian Question*. London: Zwan Publications.

Keyder, Ç., 1987. *State and Class in Turkey: A Study in Capitalist Development*. London: Verso.

Keyder, Ç., Özveren, Y. E., Qutaert, D., 1994. *Doğu Akdeniz'de liman kentleri, 1800–1914*. İstanbul: Tarih Vakfı Yurt Yayınları.

Keyder, Ç. and Tabak, F., 1991. *Landholding and Commercial Agriculture in the Middle East: Globalization, Revolution, and Popular Culture*. Albany, NY: SUNY Press.

Keyder, Ç. and Tabak, F., 1998. *Osmanlı'da Toprak Mülkiyeti ve Ticari Tarım*. İstanbul: Tarih Vakfı Yurt Yayınları.

Kiel, M., 1972. Yenice Vardar (Vardar Yenicesi- Giannitsa). *Byzantina Neerlandica* 3, 300–39.

Kılınçoğlu, D. T., 2015. *Economics and Capitalism in the Ottoman Empire*. London; New York: Routledge.

Kırmızı, A., 2007. *Abdülhamid'in valileri: Osmanlı vilayet İdaresi 1895–1908*. İstanbul: Klasik.

Kitromilides, P., 1996. *Modern Greek Enlightenment: The Political and Social Ideas* (in Greek). Athens: Educational Institute of the National Bank.

Kofinas, G., 1914. *The Economics of Macedonia* (in Greek). Athens: National Printing Press.

Kolonas, B., 2016. *Thessaloniki Outside the Walls: Illustrations from the Provincial District, 1885–1912* (in Greek). Thessaloniki: University Studio Press.

Kondylis, P., 1988. *Modern Greek Enlightenment: The Philosophical Ideas* (in Greek). Athens: Themelio.

Konortas, P., 1999. From Ta'ife to Millet: Ottoman Terms Concerning the Ottoman Greek Orthodox Community, in Gondicas D. and Issawi, C. (eds), *Ottoman Greeks in the Age of Nationalism: Politics, Economy, and Society in the Nineteenth Century*, 169–80. Princeton, NJ: Darwin Press.

Krstić, T., 2011. *Contested Conversions to Islam*. Stanford, CA: Stanford University Press.

Kuran, T., 2003. The Islamic Commercial Crisis: Institutional Roots of Economic Underdevelopment in the Middle East. *Journal of Economic History* 63 (2): 414–46.

Kütükoğlu, M., 1976. *Osmanlı-İngiliz Münasebetleri (1835–1850)*. İstanbul: Edebiyat Fakültesi Basımevi No. 1997.

Lampe, J. R. and Jackson, M. R., 1982. *Balkan Economic History, 1550–1950: From Imperial Borderlands to Developing Nations*. Bloomington: Indiana University Press.

Landes, D. S., 1988. *The Unbound Prometheus: Technological Change and Industrial Development in Western Europe from 1750 to the Present*. Cambridge: Cambridge University Press.

Lange-Akhund, N., 1998. *The Macedonian Question, 1893–1908*. Boulder, CO: East European Monographs, distributed by New York: Columbia University Press.

Lapavitsas, C., 2004. *Social Origins of Ottoman Industrialisation: Evidence from the Macedonian Town of Naoussa*, Department of Economics Working Paper, 142, School of Oriental and African Studies, available at http://eprints.soas.ac.uk/107/1/econ142.pdf.

Lapavitsas, C., 2006. Industrial Development and Social Transformation in Ottoman Macedonia. *Journal of European Economic History* 35, 661–710.

Leake, W., 1835 [1967]. *Travels in Northern Greece*. Amsterdam: Hakkert.

Lenin, V. I., 1964 [1907]. *The Development of Capitalism in Russia*, in Collected Works. Moscow: Foreign Languages Publishing House, 21–608.

Levy, A. (ed.), 1994a. *The Jews of the Ottoman Empire*. Princeton, NJ: The Darwin Press, in collaboration with the Institute of Turkish Studies, Washington, DC.

Levy, A., 1994b. Millet Politics: The Appointment of a Chief Rabbi in 1835, in Levy, A. (ed.), *The Jews of the Ottoman Empire*, 425–38. Princeton, NJ: The Darwin Press, in collaboration with the Institute of Turkish Studies, Washington, DC.

Lewis, B., 1979 [1961]. *The Emergence of Modern Turkey*. London: Oxford University Press.

Lewis, B., 1982. *The Muslim Discovery of Europe*. New York: Norton.

Lewis, B., 1984. *The Jews of Islam*. London: Routledge and Kegan Paul.

Lowry, H. W., 2003. *The Nature of the Early Ottoman State*. Albany, NY: SUNY Press.

Lowry, H. W., 2008. *The Shaping of the Ottoman Balkans, 1350–1550: The Conquest, Settlement & Infrastructural Development of Northern Greece*. İstanbul: Bahçeşehir University Press.

Lowry, H. W., 2010. *The Evrenos Family & the City of Selânik (Thessaloniki): Who Built the Hamza Beğ Câmi'i & Why?* İstanbul: Bahçeşehir University Press.

Lowry, H. W. and Erünsal, İ. E., 2010. *The Evrenos Dynasty of Yenice-i Vardar: Notes & Documents*. İstanbul: Bahçeşehir University Press.

Lyberatos, A., 2009. *Economy, Politics and National Ideology: The Formation of National Parties in Philippoupolis in the 19th Century* (in Greek). Heraklion: University of Crete Publications.

Lyberatos, A., 2010. Men of the Sultan: The beğlik Sheep Tax Collection System and the Rise of a Bulgarian National Bourgeoisie in Nineteenth-Century Plovdiv. *Turkish Historical Review* 1, 55–85.

Mansel, P., 2010. *Levant: Splendour and Catastrophe on the Mediterranean*. Great Britain: John Murray (Publishers).

Mardin, Ş., 1960. The Mind of the Turkish Reformer 1700–1900. *Western Humanities Review* 14, 413–36.

Martal, A., 1999. Osmanlı Sanayileşme Çabaları (XIX. Yüzyıl), in *Osmanlı Cilt* 3, 279–85. Ankara: Yeni Türkiye Yayınları.

Marx, K., 1992. *Capital: Volume 1: A Critique of Political Economy*, Reprint edition. London; New York: Penguin Classics.

Marx, K., 1993 [1894]. *Capital: A Critique of Political Economy*, vol. 3, Reissue edition. New York: Penguin Classics.

Marx, K. and Engels, F., 1986 [1858]. *Karl Marx Frederick Engels: Collected Works 1857–61*. New York: International Publishers.

Mazarakis-Ainian, K., 1963. *The Macedonian Struggle (Memoirs)* (in Greek). Thessaloniki: Society of Macedonian Studies.

Mazower, M., 2004. *Salonica, City of Ghosts: Christians, Muslims, and Jews, 1430–1950*. London: HarperCollins.

McCarthy, J., 2000. Muslims in Ottoman Europe: Population from 1800 to 1912. *Nationalities Papers* 28: 29–43.

McCarthy, J. and Hyde, J. D., 1979. Ottoman Imperial and Provincial Salnames. *Middle East Studies Association Bulletin* 13: 10–20.

McGowan, B., 1981. *Economic Life in Ottoman Europe: Taxation, Trade, and the Struggle for Land, 1600–1800*. Cambridge: Cambridge University Press.

McGowan, B., 1994. The Age of Ayans, 1699–1812, in İnalcık, H. and Quataert, D. (eds), *An Economic and Social History of the Ottoman Empire, 1300–1914*, 637–758. Cambridge; New York: Cambridge University Press.

Megas, G., 2011. *Hundred Years since the Visit of Sultan Mehmed Reshat in Thessaloniki, 1911–2011* (in Greek). Thessaloniki; Athens: University Studio Press.

Mentzel, P. C., 1994. *Nationalism and the Labor Movement in the Ottoman Empire, 1872–1914*. Ann Arbor: University of Michigan Press.

Meron, O., 2005. Sub Ethnicity and Elites: Jewish Italian Professionals and Entrepreneurs in Salonica (1881–1912). *ZAKHOR. Rivista di Storia degli Ebrei d' Italia*, VIII, 177–220.

Meron, O., 2011. *Jewish Entrepreneurship in Salonica, 1912–1940*. Eastbourne, UK: Sussex Academic Press.

Mielants, E., 2007. *The Origins of Capitalism and the 'Rise of the West'*. Philadelphia, PA: Temple University Press.

Moskoff, K., 1974. *Thessaloniki, 1700–1912: Analysing a Huckstering City* (in Greek). Athens: Stochastis.

Naar, D. E., 2016. *Jewish Salonica: Between the Ottoman Empire and Modern Greece*. Stanford, CA: Stanford University Press.

Nacar, C., 2010. *Tobacco Workers in the Late Ottoman Empire: Fragmentation, Conflict, and Collective Struggle*. Binghamton: State University of New York.

Nicolaidy, B., 1859. *Les Turcs et la Turquie Contemporaine*. Paris: Sartorius.

North, D. C., 1994. Economic Performance through Time. *American Economic Review* 84(3): 359–68.

North, D. C. and Thomas, R. P., 1973. *The Rise of the Western World: A New Economic History*. Cambridge: Cambridge University Press.

Obolensky, D., 1982. *The Byzantine Impact in Eastern Europe*. London: Variorum Reprints.

Ökçün, A. G., 1982. *Tatil-i Eşgal Kanunu, 1909: Belgeler-Yorumlar*. Ankara: Ankara Üniversitesi Siyasal Bilgiler Fakültesi Yayınları.

Okyar, O., 1987. A New Look at the Problem of Economic Growth in the Ottoman Empire (1800–1914). *Journal of European Economic History* 16: 7–50.

Önsoy, R., 1988. *Tanzimat Dönemi Osmanlı Sanayii ve Sanayileşme Politikası*. Ankara: Türkiye İş Bankası Kültür Yayınları.

Ortaylı, İ., 1983. Tanzimat Bürokratları ve Metternich, in *Profesör Fehmi Yavuz'a Armağan*, 361–7. Ankara: Siyasal Bilgiler Fakültesi Yayını.

Ortaylı, İ., 2011. Tanzimat Adamı ve Tanzimat Toplumu, in İnalcık, H. and Seyitdanlıoğlu, M. (eds), *Tanzimat, Değişim Sürecinde Osmanlı İmparatorluğu*, 423–61. İstanbul: Türkiye İş Bankası Kültür Yayınları.

Owen, R., 2009. *The Middle East in the World Economy 1800–1914*. London; New York: I.B. Tauris.

Özdemir, B., 2003. *Ottoman Reforms and Social Life: Reflections from Salonica, 1830–1850*. İstanbul: ISIS Press.

Özok-Gündoğan, N., 2012. A 'Peripheral' Approach to the 1908 Revolution in the Ottoman Empire: Land Disputes in Peasant Petitions in Post-Revolutionary Diyarbekir, in Jongerden, J. and Verheij, J. (eds), *Social Relations in Ottoman Diyarbekir*. Leiden: Brill.

Pakalin, M. Z., 1983. *Osmanlı tarih deyimleri ve terimleri sözlüğü*. İstanbul: Milli Eğitim Basımevi.

Palairet, M. R., 1983. The Decline of the Old Balkan Woollen Industries, c. 1870–1914. *VSWG: Vierteljahrschrift für Sozial- und Wirtschaftsgeschichte* 70, 330–62.

Palairet, M. R., 1993. *The Balkan Economies C. 1800–1914: Evolution without Development*. Cambridge University Press.

Palamiotis, G., 1914. Agricultural Study of Macedonia, Part A, Western Macedonia, *Bulletin of Greek Agricultural Society* 6 (1–2): 1–75.

Pamuk, Ş., 1984. The Ottoman Empire in the 'Great Depression' of 1873–1896. *Journal of Economic History* 44, 107–18.

Pamuk, Ş., 1987. *The Ottoman Empire and European Capitalism, 1820–1913: Trade, Investment, and Production*. New York: Cambridge University Press.

Pamuk, Ş., 1994. *Osmanlı ekonomisinde bağımlılık ve büyüme, 1820–1913*. İstanbul: Tarih Vakfı Yurt Yayınları.

Pamuk, Ş., 2004. Institutional Change and the Longevity of the Ottoman Empire, 1500–1800. *Journal of Interdisciplinary History* 35, 225–47.

Pamuk, Ş., 2007. *Osmanlı-Türkiye İktisadi Tarihi, 1500–1914*. İstanbul: İletişim Yayınları.

Pamuk, Ş., 2009. *The Ottoman Economy and Its Institutions*. Farnham, Surrey: Ashgate Publishers.

Pamuk, Ş., 2016. Economic Growth in Southeastern Europe and East Mediterranean, 1820–1914. *Economic Alternatives* 3, 249–64.

Pamuk, Ş. and Williamson, J. G., 2011. Ottoman De-industrialization, 1800–1913: Assessing the Magnitude, Impact, and Response. *The Economic History Review* 64: 159–84.

Panza, L., 2013. Globalization and the Near East: A Study of Cotton Market Integration in Egypt and Western Anatolia. *Journal of Economic History* 73(3): 847–72.

Panza, L., 2014. Deindustrialisation and Re-industrialisation in the Middle East: Reflections on the Cotton Industry in Egypt and in the İzmir Region. *Economic History Review, Economic History Society* 67(1): 146–69.

Panzac, D., 1992a. La population de la Macédoine au XIXe siècle (1820–1912), in Panzac, D. (ed.), *Les Balkans à l'époque ottoman*. Revue du Monde Musulman et de la Méditerranée 66, 113–34.

Panzac, D., 1992b. International and Domestic Maritime Trade in the Ottoman Empire during the 18th Century. *International Journal of Middle East Studies* 24, 189–206.

Papademetriou, T., 2015. *Render unto the Sultan*. Oxford: Oxford University Press.

Peacock, A. C. S., De Nicola, B., Yildiz S. N. (eds), 2015. *Islam and Christianity in Medieval Anatolia*. Surrey: Ashgate.

Petmezas, S. D., 1990. Patterns of Protoindustrialization in the Ottoman Empire: The Case of Eastern Thessaly (ca. 1750–1860). *Journal of European Economic History* 19: 575–603.

Petmezas, S. D., 2003, Christian Communities in Eighteenth- and Early Nineteenth-Century Ottoman Greece: Their Fiscal Functions, in Greene, M. (ed.), *Parallels Meet: New Vistas of Religious Community and Empire in Ottoman Historiography*, 76–116. Princeton, NJ: Marcus Wiener.

Petmezas, S. D., 2010. Bridging the Gap: Rural Macedonia from Ottoman to Greek Rule (1900–1920), in Baruh, L. T. and Kechriotis, V. (eds), *Economy and Society on Both Shores of the Aegean*, 355–95. Athens: Alpha Bank Historical Archives.

Petridis, C., 1994 [1904]. *The Kerykos* (in Greek). Naousa: Phoni Naoussis.

Pirenne, H., 1956. *Medieval Cities: Their Origins and the Revival of Trade*. Princeton, NJ: Princeton University Press.

Pouqueville, F., 1826. *Voyage de la Grece*. Paris: Firmin Didot.

Pushkin, A., 1983. *Complete Prose Fiction*, trans. Paul Debreczeny. Stanford, CA: Stanford University Press.

Quataert, D., 1975. Dilemma of Development: The Agricultural Bank and Agricultural Reform in Ottoman Turkey, 1888–1908. *International Journal of Middle East Studies* 6: 210–27.

Quataert, D., 1983. *Social Disintegration and Popular Resistance in the Ottoman Empire 1881–1908, Reactions to European Economic Penetration*. New York; London: New York University Press.

Quataert, D., 1992. *Manufacturing and Technology Transfer in the Ottoman Empire, 1800–1914*. İstanbul: ISIS Press.

Quataert, D., 1993a. *Ottoman Manufacturing in the Age of the Industrial Revolution.* Cambridge: Cambridge University Press.

Quataert, D., 1993b. *Workers, Peasants and Economic Change in the Ottoman Empire, 1730–1914.* İstanbul: ISIS Press.

Quataert, D., 1994a. *Manufacturing in the Ottoman Empire and Turkey, 1500–1950.* Albany, NY: SUNY Press.

Quataert, D., 1994b. The Age of Reforms, 1812–1914, in İnalcık, H. and Quataert, D. (eds), *An Economic and Social History of the Ottoman Empire, 1300–1914,* 759–943. Cambridge; New York: Cambridge University Press.

Quataert, D., 2005. *The Ottoman Empire, 1700–1922.* Cambridge: Cambridge University Press.

Quataert, D., 2008. *Anadolu'da Osmanlı Reformu Ve Tarım.* İstanbul: Türkiye İş Bankası Kültür Yayınları.

Quataert, D., 2014. Fabrika Bacalarından Tüten İlk Dumanlar, in Veinstein, G. (ed.), *Selânik 1850–1918: 'Yahudilerin Kenti' ve Balkanlar'ın Uyanışı,* 223–47. İstanbul: İletişim Yayınları.

Quataert, D. and Zürcher, E. J. (eds), 1995. *Workers and Working Class in the Ottoman Empire and the Turkish Republic 1839–19.* London; New York: I. B. Tauris.

Reyhan, C., 2008. *Osmanlı'da Kapitalizmin Kökenleri.* İstanbul: Tarih Vakfı Yurt Yayınları.

Rodinson, M., 2007. *Islam and Capitalism.* London, UK: Saqi Books.

Rodrigue, A. 1994. The Beginnings of Westernization and Community Reform among İstanbul's Jewry, 1854–65, in Levy, A. (ed.), *The Jews of the Ottoman Empire,* 439–56. Princeton, NJ: The Darwin Press, in collaboration with the Institute of Turkish Studies, Washington, DC.

Rostow, W. W., 1960. *The Stages of Economic Growth: A Non-Communist Manifesto.* Cambridge: Cambridge University Press.

Roupa, E. and Hekimoglou, E., 2004. *History of Entrepreneurship in Thessaloniki,* vol. 3, Thessaloniki: Cultural Society of Businesspeople of Northern Greece.

Sadat, D. R., 1969. *Urban Notables in the Ottoman Empire: The Ayan.* Rutgers State University.

Sadat, D. R., 1972. Rumeli Ayanlari: The Eighteenth Century. *Journal of Modern History* 44: 346–63.

Salzmann, A., 1993. An Ancien Régime Revisited: 'Privatization' and Political Economy in the Eighteenth-Century Ottoman Empire. *Politics & Society* 21 (4): 393–423.

Saxonhouse, G. and Wright, G., 2004. Technological Evolution in Cotton Spinning, 1878–1933 in Farnie, D. A. and Jeremy, D. J. (eds), *The Fibre That Changed the*

World, *The Cotton Industry in International Perspective, 1600–1990s*, 129–52. Oxford: Oxford University Press.

Seirinidou, V., 2008. The Greek Trade Diasporas in Central Europe, in Faroqhi, S. and Veinstein, G. (eds), *Merchants in the Ottoman Empire*, 81-95. Leuven: Peeters Publishers.

Sencer (Baydar), O., 1969. *Türkiye'de İşçi Sınıfı: Doğuşu ve Yapısı*. İstanbul: Habora Kitabevi Yayınları.

Sencer (Baydar), O., 1982. *Türkiye İşçi Sınıfı Tarihi-1*. Frankfurt: Infograph.

Seyitdanlıoğlu, M., 2009. *Tanzimat Dönemi Osmanlı Sanayii (1839–1876)*. Ankara Üniversitesi Dil ve Tarih-Coğrafya Fakültesi Tarih Bölümü Tarih Araştırmaları Dergisi 46, 53–69.

Shaw, S., 1992. Local Administrations in the Tanzimat, in Yıldız, H. D. (ed.), 150, *Yılında Tanzimat*. Ankara: Türk Tarih Kurumu Basımevi.

Shaw, S. J., 1978. The Ottoman Census System and Population, 1831–1914. *International Journal of Middle East Studies* 9, 325–38.

Shaw, S. J. and Shaw, E. K., 2002. *History of the Ottoman Empire and Modern Turkey: Volume 2, Reform, Revolution, and Republic: The Rise of Modern Turkey 1808–1975*. Cambridge: Cambridge University Press.

Stamatopoulos D., 2018. Rum Millet between Vakıfs and Property Rights: Endowments' Trials of the Ecumenical Patriarchate's Mixed Council in the Late Ottoman Empire (19th–20th c.). *Endowment Studies* 2: 58–81.

Stoianovich, T., 1953. Land Tenure and Related Sectors of the Balkan Economy, 1600–1800. *Journal of Economic History* 13: 398–411.

Stoianovich, T., 1960. The Conquering Balkan Orthodox Merchant. *Journal of Economic History* 20: 234–313.

Stougiannakis, E., 1911. *Naoussa. Makedonikon Imerologion (Macedonian Calendar)* (in Greek). Athens, 144–57.

Stougiannakis, E., 1993 [1924]. *History of the Town of Naoussa*, in Greek, 3rd edn. Thessaloniki: Society of Naoussa Graduates 'Anastasios Mikhail'.

Svoronos, N., 1956. *Le Commerce de Salonique au XVIIIe siècle*. Paris: PUF.

Sweezy, P. M., 1950. The Theory of Capitalist Development. *Economic Review* 1 (1): 56–61.

Sweezy, P. M. and Dobb, M., 1950. The Transition from Feudalism to Capitalism. *Science and Society* 14(2): 134–67.

Tekeli, İ. and İlkin, S., 1980. İttihat ve Terakki Hareketinin Oluşumunda Selanik'in Toplumsal Yapısının Belirleyiciliği, in İnalcık, H. and Okyar, O. (eds), *Social and Economic History of Turkey*, 351–82. Ankara: Meteksan.

Teoman, Ö. and Kaymak, M., 2008. Commercial Agriculture and Economic Change in the Ottoman Empire during the Nineteenth Century: A Comparison of Raw Cotton Production in Western Anatolia and Egypt. *Journal of Peasant Studies* 35: 314–34.

Thompstone, S., 2004. The Russian Technological Society and British Textile Machinery Imports, in Farnie, D. A. and Jeremy, D. J. (eds), *The Fibre that Changed the World, the Cotton Industry in International Perspective, 1600–1990s*, 337–64. Oxford: Oxford University Press.

Thurn, J., 1973. *Ioannis Scylitzae Synopsis Historiarum, Editio Princeps*. Berlin, New York: De Gruyter.

Todorova, M., 2009 [1997]. *Imagining the Balkans*. Updated edition. New York: Oxford University Press.

Toprak, Z., 2012. *Türkiye'de Milli İktisat 1908–1918*. İstanbul: Doğan Kitap.

Traikov, N. (ed.), 1957. *The Archive of G. S. Rakovski. Vol. 2. Letters to Rakovski (1841–1860)*, with explanatory notes and editing by N. Traikov, 622–5. Sofia: Izdatelstvo na BAN.

Tsakalotos, D., 1914a. A Report on the Industries of Macedonia and their Future, particularly the Chemical Industries, in Greek. *Archimedes* 15(1): January, 9–12.

Tsakalotos, D., 1914b. A Report on the Industries of Macedonia and their Future, particularly the Chemical Industries, in Greek. *Archimedes* 15(2): February, 13–17.

Turner, B. S., 1974. Islam, Capitalism and the Weber Theses. *British Journal of Sociology* 25: 230–43.

Turner, B. S., 1978. *Marx and the End of Orientalism*. London: George Allen & Unwin.

Turner, B. S., 1984. *Capitalism and Class in the Middle East: Theories of Social Change and Economic Development*. London: Heinemann.

Ülgener, S., 1981. *Dünü ve Bugünü ile Zihniyet ve Din: İslam, Tasavvuf ve Çözülme Devri İktisat Ahlakı*. İstanbul: Dergah.

Upward, A., 1908. *The East End of Europe*. London: Cambridge Scholars.

Uyar, M. and Erickson, J., 2009. *A Military History of the Ottomans: From Osman to Atatürk*. Santa Barbara, CA; Denver; Oxford: Praeger Security International.

Vakali, A., 2015. A Christian Printer on Trial in the Tanzimat Council of Selanik: Kiriakos Darzilovitis and his Seditious Books. Cihannüma, Tarih ve Coğrafya Araştırmaları Dergisi, Sayı I/2 – Aralık 2015, 23–38.

Vakalopoulos, A., 1983. *History of Thessaloniki* (in Greek). Thessaloniki: Kyriakidi Bros.

Valsamidis E. and Intzesiloglou, N., 2016. *The Communities of the Greeks.* Naoussa: The Council of Elders, Society for Macedonian Studies.

Van Zanden, J. L., 1997. Do We Need a Theory of Merchant Capitalism? *Review* (Fernand Braudel Center) 20: 255–67.

Vasdravellis, I., 1967. *The Macedonians during the Revolution of 1821* (in Greek), 3rd improved edition. Thessaloniki: Society of Macedonian Studies.

Veinstein, G., 1991. On the Çiftlik Debate, in Keyder, Ç. and Tabak, F. (eds), *Landholding and Commercial Agriculture in the Middle East: Globalization, Revolution, and Popular Culture,* 35–56. Albany, NY: SUNY Press.

Veinstein, G. (ed.), 2001. *Selânik 1850–1918: 'Yahudilerin kenti' ve Balkanlar'ın Uyanışı.* İstanbul: İletişim Yayınları.

Vlami, D., 1997. Commerce and Identity in the Greek Communities: Livorno in the Eighteenth and Nineteenth Centuries. *Diogenes* 77, 73–93.

Vryonis, S. 1971. *The Decline of Medieval Hellenism in Asia Minor and the Process of Islamization from the Eleventh to the Fifteenth Century.* Los Angeles: University of California Press.

Wallerstein, I., 1974. *The Modern World-System I: Capitalist Agriculture and the Origins of the European World-Economy in the Sixteenth Century.* New York: Academic Press.

Wallerstein, I., 1979. The Ottoman Empire and the Capitalist World-Economy: Some Questions for Research. *Review* (Fernand Braudel Center) 2, 389–98.

Wallerstein, I., 1980. *The Modern World System II: Mercantilism and the Consolidation of the European World-Economy 1600–1750.* New York: Academic Press.

Wallerstein, I., 1989. *The Modern World System III: The Second Era of Great Expansion of the Capitalist World-Economy, 1730–1840s.* New York: Academic Press.

Weber, M., 1930 [1905]. *The Protestant Ethic and the Spirit of Capitalism.* London: Allen and Unwin.

Weber, M., 1978. *Economy and Society: An Outline of Interpretive Sociology.* Berkeley: University of California Press.

Williamson, J. G., 2008. Globalization and the Great Divergence: Terms of Trade Booms, Volatility and the Poor Periphery, 1782–1913. *European Review of Economic History* 12, 355–91.

Wittek, P., 1938, *The Rise of the Ottoman Empire.* London: Royal Asiatic Society.

Yaycioglu, A., 2016, *Partners of the Empire.* Stanford, CA: Stanford University Press.

Yi, E., 2004. *Guild Dynamics in Seventeenth-Century İstanbul: Fluidity and Leverage.* Leiden: E. J. Brill.

Yildirim, O., 1998. The Industrial Reform Commission as an Institutional Innovation during the Tanzimat. *Arab Historical Review for Ottoman Studies* 17–18, 117–26.

Yildirim, O., 2000. Osmanlı Esnafında Uyum ve Dönüşüm: 1650–1826. *Toplum ve Bilim* 83: 146–77.

Yildirim, O., 2002. Ottoman Guilds as a Setting for Ethno-Religious Conflict: The Case of the Silk-thread Spinners' Guild in İstanbul. *International Review of Social History* 47: 407–19.

Yildirim, O., 2007. Craft Guilds in the Ottoman Empire (c. 1650–1826): A Survey. *METU Studies in Development* 27: 349–70.

Yildirim, O., 2008. Ottoman Guilds in the Early Modern Era. *International Review of Social History* 53: 73–93.

Zografski, D., 1967. *Razvitokot na kapitalistichkite elementi vo Makedonija (Development of Elements of Capitalism in Macedonia)*. Skopje: Kultura.

Name Index

Abdullah-i İlahi, Şeyh 12, 15n. 14, 187
  tekke 12, 15n. 14, 187
Abdülhamid, Sultan 134, 181–2, 191, 254
Abdülmecid I, Sultan 47
Aelian 15n. 14
Aigai 14
Akarli, A. O. 22, 22n. 12, 26n. 27, 30n. 37, 54, 55, 55n. 26, 55n. 27, 56, 56n. 29, 78n. 40, 80n. 43, 81n. 48, 86n. 59, 91, 91n. 70, 111n. 35, 113n. 44, 131n. 16, 161n. 96, 171n. 114
Akdağ, M. 20, 20n. 3
Albania 31, 46, 50, 69, 159
Aleppo 32, 169
Alexander, King of Macedonia 5, 10
Alexandria 83, 115, 118
Ali *Paşa*, Tepedelenli 15
Allatini, family 6–7, 118, 131, 133, 135–7, 153, 165, 167, 169, 183, 185, 204, 226, 231, 242, 258–9
  flour mill 6, 167, 169, 226, 231
  plant 135
  Villa 135
Anastassiadou, M. 5n. 4, 30n. 37, 59n. 30
Anastasopoulos, A. 14n. 13
Angelakis, family 117, 134, 136, 174
Arapitsa 12, 15, 138, 164, 196, 224
Atatürk, Mustafa Kemal 8
Austria 33, 68, 109, 112, 174, 186, 226n. 27, 231, 237
Axios (*Vardar*) 13

Baer, G. 21n. 8, 30n. 37, 116n. 56, 135n. 26
Banque de Salonique 7, 131
Barkan, Ö. L. 20n. 2, 63n. 2, 74n. 30
Beirut 5, 130
Belgium 33, 112
Benaroya, Avraam 233, 242
Bilis, family 149, 174, 187–9, 194, 218–19
  Bilis-Tsitsis plant 142–3, 161–2, 173–4, 190
Bitola (*Manastır*) 9, 39, 49, 50, 54, 55, 112, 114, 115, 157, 160, 251, 252

Braude, B. 30n. 38, 240n. 77
Braudel, F. 101, 101n. 11
Brenner, R. 87n. 62, 100–101, 100n. 9, 101n. 10
Bulgaria 31, 32, 55, 69, 70, 70n. 21, 119, 127, 154–5, 159, 163, 196, 241, 255
  Exarchate 58, 249, 251
  language 3n. 1, 13, 75, 243, 246, 248, 248n. 94, 250
Byres, T. 87–8, 87nn. 62, 63

Cakiroglu, P. 36n. 54, 44n. 1, 78n. 41, 163n. 100, 170
Constantinople, see *İstanbul*
Cousinery, E. M. 15n. 18, 17n. 19, 83n. 51, 113n. 45, 115, 115n. 59, 222n. 18

Dekazos, P. 36, 37n. 55, 91nn. 70, 72
Demetriades, V. 11n. 7, 15n. 17, 60n. 31, 75n. 33, 86n. 60, 94n. 81, 105n. 14
Dimaras, K. T. 238n. 70
Dobb, M. 97–101, 156, 209–10
  Dobb-Sweezy debate 97–101
Drama 49–50, 54–5, 128
Drazilovo (Derzhilovo) 193, 243, 243n. 88
Dumont, P. 5n. 4, 30n. 37, 227nn. 30, 31
Durzhilovich, Kiryak (Darzilovitis Kiriakos) 243–9

Edhessa (*Vodina*)
  administrative structures 49–51
  agrarian relations 90–3
  agricultural production 81–6
  çiftlik formation 70–3
  history and geography 2, 9–10, 12–14, 31
  industrialists and the state 188–96, 204
  industrialization 171–174
  population 53–61
  textile industries 138–9, 142–7, 151–2, 160–2
  trade 113–15
  workers and working conditions 228–31
Egnatia, Via (*Rumeli Sol Kol*) 9, 10

Egypt 46, 48n. 10, 74, 83, 107, 115, 116, 117, 151, 166n. 110, 192
Eldem, E. 28n. 34, 29, 29n. 36
Eldem, V. 22n. 11, 44n. 1, 55n. 26, 86, 86n. 57
Evliya Çelebi 15
Evrenos *Bey, Gazi* 11, 71–5
Evrenosoğulları, family 11–12, 94
  vakıf 15, 71–5, 86n. 60, 91–2, 246n. 91
Evrenosoğlu, Ahmed *Bey* 12, 73–4
Evrenosoğlu, İsa *Bey* 73
Evrenoszade, Rahmi *Bey* 11

Faroqhi, S. 20n. 2, 21n. 8, 112n. 40, 116n. 56, 119n. 62
France 30, 46, 48, 51, 112, 113, 115, 236, 237, 241

Genç, M. 28, 28n. 28, 28n. 31, 28n. 32, 128
Germany 83, 109, 113, 115, 115n. 51, 151
Giannitsa (*Yenice-i Vardar*) 2, 9, 10–12, 73, 94, 147, 208
  lake 10, 12, 253n. 103
Ginio, E. 30n. 37, 112n. 40, 116, 116n. 58
Göçek, F. M. 25, 25nn. 17, 21
Gounaris, B. C. 30n. 37, 35, 35n. 52, 77n. 36, 77n. 37, 80n. 45, 81n. 47, 89n. 67, 91n. 70, 130n. 12, 131n. 17, 141, 141n. 39, 141n. 40, 146n. 46, 147–8, 147nn. 48, 50, 152n. 64, 158n. 85, 160n. 93, 161nn. 95, 97, 173, 181n. 20, 187n. 39, 243n. 87, 250, 250nn. 96, 97, 251n. 99
Goutas, family 117, 150–1, 193n. 54
  Goutas-Karatzias mill 150, 161–2, 173–4, 195–6
Great Britain 22, 32, 47, 51, 81, 106–107, 109, 112–14, 128–9, 136, 139, 141, 149, 161–2, 166, 185, 235, 235n. 64, 237, 257, 258
Greece 2, 6, 14, 33n. 49, 35, 36, 46, 50, 56, 85, 112, 114, 115, 117–18, 124–5, 133, 138, 154, 159, 163, 186, 197, 198, 212, 235, 239n. 75, 241, 243, 246, 249, 251, 253, 253n. 103, 255, 259
  industrial development of 139–141
  revolution and Greco-Turkish wars 17, 70n. 20, 165, 252

Greif, A. 102–3, 102n. 103
Gülhane, Imperial Edict of 47

Hadjidimoulas, family 174, 192–3, 217
Hadjilazaros, family 118, 133n. 24, 134, 136, 174, 185–7, 203–4
  Hadjilazaros-Angelakis plant (ERIA) 155–7, 164, 173, 196–7, 199–200, 226
Hadjimalousis, Constantinos 222, 235
Hadjinikolaki, family and mill 148–9, 152
Hadziiossif, C. 35, 35n. 52, 131n. 15, 140n. 35
Haliacmon (*İnce Karasu*) 13–14
Hekimoglou, E. 30n. 37, 35, 35n. 52, 131nn. 13, 17, 18, 133nn. 23, 24, 134, 149n. 55, 153n. 68, 157n. 83, 187n. 40, 189n. 46, 193n. 52, 197n. 65, 204n. 79, 228, 228n. 34, 243n. 86, 254n. 106
Hortiatis (*Hortaç*), Mount 6

İnalcık, H. 19n. 1, 20, 20nn. 2, 4, 6, 21n. 7, 25n. 17, 28, 28n. 29, 28n. 30, 35, 39n. 58, 63n. 2, 64nn. 3, 5, 7, 8, 66n. 10, 67n. 14, 71n. 23, 74nn. 29, 31, 93, 93n. 78, 97n. 1, 119n. 62, 236n. 65
Issawi, C. P. 22n. 11, 23n. 14, 27n. 27, 93n. 75, 129n. 9, 147, 147n. 47
İstanbul (Constantinople) 2, 5, 10, 22, 28, 31, 34, 39, 45, 83, 94, 108–9, 111, 114–15, 116, 130, 138, 160, 178, 181, 183, 185–6, 202–4, 237, 242–3, 255, 258
İzmir (Smyrna) 5, 11, 31–2, 111, 130, 172

Jackson, M. R. 87n. 61, 91n. 69, 93n. 76
Japan 33, 175

Kafadar, C. 74n. 31, 236n. 65,
Kapanci, family 120, 122–3, 134–5
Karacaabad/Karacaova 13
Karatzias, family 151, 174
Karavas, S. 186n. 37, 252n. 101, 253n. 103
Karpat, K. 20, 20n. 5, 44n. 1, 53n. 21, 241n. 81
Kazazis, family 157
Kelemeriye (Kalamaria) 8, 198

Keyder, Ç. 5n. 3, 26nn. 24, 25, 26, 63n. 21, 65n. 8, 97n. 1
Kiel, M. 11, 11n. 7
Kirdzhali Georgii 70n. 20
Kitromilides, P. 238n. 70
Kofinas, G. 36–7, 37n. 55, 228n. 34
Kokkinos, family 92–3, 117, 151, 189, 192–6, 218–20
  mill 204–5
Kondylis, P. 238n. 70
Konortas, P. 240n. 77
Krstić, T. 239n. 74
Kyrtsis, family 117, 123, 134, 144–6, 152–3, 174, 189

Lampe, J. R. 87n. 61, 91n. 69, 93n. 76
Lanaras, family 117, 156–7, 174, 198, 223
Lapavitsas, C. 37n. 55, 56n. 29, 82n. 50, 161n. 97
Lapavitsas, family 92–3, 117, 125, 151, 172–4, 193–5, 222–3
Lappas, family 117, 174, 192
  Lappas-Hadjidimoulas mill 151, 162, 173–4, 192–3
Leake, W. 17n. 19, 83n. 51, 113n. 45, 113n. 46
Lenin, V. I. 87–8
Levant 5n. 3, 111
Levant, Company 136
Levy, A. 132n. 20, 214n. 11
Lewis, B. 25n. 17, 236n. 66, 241n. 80
Longos, family 117, 140, 153, 189–90, 217–19, 222
  Longos-Kyrtsis-Tourpalis plant 115, 118, 134, 139–43, 158–62, 173–4, 182–7, 195–6, 200–203, 224–5, 231, 254
Lowry, H. 11n. 6, 11n. 8, 11n. 9, 73nn. 25, 26, 27, 74n. 32, 94n. 80
Lyberatos, A. 251n. 98

Macedonia
  geography 6, 9–17, Plate 2
    historical writing on 34–7
    industrial capitalism 2–4, 5, 10, 29–34
Mahmud II, Sultan 44, 47, 51, 178n. 3
Marx, K. 25, 25n. 19, 97
  Marxist analysis of capitalism 25, 30n. 37, 87n. 62, 97–100
Mazarakis-Ainian, Constantinos 252–3, 252nn. 101, 102, 103

Mazower, M. 5n. 4, 30n. 37, 136n. 27, 242n. 84
McCarthy, J. 38n. 57, 44n. 1, 52n. 20
McGowan, B. 28, 28n. 33, 45, 45n. 2, 63n. 2, 65n. 8, 212n. 5
Mehmed II, Sultan 72
Mehmed Ali *Paşa*, Kavalalı 46–7, 107, 117
Mehmed Emin Abu Lubut *Paşa* 17
Mehmed Reşad, Sultan 254–5
Meron, O. 132nn. 19, 21, 134n. 25, 153n. 66
Midhat *Paşa* 48
Mieza (Gardens of Midas) 15n. 14
Misrachi, family 133–34, 153
Modiano, Eli 7
Modiano, family 118, 131, 133, 135–7, 167, 204
Moskoff, K. 36, 36n. 53
Mount Vermion (*see also* several other subject entries)
  Ağustos Dağ/Karakamen 14
  capitalist class 217–27
  historical and geographical background 9–17, 29–39
  modernization and industrialization 2–6, 138–50
  nationalist conflict 251–5
Mustafa Reşit, *Paşa* 37, 48

Nakşibendi 12
Naoussa (*Ağustos*)
  administrative structures 49–51
  agrarian relations 90–4
  agricultural production 81–6
  çiftlik formation 70–1, 74
  çorbacı/industrialists 217–23, 235, 252–5, 259
  Greek school of 215
  history and geography 2–4, 10–17, 31–3
    in the *vakıf* of *Gazi* Evrenos 74
  industrialists and the state 182–205
  population 53–56, 60
  textile industries and industrialization 138–74
  trade 113–25
  workers and working conditions 228–31
North, D. 102, 102n. 12

Olympios Giorgakis 70n. 20

Ottoman Bank 7, 118, 130
Owen, R. 23n. 14

Palairet, M. 23n. 14, 30n. 38, 31, 31n. 43, 35, 44n. 1, 52n. 17, 52n. 19, 55, 55nn. 25, 26, 68n. 16, 69n. 18, 70n. 21, 71n. 22, 91n. 71, 127n. 2, 127n. 3, 141n. 39, 155, 155n. 76, 158, 158n. 86, 160n. 92, 160n. 94, 166, 167n. 112, 174n. 116, 181, 181n. 21, 260nn. 2, 3
Palamiotis, G. 36, 37n. 55
Pamuk, Ş. 23n. 14, 26n. 27, 28, 28n. 34, 28n. 35, 33, 33n. 49, 33n. 50, 65–6, 65n. 6, 66n. 12, 97n. 1, 107, 107n. 15, 108n. 20, 110nn. 30, 31, 129n. 8, 166n. 111, 177n. 1
Papademetriou, T. 237n. 69, 239n. 76
Paul, the Apostle 14
Pehlivanos, family 92–3, 117, 174, 197–8, 205
  Pehlivanos-Lanaras mill 155–7, 173–4, 200
Pella 10
Petmezas, S. 70n. 21, 80n. 43, 85n. 54, 85n. 56, 122n. 65, 127n. 2, 128n. 4, 212n. 6, 213n. 7, 213n. 9, 216n. 14, 260n. 2
Philip, King of Macedonia 5, 10
Pirenne, H. 99–103, 99n. 7
Poselli, Vitaliano 8
Pouqueville, F. 15n. 18, 17n. 19, 83n. 51, 222n. 18
Pushkin, A. 70n. 20

Quataert, D. 5n. 3, 19n. 1, 22n. 13, 23n. 14, 26nn. 24, 27, 28n. 29, 30nn. 37, 38, 31, 31nn. 40, 41, 44, 32n. 45, 35, 35n. 51, 46n. 4, 47n. 6, 51–2, 51n. 13, 52n. 18, 63n. 1, 66n. 10, 91n. 69, 107, 107nn. 15, 16, 110n. 32, 127n. 1, 129n. 10, 130n. 11, 141n. 38, 149n. 57, 154–5, 154n. 70, 155nn. 78, 79, 159n. 88, 161n. 97, 162n. 101, 163, 163n. 103, 179n. 10, 180nn. 14, 16, 227n. 31, 228, 228nn. 35, 36, 39, 40, 232, 232nn. 48, 49, 50, 51, 233n. 56, 257n. 1

Romania 55, 250, 251
Rostow, W. 22, 22n. 11

Rumeli 39, 48, 51, 74
  railways 130, 181
  vilayet 224–5, 253
Russia
  capitalist development 33, 88, 175
  imperial and military pressure on Ottomans 23–4, 34, 46–7, 68, 70n. 20, 249
  Russo-Turkish wars 51, 78, 110, 165, 204

Sadat, D. R. 45n. 3, 70n. 21, 127n. 2, 212n. 4, 213n. 8, 214n. 10,
Saias, family 7, 141, 158, 160, 161n. 96
  mill 7, 141, 158, 160
Selim, I Sultan 74
Serbia 31, 48n. 10, 159, 163, 241, 255
Serres (*Serez/Siroz*) 49–50, 54–5, 76, 109, 112, 114–15, 154, 171
Skylitzes I. 13, 13n. 12
Sossidis, family 118, 123, 134, 149, 194
  Sossidis-Faik plant 147–9, 161–2, 205
Stoianovich, T. 17n. 20, 20n. 6, 65n. 7, 69n. 19, 109, 109n. 23, 109n. 24, 109n. 28, 117n. 60
Stougiannakis, E. 37, 37n. 55, 91n. 72, 119n. 64, 141, 141n. 37, 187n. 39, 202, 202n74
Süleyman, Sultan 74
Svoronos, N. 30n37, 109n28, 116n57, 209n2
Sweezy, P. 97–100, 97n. 3, 99n8, 103, 106, 209–10

Tekkealtı 12, 187
Thessaloniki *(Selanik)*
  historical and geographical background 5–9
  Jewish community of 9
  modernization 2, 4, 6–9
Thrace 2, 10, 11, 69, 159, 182
Torres, family 134, 204
  Torres-Misrachi plant 141, 158
Tourpalis, family 117, 119, 134, 152, 157, 173–4, 195, 197–200, 204
  Tourpalis-Kazazis plant 157, 173–4
Tsakalotos, D. 36–7, 37n. 55
Tsitsis, family 117, 151, 153, 174, 187, 195, 218–19, 223, 234

Name Index

Tsitsis plant 115, 144, 152, 161–162, 173–4, 189–90, 196n. 62, 204, 229–31, 253
Turkey 33, 33n. 49, 35, 40, 149
  'in Europe' 1, 3, Plate 1

Upward, A. 228n. 39, 228n. 40, 235, 235n. 64

Veroia (*Karaferye*)
  administrative structures 49–51
  agrarian relations 90–3
  agricultural production 81–6
  bishop of 222–3
  çiftlik formation 70–3
  history and geography 2, 9–14, 31
  industrialists and the state 194, 205
  industrialization 171–2
  manufacturing 128, 138–9, 150, 154
  population 53–61
  textile industries 142, 147–9, 152, 161–2
  trade 113–17
  workers and working conditions 228, 231
Voras (*Kaymakçalan*), Mount 13

Wallerstein, I. 25–6, 26n. 22, 26n. 23, 26n. 24, 101, 101n. 11
Weber, M. 24–5, 24n. 16, 25n. 17
Wittek, P. 236n. 65

Yaycioglu, A. 45n. 3, 69n. 17, 212n. 5
Yedikule
  fort (Thessaloniki) 6
  mill (*İstanbul*) 160
Yildirim, O. 21n. 8, 21n. 9, 22n. 10, 116n. 56, 179n. 12,
Ypsilantis, Alexandros 70n. 20

Subject Index

aba (coarse woollen cloth) 114, 153, 154, 166, 257
agriculture 3, 4, 20, 26n. 25, 63, 63n. 1
   commercialization of 66–70
   emergence of capitalism in 43, 87–90, 94–5, 104
   in Macedonia 36, 70–1, 90–2, 104–6
      output in Veroia, Edhessa and Naoussa 81–7
      output in the *vilayet* of Thessaloniki 76–81
   sharecropping 3, 34, 69, 76, 86, 88, 89–90, 93, 105, 211, 260
   smallholdings 3, 4, 63, 64, 65, 86, 88, 89, 91, 169, 211, 234, 260
askeri (social layer) 67–8
ayan (notables) 15, 215, 238
   relations with merchants 46, 210–13
   rise of and conflict with the Porte 44–7, 45n. 3, 66–9, 69n. 17
   warlords and *çiftlik* owners 70, 75, 91, 92n. 74, 210–13

Balkan wars 1, 31, 36, 150, 241, 255, 262
banking 7, 34, 118–19, 123, 130–1, 132–6, 133n. 24, 150, 161n. 96, 198, 208, 228, 254
Byzantine Empire (Eastern Roman) 5, 6–8, 13, 13n. 12, 14, 64, 72–3, 82, 223, 238, 239n. 76

capitalist class (bourgeoisie) 24, 25, 34, 43, 97n. 1, 101, 105, 153, 167, 192, 211, 216, 218, 219–20, 261, 262
   in Mount Vermion 217–27
   in Thessaloniki 135–7
capitalist transformation of Ottoman Empire 5, 6, 10–11, 13
   communal and religious aspects 43, 131–7, 207–9, 214–15
   theoretical debate on emergence of capitalism 97–104

Christian (Greek) Ottoman community 27–8, 212–13
   of Naoussa
      economic activities in Thessaloniki 152–3, 157, 198–9
      educational mechanisms 190, 214–15, 223, 235
      juridical mechanisms 194–5, 223–4
      political mechanisms 220–2
      relations with the Ottoman state 106, 137, 182, 193, 208–9, 226–7, 231, 233–5, 236n. 65, 237–41, 254
   role in industrialization 4, 207–9, 210
   of Thessaloniki 8–9, 136–7
çiftlik system 20–1, 45, 65, 65n. 8, 69, 125, 135
   and capitalist development 104–6, 210–13, 260
   çiftlik estates in Macedonia 45, 70–1, 77, 86–87, 86n. 60, 91, 136, 151, 171, 173, 192, 193, 198, 208, 251, 253n. 103
   Muslim and Christian *çiftlik* 90–4, 92n. 74
   rise of *çiftlik* estates 66–71
   and sharecropping 89–90, 93
çorbacı (social layer) 125, 173–4, 190, 193, 198, 212, 235, 252, 253
   and capitalist transformation 217–22
   and community control 190, 214–15, 222–5
   compared to *ayan* and *kocabaşı* 212
   and Greek national identity 250–51
   internal frictions 193–5, 194n. 55, 196, 224–6
çuka (fine felt) 178, 197
cotton
   cloth 11, 31, 128n. 7, 154, 161, 166, 169, 171
   raw 32, 128, 162, 166, 169, 170–2, 171n. 114
   yarn 3, 31, 80, 95, 105, 115, 119, 139, 141, 151, 154, 157, 159, 160,

161n. 99, 166, 169, 171, 171n. 114, 178, 190, 200, 202

enterprise application procedure 182–5, 188–9, 191, 199–200, 201–2, 204, Plate 7
'enterprises with concessions' 180–4, 201, 204, 226, 260

feudalism 25, 64, 88
　transition to capitalism 97–104
flour mill 6, 134, 138, 138n. 31, 165, 167, 187, 197, 202, 203, 209, 231, 258
Free Trade Treaty (Convention) of *Balta Limanı* 46, 66–7, 106–7, 117, 128, 177, 179

gaytan (braided woollen cloth) 196
gedik certificate 21–2
'Great Depression' 81, 110, 110n. 30, 258

iltizam (tax farming) system 21, 67
　malikane (life-time tax farming) 21, 67–8, 211
　mültezim (tax farmer) 21–2, 47
industrial capitalism/industrialization 1–3, 5, 6, 10, 11, 13, 15, 16, 29–30, 137
　in cotton spinning 158–62
　domestic and rural origins 127–8
　economics of industrialization 165–9
　in Mount Vermion and Thessaloniki 138–57
　predominance of Naoussa capitalists 172–4
　responding to imports 129–30
　state-led 177–9
　and steam power 141, 160, 167
　textile network in Macedonia 165–72
　and water power 13, 15, 114, 124, 138, 139, 140–1, 143, 144, 146, 149, 160, 168, 184, 187, 189, 192, 193, 195, 201, 229
　weaknesses of industrial development 174–5, 260
　in wool weaving 162–5
Industrial Reform Commission (*Islah-ı Sanayi Komisyonu*) 179, 179n. 10, 179n. 12, 184

IMRO (Internal Macedonian Revolutionary Organisation) 251–2, 252n. 100, 254
Italy 31, 132–3, 161–2, 204, 226, 241

Janissaries (*yeniçeri*) 46, 51, 68, 107, 257
Jewish Ottoman community
　educational mechanisms 135, 242–3
　Francos 132, 242
　internal organization 241n. 11
　relations with the Ottoman state 132–3, 135, 158, 182, 207–8
　of Thessaloniki 6–9, 27–28, 133–5
　　Askenazy 241
　　and industrialization 4, 30, 132–3, 207–9, 210
　　Sephardic 30, 132–3, 242
　of Veroia 9
joint-stock enterprises (cartel and oligopoly) 155, 162, 197, 197n. 67, 198, 226

kazmir (cashmere) 196, 197
kırcalı (rebels) 68–71, 70n. 20, 238

merchants 1, 3, 22, 55, 77, 95, 131, 135–6, 262
　and capitalist development 97–104
　commercial correspondence
　　from Naoussa 124–5
　　from Thessaloniki 199
　growth and fluctuations of Thessaloniki trade 106–10
　in Macedonia 104–5
　　Greeks 3–4, 17, 106, 109–10 116–23
　　Jews 8, 118–23
　　Turks 118–23
　Ottoman trade protectionism 107, 128–30, 258
　relations with *ayan* 66–8
　tariffs and taxes 106–7, 177, 179, 180, 201, 258
　trading in Veroia, Edhessa, and Naoussa 113–16
　in the transition to capitalism 97–104
millet (official communal organization) 214n. 11, 240–1, 240n. 77, 249
'Modern Greek Enlightenment' 238

Subject Index

money lending 68, 75, 86, 90, 105, 136, 193, 211, 212, 213, 216, 217
Muslim (Turkish) Ottoman community 27–8, 216
  educational mechanisms 240–1
  of Naoussa 16–17
  relations with the Ottoman state 136, 250
  of Thessaloniki 8–9, 135–6
mütevelli (trustee) of *vakıf* 15, 72, 75

nationalism
  Bulgarian 243–9
  conflict 243, 248–9, 250, 251–5, 253n. 103
  Greek 237–8, 243, 249, 251, 253n. 103
  Jewish (Zionism) 241–3, 242n. 84
  language and religion 236–9
  and the 'Macedonian Question' 209, 250n. 96, 253, 255
  social underpinnings 249–51
  Turkish 240–1, 250
Napoleonic wars 46, 109, 122

Orthodox Church (Patriarchate) 58, 214n. 11, 223, 237, 239–40, 240n. 77, 241n. 79, 243, 248, 250, 251
  communal power 222–3
  juridical role 194–5, 235
  provision of education 223, 235
  tax collecting 212–13, 237
Ottoman archives 40–1, 59n. 30, 118–19, 138n. 31, 139, 148–51, 161n. 97, 162, 165n. 106, 165n. 108, 183n. 26, 185–200, 201, 225–35
Ottoman Empire
  emergence of capitalism 1–4, 30n. 37, 29–34, 104, 106, 150, 234, 262
    communal aspects 27, 33–4, 43, 48–50, 104, 131–2, 130–7, 200, 207, 209–16, 259
    religious aspects 27, 33–4, 43, 215–16
    theoretical analysis 22–9
  communities 10, 130–7
  'decline' 19–24, 63
  modernity 1–2, 5, 6–9, 9, 22n. 11, 22–3, 34, 47, 145, 216, 218, 220, 240, 255
Ottoman Public Debt Administration (OPDA) 83–4, 110, 180n. 13, 258

Ottoman state 1, 3, 19, 20, 22, 23–4, 25, 30, 38, 64, 69n. 17, 73n. 26, 155, 162–3, 213, 224–5, 246, 249
  administrative reform 39, 44–8
  and capitalist transformation 27–9, 34, 164–5, 260–2
  and education 47, 240–1
  economic intervention 177–82
  fiscalism 28, 67
  fiscal crisis (bankruptcy) 34, 110, 179–80
  infrastructure investment 130, 178, 180n. 14, 181–2
  population censuses 51–3
  provisionism 28, 66, 116, 128
  relations with communities 34, 51–3, 106, 213–16, 214n. 11
  relations with Macedonian capitalists 41, 43, 182–200, 204–5, 259
  support for private industrialization 180–2
  trade protectionism 107, 128–30, 258, Plate 8
'Ottomanism' 240–1, 242, 254, 261, 262

population 20, 38, 39, 43, 74, 75, 113, 132, 236
  estimation problems 39–40, 43–4, 44n. 1, 51–3
  size and ethnic mix
    Edhessa 13, 56–8, 59–61
    Giannitsa 11–12
    Naoussa 56, 60, 74, 215
    Thessaloniki 5, 53–7, 58–9, 86, 172
    Veroia 14, 56–57, 59–61
Porte (Sublime) 15n. 16, 17, 40, 41, 50, 72, 132, 165n. 106, 177, 186, 237, 239, 240, 240n. 77, 249, 257
  conflict with *ayan* 44–47, 66–70, 69n. 17, 212–13

railways 39, 56, 112, 115, 115n. 54, 130–1, 131n. 14, 146–7, 147n. 49, 148, 159, 160, 171, 181, 181n. 20, 259
reaya (social layer) 66, 67, 215

şayak (woollen cloth) 164, 166, 257, 259
  production method 114, 119
  production volume 138, 138n. 10, 139, 154

traders become industrial capitalists 122–5, 139, 151, 153–7, 167–8, 174, 184, 187, 193, 195–8, 202
trading in 113–15, 118, 138

Tanzimat (reforms) 28, 37n. 56, 41n. 59, 47–8, 47n. 7, 49–51, 76, 92, 182, 220, 222, 240–1, 241n. 79, 242, 257
tevzi (local tax system) 212–13
tımar system 20–1, 72, 63–5
    iqta and pronoia 64
    tımarlı sipahi 63–64

vakıf 71–2, 86n. 60, 91, 216
    of *Gazi* Evrenos 11–12, 71–5, 92n. 74, 246n. 91
vilayet
    of Bitola (*Manastır*) 111n. 33, 170, 252
    of Kosova 111n. 33
    law (*Teşkil-i Vilayet Nizamnamesi*) 220
    of Skopjie (*Üsküp*) 170
    of Thessaloniki (*Selanik*) 5, 5n. 2, 36, 41, 71, 75, 86, 108, 138, 1 50, 154, 162n. 100, 169, 179, 258, 261
        administrative mechanisms 49–51
        agricultural output 76–81
        çiftlik formation 86–91
        ethnic composition 58–60
        population 51–8
        stagnation of agriculture 85–6
        trade 110–13
Vlachs 109, 114, 149, 154, 164, 240
voyvoda 15, 15n. 16

watermill 119, 123, 139, 143, 185, 187
Western Europe
    advanced capitalist development in 33, 65, 99, 101–2, 106, 108, 174
    imperialist pressure 23–4
    as model 47, 177–9, 214
    and nationalism 235–42
    trading relations with 30, 66, 77, 83–4, 116–17, 122, 129, 163, 257
wine 15, 82, 83 91, 111, 113, 114, 115, 115n. 51, 118
wool
    cloth 3, 30–1, 32, 92, 106, 113–14, 118, 119, 132, 154–7, 163–4, 166–7, 169, 173, 196, 210
    weaving 32, 119, 122, 259
    yarn 202
working class (wage labour) 1, 8, 34, 43, 86–7, 90, 99, 100, 135, 207, 211, 227, 258, 259, 260, 261
    labour organization 159–60, 232–5
    'Poupoulo' 234–5
    Socialist Workers' Federation 233
    in Mount Vermion 136–7, 210, 228, 234
    in Thessaloniki 210, 216, 227–8
    wage levels 159, 227, 228, 232
    working conditions 227–32

Yearbooks of the *vilayet* of Thessaloniki (*Selanik Vilayet Salnameleri*) 36, 37–40, 43, 53–61, 78–85, 111–16, 138–71
Young Turks 2, 11, 134, 182, 191, 199, 208, 226, 231, 232–4, 241, 242, 249, 254, 261

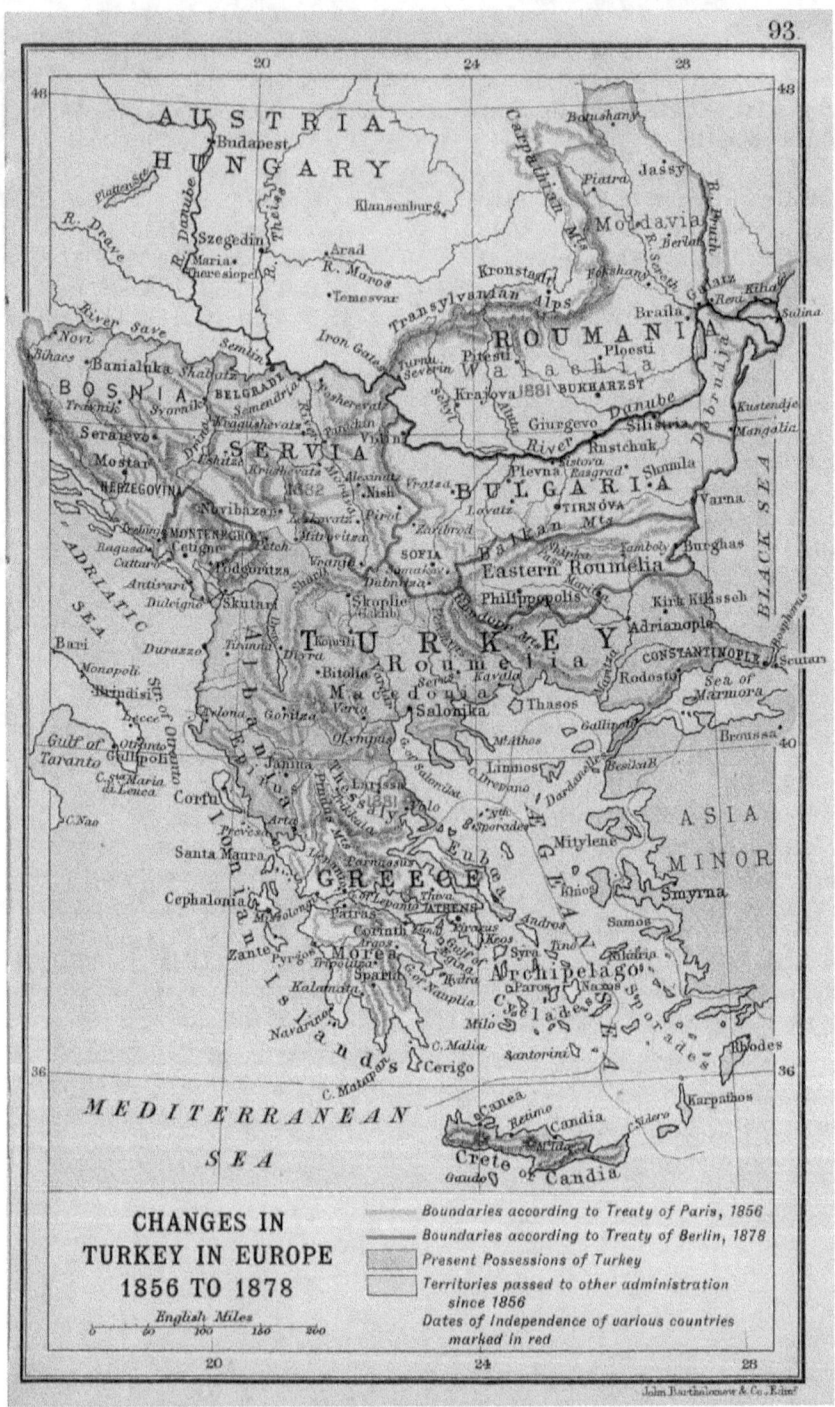

Plate 1 European territories of the Ottoman Empire at the end of the nineteenth century

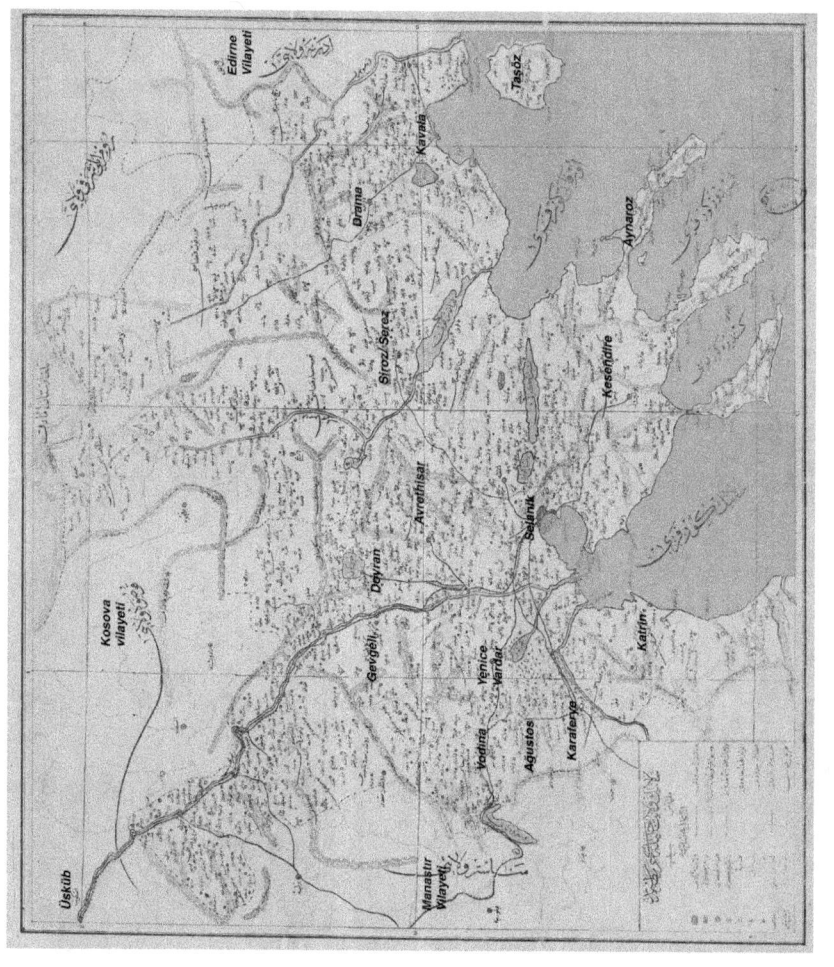

Plate 2 The Ottoman *vilayet* of Thessaloniki (*Selanik*) and its provincial urban centres

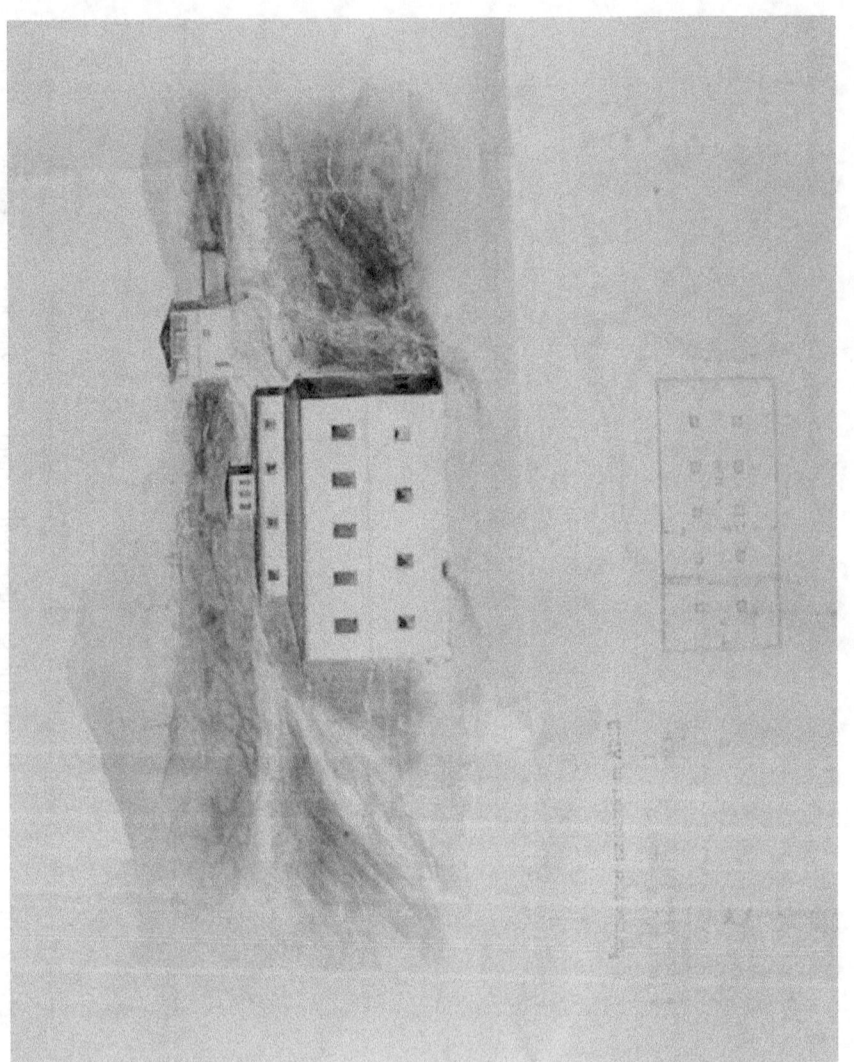

Plate 3 The original plant of Longos–Kyrtsis–Tourpalis in Naoussa, 1870s

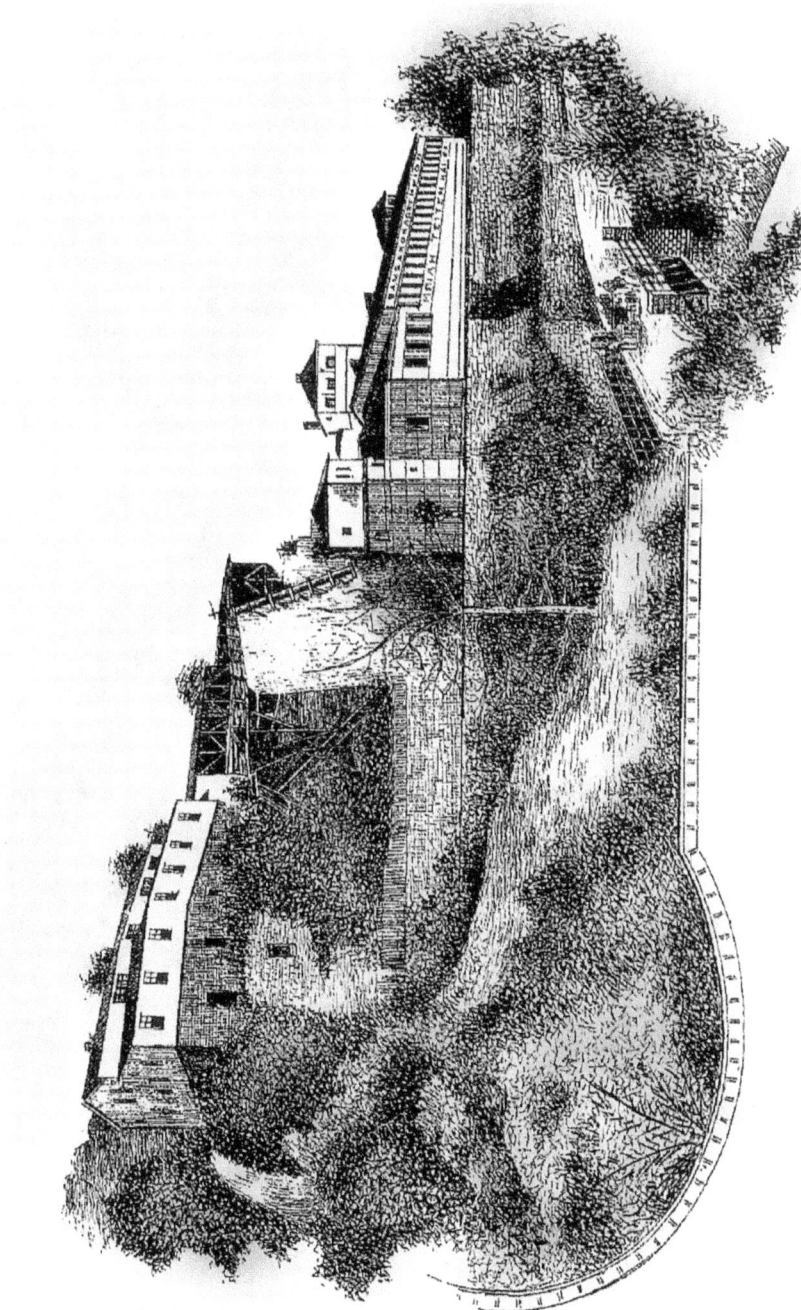

Plate 4 A drawing of the Bilis–Tsitsis plant in Naoussa in the early twentieth century

Plate 5 Commercial publicity of the Goutas–Karatzias plant

Plate 6 Commercial publicity of the mill of Longos–Tourpalis in the early 1900s

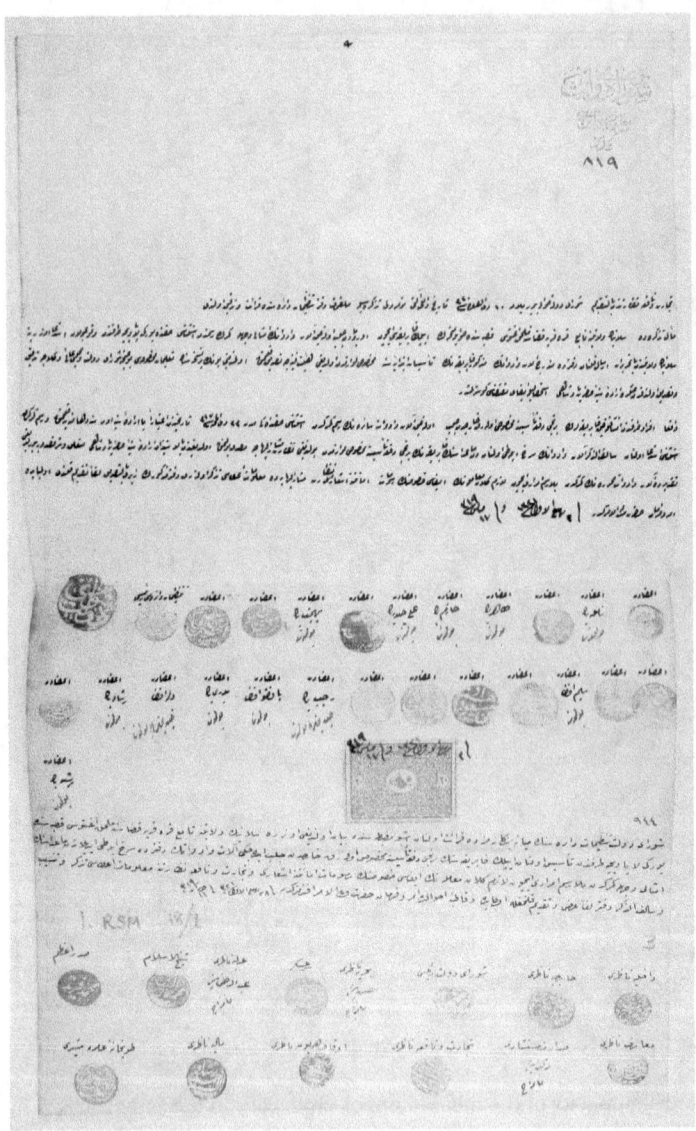

Plate 7 The approved application of Georgios Lapavitsas for a spinning mill in Naoussa

- 2 -

48 Rideaux à mousse pour défonceuses .... ؟ ؟ (نسيج) ٤٨ ستار من الصوف يستعمل في ماكينات تصفية الاصباغ

10 Kilo petits clous à corde .... ١٠ كيلو كلوب قدر جميزى

500 [illegible] .... ٥٠٠ [illegible]
100 [illegible] .... ١٠٠ [illegible]

6 [illegible] .... ٦ [illegible]

100 Yards de drap pour nettoyer les machines .... ١٠٠ ياردة قماش لتنظيف الماكينات

20 doigs ciré pour couvrir les tables de pression .... ٢٠ اصبع من الشمع لتغطية [illegible]

400 Yards de drap .... ٤٠٠ ياردة قماش

1 Barils d'huile 400 gall. .... ١ برميل زيت ٤٠٠ جالون

500 Kilo, cuisine de divers genres .... ٥٠٠ كيلو اوانى من انواع مختلفة

200 grosses baguettes pour les bancs .... ٢٠٠ جروسة عصى كبيرة تستعمل في البنك

20 toujours tige à nappe .... ٢٠ طويل درجة عمود زينك

2 Pompes à huile de toiles à anneaux .... ٢ طلمبة زيت لنوع درجى محتوى درجين

12 [illegible] .... ١٢ [illegible]

2 long Bancs à main .... ٢ بنك طويل اليد

6 Collection d'outils tels que marteaux ciseaux, limes, clefs, etc .... ٦ مجموعة من ادوات مثل شاكوش ازميل مبرد مفاتيح الخ

2 Balances pour peser les nappes .... ٢ ميزان لوزن الزينكات

2 bacs pour mesurer les chaletts d'encres .... ٢ حوض لقياس الاحبار

2 Tambours pour mesurer les mèches .... ٢ طبلون لقياس الفتائل

2 Appareil, pour unir les cylindres de pression .... ٢ منسيجات تستعمل لتوحيد ماكينة الضغط

www.ingramcontent.com/pod-product-compliance
Lightning Source LLC
Chambersburg PA
CBHW070016010526
44117CB00011B/1599